HORSE WISDOM

HORSE WISDOM

by

Henry Blake

SOUVENIR PRESS

ISBN 0 285 62756 2

Printed in Great Britain by
WBC Print Ltd, Bristol

Contents

PART I

TALKING WITH HORSES

A Study of Communication between Man and Horse

Foreword

This book is based on forty years' work with horses, the last twenty of which have been spent studying how they communicate, with each other and with man. My wife Leslie and my daughter Paddy have both taken a full part in this research – hence the frequent use of the pronoun 'we' in the text.

My motivation was simple – I wanted to achieve a greater understanding with my horses, and so to attain better performance on the racecourse and in competitions; and the way to such attainment I soon found to be through increasing the horses' own enjoyment of life. It was only towards the end of our research that we began to think our work might be of interest to other people. This book has been written in the hope that others will benefit from, and in due course build on, what we have learned.

H. N. Blake

1: *Horses I have Learned From*

Maybe I am not quite sane, but horses have been my whole life. For me they are a drug more potent than LSD and more lethal than heroin. My friends tell me that my addiction has already produced deterioration of the brain. And unlike any other drug, horses are a drug for which there is no known cure: for me life without horses would be only a living death.

My earliest memories are of horses rather than people, and horses rather than places or people have represented the milestones of my life. I am a true centaur, half man, half horse.

The first thing I remember is sitting on a horse in front of my great-uncle Harvey Blake: I must have been little more than a year old. And I remember that just after this my father bought a black thoroughbred gelding called Masterpiece, a horse that was extremely difficult to handle, for he used to kick and strike out with his front legs at anybody who came into his stable. I had not been walking for very long when a general panic was caused in the household, because I was missing and could not be found anywhere. After a considerable time my mother and father, nursemaid and the farmhands, all of whom were looking for me, found me in the stables coolly playing under Masterpiece's manger. When they tried to get me out, Masterpiece used his feet and teeth to prevent anybody passing the door. Eventually I had to be tempted out with a sweet from the doorway, after which I always used Masterpiece's stable as my favourite refuge, where I could play undisturbed with the horse protecting me. I used to wander about under his legs and feet and thoroughly enjoy myself, as a small boy will, getting myself filthy. Further, being rather an unpleasant child, I quickly found that when

I was naughty I could escape punishment there as long as I wanted, while my nursemaid and parents fumed outside the door. I used to refuse to come out until they promised not to spank me. This experience taught me at a very early age that horses were my friends and protectors.

In the autumn of 1933 my parents went to Bridgwater Fair and paid two pounds for a small black Dartmoor pony. Inevitably she was called Black Beauty and she became the guide, teacher and friend of the whole family. A great individualist, she could untie any rope and open any door. On one occasion when we were trying to corner her in the yard, she escaped by going through the back door of the pantry into the kitchen, out to the hall and then out through the front door. And when we were sick, she would be brought up the stairs to our bedrooms to keep us company as a reward for good behaviour. A very stern disciplinarian, she punished any bad practice in a rider by depositing him firmly on the ground, and then waiting to be remounted, teaching me very early in life that a horse will retaliate instantly against any infringement of its code of conduct.

When the time came for me to go to school the obvious way to get me there and back was on a pony, and when a year or two later my younger sister joined me, she used to ride behind. We always rode bareback, as my father was of the opinion that the only way to learn a true seat on a horse was to ride without a saddle. We learnt to trot, canter and even to jump long before we had a saddle, which we were allowed to have when we were seven.

And so for the next five or six years, until I went to boarding school, I rode to school every day. Occasionally, if we were very very lucky, we would go down in the morning to find that the ponies had got out of the field; and provided the weather was nice, that would be a 'red letter' day, spent looking for ponies and being damned careful not to find them.

The next horse who played a really significant part in my education was a New Forest thoroughbred-cross chestnut mare, who had been bred as a polo pony. Chester was very difficult to handle in the stable. Since she had a very thin skin and was very ticklish, she would kick and scream in temper if anyone touched her legs or tried to groom her. But she was the first horse with which I ever established a real understanding and empathy, and I found after a while I could anticipate what she was going to do before she did it, and that she in turn would reflect my moods. As a result she was a fantastic gymkhana pony and for two years I supplemented my pocket money with her winnings.

While I still had Chester, another horse arrived who was to teach me a great deal. One day the local knacker man, Bert Newman, who for years had sold my father horses he thought too good to kill, telephoned to say he had a bay sixteen-two-hand three-quarter-thoroughbred mare, four years old, and he would let my father have her very cheaply for ten pounds. My father said that there were too many damned horses about the place and he did not want another one, so Bert said he would let my father have her for a fiver. 'No thank you,' was the reply. The exchange ended with Bert saying that, because of their long-standing friendship, he was giving the mare to my father and would send her over at once. I was thirteen at this time and still riding to school. When I got home that evening, the mare had been unloaded from the lorry into a covered yard with some heifers, and I managed after some argument to persuade my father to let me ride her to school the next day.

The following morning I went out to the yard to catch her and bring her into the stable. But instead of eating from the proffered bowl of oats, she attacked me with her teeth and front legs, so I clouted her across the nose with a halter and told her not to be a bloody-minded cow. I put the halter on, saddled and bridled her and rode her off to school.

About five minutes past nine Bert telephoned. He had had a bad night nagged by a guilty conscience, he said, and my father was not to touch the mare as she was dangerous. When he heard that I had already ridden her to school, the full story came out. Fearless had killed her previous owner, a Devonshire farmer, and Bert had been paid to take her away. He had intended to shoot her as soon as she came off the lorry, but unfortunately an R.S.P.C.A. official had arrived and insisted that she be put down with a humane killer in his presence, and since this was clearly impossible Bert had thought of my father.

I rode Fearless to school for the next two weeks, and apart from the fact that she was inclined to take a piece out of me with her teeth and strike at me with her front legs, I had no trouble whatsoever. We kept her until she died and she repaid us a thousand times, as she saved me twice from serious injury and on one occasion saved my father's life.

My father was driving home with her and a young horse as a pair in a wagon, when the young horse bolted at an American Army convoy. Fearless steered the cart and the other horse in and out of the convoy and the oncoming traffic, and eventually managed to stop the other horse. This she did by swinging away and pulling the young horse with her when she wanted to go to the left, and when she wanted to go to the right by swinging her head and biting the young horse to make it shy away. My father could not do anything with the reins since the young horse had panicked and was completely uncontrollable, but Fearless could control him, and she managed eventually to stop him after about two miles.

Fearless was always bloody-minded, but there was no horse like her. My first encounter with her had taught me a lesson I have remembered ever since : that with horses, if you are without fear and confident of yourself, you will be able to master any situation.

Fearless was such a good worker we never chose to breed from her, but finally when she was eleven years old her frustration got the better of her, and one night she got out into the neighbouring field where we had a bunch of yearlings and two-year-olds running. Among them was an immature uncut two-year-old thoroughbred who was barely fourteen-

two. Fearless was well over sixteen-two, and my father always
swore that she went up into the yard and borrowed a step-
ladder; but anyway, during the night she somehow managed
to persuade the young Corsican – that was the two-year-old's
name – to serve her, and eleven months later, full of pride
and joy, she produced a son and celebrated the fact by taking
a piece out of me when I went down to congratulate her.
There was only one name that he could be called and that
was Folly. He became the property of my sister Olive, and
for the next five years he grew and thrived.

When he was three years old he was broken, and after
breaking him I taught him to buck on command. I could
always make him buck in a dead straight line, a very big and
powerful buck that was nevertheless extremely easy to sit, so
at the age of eighteen this was my standard party piece
when I wanted to show off to my girl-friends. My father
played polo on him and my sister Olive hunted him.

Eventually, just before she went out to New Guinea as a
medical missionary, Olive decided she would like to fulfil
an old ambition and ride in a point-to-point. Since she weighed
twelve stone seven pounds and stood five feet ten inches, this
was clearly a piece of madness. But when Olive makes up her
mind to anything there is no arguing with her, so she entered
Folly for the ladies' race at the Axe Vale point-to-point.
For the whole of that season two horses had been dominating
the ladies' races in the West Country – Ching Ling and
Shepherd's Pie. So unbeatable were these two that everyone
else eventually gave up, and when we got to the Axe Vale
we discovered there was nothing else in the race : only Ching
Ling, Shepherd's Pie and Folly.

Olive borrowed my breeches, racing colours and boots, and
ate a hearty breakfast. Apart from instructing her that even
if she broke her neck, she was to get back to the paddock
to give me back my racing colours, there was not much else
I could do to avert the coming disaster. She also insisted
on riding in a hunting saddle, since she had never ridden in
anything else.

Olive and Folly clearly decided that this was a first-class hunt and nothing more, so they proceeded for two-and-a-half miles at a steady speed. At last, half a mile from home, Olive decided that now was the time to do something about winning the race, and since Ching Ling and Shepherd's Pie were then a fence and a half in front of her, I thought she was leaving it a bit late! But Folly went; and it was only because he was giving two-and-a-half stone away to the two best ladies'-race horses in the West of England, that he was beaten by five lengths. What he would have done if he had started his run in good time, I clearly do not know. I am quite sure that the public, none of whom had backed Olive, would have lynched her if she had won, so it was probably just as well she took her time. But they both enjoyed themselves, and that little story only shows just what a good horse will do for its owner when he really puts his mind to it.

The following year Folly was sold to some friends of ours and he was still hunting and hunting well when we left the West Country ten years ago.

Shortly after the experience with Fearless, my father realized that in handling unmanageable horses he was on to a good thing. So he put a series of advertisements in the *Horse and Hound*: BAD'NS AND MAD'NS BOUGHT AND BROKEN.

For the next five or ten years a series of unbreakable and unrideable horses arrived at Martock and Crewkerne Stations, each of which was about four miles from my home. It being war time, and help being scarce, I was sent to fetch them, and was always given strict instructions to lead the horses home. But I was bone lazy as well as disobedient, and saw no reason why I should walk when there was a horse to ride, so apart from the first and last half mile, I used to ride them home in a halter. I got plenty of secret amusement out of the next day, when my father went through the full breaking procedure before considering the horse safe for me to mount. I realized of course that the reason I found these unrideable horses easy to ride was no virtue of mine, but that, after being bumped and banged about in the train for ten or twelve hours, they would have proved friendly towards anybody who rescued them from their misery and treated them kindly. After petting and talking to them for ten minutes I was their friend for life, and I could do anything with them. They were all horses of great brain and character and taught me a lot, mainly that friendliness and gentleness and firmness can cure any vice.

I was about fourteen when a horse arrived who did not have much brain or character. But what he taught me was fundamental to all my future handling of horses. He was a thoroughbred called The Toff, and we got him because he was completely uncatchable. After we had had him for a week, I decided it was time to teach him to be caught. He was grazing by himself in a two-acre field. I started directly after breakfast, and for the next nine hours I walked after The Toff round and round and up and down the field, and when I walked The Toff walked, always refusing to let me catch him. After the first half-hour he got so bored that he moved only when I got near him; but he still kept walking away, walking away, walking away. This went on for nine hours. But eventually he gave in. He let me catch him and put the halter on. Even at that time I had enough sense to know that the first thing to do when I had caught him was to make a great fuss of him, and the second thing was to turn him loose again. Then for the next hour and a half I walked after The Toff, up the field and down the field, and round and round and round the field again. Then I caught him for the second time and made a fuss of him, and turned him loose. For the next twenty minutes I walked after The Toff, caught him for the third time, made a fuss of him and again turned him loose. I went on like this until I could catch him at my will and turn him loose, and after fourteen hours I went back to have my tea. He taught me one thing: when you start a thing with a horse, you must finish it, no matter what happens. You go on until you have done what you have set out to do, you must have endless patience, never lose your temper, and when he has done what you want, make a fuss of him; and then do it again and again until he does it without question. I do not know what happened to The Toff as he has completely gone from my memory; but I shall always be immensely grateful to him for teaching me what is basic to all my knowledge of handling animals.

Since it was war time, my father, to salve his conscience, made all the horses work on the farm. Thus he could keep horses and feel that he was doing it for the good of the nation rather than for his own pleasure. I remember we had one magnificent thoroughbred gelding called Caravan and he used to have to work in harness and pull one of the farm carts, but he did not approve of it, and used to bolt occasionally, much to everyone's consternation, because he really could travel. I remember driving him out of the yard one day, just as a builder was finishing repairing the gatepost and wall which the horse had demolished when he had bolted only a fortnight before. I drove half a mile down the road and got out to open the gate in the field, only to find that Caravan had swung round, cart and all, and was going flat-out back up the hill. When he got to the yard, the builder, who had just finished the wall, was standing back to admire his work. Caravan came around the corner and the new wall was flat again. The language was blue.

Caravan was a wonderful horse, however, for he had courage as well as determination. During the winter he was sound only one morning a week, and that was the day I was taking him hunting. If on Monday morning I was going hunting, Caravan was sound. He would be lame coming home from hunting and he would be lame until the next hunting day, when he would be sound again. This started me wondering how he knew before he saw me that it was hunting morning.

Of all the mad'ns and bad'ns we had, in fact none was bad, and none was mad. All of them had more than average intelligence, and an awful lot of temper with it. They were horses who had been misunderstood. They were horses who had been ill-treated. They were horses who had been spoilt by kindness. The bad'ns were strong-charactered horses who had been owned by weak-charactered people, and one or two by brutal people. One of them in particular sticks in my mind, a horse called Breakspear, who had a reputation of being a terrible bucker. My father and I went over to Arthur Brake's farm to see him, and my father bought him on the yard. He decided to ride him home. I was fifteen at the time and had broken a leg playing rugger, so had plaster on it from thigh to ankle. My father threw the horse preparatory to mounting him. He was very easy to throw and he behaved himself, did everything perfectly. I remember my father saying that either he was a very bad horse, or there was nothing wrong with him at all. He put his foot in the stirrup and then got on him. Breakspear put on the hell of a buck, my father went up and up and up into the air, then came down and hit the ground very hard. He got on him again and came off him again. After three times he managed to stay on. Then came the problem of getting the car home, so, full of youthful confidence, I said I would drive the car behind my father. I had driven it once or twice about the farm, so I got into the car and proceeded to go in jerks and stalls across the yard of Arthur Brake's farm. By the time I had gone half a mile down the road, my father was waiting for me. He had decided that since he had two more sons at home, he could, if necessary, afford to lose me, but during war time he had no hope of getting another car. So he took me out of the car, and Breakspear, who had had him off another five times in the half-mile, stood absolutely quiet whilst I got on him, one leg stiff in plaster, and took me home as if he was an old plug. He knew I could not do anything if he bucked, so he carried me safely and carefully all the way home. This incident shows the kindness and consideration even the most difficult horse has for a rider who is put in his care.

The horse that followed him displayed the opposite tendency. This was a sixteen-two strawberry-roan mare which we got from the late Arthur Palmer. She was a magnificent horse, but she had one unfortunate tendency : as soon as anyone got on her back, she would go flat out to the nearest tree and try to jam the rider into the trunk or knock him off under the branches. She tried it with me once and got me off. The second time she went straight for a big elm tree, and at the last second, finding I had no hope of steering her away from it, I swung her head the other way hard into the tree so that she went flat-out head-on into the tree. I went flying and she dropped to the ground as if she had been shot. I thought I had killed her. She did not move for about five minutes. When eventually she staggered to her feet very groggily, she was a sadder and wiser horse. I got on her again and rode her around the field, and she never tried that trick on again. But the story shows that an instantaneous reaction, an instant punishment, will cure a horse of most vices. After she had got me off the first time I did not curse at her, I did not swear, I just got on again; but the second time she went into the tree and knocked herself out. When she woke up there I was standing by her talking quietly and gently to her, and after a month or two she lost all desire to hurt human beings, and came to understand that we were her friends.

Early in 1946 my father went to Taunton races. Steeplechasing had started again just after the war and in the paddock of the three-mile race was a steelpoint gelding called Lucky Bargain. What attracted my father to him was the fact that he bucked his jockey off three times, eventually putting the poor man across the rails so that he could not ride him in the race. My father bought him for £25 from his somewhat disheartened owner. Lucky I will swear could count. It did not matter when you rode him, he always bucked you off three times. After he had had you off three times, he was quite content to let you ride him for the day. He was a very good horse. But he was a horse that taught me to sit a buck, he would twist and turn, and buck in a straight line, he would go flat-out bucking and then he would stop and buck in the same place. He was almost impossible to sit. But at the same time he was an extremely kind and gentle horse, for having bucked you off, he would always wait for you to get on. When you hunted him or raced him he would always give everything he had. He was very generous.

On one occasion my father sold him, warning the man that he bucked, and he went into training. After three months the trainer had had enough and my father bought him back in Exeter market, then we kept him until he died.

Over the next five years I had a number of horses, and through them learnt more and more, because it is only by watching and trying to understand a large number of horses that you can learn what pattern of behaviour is general to each breed, and what is applicable to horses in general rather than to horses in particular.

We had one horse, for instance, who had been completely soured by racing. He was a big chestnut called Tomahawk II and he was French-bred and had won a lot of hurdle races and two-mile steeple-chases. But he had taken a dislike to racing and would refuse to start. He would just run backwards. He could move backwards as fast as many horses could trot, and his trainer and owner had given him up as a bad job and sold him to Bert Newman's son George, who passed him on to me for £15.

I rode him for some time, and on one occasion my wife rode him down to the village of Banscombe, which is half a mile to a mile long, and proceeded down the whole street backwards. We eventually cured him of running backwards by just using patience and not trying to make him go forward. We would sit on him until he wanted to go forward and then he would go forward quite steadily and happily. Within three months we had him going right. He was the sort of horse who really made life worth living: he came to us miserable, unhappy and disliking men in general, but when we passed him on eighteen months later, he was happy, kind and ready to look upon everyone as his friend.

I have always had to sell my horses once they were going right, simply because I have never been able to afford to keep them. My horses have had to keep themselves and help to keep me. But there is another reason why I have allowed horses to come and go. I have always felt that since I have a gift with difficult horses, the gift must be used. If I had concentrated it on one horse and one horse alone, many of the other horses I have had in my life would never have been rehabilitated, and probably ended up in cat-meat tins.

There is one incident in this period that stands out in my mind. I was living down near Lyme Regis at the time, running a pig farm, and we had five unbroken three-year-olds on the place. One day the hounds met nearby, but I decided not to go out hunting, because my horse was down in the village. I was working on the farm when the hounds found, so I caught the nearest three-year-old and put a bridle on it, and even though it had never been ridden before, it went quietly for me and I hunted it for half an hour until the hounds came back to the farm, and I turned it out. I had hardly turned it out before the hounds found another fox, and since the horse I had been riding was a little tired, I caught the next one of the five – and so on for the rest of the day until I had hunted all five. They all went absolutely quietly, except the fifth, which bucked for about five minutes and that was all, and that taught me a very significant thing : the barrier against riding a horse for the first time is not in the horse, but within the mind of the man who rides him. It is a mental barrier.

In February 1954 I had got married, and in March 1955 my daughter was born. Arguing that the labourer is worthy of some reward, my wife asked me to buy her a horse, so I went down to Exeter market at the beginning of April. I could not see anything I liked at all. I was talking to Arthur Brake, from whom we had bought Breakspear some ten years earlier, when suddenly I heard a commotion, and saw a three-year-old rearing and plunging about. It was being held by two people on the end of a long rope, and the crowd around the ring scattered like confetti. The challenge was too much for me. I bought him for a maiden bid of £27. That horse carried my wife for some twenty years' hunting – we called him Cork Beg after her home – and he proved the horse that taught us most about animal communication.

I will not say much about him here as he will reappear in the pages of the book time and time again. But our relationship had an interesting beginning. I had great difficulty in getting him into the lorry to drive him home, and had to drive him up a cattle chute. When I got home, I unloaded him into the cattle yard to catch him, and noticed that he was frightened about his head and had a very quick temper. So, about two months later, after I had got him riding, I decided I had to make him submit to having his ears touched. I took him out into the yard and got on his back, then I ran my hand up his neck. He threw his head about. I ran my hand up his neck again and he threw his head about again. I kept on doing it for about ten minutes and finally the fragile fragments of his temper went, and he went straight up the road flat-out. Finding he had not worried or dislodged me, he swung to one side and jumped a five-foot barbed-wire fence, landing on the top strand. We both crashed to the ground. I have never been slow to make use of a golden opportunity, so I sat on his head so that he could not get up, and for the next half-hour proceeded to roll my hands all over his head and neck. It did not cure him but he was never quite so bad about his head again, though for years he used to pretend that he was petrified of anyone touching his ears.

For the first four or five years we had him, he was difficult to shoe or clip. When he was being shod the blacksmith, myself and anybody else who was about usually ended up in the yard on the dung heap. As time went on he got better, but for the rest of his life he refused to be shod unless I was there, though for the last ten years I had only to sit and talk to the blacksmith and he would allow himself to be shod.

He was a great character. My wife looked after him herself and I was only asked to help when he was being bloody-minded. Whenever he saw me coming on such an occasion he would gird up his loins for battle, and we would have a battle, enjoyed by both of us. It usually ended with my wife losing her temper and cursing me, but that was all part of the horse. He eventually died at the age of twenty-two.

Nine months before he died, he created what is probably equine history. He was turned out with his current girl-friend – the old man always had to have a girl-friend with him – in a boggy field, and she went across a bog, so he, forgetting his age, decided to follow her, and got himself stuck. When we found him he was half-buried with only his back, head and ears showing. After an hour-and-a-half of hard work, my wife and I managed to roll him on to a piece of dry ground, still in the middle of the bog. It was one of those times: usually when anything goes wrong, there are a thousand people on your doorstep straight away to help, but on this occasion we did not see anyone pass us for nearly two hours, and we were faced with the problem of getting the old man across fifty yards of bog. So I went home and got three five-foot by four-foot sheets of plywood, and made a platform on the bog. The old man was only on three legs, but he managed to hop from the island on to the first piece of plywood, and then on to the second, then on to the third, by which time I had managed to get the first piece in front, and so we went on. Slowly and steadily the old man followed my wife from one piece of plywood to the other. When he was quite sure that it was safe and secure, he would hop on to it. So we got him home. But by this time his back joint was very badly swollen. I thought he must have pulled a tendon in the joint, so we left him hobbling around, and for the next two months, three or four times a day, he would give a screech to let us know that he was lying down and could not get up, and my wife and I would have to go out. She would take his head and he would get his front legs up, and I would get under his hind quarters and heave, until he got his good hind leg from underneath, and could get up. He never seemed to worry. He would hobble around quite happily with his girl-friend, and after about five weeks he was putting his foot to the ground a little bit. By September, about six months later, he was back on his leg again, though a little stiff in the joint. When the old man died on 17th October we had a post mortem on the leg, and found that the joint had broken right across and had healed itself.

A year after I had bought Cork Beg I went back to the market again, looking for a horse myself, and suddenly from a pen at the back of the market I seemed to get a message: 'for God's sake get me out of this.' I was drawn as if by a magnet to a sixteen-two-hand dirty brown thoroughbred horse, who was as thin as a rake. When he came up in the auction I purchased him for £40. This horse was Weeping Roger, and he it was who set me seriously to study how horses communicate with each other and how man communicates with horses.

From the very start Roger and I seemed to have an affinity for each other, and it was handling and working him that first made me realize the power a man may have over a horse, if he really applies his mind to its control and handling. This set me thinking about the whole question of communication between man and horse, about how much it seemed to depend upon *mental* control. If this were true, conventional training methods were wasteful and inefficient.

I decided to test out my ideas. At about this time my father had bought a four-year-old thoroughbred gelding, who had been used as a stallion for two years and then castrated, so I asked him to let me try a new breaking method. I worked on the horse intensively for seven days: handling him, gentling him and working him. I got on him on the second day, and then rode him for an hour in the morning and afternoon for the next five days. This was a completely unbroken horse, yet on the seventh day we took him down to Taunton, where my father and I were both playing polo, and I was able to play him in a slow chukka and he went extremely well. On the following Wednesday, that is ten days after the horse had first been handled, I played him again, this time in a fast chukka, and he never put a foot wrong. He turned out to be a really first-class polo pony who loved the game.

It normally takes at least two years' schooling to make a polo pony; yet by using mental control to get the horse to want to do what I wanted him to, I had done two years' work in ten days!

I was immensely excited: it seemed to me that I had stumbled on the edge of a real discovery, the meaning of which I was determined fully to grasp. What exactly was the 'mental control' I had exercised over my father's gelding? What precisely was the affinity I felt with Weeping Roger? I was to spend the following years trying to solve these mysteries. Meanwhile I was to have further evidence of the extraordinary sympathy that can exist between human being and horse. One such piece of evidence concerned a pony I bought for my daughter Paddy.

When Paddy was about three years old I went back to Exeter market again, and bought a three-year-old Dartmoor-cross Shetland pony who stood a bare nine hands high. He was obviously too small for me to break, so I got the daughter of a neighbour to break him for me. Darwi (that was his name) and Doreen got on like a house on fire and developed so close an affinity for each other that Darwi, who could get out of any field, whenever he got lonely or bored at night used to take himself the two-and-a-half miles to Doreen and bang on her window until she came to talk to him. Doreen did not mind, but her parents used to object strongly.

Darwi did Paddy extremely well for a couple of years, and then we passed him on to a friend who wanted a child's pony for his daughter. And that was the last we heard of him for eight years. We came to Wales, and Doreen went off to a job somewhere. Then seven or eight years later, my father was at a gymkhana and who should greet him in her rather distinctive voice, but Doreen. My father had not been talking to her for more than five minutes when their attention was drawn to a pony who was whinneying its head off at the far end of the field. Suddenly they could see a pony bolting out of control with a very small child on its back. Child and pony came round the ring flat-out, straight to where my father and Doreen were standing, and skidded to a halt. My father rescued the child, and the pony proceeded to greet Doreen. After eight years he had recognised her voice from the other side of the field. I do not suppose Doreen had handled Darwi for more than three or four months. But a bond was there between them even after eight years.

These experiences redoubled my enthusiasm for the work we were beginning to do on animal communication, and encouraged me to start trying to make some sense out of the signs, sounds and other signals we could observe the horses using to make their intentions and wishes plain to each other.

2: *Horses in History – Man's Unique Bond with the Horse*

Basic communication with horses is quite simple, and there is nothing superhuman about it. The horse can easily be trained to communicate with man, and to understand man's communication. If you sit on a horse and pull the reins, it will stop quite easily – it is trained to stop when it feels the pressure of the bit. When you touch it with your heels it will go forward. You can steer it to the right, you can steer it to the left. You can teach your horse very quickly to do anything it is physically capable of doing. This is all communication, because man is communicating to the horse through a language which they both understand, a language of signs taught to the horse by man.

But the horse himself also communicates with other horses, and it is this communication that I have set out to understand. Over the past twenty years I have concentrated my energies on grasping the language that horses use themselves, not only to understand other horses but to communicate also with man. For I was convinced that there is another and more subtle level of communication between man and horse than the simple pressure of heel and rein. But of course I realized that before I could do anything, I had to understand how much was already known to man.

I was between twelve and fourteen when I first started to wonder why man rode horses and not cattle, sheep or pigs, and so I experimented a little. I tried to ride the heifers and pigs on the farm, and after being deposited a great number of times on the ground, concluded that the reason they were so difficult to ride was that they would simply not co-operate and work *with* you as horses do. Yet this conclusion itself poses a problem : *why* would horses let you ride them and not other animals? It was obvious that the horse was more intelligent than either the cow or the pig. It was just as obvious that it was stronger. Yet cattle are much more docile than horses, they drive more easily, they are quieter and steadier and much safer animals to handle. Yet you cannot ride them. It could not be an instinct of self-preservation which made the heifer shake the rider off its back, since the same animal preyed on both the cattle and the horse. I could only suppose that there was some unique rapport, a special relationship, between man and horse which does not exist with any other animal, excepting possibly the dog. Why this should be so I did not know at the time, but I was to find out later from reading and from my own experience.

From my reading I discovered that horses featured in the cave drawings of prehistoric man first as prey for food, and later as mounts for man in hunting and in battle. Pictures of horses are engraved on the tombs of the Pharaohs, horses are embodied in the Greek myths. Greek sculptors carved horses on their magnificent friezes. It was Xenophon, the famous Greek general, who said : 'horses are taught not by harshness but by gentleness.'

Alexander the Great was able to conquer a great part of the then known world largely by his use of his fine cavalry; and he it probably was who first discovered the value of crossing the hot-blooded Arab with the cold-blooded horse of Europe. His closeness to his own mount is shown by the fact that his horse Bucephalus is one of the first to be mentioned by name in history.

The great myth of the centaurs who were supposed to be part man, part horse was probably based on travellers' reports of the Mongolian tribe, the Hsiung-nu, who were later to appear as the Huns under Attila who tore the Roman Empire apart. The Hsiung-nu were nomads who controlled the whole of the central and Eastern European plain and were herdsmen and warriors. They kept their herds on the oceans of grass extending from the Hungarian plain to Manchuria and the great wall of China. Always searching for food, in the winter they sheltered under the lee of the mountains and in the spring they moved north and east to find fresh grazing. They waged war on everybody, even on sections of their own race, and on all of the northern civilized world. They were said to be born on horseback and could ride before they could walk. They used their horses for everything: they would no more think of walking more than two or three steps than they would dream of flying, and so no doubt gave rise to the legend of a race that were part man and part horse.

By the end of the second century BC the Hsiung-nu ruled a large section of the world. The Emperor of China, Wu-ti, was in such terror of them that he developed a very formidable cavalry force, and about 142 BC the brilliant Chinese General Hoc'u-P'ing managed to split the main Hsiung-nu army; but even then the Chinese cavalry proved inferior. So the Emperor Wu-ti sent an army of three hundred thousand men three thousand miles to Western Afghanistan to capture a superior breed of horse. The whole army died on the way. Nothing daunted, Wu-ti sent out a second army, and enough of these survived the three thousand miles to Afghanistan and three thousand miles back to bring back thirty breeding animals. They were probably a strain of Arab, reported to be able to travel three hundred miles a day and to sweat blood. Almost certainly they were descendants of Arabs who had been carried eastwards by Alexander the Great's troops.

The success of Julius Caesar in establishing Roman rule over so much of Europe was almost certainly due to his brilliance as a cavalry general. Again, he and his horse were reported to be inseparable. The Emperor Caligula, indeed, thought so much of his horse Incitatus that, according to legend, he made him a Senator, claiming that he was both wiser and more loyal than any other member of the Senate. The Roman Empire survived 500 years, until the superior horse power of the Hun army, which had already conquered the northern world, finally sacked Rome in AD 408.

Later these same Mongolian horseback tribes were to re-appear as the hordes of Ghengis Khan, who were also supposed to be conceived, born and married, and finally to die, on their horses. On one occasion Ghengis Khan's troops conquered a town by climbing a cliff on horseback which the defenders thought to be unscalable by man.

Central to all this history lies the uncanny relationship between man and horse. Later Norman knights in armour and the fabulous Ottoman cavalry took their turns to conquer the then-known world. In each case a key to victory was the understanding and use of the horse; for these ancient armies were made up of riders who knew how to communicate with horses.

There is a story told of an Arab chief named Jabal who owned the fastest horse in the world. Hassad Pacha, then governor of Damascus, wished to buy the mare and repeatedly made Jabal the most liberal offers, which he steadily refused. The Pacha threatened him but with no better success. In the end he persuaded a Bedouin called Gafar, from another tribe, to steal the mare, offering as a reward to fill the mare's nosebag with gold. News of this bargain got out and Jabal became more watchful than ever and secured his mare at night with an iron chain, one end of which was fastened to her hind fetlock and the other to the ground under Jabal's bed. But one night Gafar crept silently into the tent and succeeded in loosening the chain. Just before he started off with the mare, he caught up Jabal's lance and poking him with the butt end, cried out 'I am Gafar, I have stolen your noble mare and give you notice in time.' This warning was in accordance with the customs of the desert, for to rob a member of another tribe was considered to be an honourable exploit, and Gafar wanted the glory of the theft. Jabal when he heard the words rushed out of the tent and gave the alarm, jumped on to his brother's horse and, accompanied by some of his tribe, pursued the robber for four hours. The brother's mare was of the same breeding as Jabal's horse, but was not quite as fast as she was. Nevertheless she out-galloped

all the other pursuers and was on the point of overtaking
the robber, when Jabal shouted at him 'pinch her right ear
and give her the touch of the heel.' Gafar did so and went away
with the mare like lightning, speedily rendering pursuit hopeless. The pinch of the ear and the touch of the heel were the
secret signs by which Jabal had been used to make his mare
increase her speed. Jabal's companions were amazed and
indignant at his strange conduct. 'You are the father of a
jackass,' they cried, 'Fancy enabling the thief to rob you!'
But he answered them by saying 'I would rather lose her than
spoil her reputation. Would you have me suffer it to be said
among the tribes that another mare had proved greater than
mine? I have at least this comfort left to me. I can say she
has never met her match.'

This is a lovely legend, and the point of it is that until
the correct form of communication was used, the mare
did not know what to do, but as soon as the correct command was given, she settled down and galloped like the
wind.

In America too there are countless stories of the horse,
but the only American Indians who set out to study and
understand the horse were the Mohicans. They did not break
the horse's spirit by getting on it and riding it until it gave in.
They used to spend days handling it, talking to it and feeding
it, and gently, gently, gently getting on its back. They would
work for hours over a horse's back with a blanket, and when
the horse understood what they wanted, they had no trouble
in riding it.

Over the last century there have been men all over the
world who have gained fame as horse-tamers. In America
there was Reary, in Australia Galvin, in Ireland Dan Sullivan
the Whisperer, and in this country Palmer and later on Captain Hayes. The stories about them are legion, but basically
they have one feature in common, and this is the hero's
ability to control and dominate a horse no matter how difficult or how wild. Their methods varied. Reary had a system
of ropes and throwing a horse to train it. Galvin had a

number of 'humane twitches', as he called them. Some, like Palmer, had 'taming oils', for which there were various recipes, one involving grinding the chestnut of a horse's leg into a powder, and blowing it into his nostrils. Oil of rhodium was sometimes used, so was origanum, and some people simply used the sweat from their armpits. These techniques have one virtue in common: they all gave the person using them a certain amount of confidence in handling a difficult horse.

But Sullivan the Horse-Whisperer was probably the greatest of all the old-fashioned horse tamers, for he used nothing but his own ability. He would go up to horses, who were killers, kickers or unbreakable in some other way, and he would have the door shut on him. After an hour or so he would open the door, and walk the horse out on a halter absolutely quiet. The Whisperer never took any pupils and he never taught even his own sons his skill. He was so jealous of his gift that even his priest at Ballyclough could not get the secret out of him in confession. Sullivan's sons used to boast about how His Reverence met the Whisperer on the road towards Mallow and charged him with being a confederate of the devil. The Whisperer made the priest's horse bolt for miles until the holy man promised in despair to let Sullivan alone with his secret for ever. Only one of the Whisperer's sons practised his art, but he had no real knowledge of how to do it and neither of the other two pretended any skill at all. The Whisperer had a great fascination for me because I had this ability to handle difficult horses myself, and I often wondered how his gift compared with mine. But I think he used something similar to the system that we practice ourselves when we gentle a horse. I believe he used to get his hand on to the horse and simulate the movements of a mare nuzzling her foal, and as soon as the horse understood the familiar signs, he would relax, and all the time Sullivan would be talking with his gentle sing-song Irish voice, until he could get both his hands on the horse and relax him, and create a bond of understanding between him and the horse.

Palmer, the English horse-tamer, used taming oils which he would put on his hand, then put his hand under the horse's nose and blow it up his nostrils, and the horse would immediately become docile. Barbara Woodhouse relates how a similar practice is still used in South America, though without the oils, probably taken there from this country about the middle of the last century. There is nothing strange about this custom: when two horses meet, they will blow through their nostrils, strongly or gently depending on their mood. Two horses that are hostile to each other will almost trumpet through their nostrils; while a mare caressing her foal will blow so gently that you can hardly hear her. When Palmer blew up the horse's nostrils, all he said was 'I am friendly, I will not hurt you.' If you are doing this yourself you should next get your hand on to the horse and get your fingers into physical contact. The horse again will understand; because when two horses are frightened, they will push together to get physical contact.

This principle is similar to that behind the system practised by the American Mohicans. They too would get physical contact with their horses, and as soon as physical contact was established the horse began to understand, because the signs that he used himself were being used.

It should now be clear that these methods all had one thing in common: they all used the signs that the horses use themselves, and so instead of using foreign signs and sounds to train a horse, they used signs and sounds the horse already understood.

Captain Horace Hayes' methods are so well known that there is no need for me to go into them here, but the point of interest is that a pupil of his was Captain Ward Jackson, who was my father's Company Commander in India during the First World War, and Ward Jackson took my father as a pupil and taught him Hayes' methods, and in turn of course my father taught me, so I always feel a very close contact with Horace Hayes. There is a lovely story about him, which as far as I know has not been told before. When Hayes was in India he dined one night in a neighbouring mess. The wine was good and it was well sampled, the whole party got rather high, and everyone was talking expansively. Now it so happened that the Colonel of the regiment owned an un-manageable horse and late in the evening he sold it to Hayes, and then bet him that he would be unable to ride him on parade the next day. They settled for a bet of five hundred rupees. Horace Hayes, anxious to win his bet, left the party and spent the rest of the night working on the horse to get it going. The following morning Hayes rode the horse out on parade, and the horse went beautifully for him. The Colonel, anticipating the loss of his five hundred rupees, ordered the troops to fire a *feu-de-joie*, which meant that they fired off their rifles at random. When this happened all the other chargers disappeared with their riders over the horizon; but not so the horse Hayes was riding. He stood like a rock, still and relaxed. As soon as the order was given, Hayes had kicked his feet out of the stirrups, pulled out his pipe and lit it. He was so relaxed that his horse took no notice of the rifles being fired. The other officers on the other hand, fearing that the horses were going to bolt, pulled them together, and in doing so, frightened them even more than the rifles had done. This story finely illustrates the great control that man can have over a horse by controlling him mentally as well as physically.

Such control and understanding no doubt not only applies to horses, for it is probably the great art of stockmanship in general to know and understand the animals that you are handling and sense when something is wrong with them. I remember an incident that took place when I was about twelve years old. By some miracle I had beaten Les the cow-man into the cowshed one morning. (This was the only time it ever happened that I was up before Les.) I remember him coming into the cow stall, and almost before he was through the door, saying 'What is the matter with Pride?' He could not see Pride, but sure enough, when he walked down to the far end of the cow stall, Pride was lying down with milk fever. There was a bond between Les and the cows of much the same kind as I feel with horses.

Similarly, a shepherd may have an intuitional sympathy with his sheep. I have heard a shepherd claim that at lambing time he often got up in the middle of the night, without quite knowing why, to go out to the sheep; and to use his own words 'Hardly a journey was a wasted one.' There was always something wrong that needed his attention.

Animal communication has become a problem of increasing concern to modern mankind over the past twenty years. The Russians were the first people to start serious research just over twenty years ago, and more recently the Americans have taken an interest. The Russians however, seem to have started off on the wrong track. They based their work on observations on dogs and rats and the thing that I think led them the wrong way is the fact that the rat has a number of signals with definite meanings, that are easy to discern, and researchers have thus been encouraged to try to make patterns of other signals and sounds, or of the signs made by other animals. For example, the rat has a definite signal for distress and other signals for alarm : these are vocal signals designed to carry a very large distance. It also has an ultrasonic squeak which it gives when meeting another rat, the note of the squeak denoting its place within the social hierarchy. The dog equally has a number of sounds which have definite meanings. But to observe these sounds without taking into account other forms of communication leads only to a dead-end. They are only *part* of the animal's communication system.

The Americans have done a lot of very good work, though they have also concentrated on sounds. Their work was on dolphins, however, whose main form of communication is in sound : because a lot of dolphin communication takes place when the animals are out of sight of each other, the dolphins seem to have a developed vocal language which most animals do not.

This primary mistake of the early researchers, who tried to make a pattern out of the sounds the animals made, was largely the result of assuming that man's behaviour pattern was similar in this respect to that of animals. Since people of the same race use a set language it was argued that man as a whole uses a set language, which he does not. Mankind as a whole uses a number of languages. It was also assumed that man communicates using sounds alone, and this again is wrong. Man does not use sounds alone to convey any meaning, since he also uses signs and facial expression, which itself is a sign. The major error in these three basic assumptions has resulted in only part of each animal's language being investigated – that is, only sounds or signs – and it is obviously impossible to understand any language by only understanding part of it.

As we will show later, man's behaviour pattern in communication cannot be directly related to forms of comunication used by animals. Each species of animal is different. You cannot conclude that the form of communication used by one species is in any way parallel to the form of communication used by a completely different species. Very fortunately in this country, the little research that has been done in communication has been done in conjunction with research into animal behaviour. This has meant that research has not followed the pattern that has dominated the Russians and the Americans. Doctor Martha Kylie has done some research with cattle, and Meek and Ewbank have done a certain amount of research at Liverpool University. (In a similar spirit some very good work has been done in Africa on apes and chimpanzees.) Very little practical use has been made so far of any of this research into animal communication, however.

The Americans on the other hand have used their research to train dolphins for military purposes, and incidentally for use in the movies. The film *The Day of the Dolphin* is a fascinating example of how research into animal communication can be used. The six dolphins in this film were

caught by the trainer Peter Moss off the coast of Florida. He
was to remark later that there was something more than a
man-animal relationship in the situation that developed
between George C. Scott, who was the star of the film, Mike
Nicolls, who was the director, and the dolphins. So great
was this rapport that one observer who watched the dolphins
at work insisted that the the dolphins were actually 'expressing
themselves' – that they really could act. Nicolls himself said
he found himself reacting to the dolphins just as if they were
temperamental actors. Some days he loved them, some days
he hated them. Since the dolphins' life is all play, their
favourite game was rearranging the underwater lights used
in the film, which at times made the filming impossible.
Nicolls would get furious with them when they refused to do
something they knew how to do, but then two minutes later
they would come and rub their bellies on his feet and nibble
his toes as if saying, to use his words, 'come on, don't be
mad'. On one occasion Nicolls was sitting by the pool
reading the script for the next day's scene, with one hand
lightly scratching the tongue of the dolphin who was playing
the male lead. The dolphin had been christened Buck, and
Buck just lay there with his head on the side of the tank
and his mouth wide open. Then Nicolls looked at Buck,
and suddenly knew he was ready to be filmed. Right on cue
the dolphin swam to the side of the tank, pushed himself
under the arm of the boy who was playing the scene with
him, and then proceeded to dive and swim right through a
narrow opening, still with the boy in tow. Such was his timing
that he got the actor to the position right on cue to say his
two lines. In all, Buck and the actor repeated the movement
ten times, but each time they were failed by sunlight. Then
on the eleventh attempt, Buck, who had not made a mistake
throughout, reared out of the water, began to make a series
of sounds which built up into a noise like a football cheer,
turned abruptly and swam away. 'That was what I was
afraid of,' said Moss, 'it was boring him.'

Peter Moss had no trouble in teaching the dolphins to

perform specific actions. But when one of the dolphins had to have a worried, apprehensive look, that was more difficult. In the end it was Nicolls who taught the dolphins to look apprehensive. Moss himself says that if he described the relationship that grew up between the dolphins and the director, people would say that he was mad.

It had been decided that at the end of the film the dolphins would be allowed to go free. Nicolls said that in the event there was no choice about it: as soon as the two main dolphins had finished their last shot they made their own decision, turned round and swam out to the ocean. They took care of their fate themselves; but only when they knew the film was finished.

This story may be dismissed as a typical piece of Publicity Office ballyhoo, but to anyone who has experienced the amazing results that can be obtained by communicating with animals in the language that they understand, and developing a real relationship with them, it has that unmistakable ring of truth. There are things in the story that even Hollywood could not dream up: even in this permissive age to suggest that one of its directors and a male dolphin could form a special relationship, is a little outrageous!

I was reminded by this story of something that happened to me in 1970 at the Royal Welsh Show. The Welsh Cob Society had been asked to put on a display in the main ring and I was to do a special demonstration at the end, showing the versatility of the Welsh Cob. I had an awkward bloody-minded little horse called Trefais Comet. He was also without any doubt one of the most versatile horses of the breed, and I had developed a tremendous relationship with him. For the demonstration I had prepared a number of exercises, one of which was a full pass, which means that the horse walks at right angles to itself sideways. When I tried to teach him this, I took him up to a four-foot forestry fence, walked him up the fence once sideways then down sideways and then up sideways again. I was feeling very pleased with myself, so I decided to do it once more. I went down sideways, then he took half a step back and went straight over the four-foot fence and that was that. I decided I could not do it at the Royal Welsh. But on the first day we had a wait before the display, so I was thinking about this when Comet suddenly, without any prompting from me, did a full pass one way and a full pass the other, and so that went into the demonstration. On the second day I was asked beforehand what I was going to do, so I told the officials, and Comet went straight into the ring and did everything exactly as I said I was going to do it, plus something that I would have thought was impossible, which was jumping into the air and turning in the air to face in the opposite direction. After his performance, he so loved the crowd's applause that he proceeded to invent things for himself to excel in. He was very fast and excitable, and one of the things I knew I could not do was stop him dead, but nevertheless he finished his demonstration completely out of control, galloping straight towards the president's box and then at the last second stopping dead and standing on his hind legs. I had wanted him to do this and he knew I had wanted to do it, so he put it in himself. This is the kind of phenomenon that is possible once you are communicating with your horse effectively.

In the early days of our work, which began in 1955–6, we dealt mainly with Weeping Roger and Cork Beg. This meant that our research was largely limited to the signs and sounds used by those two particular horses. We knew that there was more to 'Equine Communication' than signs and sounds, but we felt it best to begin by trying to understand what the horse was saying, and why and how he responded to the signs and sounds used by another horse. This knowledge would be the basis for future work. But it was soon obvious from our observations that the horses were using the same signs and same sounds to convey a large number of meanings, so we concluded that there must be something more than signs and sounds at work to distinguish one meaning from another, and we called this unknown factor 'attitude' or 'feeling'. It was only later that we used the terms 'telepathy' and 'extra-sensory perception' : in fact it was ten years before we came round to doing so.

Research into the communication between animals is of comparatively recent origin, but knowledge and understanding of animal communication is as old as man himself, and primitive tribes today have far more knowledge of animal communication than civilized man. Laurens Van Der Post in his travels among the bushmen discovered that the witch doctors could put themselves into a trance by gazing at the cave drawing of an antelope, and then describe where the antelope were to be found. In other words, the witch doctor could put himself in mental communication with any antelope within ten or fifteen miles' radius, so that the hunters of the tribe could go out and kill it for food. Van Der Post calls this facility 'empathy'. But from our own work, we know it to be the one we call telepathy : the ability that animals use to transfer mental pictures to one another.

Much modern research into animal communication has been complicated by the fact that it has been limited to only one means of communication, usually sound; and this is as fruitless as trying to understand English by learning only the verbs. If we are to understand what horses are trying to say, and to make ourselves easily understood by them, we must use and understand the whole language, and not just one part of it. We must thus learn to think and react as the horse thinks and reacts, and guard against the sentimentality of anthropomorphism : that is, against endowing the animal with human characteristics. Indeed the man must reverse the process and when handling horses become half-horse. Alex Kerr, the lion tamer, was once asked if he would allow his daughter to tame and train big cats, and he said no. Asked why, he said, 'Well, it is quite simple. To do it successfully she must think like a lion or a tiger, and if she thinks and acts like a lion or a tiger, the lion or tiger will look upon her as a lion or tiger, and that would mean that when she came into season, as human beings do just as animals do, the cat would know. And since the way a lion denotes affection is to pick the female up by the scruff of the neck, that is what he would do. And he would break her neck.' This is the essence of our communicating work. Alex Kerr probably had more understanding of how felines think than any living man and his book *No Bars Between* is unequalled.

The first person in recent times to claim to be able to communicate with animals was the Englishman Archie Delany, who masqueraded for a long time as an Indian half-breed called Grey Owl and wrote two famous books, *Tales of an Empty Cabin* and *Sasho and the Beaver People*. He was also the first man to advocate conservation, and he started the first of the modern nature reserves. Although in some things he was a fraud, he was also a very great man with a very great understanding with wild animals, especially beavers, on whose habits and behaviour patterns he did some outstanding work. The beavers accepted him so completely that they made their lodge within his cabin at the side of a lake. He claimed to have produced a dictionary of beaver language, but I have unfortunately not been able to obtain a copy of this dictionary, and those reports I have of it indicate that it has been of little use to other people.

One of the many people to visit him was Mr John Diefenbaker, later Canadian Prime Minister, who visited him in late 1935 or early 1936. When he got there with a party of people, Delany said he would have to go and ask the beavers if they would receive him. Then he came back and said that the beavers had said they would. This was obviously pure showmanship, but there is little doubt that in spite of his masquerade Delany did make a magnificent breakthrough in the study of animal communication. It was nearly twenty years before anyone else even attempted to communicate with animals, and very little use has been made of his work, mainly, I suspect, because of the academic's inbuilt prejudice against any research done by a person living and working outside a university. But it is my feeling that it is to people like Alex Kerr and Grey Owl that we have to turn if we wish to extend our present understanding of animal communication and behaviour.

There is a real difficulty in this experiential approach to study. For to understand the horse you must become a horse, you must think like a horse and act like a horse, research becomes extremely difficult, since it is difficult to be analytical at the same time as trying to think and react as the animals will do : animals are simply not analytical! But we are not, nor have we ever been, concerned with orthodox research. We are interested only in gaining a greater understanding of our horses, and we hope that other people will reap from the ground that we are now sowing. It will be for them to take the work that we have done and analyse it, and carry out orthodox research on the foundations that we are now building.

3: *The Language of Horses*

It is already clear that there is a great deal of communication between man and horse in the ordinary process of handling. First man communicates with a horse with his voice in his basic training of his animal. He teaches him certain words of command: 'whoa,' 'walk on,' 'trot on,' 'steady,' and so on. These words the horse learns and his rider hopes that he will obey them. In turn, man learns the significance of some of the sounds used by the horse. He quickly learns to recognize the whicker of welcome, the neigh saying 'is anybody about,' and the squeal of anger.

Man also teaches his horse a number of signs: he touches the horse with his heels to tell him to go forward and he pulls at the reins, that is he exerts pressure on the horse's mouth, to make him stop. He caresses him when the horse is good and he hits him when he has done wrong. These exchanges are all basic to communicating with any animal. A vet trying to diagnose an illness will observe other signs made by a horse: for instance if a place hurts the horse will wince if you touch it. The horse will also tell you if you are hurting him by a sharp intake of breath. You can also tell if the horse is sick and out of sorts by his listless and dejected attitude. All these are the ways a horse communicates by signs with you. He will equally tell you if he is excited and he will tell you if he is tired, by the way he carries himself.

When we started research into animal communication, we decided to try to compile a short dictionary of horse messages, and for this we started by following the path that had been trodden by most people in the same field. Since we use sounds ourselves to communicate, it seemed obvious to start by studying horse sounds, so we decided to try to deduce some pattern from the sounds horses make. In these early stages we had a certain degree of success. We found that the whicker of welcome and the neigh of alarm were sounds that were common to very nearly all horses. But the more research we carried out, the more we discovered that we could not rely on set patterns as a guide to interpreting the sounds used by horses as a species. It became clear that different horses use the same sequence of sounds to convey different meanings, each horse having its own language, only similar to that of its associates and not identical. So we had to go back and start again.

We did this first by looking at how human beings communicate, and we discovered that as much is conveyed by the tone of voice and the manner of delivering a phrase as by the actual words themselves. For example, an Englishman, an Irishman, a Scotsman and a Welshman all speak English. They can understand each other, but their means of conveying any meaning is different. They will use different words, different phrases in different forms. In other words, people of different cultural background, even though they speak the same basic language, will use different words and phrases to convey a single meaning. And even within one culture, people of different nature and temperament will use divergent word-forms to convey a single meaning. Certain sounds on the other hand are standard to all people of the same race and are used at certain times: the word 'hello' for instance is common to all English-speaking people. It is in the same sense that the whicker of welcome is common to all horses. And just as the cry of 'help' is used by all people who speak English, most horses have a neigh or scream of alarm.

We also looked at the importance of the tone of voice to meaning. We found that the tone of the voice used by human beings to convey a standard message can vary both its meaning and its force. For example, a man or a woman using the phrase 'come here' can vary its whole sense by the tone of voice. If the words are murmured by a woman in a soft and seductive voice, it can be an invitation to make love. If the tone of voice is sharp or harsh it is a command to be

obeyed instantly, and if screamed 'come here' can be a cry
for help. In the same way the horse can vary its message by
a raising and hardening of the voice, so that similar sounds can
mean anything from 'come here, darling' to, in its highest and
hardest imperative, 'if you do not come here immediately
I will have your guts for garters.' And exactly the same
message can be used as a cry for help.

The second thing we found we had to take into account
was that habits of communication vary according to sex;
and whereas among human beings there are only two sexes,
male and female, among domesticated horses there are three
sexes, male, female and neuter. This is important, since the
note and tone of each sex is different: the range of
notes used by a stallion and a mare are completely different, and the gelding will come somewhere between the two.
This is not so important when you are in contact with a
single horse, but it is extremely important to remember if you
are handling a large number of horses, or are trying to
understand what a strange horse is saying, since the same
sequence of notes used by a mare, a gelding and a stallion
can mean different things.

Before you can even start to interpret a message made by
sound, therefore, you have to know the sex of the animal.
We also discovered that it is important to take into account
the age of the horse, because obviously the range of tones
and notes used by a foal is completely different from the notes
and range he will use as a stallion four or five years later.

On the other hand the stallion, mare, gelding, foal and
yearling will all have the same number of tones and notes,
and they will be made in eleven different ways. Nine of the
eleven different tones of voice are made by exhaling, that is
to say they are made by breathing out. First there is a snort,
which is made by using the nostrils alone as a sound box,
and at times the imperative is expressed by crackling the
nostrils at the same time. The stronger note with the crackling
of the nostrils is used to draw attention as a signal of alarm,
as a sign the horse is excited or to denote strong emotions.

The whicker is also made by using the nostrils as a sound box, but this is a much more caressing note and can vary from a very gentle blowing through the nostrils to quite a strong sound, used usually as a greeting or to show affection of some sort. Then there is the whinney, which is a much higher-pitched enquiring sound, and the neigh, which is stronger again than the whinney. In these two the voice box is used. In addition we know the squeal of the mare, and the bell of the stallion, each of which can have a distinctive sexual tone to them, or may sound aggressive or be used as a warning. These both come from the upper nasal regions of the voice box and are used in sex play, in anger or to display temper. The stallion has a whistle which he uses to call the mare; and all horses have a scream of fear, pain or anger which comes as a gust of terror from the lungs. These are all exhaling sounds. The breathing-in sounds consist of a snuffle, which corresponds to the gentle blowing out, and a sniff, which corresponds to the snort. Each of these notes has a definite meaning for another horse.

The stallion has the greatest vocal range, and some of his notes are frightening, while others will be very beautiful to hear. But he has a somewhat limited range of messages to deliver with his voice, simply because in his natural state he is concerned only with three things: sex, danger and food. So his messages are confined to these three subjects. In fact you might say he has only got three subjects of conversation, fear, food and female, which makes him very like man, except that man has one further topic of conversation, and that is how best to avoid work. So in addition to 'let's eat', 'let's make love', 'let's bugger off', mankind also adds 'let's strike'!

A mare on the other hand, while she has her sexual sounds and her sounds for food and danger, also has a range of sounds for the care and protection of her foal, and probably her yearling as well. She has to call her young to her for food, she has to call them in case of threatened danger and she has to teach them discipline, so her range of messages will be far greater than that of the stallion. A gelding, which of course does not exist in the wild, has a vocal range which may vary from that of a stallion, if it has been cut very late, to that of a mare if it is over-protective to the person who looks after it. A foal equally will have its own messages and vocal range concerning food and fear; it will have no sexual messages but it will have a range of sounds asking for protection and reassurance, and these will change as he gets older. He will retain some of his foal phrases as a yearling and even as a two-year-old. Then, when he starts feeling a man in his two-year-old summer, and certainly as a three-year-old, unless he has already been cut, his messages and voice will change to that of a stallion; or a filly will develop the language of a mare.

Contact with man too increases a horse's vocal range. This makes for complications, since it is almost impossible to differentiate between the messages that are natural to the horse and those that result from contact with man. If feeding is late, for example, a horse that has been in contact with man will whinney or bang his manger, or make some other sign to remind you it is time to feed him. This action is completely unknown to the horse in the wilds, since his food is always there, and he does not have to draw man's attention to the fact that he is hungry. We note from observation that when a horse discovers the messages that he is trying to convey are understood, either by another horse or by man, he will use it again: that is, he extends his own vocabulary. The most extensive vocabulary we have ever come across was that of Cork Beg whom we owned for twenty years, and we observed that other horses who had had little or no contact with man learned phrases from him and thus extended their vocabularies.

We were taught just how much one horse can learn from another by another horse belonging to my wife, Rostellan. When Cork Beg was getting somewhat arthritic and stiff and no longer enjoyed a long day's hunting, it was important to get another horse to help him out. We were very fortunate in that we had a registered Welsh Cob, Trefais Dafydd, who seemed to fill the bill perfectly. Trefais Dafydd being such a mouthful, we called him Rostellan after an estate near my wife's home in Ireland. (Cork Beg had been named after her home.) He arrived at our place in a lorry-load of nine horses, none of which had ever been handled in any way. He was a big, black three-year-old. By the autumn, when we decided to keep him, he had filled out considerably and had established his own particular place in the establishment. The only way my wife could find time to exercise two horses during the winter was to ride Cork Beg and let Rostellan follow behind with her labrador, Dora. He soon learnt to follow very closely to heel and never tried to pass Cork Beg. If he did Cork Beg would swing his head round and threaten to have a large piece of his anatomy for breakfast. Having established the correct order in the herd of two, Cork Beg was quite pleased to take on an apprentice and to teach him the tricks of the trade, and just how much the pupil was learning from the master I discovered one day when I went out after lunch. Cork Beg had a habit of standing with his head out of the stable door with his bottom lip flapping in the wind. This particular day was a nice sunny day and I came round the corner, and there were the pair of them, Rostellan imitating Cork Beg with his lip flapping completely relaxed. Rostellan had added his own touch to it by sticking two inches of tongue out as well.

Some things however were not quite so easy to teach. For example Cork Beg had a habit of standing with his hind legs crossed, that is with one hind leg resting in front of the other. The only time Rostellan tried it he ended up sitting on his bottom in a very undignified position, and he did not try that particular trick again. But mostly Cork Beg concentrated on teaching Rostellan the things he needed to know : for example he taught him exactly what he had to do when my wife was depressed. She, as everyone else, at times feels the weight of the world very heavy on her shoulders, and on these occasions she used to take Cork Beg out and Cork

Beg would proceed through a whole gamut of tricks to make her laugh. The first one he would try on going out through the gate was to make a dive at Dora, who used to bark, pretending to bite his nose. Then he would walk sedately down the road until he saw a convenient object to shy at. He would shy right across the road as if it was the most terrifying think he had ever seen. It might be a fencing post or it might be a leaf blowing along the road, or a robin flying out of a fence, but Cork Beg would react to it with one bound and jump from one side of the road to the other, and stand cowering and shivering in the ditch. If this did not succeed in cheering my wife up a little bit, he used to take even sterner measures. He would wait until there was a grassy stretch on the roadway, then he would jump forward in a series of bounds, and gallop off in pursuit of Dora. Having gone five or six strides and made sure my wife was quite firm in the saddle, he used to proceed to put in a series of four or five bucks. I have even seen him on occasion, when he had unseated my wife, dodge to one side on landing and catch her as she came down. This trick was almost infallible, because he would not stop bucking until he had her laughing.

One of the greatest advantages we have for working a horse is the fact that we live on the edge of 2,000 acres of Forestry Commission land, where we have the benefit of any number of grassy rides. One of the things the old man loved doing was to walk along pretending to be half asleep until he came to the corner of one of these rides, then he would suddenly dodge to one side round the corner and dash flat out as fast as he could with Dora in pursuit, and this was another infallible trick for making my wife laugh. One of the amazing things about him was that no matter how arthritic and stiff he was, even after he had broken his leg, he still used to go through the whole gamut of his tricks, and after doing them he would dance along as if he was a completely unmanageable and unschooled three-year-old.

Another thing he had to teach Rostellan was of course that

whenever I appeared on the scene in the stable, set on doing something, he had to put up a show of being a wild unmanageable horse, completely terrified of the boss. I could go into the stable fifty times to do my stable chores, and have a job to get the old man to move over. But if I went in with a brush to groom him, to get the worst of the mud off after a day's hunting, then it was a case of battle stations.

Yet another thing the old man had to teach Rostellan was that when you are competing, if the missus was on board everyone was out to enjoy themselves. It was not important whether you won a prize or not, provided a good time was had by all. But when the boss got on you were really competing and you had to get down to it and give every ounce you had. I used to compete with the old man once or twice a year and I never took him anywhere without winning a prize with him. He was placed three times point-to-pointing, won several hunter trials, and I even used to play polo on him. He was an absolutely superb horse.

Whilst Rostellan was not as intelligent as Cork Beg and was built differently, being a Welsh Cob instead of a three-quarter thoroughbred, he was a very willing pupil and over the course of the next three years he learnt most of what Cork Beg could teach him. This was a case where over a period of time one horse took on part of the personality of another.

The story of how Rostellan's character was changed by the influence of my wife and Cork Beg is only one example of how the character and behaviour pattern of a horse can be completely altered by a change in environment. And an alteration in the horse's environment has of course considerable consequence for equine communication, since change in his needs and habits means also that the horse needs a new and extended vocabulary to meet these new demands. Perhaps I can best explain what I mean in human terms. I live on Llanybyther mountain in North Carmarthenshire, my neighbours are farmers, as I was myself at one time, and the topics of conversation are horses, hunting, the weather, sheep and cattle, in that order – together with the latest bit of local gossip of course. The words we use are relevant to these subjects. Now if I were to move to London or the Midlands and take a job in an office or a factory, the topics of my conversation would change to football, cricket, cars, the theatre and music, and I would use words and phrases which at present I never use. Equally, when horses are in their natural environment they live within a group with a fixed pattern of behaviour and a distinct social structure, descending from the lead mare to the lowliest yearling – the stallion will be outside the herd, usually unattached temporarily, though there may be immature males within the group – and their communication will be conditioned by the needs of that situation. When that herd of horses is gathered off the mountain and confined within a field its behaviour pattern is broken. The horses' freedom of movement has gone, which means that the signs concerned with that movement will no longer be used; and they will be in much closer proximity to each other and so certain signs and sounds will be used less and others will be used more. When they have been broken and handled by men the variation in the signs and sounds used will be even more marked, especially if the horses are permanently stabled. Some signals, such as those of alarm and those of movement, will almost never be used, and others such as those signalling impatience or demand for food will have to be evolved by the horses themselves, either through imitating other horses or out of their own ingenuity. Since the horse has only eleven different tones of voice and is unable to create new tones to convey new messages, this means that he has to adapt and duplicate his existing vocal messages to meet his new needs. Whilst he will be able to adapt a large number of his existing signs, he will also need to invent a number of new signs, and this he will do either by imitating a sign used by another animal (usually, but not necessarily, another horse), or he will find that a sign he uses at random gets a particular response and he will then use that sign again to gain that response.

One of the experiments we used to show how a horse extends its vocabulary is very simple to reproduce. We would take a wild pony from the mountains and put him or her with my wife's hunter, then, when it was feeding time, old Cork Beg would whinney for food, and within a very short time his companion would be whinneying in imitation. When segregated the young horse would still ask for food when hungry, but not necessarily in the same way as Cork Beg. Of some one hundred and twenty-two observed cases, only three had not learnt to ask for food within seven days of contact with horses who were already asking for food. We found that there are four basically different ways of doing this and it is unlikely that any two horses within a small group will ask for food in precisely the same way, but in each case there will be little doubt as to what he is saying, and he will be easily understood. Since we found it almost impossible to differentiate between those sounds learned from association with man and other domesticated horses, and those messages which are natural to the horse, we decided in our dictionary of horse messages, which we were then beginning to compile, to list the meanings of all signs and sounds used, as they are all intended to convey a meaning and can be understood by other horses and by man. The distinction between 'natural' language and language learnt in domestication is further obscured by the fact that some sounds may be used comparatively rarely in the wild, then after contact with human beings and domesticated horses become common. One example is the message of welcome. In the wild the horse will stay in a reasonably settled herd, and a horse returning to the herd is greeted by gentle blowing through the nostrils, or a low whicker, or a nuzzle, all of which mean 'welcome'. The same phrase will be used by a mare calling her foal to her, by a mare reassuring her foal, and occasionally by other horses in the herd greeting each other, but it is not in common use. As a result of contact with man, it becomes very commonly used. When I pass my horses, I talk to them, I say 'hello' and they greet me in return. Some will blow through their nostrils, some will nuzzle me, some will give me the whicker of welcome, and my mare Iantella will kiss me. They will use the same phrases also when I feed them, and they will greet their friends on return to the stable with the same whicker of welcome.

To anyone interested in academic research, it is crucial to discover whether a particular sign or sound is natural to an animal in the wild, or merely acquired from association with man. But to the practical horseman who only wants to understand his horse, the distinction between natural and acquired language is unimportant.

4: *How a Horse uses Sound*

One of the early difficulties we discovered in studying the sounds made by a horse and trying to make sense of them, is that unlike man a horse uses no set sequence of sounds to convey any meaning. In compiling our dictionary we very quickly found that, apart from a few exceptions, it is impossible to say that a certain sound means a certain thing, but it is possible to say that within certain limits a horse will convey a particular message in one of a number of ways. To try and understand this, we had another look at the human languages, and we realised that to convey a certain meaning the human being might use a thousand different sounds, but you could not be certain that any particular sound used by a human being would mean a definite thing. This may sound complete nonsense at first sight, but if you look at it you will see that it is so. The human species is made up of a myriad different nations, and each nation has its own language and dialects. If you take a common phrase like 'I love you,' each race, each nation and each tribe will have a different set of sounds in common use to convey this one phrase. Even within a single language, such as English, there are different ways of saying 'I love you.'

So in our dictionary of horse phrases, we have set out each message in English, and against it listed every individual way we know of that a horse uses to convey that message. We have taken for instance the simple phrase 'I love you,' using it as a broad way of denoting all signs of affection, and against that we have listed the various ways in which the horse denotes affection. We start with breathing out with two imperatives, breathing in with two imperatives, the whicker of welcome with three imperatives. These are the vocal ways by which the horse shows affection. Then there are in addition a very large number of signs, and we have found twenty-six variations of these. That is to say that we conclude that most horses will show affection in one of twenty-six various ways. You will of course get an odd individual who will be outside the mainstream and show affection in a very odd way: for example Fearless denoted affection, when I came back from overseas, by galloping up with her ears flat back, skidding to a halt and licking me all over, then picking me up in her teeth and shaking me. We had another case of a Welsh pony stallion who had been recently castrated and who had been running with cattle, who denoted affection for a mare by smelling her urine as she made water. There are also one or two signs of attraction in sex play, but we do not include those with the phrase 'I love you' as they really mean something completely different. The girlish giggle of the mare when she squeals, and the stallion's whistle, are both sexual in impulse, not affectionate, for it is unusual for anything except sexual attraction to be involved in the mating of horses.

In effect, then, we have compiled an English-Horse dictionary. In it we have taken each of forty-seven phrases used by the horse, together with fifty-four sub-messages, and we have noted the various ways in which most horses will convey each meaning. This method is the opposite to that of most other people working in this field, who have tried to allocate a meaning to each sign or sound. This approach seems to us merely to increase the difficulties. But to make a dictionary of the more common phrases and messages used by a horse is a comparatively easy task. First you select a horse that you know well and are handling daily, and use him as the primary object of your study. You list the phrases, that is the signs and sounds, he uses that you understand. Some of these will be conveyed by signs alone, some by sound, but most by a mixture of signs and sounds. You will be surprised to find how many you already understand. This will probably be about half of what he is saying, and then by observation you will try to interpret the other phrases and sentences he uses. Since you will already know about half of what he is saying, these other signs and sounds will be comparatively easy to put a meaning to. After anything from six weeks to a year, you will find that you have got a list of between twenty-five and thirty-five basic messages that your horse frequently uses. Then, when you can understand everything your horse is saying, you can start observing other horses, and against the basic messages that you have listed for your own horse, you can list the ways that other horses have of saying the same thing. You will find that some of the horses will use phrases your own horse, that is your primary subject, used, and some will convey messages that your primary subject did not even attempt, and this will add to your list of common phrases.

In time – anything up to about twenty years! – you will perhaps have all the forty-seven basic messages used by the horse. Some of these, such as the scream of rage or terror, you may never hear, others which are confined to set situations such as lovemaking, or mothering of a foal, you will not often come across unless you keep breeding stock. So your list of basic messages may be less than my total of forty-seven basic messages and fifty-four sub-messages, but you will still have a list of all the messages used by the horses you come into contact with, and this can be added to from time to time. You will find that with some messages there are very few variations in the number of ways a horse will express himself, but for others you will find up to thirty variations, and the list is never complete. There is always one particular horse who will say something in a way you have not come across before.

As one example of the range of variations, the phrase 'where is my bloody breakfast' can be said by a horse in sound alone, by using the basic phrase 'welcome', and its six imperatives: that is, two degrees of blowing through the nostrils, a low whicker, a high whicker, a low whinney and a high whinney. A horse may also use a snort or even a neigh. Then there are a dozen or so signs or combinations of signs and sounds.

The fact that the phrase 'welcome' can also be used to mean 'where is my bloody breakfast' highlights the difficulty in getting any sense out of any set sequence of notes. The whicker of welcome which is used by a horse when he is greeting another, can become at feeding time 'where is my bloody breakfast.' Equally the mare can use the same set of notes to call her foal to her, or a stallion and mare can use it as a prelude to love play. The same sound can mean a number of things, depending on the circumstances in which it is used.

Old Cork Beg, for instance, uses the same call to say 'hello' to my wife or another horse, to say 'good, here is breakfast,' to me, or 'come here darling' to his current girl-friend. But this call can change to the imperative. If I am slow feeding him, or I feed another horse first, the notes he uses in his whicker of welcome quickly rise and the message becomes 'where is my bloody breakfast.' If his current girl-friend does not come when he calls her first, the note will rise and change from 'come here darling' to 'get over here you lazy little bitch.' The degree of imperative used depends in part on the personalities of the two horses concerned. Just as when my wife is handling the horses and says 'stop it,' it is a far stronger threat than if I say 'if you do that I'll have your guts for garters,' and the horses know it, so one horse might quite naturally use a much higher note of imperative to convey the same meaning than another. The increase or decrease in the imperative will be shown by raising or lower-ing the voice, as in human beings, as well as by adding to the original phrase or sentence. A man for example may increase the imperative by raising his voice in using the words 'come here,' or he may change the phrase from 'come here' to 'come here immediately.' The horse may increase the imperative by using a sign as well as increasing the volume of sound.

This approach to equine communication – instead of

putting our emphasis on the sound a horse makes, such as most researchers have done, we have put the emphasis on the meaning conveyed by *sounds and signs as a whole* – has been our major breakthrough and is I think our major contribution to the understanding of animal communication.

The volume and pitch of the voice is also determined by how far the horse is from the horse he is speaking to. For example when I am four or six hundred yards from home on one of my horses, he will shout at the top of his voice 'hello is anyone at home,' to which one of the horses in the stable will answer 'I am here.' The closer he gets to home, the lower he will have to pitch his voice to make himself heard, and the two horses will drop their voices the nearer they get to each other. When I get to the stable door they will still be saying the same thing, but instead of shouting at the top of their voices, they will just be blowing through their nostrils to each other. My horse will go on saying his welcome until he gets within sniffing distance of the other horse, and then he will stop saying welcome and use one of his calls to show affection. Now to anybody listening there is absolutely no difference in tone between the first call and the second call after he has been answered by another horse. A human parallel, perhaps, is in the words 'hello there'. If you go into the house of a friend, you might shout 'hello there,' to find out if there is anybody at home; he may answer you from upstairs, 'hello there,' and then when he comes downstairs you will greet each other quietly with the same word, 'hello'.

All these welcome calls could perhaps be translated by the world 'hello'. But we have not done so mainly because this would obscure the great variation in actual meaning. A mare welcoming her foal is conveying a very different message from the stallion trumpeting a challenge. The initial call of the stallion – 'is there anybody about' – will change very little in sound when it is answered, but the meaning of his call will change to 'come and fight,' if answered by another stallion, and will then go on to increasing provocation until they meet. But if he is answered by a mare he will go on calling the same call, but in this case 'is there anybody about' changes to 'come and make love,' and he will go on using this until he gets closer to her, when the imperative will drop to welcome, and she will either snap and kick at him, telling him to find another fancy piece, or she will give a girlish giggle and they will start their love play. And if a gelding answers, the stallion will tell him to bugger off in no uncertain terms. In every case the stallion's call will sound much the same, but the message will be completely different. The voice of the horse is only a guide to the meaning of the message, it does not convey the message itself, as the speech of a human being does.

It is of course also possible for a human being to make himself understood by someone who speaks a different language, simply by the use of signs and the tone of his voice. If you do not believe this you only have to observe any sailor landing in a foreign port. In a very short time he will have made his needs known and had his requirements fulfilled – usually booze, women and entertainment in that order – and he will not need a word of the language to make himself understood.

With horses, the context of the call gives you the meaning. This is why the work done on tape-recordings of horse calls has been so difficult to understand – no tape-recording can give you the context of the signal. Of course it is possible to misinterpret calls – I have seen a horse misinterpret the call of another horse. My wife's Welsh Cob Rostellan once answered the call of a stallion I had recently purchased and had castrated. When he was turned out for the first time, the stallion trotted into the field and called 'is there anybody about?' and Rostellan answered. They proceeded to call to each other until they were within sight of each other, then Rostellan trotted over to the stallion thinking he was saying 'welcome,' and got kicked in the ribs for his pains.

Since as well as understanding what your horse is saying, you want him to understand what you are saying, it is vital that you use your voice correctly in speaking to him. Unless you are an animal imitator by profession, it is of no use whatever to try to use the notes and tones that he uses, other than those in the lower ranges – that is, breathing in softly and breathing out softly. You can also get a very low whicker from your own vocal range. But further than this, it is pointless to try to imitate another horse, and in any case the horse will soon be able to interpret your own normal tones. Most of the rider's verbal control of his horse depends on simple commands in English, such as 'whoa', 'walk on', 'trot on', and the horse will learn to respond to these extremely quickly provided you use a correct method of training. When the horse responds to the word of command, he should be praised and caressed. He should be taught by encouragement, not punishment. For if you say 'whoa' and he moves on and you catch him a clout, he will very quickly associate 'whoa' with being hit and will never learn the word of command. Certain commands will in any case get an automatic response from a very high percentage of the horses you handle, and 'whoa' is one of them. About seventy percent of horses who have never been handled, will respond naturally to the word 'whoa'. Similarly, if you click your tongue the horse will go forward and become excited. If you say 'stand up', the horse will draw himself together naturally. These sounds seem to produce an automatic response in the horse, and should not be confused with commands that have to be taught him.

Of course when you are commanding your horse, the tone of the voice is extremely important. I have already referred to the Irishman, Dan Sullivan, who was known as the Whisperer. If you whisper to your horse very softly, he will find that the tone caresses him and it has almost exactly the same effect as caressing him with your hand. If you talk to him in a singsong gentle voice (I usually recite a little verse, 'there's a clever boy, there's a clever boy, there's a clever little fellow'), you will find it automatically steadies the horse and settles him if he is excited. If you speak to him in a sharp voice he will draw himself together and become alert. If you shout at him he knows you are angry. All these tones of the voice and those in between will draw an automatic response.

But you have to be extremely careful how you use them. Four or five years ago I had a very brilliant sheepdog who had the makings of a champion, but she was so keen and so enthusiastic that she was not very obedient to command. After some three months of training, unless I shouted at her and said 'Damn you Fan' before I gave the command, she would go on with what she was doing. And this was simply because when she was extremely disobedient, I used to curse her by saying 'Damn you Fan', and throwing a pebble in her direction so that she would know that she had to do what I told her to. So after this all my commands had to be prefaced with 'Damn you Fan'.

The horse is of course extremely responsive to the voice. On one occasion I was hauling cowdung with Fearless and a young cart colt which we were breaking, up into a very steep field. The cart colt was in the shafts and Fearless was in the trace harness. To get up into the field you used to have to take it as fast as you could, which meant the horses were cantering and you were running beside the horse in the shafts, and on this particular occasion, just as we got into the gateway, I slipped and my leg went under the cart and the colt's hind legs. I shouted 'Whoa Fearless' in a desperate voice, and Fearless stopped immediately and kicked the cart colt in the face, so that he stopped and threw himself back into the breeching. The wheel had stopped just on my leg, you could see the mark of the wheel on my thigh, but if it had gone over me, with ten or fifteen hundred weight of dung in the cart, I would never have walked again. This is a perfect example of the way a horse will respond to the tone of your voice. If I had said 'Whoa Fearless' in a normal tone, it would have been an even chance that she would have taken no notice of me whatever, but on this occasion she stopped instantly and stopped the colt as well. That was one of the reasons I had a very great affection for the old cow.

My father had a theory that when you were breaking a young horse it was very important to throw him on to the ground and teach him to lie down when you told him to. He used to throw the horse, and once it was down, sit on top of it and smoke his pipe or a burma cheroot, which he was very partial to, and recite marathon verses: usually 'The Man from the Snowy River' or 'Kissing Cups Race'. By the time he had recited those two, he used to swear that any horse would be quiet, and usually it was. This was in fact an extreme test of obedience, because anything that could stay within half a mile of the boss when he was smoking one of his burma cheroots at full steam must have been under remarkable control. But the principle of reciting verses is an extremely sound one, for we have found repeatedly with the untouched horses that we get here that reciting or singing to them anything that is soothing and rather monotonous, will settle and relax them, and, which is probably just as important, make you relaxed. For if you are close to the horse your emotions and feelings will be reflected by him; if you are nervous, he will be nervous, and if you are relaxed and speaking in a relaxed way, he will be relaxed as well.

5: *How a Horse uses Signs*

In the preceding two chapters I have tried to show how the horse uses his voice to convey a meaning. But it must be obvious to anyone who has observed horses that a horse also uses signs in various ways: to convey an intention, to draw attention to an object, as a warning, and sometimes to express an opinion. He will tend to look to the left if he is going to turn to the left and he will look to the right if he wants to turn to the right – that is the way he tells you which way he is going to go. He will raise his head and prick his ears and look intently at an object to draw your attention to it. He will put his ears back and raise his hind leg to warn you that if you come any nearer he will kick. If you give him something to eat which he does not like, he will take a mouthful and spit it out again, thus telling you what he thinks of it.

The use of sign language is of course not just confined to horses. All animals, including human beings, use signs as an integral part of their communication with other members of the species. We get the meaning of a conversation as much from the expression on the face and the use of the hands as we do from the tone of voice. The words 'I hate you and I am going to make you suffer,' used in one context are threatening and aggressive, but used by a man who is kissing and caressing a woman they mean a different thing altogether. I have already described how Cork Beg, when he uses the welcome tone, can mean 'welcome', 'good, here is break- fast' or 'come here' depending on whether he is nibbling my wife's coat, pushing his food basin around, or calling his girlfriend in the field. Equally, if a mare puts her ears back, squeals and raises her foot to kick, she is saying 'if you do not go away I will kick your teeth in.' But if on the other hand she squeals, kicks and raises her tail when a stallion is around, she is horseing and it means a different thing altogether. We call this her girlish giggle. So you can see that with the addition of a different sign, the same vocal note can mean two totally different messages: in fact two diametrically opposite messages, 'go away' and 'come and make love.'

The sign language is in fact much more easily understood than the vocal parts of the message, and it has always been a mystery to me why, with the exception of Meech and Ewbank in their work on pigs at Liverpool University, and one or two others, the modern researcher has not concentrated more on the sign language in work on animal communication. With horses at least, signs are of a much more regular pattern than sounds, and the intention of the horse is easily interpreted from the signs he uses. Added to this is the fact that sign language is similar in all breeds, ages and sexes of horses, though there are one or two exceptions, such as sexual sounds, and those limited to use by a foal calling 'I am only small.' The foal says this last when he is approaching a bigger horse that he is not sure about, by putting his head down as if he is going to suckle a mare, opening his mouth slightly, curving his lips back and making sucking motions with his tongue. He does this because he knows a bigger horse will then realize he is a foal and not kick or bite him. This is a sign common to very nearly all foals, though you get it also in some yearlings, and I have seen it done once by a four-year-old gelding. Sign language is almost universal among human beings too, and is the same irrespective of what race a man belongs to.

It is of course almost impossible to give a definite meaning to any movement taken in isolation. For example, if a horse waves a hind leg, he may mean 'I am going to kick,' or he may mean 'my foot hurts.' The vigour of the movement, the situation in which it is made, and the sounds made before and after all go to indicate meaning. Anyone who knows the horse well will be able to interpret the meaning of the signs very easily indeed.

There are between seventy and eighty different signs used by a horse. These depend on the age of the horse, and whether it is a stallion, mare or gelding. All these signs are used as part of the forty-seven basic messages and fifty-four sub-messages, and are usually used in conjunction with sounds, though there are certain cases when the message is conveyed solely by signs, especially when the horse uses only his head and ears. When a horse is conveying a message by signs he uses his muzzle, nose, mouth, eyes, ears, the whole head and neck, his skin, his tail, his legs and his feet. The legs and feet can be used either singly or as a pair: that is, the front legs may be used singly or as a pair, and so may the hind legs. A horse in the wild will normally use his hind legs only as a defensive weapon, and his front legs and teeth as an offensive weapon, though it is very little consolation to someone lying in hospital with a broken leg to know that the horse was only defending himself.

The unusual thing about sign language is that you sometimes come across very odd signs indeed, often acquired by the horse from other animals. I have already mentioned our eleven-two Welsh pony who had not been much in contact with other horses most of the year, and had been running with a herd of cattle, so when a mare made water, he would put his nose under it and sniff at it in exactly the same way a bull would sniff that of a cow. This is the only time I had come across this habit in a horse, and I have no doubt that he had acquired it from the cattle he had been running with.

Another pony we had cocked his leg like an immature dog, and when I traced this back, I found that the sheepdog on the farm he came from used to sleep in his stable. He and the pony were very great friends, and the pony had acquired the habit of cocking his leg by imitation of the dog. But funnily enough he would do it only over a spot where a mare had made water and not where a gelding had done so.

In the horse's sign language the head and neck are of course the most used parts of the body. They may be used as a whole to convey a message, or the various part may be used separately. The muzzle and the lips are used mainly to indicate affection – to caress and reassure a foal or another horse, and in love play – though they may also be used to investigate something and to draw attention to a special object. When a horse nuzzles you or when he nuzzles another horse, he is using his nose to show affection for you. When a foal is frightened it will run to its mother and she will nuzzle the foal to reassure it. In effect one horse nuzzling another is using its nose as an extension of the welcome sign, but when a mare nuzzles her foal to reassure it, she is saying, 'all right, mummy's here.'

Most people, when they are bitten by a horse, know only that it hurts and that they do not like it. But in actual fact there are four completely different sorts of bites from a horse. In love play, the mouth, teeth and lips are used a great deal and all four different types of bite may be used. A stallion will approach a mare and nip her. The mare will then swing her head round and snap at the horse, and the way she uses her head and neck is an indication of how she is receiving the stallion's attention. She may just swing her head round and nip him affectionately, or she may swing her head and snap at him, telling him to go away. She may even punch him with her teeth, or bring her head round and fasten her teeth in his skin, really biting him in rejection. If his intentions are received in any sort of encouraging manner, the stallion will nip and caress the mare's flanks and loins with his lips, and very often he will grip the mare's neck with his teeth, without actually biting her. Thus in a single sequence the stallion has nipped the mare as a token of affection and gripped her in his teeth to indicate his passion. The mare in return has either nipped the stallion with affection, snapped at him or punched him with her teeth, or in an extreme case really caught hold of him in anger.

Each of these four gestures means something completely different. When the mare nipped him, she said 'darling stop it' and when she snapped at him, she said 'go away and leave me alone.' Then she either punched him with her teeth or really bit him. The punch with the teeth is more commonly seen. The teeth and head are brought forward in a lunging or swinging movement and the teeth hit the other horse. They are not closed and it is a blow not a bite, though it is often confused with the bite, which is a similar movement of the head and neck, though the teeth in this case are closed on the opponent. If they are promptly opened again, this is a snap. But the horse may hold on, closing his teeth with all his power, though this is very rarely seen, and is used normally only in the wild by two stallions fighting. The punch on the other hand is often seen, most commonly as a warning, though if the warning is not heeded, the horse will go on to snap or bite. It is generally wise to heed the warning, for if a horse really catches hold of you, you will be hurt. If he catches hold of your arm, he will probably break it. If he catches hold of your shoulder, he will pick you up and shake you, (though this is most uncommon, and you must only hope that it never happens to you).

Unlike the eyes of a human being, which speak a language of their own, the eyes of a horse change expression very little. They are used only to indicate what the horse is looking at. But the ears on the other hand, which are scarcely used in the sign language of humans, have an infinite variety of meanings to express. They are used not only separately, but also with other parts of the body, to convey an intention, to draw attention to an object or an incident, and above all to convey the mood of the horse. Most people know that when a horse lays his ears flat back as far as they will go, he is hostile, and he is warning you to keep away. When the ears are half-way between the upright and back position, it usually means that he is relaxed and doing nothing, and not worried about anything. But if the ears are set in this position, and not just lying there anyhow, it means that he is looking at you behind him, and possibly listening to what you are saying to him. When I am riding and handling a horse I talk to him a great deal of the time, and the horse keeps his ears half-back, just listening to the tone of my voice. I always say that he is listening for my words of wisdom, but in actual fact he is only listening to the tone of my voice. A horse also points his ears sideways, to one side or the other to draw attention to an object. He will look at an object and appear to be listening to it at the same time, probably listening to hear if the object is making a hostile sound, at the same time as he is looking for a hostile movement. When a horse has his ears three-quarters pricked it means 'I am awake and alert, let's go,' and when the ears are fully pricked it means that the horse is drawing attention to or looking at an object. But when the ears are stiffly pointing sideways it is a sure indication that the horse is going to have a go at you. Like the ears laid back, this position means that the horse is hostile. But whereas when the ears are flat back the rest of the body may be half or three-quarters relaxed, when the ears are pointing sideways every muscle of the body will be taut as well. He may be going to buck, kick or rear or have a go at you with his teeth. The ears can be used as a guide to the horse's mood in nine hundred and ninety-nine cases out of a thousand.

We did have a horse some years ago, a registered Welsh Cob, who was just plain mentally unbalanced. No matter what he was going to do, he always had his ears sweetly pricked as if he were a kind and gentle horse. But this horse was the worst horse I have ever handled. I have seen him buck, rear, roll, throw himself over backwards, spin round bucking, spin round rearing, try to knock you off against a tree, try to crush you against a wall, kick, and strike out with his front feet. Yet he would do all of these things as if he were going as sweetly and kindly as a baby. Three or four people had tried to break him, two of them very cruelly and the third had made him completely hostile to human beings. Though after having him for about three months I could do anything with him, he was still dangerous to any other human being. Horses will very often buck for pleasure and they will enjoy doing so, particularly when their owners themselves enjoy their horses bucking, and in this case the horse will very often buck with his ears pricked. But here the buck is *joie de vivre* and there is no intent to get you off. Old Cork Beg used to buck with my wife until he got her laughing, as I have already described.

The head and neck when used together to make a sign are used to draw attention to an object, or to convey an intention of going in a certain direction. When the neck and teeth are used either to bite or punch, they are used to make a threat against another horse. The legs, teeth and tail of course are generally used to convey a warning of hostile intent; but it must always be remembered that the raising of the foot can mean 'my foot hurts', as well as 'I am going to kick you.' The difference between a warning and a definite threat is usually conveyed by the vigour of the movement, but this varies from horse to horse, as does the degree of violence of language among human beings. One horse may lift his leg and wave it and mean absolutely nothing, the second horse doing exactly the same thing may be making a very real and definite threat, and you may get a third horse which will raise his foot only a couple of inches from the ground as a warning. If you do not pay attention the next thing you know is that you will be picking your teeth out of the gutter. The vigour of the movement in the horse or the strength of the language in the human being are an individual thing and you must know the individual before you can gauge the strength of the message.

The skin of the horse also speaks. It is usually used to convey a response; for example, if you touch a sore part of the body and the horse twitches his skin and flinches, he is saying 'that hurts.' On occasion horses will twitch their skin spontaneously to tell you that that part of the body is sore. The muscles will indicate the mood of the horse, whether they are taut or relaxed. According to which muscles are being tightened or relaxed, they will also convey to you exactly which part of the horse is going to react next. For example, if the back muscles are tightened it shows you the horse is going to buck. And the tail is used to convey hostile intent; or to indicate sexual response (in a mare). Or if it is held up and out it simply shows that the horse is alert and awake – in effect the the horse will use its tail to say 'let's go'. The tail tends to be used in conjunction with the head and neck – if the head is raised, the tail will be, if the neck is relaxed the tail will rest into the buttocks.

It must also be remembered that all these signs can be, and very often are, used with the vocal part of a message. This may only be a sharp intake of the breath or a blowing through the nostrils, or it may be a squeal of rage. Unlike the vocal range of the messages, the number of signs varies very little from horse to horse, but combined with the voice and e.s.p. the number of messages conveyed by signs varies considerably.

One of the most emotional moments of my life happened whilst I was in the Army. I had just come back from overseas, and when I came home the first thing I did was to go out and see the horses. They were all grazing at the far end of a ten-acre field, which was about six hundred yards long. I stood at the gate and shouted 'come on my darlings'. They all looked up and came flat-out up the field, led by Fearless. She was galloping as fast as she could with her head stuck out and her ears flat back and her mouth open. Even after eight years she was still liable to have a piece out of you or to clout you with her front feet, and since I had gone too far down the field to make a run for it, I stood still. When she got to within ten yards of me she stuck her four feet into the ground and skidded to a stop. Then she took two steps forward and licked me all over from head to foot, and when she had done this for about three minutes the tears were running down my cheeks, so she thought that was enough of a good thing. Just to show me the status was still quo, she caught hold of me with her teeth and lifted me from the ground and shook me slowly backward and forwards four or five times, then she put me down, and rubbed me with her nose. I have never been so touched in all my life, the display of affection was somewhat unusual in form, but it was fantastic.

Another example of unorthodox display of affection befell a friend of mine. I sold him a very nice quiet gentle mare. He did not know a lot about horses, but he and the mare got on extremely well for a long time, until one day I had a desperate telephone call from him. The mare was in pain and would I go over. So I went straight out to his place and asked him what was the matter. He said 'Oh she seems all right, until I go into her stall, and as soon as I go in and touch her, she squeals and waves her hind leg and makes water.' Then he took me out and showed me. As soon as I got there I saw what had happened. It was merely that the mare was horse-ing. She had fallen in love with her new owner as if he were a stallion, and she was showing her affection the only way she knew.

6: *Our Dictionary of Horse Language*

I have been referring to messages, sub-messages and variations. These terms of course are rather vague and indefinite. This is because animal communication itself is very indefinite since the interpretation of any message is a personal matter. A message as we define it is an intention, a threat or an enquiry, a feeling or a statement made by a horse. A sub-message is a response to or a development of a message. The term 'variation' is an abbreviation of the self-explanatory phrase, 'variation from the most common way of conveying a message or a sub-message'. Some messages can be conveyed in a number of different ways, by signs, sounds and various combinations of the two. In our observation of some three hundred horses, we have noted thirty different ways of saying 'welcome', and also about thirty variations on 'where is my breakfast.' But the foal's 'I am only small' is said in only two or three ways, and most messages have six to ten variations.

In our dictionary of signs and sounds we have not listed most of these, but for the purpose of this book we have abbreviated the list to the most common ways of saying each phrase. The phrases we have used to convey any particular message have just happened, there is no particular thought behind them, though of course we have tried to convey the feeling of the message by the words and phrases we have used. You will see in the dictionary that some similar messages will be described by two or three different phrases, but you will also see that the context of the message is different and therefore the message itself is different. This applies particularly to messages that are almost sub-messages in that they are developments of an original statement, but since they are at times used alone, we have listed them under messages. Anyone who is interested in equine communication will in any case need to compile his own dictionary and will of course use his own words to describe each message – he may decide to dispense with the distinction we have made between messages and sub-messages; or include some imperatives or some variations as separate messages. Since each horse will convey his oral and visual messages differently, so each person's dictionary will be laid out differently. But as a guide to anyone who wants to understand his or her own horse I am including a very abbreviated form of my own dictionary. I have made first an alphabetical list of English phrases, noting the number of sub-messages attached to each phrase, and a reference by number to the full translation set out below. Thus, if you want to know how a horse communicates the idea 'I love you' and its two sub-messages, you turn to number 16 below.

Phrase	Number of sub-messages	Reference number of message
Come and drink	1	24
Come and fight	4	18
Come and get it	–	20
Come here	1	5
Come on	3	11
Come on then	–	37
Don't do that	2	25
Don't go away	2	6
Don't leave me behind	–	38
Don't worry	–	32
Gangway	1	34
Go away	2	12
Help	–	30
I am boss	1	33
I am enjoying this	–	39
I am frightened	–	28
I am here	–	9
I am hungry	3	36
I am king	–	19

Phrase	Number of sub-messages	Reference number of message
I am only small	–	27
I am thirsty	–	26
I am tired	1	41
I cannot	1	42
I hate you	2	17
I love you	2	16
I suppose I will have to	–	43
I will buck	–	44
Is anybody about?	–	7
It is good to be free	–	47
Let us get the hell out of here	–	29
Let us go	1	40
Look	4	4
Mummy loves you	1	23
Oh my God	–	31
Scratch here	–	46
Stop it	2	13
That hurts	1	14
That is nice	–	15
That tickles	–	45
There you are	–	10
We are good girls here	5	22
Welcome	–	1
What's this?	2	3
Where are you?	–	8
Where is my bloody breakfast?	6	35
Who are you?	2	2
You will be quite safe with me	4	21

1. *Welcome.* This is used to generalize all calls and signs of greeting used between horses, the most common of which is the whicker of welcome. The strength of the call and the vigour of the movement indicate the degree of imperative. The context, and the carriage of the head and tail, indicate the purpose of the welcome.

2. *Who are you?* is used by two strange horses on meeting. It is an extension of the 'welcome' phrase and is said by sniffing or more usually blowing at each other. The attitude of the two horses towards each other is indicated by the harshness or the gentleness of the blowing and the carriage of the head and tail. This procedure leads to the sub-messages, (1) *I am a friend,* said by continuation of the gentle blowing and other friendly movements, or (2) *go to hell,* a snap or nip by one or other horse, a stamp on the ground with a front foot, a threat to kick, or a squeal.

3. *What's this?* is used in reference to objects which are close at hand, usually said by a sniff at the object; but a horse may paw the object with his front foot. This gesture leads to the sub-messages, (1) *it's all right,* shown by approaching and inspecting and then ignoring strange objects, or (2) *it's dangerous,* shown by moving away, by shying at the object or attacking the danger.

4. *Look,* used to draw attention to an object and denoted by raising the head and tail and snorting or whinneying to attract the attention of other horses. Similar, and a sub-message to 'look', is (1) *what is that,* which is said by raising the head high and pricking the ears and looking at a strange object. There is no sound as a secondary reaction to 'what is that'. The horses will either respond *it is all right* or *it is dangerous.* Another sub-message is (2) *let's go this way.* The horse says this by looking in the direction he wants to go and moving in that direction. A second horse responding to 'what is that' will look at the object, and if he recognizes it will say (3) *nothing to bother about,* or (4) *look out,* using a snort or a neigh of warning.

5. *Come here.* This starts as a whicker of welcome rising in the imperative, which may also be shown by shaking the head back and forwards if there is no response. The message may be changed to *if you do not come here, I will have your guts for garters,* which is shown by a threatening movement and will draw the response, (1) *all right I am coming,* usually said by a low whicker.

6. *Don't go away*. This is a whicker or whinney to call a companion back, and varies from a whicker of welcome to the 'where are you' neigh. This is often used also for the sub-messages, (1) *where are you going?*, or (2) *wait for me*.

7. *Is anybody about?* A loud neigh repeated several times. This has an enquiring note and is used with the head and tail held high. When it is answered – with another loud neigh meaning 'I am here' – the first horse will then use the following message :

8. *Where are you?* 'Where are you' may thus be a sub-message of 'is anybody about?' When it is used by a mare looking for her foal, or by a horse looking for a friend. 'Where are you?' will be a whinney rather than a neigh.

9. *I am here!* is a loud neigh used in answer to 'is anybody about?' This will be repeated until the two horses are in sight of each other. This again my be used as a sub-message as in the sequence described in 7 and 8 above.

10. *There you are*. This is used at a distance in answer to 'where are you?', and is usually a whinney as the two horses approach each other, which will change to a whicker of welcome as they meet.

11. *Come on!* This is used when two horses are grazing together or resting, and one wants to move away or play. He will indicate this by nudging his companion or dancing round him and nipping him. He may give a whicker or just walk away hoping his companion will follow. He may get the responses (1) *oh all right*, shown in the reluctant carriage of his companion; or (2) *yes let's* – an enthusiastic response – or (3) *I'm damned if I will!*, shown simply by a negative response or even by threatening or snapping.

12. *Go away!* This is a defensive sign and is designed purely to protect. It can be a mild threat, usually made with the teeth or hind legs, possibly only one hind leg. If this is ignored the stronger warning *go away or I will clobber you* follows. This is a definite and hostile movement and quickly becomes *you have asked for it*, which is an attempt to bite or kick the tormentor.

13. *Stop it!* This is a response to an action by another horse or a human. It varies from twitching the skin to striking with the front leg, kicking or biting. This has a response (1) *sorry*, shown by a rapid evacuation of the area with an air of injured innocence or (2) *I will if I want to*, which is shown by intensification of the annoying action.

14. *That hurts.* This is shown by flinching or twitching the skin and shying away from the aggressor. It has a sub-message (1) *my foot hurts*, shown by lifting up the foot and limping. Variations include *my back hurts, my neck hurts, my head hurts*, or anything else, but we have counted this as one sub-message.

15. *That is nice!* is a response to any action that is pleasing to the horse and it appears three times in sub-messages, but it is used as a message in its own right and as a plea to continue. It is shown by an increase of pressure on the partner and is used when two horses are in close contact, maybe accompanied by a grunt of contentment or by breathing out.

16. *I love you.* We use this phrase to show affection other than maternal or sexual. There are thirty or more ways of showing this, the most common being a gentle blowing through the nostrils or rubbing with the nose and head. This can draw the response, (1) *I love you too*, or (2) *go away*.

17. *I hate you.* The signs and sounds used in this case are different from *go away*, and are of an aggressive rather than a defensive nature. The front legs and teeth will be used, which is a definite sign of antipathy between two horses, and if it draws the response (1) *I hate you too*, a fight will ensue. It may draw the response (2) *I am sorry*, as in message 13: the same sorry signs will be used, but they will also include the defensive actions, that is the hind quarters will be presented or a pair of heels may be used on the aggressor.

18. *Come and fight.* This is a response to a stallion's challenge and is a high-pitched neigh, or perhaps a scream of rage. This is followed by (1) *I will pulverize you*, which is part of the preliminary manoeuvring and threatening to

try and establish a psychological advantage before fighting the battle. After the battle the loser will say (2) *I am sorry, I am going.* He does this by fleeing with his tail tucked in, and the winner in his triumph, threatens (3) *if you come back I will kill you.* The stallion will then go to his mares and say (4) *did you see that, girls, I murdered him.* He may do this by snorting and dancing round his mares, and he may also drive them away to safety. This cavorting signal of sheer triumph may also be used by a mare or gelding who has got the better of another horse or human being.

19. *I am king* is the bugle note of a stallion, which is either a challenge, or a call to a group of mares. This will be repeated again as he goes towards the mares.

20. *Come and get it.* This is the horseing mare's neigh in response to the stallion's bugle, and will be used as the horseing mare leaves the group to meet the stallion.

21. *You will be quite safe with me.* It is the first phrase of love play used by the stallion, and is said by blowing through his nostrils. Unless he gets a definite 'no' from the mare he will continue with this until he gets a girlish giggle, when he will say, (1) *I like you.* He does this by titillating the mare on her neck and flanks with his lips, and then (2), in a more urgent manner, he will say *let's make love* by nipping her with his teeth. Next he progresses to (3) *come on then*, which can be shown by gripping the neck with his teeth, by trying to mount her or by actually mounting the mare. The next sub-message will be (4) which is *that was good.* After he has served the mare he will dismount and arch his neck and nuzzle the mare, or he may snort, or otherwise show his affection.

22. (*Go away*) *we are good girls here.* This can be shown by a very aggressive action indeed towards the stallion. The lead will be taken by a very strong mare protecting the virtues of the rest of the herd from a rather immature stallion. This response may then change to (1) the girlish giggle, which is used in response to the stallion's 'you will be quite safe with me.' This is a squeal by the mare, and she may also wave her

hind leg, and may lead to (2) *what are we waiting for?* This is usually the phrase of a highly sexed mare, who will make water and stand with her hind legs open and her tail raised; or she may open and close her vuvula or stand with her vulvula slightly open. But mares are as unpredictable as women in their response to the male, and in her love play the mare can change very quickly from saying 'go away I am a good girl' to 'come and get it, what are you waiting for.' It all depends entirely on the mare. She may use all three messages as separate messages or start with 'go away' and use the other two as sub-messages. When the love-making is over she may say (3) *that was hard work*. She will say this by grunting, puffing and blowing and complaining thoroughly. She may say (4) *is that all?* by simply shaking herself and walking away to graze, or (5) she may say *that was nice, let's do it again.* Here she will whicker and try to initiate further love play.

These events, with any luck, will lead after eleven months to the birth of a foal the following spring, and the need for a further group of messages for use by the mare in the care of her foal. The first of these is :

23. *Mummy loves you.* The mare does this by nuzzling her foal and blowing gently through her nostrils. If her foal is frightened she will reassure it and say (1) *you will be quite safe.* She will do this by pushing the foal into her flank on the other side of danger.

24. *Come and drink.* She does this by a low whicker or whinney, moving one leg slightly sideways and offering the udder to the foal. If she does not want the foal to feed, she will say sub-message (1) *there is none there*, pushing the foal away with the upper part of her hind leg or her stifle joint or her nose. If the foal is naughty she will say :

25. *Don't do that.* This is different from the normal 'stop it' used between two horses, because 'stop it' will be said when two horses are in close proximity, and usually by signs. But the mare may warn her foal from a distance, usually in a sharp whinney while she threatens it with her head. This is followed by *mummy warned you!* raising the tone of voice

and increasing the vigour of movement. If the foal is still disobedient she will say, *right you have asked for it* and punish the foal, usually by nipping it. The foal itself will use a lot of the adult messages, but will have two of its own:

26. *I am thirsty*. This is shown by nuzzling the mare's flanks and trying to get to her udder.

When the foal is threatened by a bigger horse it will say:

27. *I am only small*. He says this by holding his head and neck out straight, sometimes holding the nose up slightly and moving the mouth as if sucking. When he does this it is most unlikely that another horse will hurt him.

28. *I am frightened*. This can be shown by a snort or a neigh, and if they are in a confined area the horses will lean against each other and gain reassurance from the group.

29. *Let us get the hell out of here,* is said with a snort or a neigh with the head and tail held high ready for flight, which in turn will draw a response of 'yes, let's', or 'nothing to worry about'.

30. *Help!* This is a scream of fear and is seldom heard. I have heard it only once but it is unmistakable.

31. *Oh my God!* This is a scream of pain and is only uttered by a horse suffering unbearable pain. Again it is quite unmistakable.

32. *Don't worry,* is used by a calm horse to steady a frightened one. It can be conveyed by a whicker, by offering protection to the other horse with the body or merely by reassuring bodily contact.

Another group of sounds is concerned with herd discipline. There is a definite social order within the herd, descending from the lead mare to the yearlings, small foals being usually disciplined by their mothers. Even in domestication this herd discipline will still be observed within a group. The senior member of the herd takes precedence in feeding, watering and moving, and may demand her rights with the threat:

33. *I am boss*. This is said to an inferior within the group,

usually by threatening with the head and teeth. The boss will also say *go back*, by swinging the head and threatening any inferior that tries to pass her. Next comes either *I will bite you* or *I will pulverize you* which involves driving the inferior away with her teeth and front legs. If the second horse is a social equal, it will respond to the statement 'I am boss', by saying (1) *no you are not*. This is expressed either by ignoring the threat altogether, or by threatening the other back. Similar messages are used in other situations – for example, *go back, I will kick* or *I will bite* may be used when the boss horse is feeding and an inferior horse approaches. In this case a threat to kick may be made.

34. *Gangway!* This is said by a boss horse by pushing through a herd and laying about the others with his head. On the other hand the sub-message (1) *Excuse me*, is used by an inferior horse trying to pass a boss horse.

There is another group of signs and sounds which have been developed by horses through their contact with man. Many of these deal with feeding. The first and possibly oldest of these is easily understood :

35. *Where is my bloody breakfast?* This is shown in a multitude of ways, from the whicker of welcome to a bang on the food bin. Each horse-owner will know how his horse does it. The sub-messages are several. (1) *I want water* is often expressed by knocking the water bowl about and whinneying. (2) *I want hay* may be said by walking to the hay rack looking disgusted. When he has been fed (3), the horse will say *thank you*, usually by using the whicker of welcome or saying *I love you* and showing affection. He will of course indicate whether or not he likes his food and will say (4) *this is nice*, by eating his food greedily with bits falling out of his mouth; or if you are feeding him tit-bits he will say (5) *give me some more*, by whickering and nuzzling at your pockets and nudging you to remind you he is still there. If he does not like what you give him he will say (6) *that is horrible* by spitting it out and wrinkling his lips and making ugly faces.

Whereas 'where is my bloody breakfast' is used by horses accustomed to being fed regularly, a horse which has never been fed will also say:

36. *I am hungry, or thirsty.* He will say this by whickering when he sees you, and putting on the appearance of being empty and miserable. Sub-message of this is (1) *I am wet,* which is very similar and said by standing in the rain with head down looking very miserable. If a horse has to go out into the rain he will say (2) *this is horrible* by turning his head away from the rain and going into it with reluctance and disgust. He can also say (3) *I am cold,* by shivering and again looking miserable.

When you are riding a horse there will be a continuous contact and interplay of messages. We will ignore the messages used by man to convey his wishes, as these are a matter of taste and training; and we have also dealt with a lot of the signs used by the horse already, because they are also used by horses between themselves; but they also use them in communicating with man. The first sign specific to riding, however, is:

37. *Come on then,* said by whickering and dancing round a little to show his desire to go out and enjoy himself. A companion left behind will shout:

38. *Do not leave me behind.* This is said with a neigh or a whinney and the horse may try to demolish the stable door in his anxiety to follow his companions. Once you have started your horse may be saying:

39. *I am enjoying this,* which he does by dancing about or walking along with his head and tail held high and generally showing his enjoyment. If he is feeling particularly well he will show his *joie de vivre* in an unmistakable way – *I feel fine* – by cavorting around and giving a little squeal or pretending to buck.

40. *Let us go!* is said by dancing around and reaching for his bit and showing a general desire to go faster. A sub-message to this is (1) *yes let's,* shown by an enthusiastic response to a request or an order to do something. After his work

he may be tired and he will say this too in an unmistakable way :

41. *I am tired.* He will communicate this by the way he carries himself. The sub-message is (1) *not again,* which he says by his reluctance to repeat an action. Of course not all horses are willing and keen, and at times they may refuse to do what they are asked to do and say :

42. *I cannot,* by refusing to do whatever it is. The sub-message (1) *I will not* differs from 'I cannot' only because you know quite well that he *can* do it. So if you can make him he may give in by saying :

43. *I suppose I will have to,* and he will show his reluctance in much the way that Shakespeare described the school-boy 'creeping like snail unwillingly to school'. But before he capitulates he may well threaten :

44. *I will buck.* He points his ears sideways and arches his back and makes as if to buck. There are similar messages *I will rear,* said by throwing his head up and lifting his front feet off the ground, and *I will kick* or *I will bolt.*

45. *That tickles,* he says by twitching the skin and possibly waving a leg, stamping or squealing.

46. *Scratch here,* is shown by rubbing where the itch is. If he is with another horse, he will scratch the other horse with his teeth to show where he wants to be scratched.

Finally, here is the last message. When you turn a horse into the field he will say :

47. *It is good to be free!* And *joie de vivre* is something every horse expresses in his own individual way.

7: *E.S.P. and Weeping Roger*

Early in our researches we realized that the air and manner of the horse when he was delivering a message was all-important to interpreting what he was trying to say. But we quickly discovered also that there was more than this to the way we were receiving messages from our animals. It was not just the air and manner of delivery that was giving us the clues. There were also times when we knew instinctively the meaning of the message. And even when we could not see or hear the horse, we found that in times of stress or difficulty we could feel the uneasiness and know that something was wrong. Over and over again, when we went to see what was the matter, something was wrong.

Funnily enough the first time this happened after we had started on our research into animal communication, it was not a horse but a cow that was involved. Normally I sleep like a log and do not hear anything, but on this night I woke up with this powerful feeling that something was amiss, and went out to the animals. The cow was calving, but it was a breech delivery so she was in difficulties. Thinking about it afterwards, I worked out that I had been awakened by the feeling that something was wrong; and been drawn sub-consciously to where the cow was. This started me thinking in a new direction and, step by step, I came to the somewhat startling conclusion that I could feel the moods of the horses rather than see or hear them. This faculty is what we call extra-sensory perception, perception outside the range of our normal five senses. And we realized that animals can use this faculty to convey moods, emotions and certain limited ideas. Since it is used in conjunction with other forms of com-munication – sounds and signs – it can be compared with the air and manner of delivery of speech in a human being; but it is more than this, because you *know* the mood and feel it within yourself. If a horse is excited, you feel it, and the horse will feel it when you are depressed and this is a matter of instinct rather than visual, aural or tactile perception.

This is the part of our work about which there is considerable controversy. I have been warned that entry into so highly contentious an area may tend to devalue our work on animal communication as a whole, in the eyes of the academic world. I have often been told that while our work on signs and sounds is far in advance of anything anybody else has done, our involvement with animal extra-sensory perception makes us suspect – even puts us in the same class as charlatans and music-hall acts! For scientists have been arguing for the past fifty years about whether extra-sensory perception exists or not: who are we to rush in where scholars fear to tread, and claim to have proved not only that it does exist, but that it exists among animals and is an integral part of their communication?

However, I must stand by my own view. The scepticism of some scientists does not of itself invalidate my conclusions. Until Faraday started his work with frogs and the single-cell battery, no doubt a section of the scientific world said that electricity did not exist, for any new field of research has been looked upon with suspicion by the scientific conservatives. We are absolutely convinced by our own experience that e.s.p. does exist, and we have proved, to our own satisfaction anyway, that it does. We know that we cannot have complete communication with horses without using e.s.p. We know that horses use it in communicating with each other. Therefore we must continue our researches into it, and I would be insincere if I did not deal with it in my account of the work we have done with horses. In fact, to carry out research into equine communication *without* taking into account e.s.p. and telepathy would be equivalent to trying to study English by studying only the nouns and verbs and pretending that adverbs and adjectives did not exist. Since our work is primary research and not secondary research, we have to study

equine communication as a whole, not its parts. Subsequent
researchers may, for example, be able to do more detailed
studies on the use of sounds or signs or e.s.p. alone, but they
will have the work we and other researchers have done into
communication as a whole to give their detail a context.

A further area of argument about our work on e.s.p. with
horses, even among those who do not totally reject the idea,
has been around the degree of unconscious perception involved. When you are perceiving consciously, the argument
runs, you can consciously see, hear and understand the signs
and sounds made by a horse. But you also exercise a certain
amount of unconscious perception: that is, without consciously knowing you are doing it, you see and hear certain
things which help you understand the message which the
horse is trying to convey. The charge is that we are confus-
ing, to whatever extent, unconscious perception with extra-
sensory perception. Now we have always realized that in a
large number of cases this may be so, because when you are
handling a horse, you do unconsciously observe and anticipate
what he is going to do, and you do tend to put your understanding down to 'instinct'. Equally, no doubt, a herd of
horses will realize unconsciously what you are feeling simply
from your facial expression, your movement and the way
you carry yourself. This is all unconscious perception, and
we know that it is, but since it is not conscious we have,
rightly or wrongly, included it under e.s.p., since we find it
extremely difficult to set an exact border line between the
unconscious and true e.s.p. There is of course room for considerable research here, and we may find when this has been
done that we have mistaken a very large amount of unconscious perception for e.s.p. We are not really concerned
at present – though we will be later – with whether unconscious perception is a fifth means of communication or
not. Our research from the beginning has been very much a
question of following a path to see where it goes. All the experimental work we have done on e.s.p. has in any case been
designed in such a way that it can be duplicated at a later date

by other people in other places, so that our own work can be verified, and anyone doing later research into equine communication has some standard experiments to carry out before he goes on to experimental work of his own design. We hope that this will be done time and time again, and that once sufficient work has been done in the field of signs and sounds, systematic experiments will be carried out on e.s.p.

We have done some experiments specifically on e.s.p., one of which was a feeding experiment carried out between two horses who had no visible or audible contact with each other; but we cannot be absolutely certain that our horses' sense of hearing does not allow them to pick up distant sounds unconsciously, and even less can we be certain that part of equine communication is not the unconscious perception of certain sounds that are normally considered to be inaudible. We are led to believe by other scientific research that horses' hearing is much the same as ours and that the horse does not hear ultrasonic sounds: that is, previous scientific experiments on horses have shown no reaction to ultrasonic sounds. On the other hand it is quite possible that there are certain sounds which are inaudible to us, which a horse will hear unconsciously, though we do not think that this is so. On the other hand it is not without significance that in our experiments we did not get any conclusive results except with what we call empathic pairs.

The point is that any horse cannot communicate mentally with any other horse, just as any human being cannot communicate mentally with any other human being. It is only if you are very close to someone that you may be able to sense what they are feeling without seeing them and talking to them. When two horses are mentally and emotionally on the same wavelength, then they too can sense what the other is thinking and what the other is doing.

Now it is common practice for a horse handler, faced with a very frightened or nervous horse, to use another horse that is confident and relaxed to give the anxious one confidence and relax him. We very often get sent a bunch of seven or eight three- and four-year-old cobs, horses and ponies which have never been handled and are completely wild, and we use one of two ways to get them settled and quiet. One is to approach the most settled cob in a quiet way and get him quiet, so that slowly the other horses in the bunch will become settled too, in tune with the horse we are handling. The second method, which we use more often, is to put the wild ponies in the stable together with one or two of our own horses. We leave them for half-an-hour to get accustomed to each other, then we go in to them. They will belt around the stable trying to get away from us, but our own horse will come over to talk, and we talk to him and feed him a few horse nuts, and we can then feel the others becoming gradually more relaxed. He will give them confidence in us and confidence in themselves.

Now it is obvious that the wild horses relax a certain amount from the example of the other horse. But we have found that we can do exactly the same thing with horses that are out of sight and sound of each other, *if the two horses are an empathic pair,* that is, if they are mentally in tune with each other. We can settle one horse by relaxing the other, or make one horse excited by exciting his companion.

This is one of our standard experiments. But it is in fact based on a trick as old as man's contact with horses. One of the earliest books on breaking horses for harness instructs you to take a colt and couple him to an old horse who will teach the young one to work. This method of horse-training has been used for hundreds of years. The South American *gauchos,* when they want to control a herd of horses, turn an old mare out with them and put a bell on her. The other horses will follow the old mare, and she will get them going quietly and steadily. The *gauchos* can then find the herd by the bell, and the old mare will make it possible to drive the young horses into a corral.

My early memories of seeing horses broken at home include

seeing Black Beauty, our pony, always in attendance 'as a schoolmaster' to tell the others what to do. Those were my father's words: he said that Beauty had to be there to tell the young horses what to do, and for some fifteen years we used Cork Beg for the same purpose. The older horse settles the younger horse and the young horse will imitate his senior. When a young horse is being asked to do something new his first reaction is to say 'I can't.' Seeing another horse do it will show him that it is not impossible, but seeing another horse can do it does not necessarily convince him that he can, so he may still say 'I can't.' However, if he can feel the other horse *enjoying* himself he will want to enjoy the experience too, and that is where extra-sensory perception comes in.

E.s.p. between animals is not a conscious mental process, it is an unconscious process and to a certain extent it is an automatic reflex. If an old hunter hears the sound of a hunting horn and hounds in full cry in the distance, he will become excited. This is because he associates the sound of the hunting horn and the cry of the hounds with being excited. But if he has a companion with him who has never heard hounds and does not know what a hunting horn means, the companion will become excited because the old horse is excited, without knowing why. The old horse's excitement is an automatic reflex and the young horse's excitement too is an automatic response. If you go into a stable and frighten a horse, his empathic companion, even though he may be out of sight and out of hearing, will also show signs of being frightened.

An empathic pair is simply a pair of horses mentally and emotionally close to each other, and the phenomenon comes about in one of two ways. Two horses may simply find themselves automatically in tune with each other from the first time they meet. These will probably be of the same breed and type. Or alternatively, they may become mentally in tune with each other through close and constant companionship. They will initially think roughly upon the same mental lines, but by close association they will attain complete empathy. If you get two thoroughbreds and turn them out with a herd of ponies, they will in most cases tend to graze together, probably away from the ponies, and in time they will become an empathic pair. Or if you have a mare and a gelding and turn them out together for a long period, perhaps several years, they too may in time think as one.

A truly empathic pair is a pair of horses who literally think as one, the perfect union. The nearest analogy I can think of is that of a pair of tuning forks. If you strike one tuning fork, it will hum, and if you put an exactly similar tuning fork beside it that will also begin to hum, in unison. If the second fork is not exactly similar – that is, it makes note D while the original is an E – the response will be less marked. And the further the second fork is from the note of the original tuning fork, the less the responding tuning fork will hum. So it is with e.s.p. and empathy: if you apply a stimulus to one horse of an empathic pair, the other, even though he is not in physical contact, will respond too. The less the sympathy between the two horses – the further from an empathic pair – the less the response will be, until two horses which are not in mental communication at all will make no response whatever!

I had my first experience of this phenomenon when I was quite young. Along with Beauty we had other ponies, and one pony we had had for a very long time was called Bill the Baby. When Bill did not want to be caught, we could not catch Beauty, and countless times I have driven Beauty and Bill into the corner of the field to try to catch them. I would approach them, and they would be standing quietly and quite happily looking at me, until I got to within five or ten yards of them, and then, without any signal I could see at all, one would shoot to the left of me and the other to the right of me, and on no occasion did they both try to go the same way. They would always start at exactly the same instant, so that there was no possible way of stopping them, and it was a good twenty years before I realized how they did it. I used to spend hours and hours trying to work out the signals that they were giving, so that I could stop them beforehand, but I never could. I can read those signals to a certain extent now, but now I know enough never to corner a horse if I want to catch it. I always make him come to me.

There is still a great deal of work to be carried out into exactly how one horse communicates with another horse using e.s.p., and into how a human being can communicate mentally with a horse or with another human being. Equally, we know little about why one person has this faculty and not another. The Russians and Americans have done a lot of work on e.s.p. and telepathy between human beings, mainly on telepathy, which is by far the less common phenomenon. But there has been very little work done on e.s.p. between animals, apart from our own. And we, I must emphasize, have only scratched the surface of the subject. We have researched only into communication between horse and horse, and horse and man. But we have found that if one is to do any animal-communication research, it is essential to concentrate in the beginning on one animal, and it must be an animal that has been selected as the one you are naturally mentally in tune with. Equally, if you are carrying out research into communication between two horses, it is essential to get two horses of similar breeding and type, and two horses that are naturally mentally in tune with each other.

We can sometimes find two horses with a natural empathy when we go to a sale; if we see two horses which come from different places yet are immediately friendly to each other, and start whickering and talking to each other, we know these two horses are mentally in tune. Normally, if you walk down the line of horses at a horse sale, you will see that most of the horses are standing in apparent mental and physical isolation from the horses on either side. But just occasionally you will see two horses, usually of similar type and breeding, who are acting in a friendly way and talking to each other. These are likely to be a naturally empathic pair.

In the wild, when a strange horse approaches, the natural reaction of the herd is to reject it; and to begin with, even a domesticated horse, if you introduce a strange horse to it, will react by snapping at him or telling him to bugger off. He will in fact be saying 'this is our home, you get the hell out of here, this is our territory.' This is the natural and automatic reaction of a horse, just as it is with human beings, who tend to reject advances from strangers. As evidence of this, you have only to look at a bunch of people travelling in a railway carriage, each sitting in defensive isolation. A naturally empathic pair, however, will drop their reserve at once.

It is only when you have obtained a horse that you think you are mentally in tune with, and obtained a companion horse which is also in tune with him, that you can start your research. You will start by concentrating on trying to communicate mentally with your subject, and at the same time observing his behaviour with his companion.

The first horse that I knew I had this empathy with was Weeping Roger. I have already briefly described the extraordinary circumstances in which I met him, one day in Exeter market. I was just having a look, and talking to a friend of mine, when suddenly behind me I could feel dejection invading my mind and body as if someone or something was screaming 'for God's sake get me out of here.' I turned around, and there was a horse just waiting to go into the ring, a dirty-brown lop-eared half-starved sixteen-two thoroughbred. I just had to buy him. My wife, who was standing some distance away, saw what was going to happen, and, realizing that a desperate illness required a desperate remedy, saw a very attractive girl, to whom she had just been introduced. By this time Roger was in the ring, and I was bidding for him. She grabbed this unfortunate female and dragged her over, hoping to distract me from the horse. The poor girl got one glance from me, 'hello', and I turned my back and went on bidding. Fortunately no one else wanted a lop-eared sixteen-two half-starved thoroughbred and I got him for £40.

I took him home, having learnt he had been on Exmoor all winter (this was the end of February). I put him inside and started stuffing food into him. I took him out hunting with the hounds three or four days later, and he loved it and I hunted him a dozen times more before the end of the season. Then just ten days before the local point-to-point at Cotley, the horse I had been going to ride in the hunt race died. So I entered Roger.

On the day of the point-to-point, I was so ashamed of his condition and appearance that I did not take him out of the lorry until the very last minute, and then took him straight down the paddock, once round, and down to the start. I always had a half-crown bet on the race with my friend Pat Frost, on who would finish first. But this time I had so little confidence in my mount that I made the condition that the loser would have a double scotch afterwards. I thought I was being very smart. There were about a dozen to fifteen horses in the race as far as I can remember, and they were off to a very ragged start, but away we went with me settling Roger down on the tail of the field.

On the Cotley course, you go first about half a mile uphill, then you turn downhill towards the finish, then away uphill again. By the time we got to the top of the hill the first time, I was two lengths behind the last horse, but Roger was going very well, taking his fences with great enthusiasm, and as we went down the hill, I was surprised to find that I was still in reasonable touch with the bulk of the field. Down past the finish, to the bottom of the hill, and away up the hill again – then the horse just in front dropped back past me, and I thought 'well that is good, I will not be last anyway.' Then we passed another horse and another and another. By the time we got to the top of the hill there were only two horses in front of me, and I thought I had better do something more vigorous, since Roger was hardly sweating. So I set him alight, and went in pursuit of the two riders half a fence in front of me, and slowly and remorselessly I found I was catching up with them. Three fences from home, the horse that was lying second fell, and by the time we reached the winning post I was within three lengths of the winner. I just could not believe it, that this skeleton of a horse had beaten some of the best horses in the West Country. Roger literally danced past the winning post, as if he had won the Grand National, his head and tail up and never more than one foot on the ground at a time. We went into the unsaddling enclosure and it took me five minutes to get the saddle off, he was dancing around so much with pride and excitement.

After this I really set about getting him fit to race, for I suspected I had a very good horse indeed. After breakfast each morning I used to take him out for exercise, and since it was very cold weather and I never had gloves with me, I used to put my hands into my pockets and they stayed there until I got home. I would direct him and control him entirely by e.s.p. I could make him trot, walk, turn left, turn right entirely by mental concentration.

Roger had another very useful function. He was a superb nursemaid. My daughter Paddy, who was then about eighteen months old, used to love horses, and the sure way of keeping her quiet and happy was to put her on the straw in Roger's box, and let her play under the manger and around his feet. She learned to walk by pulling herself up by his tail, tottering from one leg to another. When she fell down and bumped herself, Roger would blow at her, and she rolled over on her back quite happy again.

But we could never get any condition on him, and we were always ashamed to take him racing because he looked so terrible in the paddock, and the only consolation we had was that the worse he looked in the paddock, the better he was going to run. If he stumbled around and looked as though he would have a job to totter down to the start, we knew that he was really going to go that day, and we could get our money on. I won two or three races on him, and I always enjoyed riding him, because he was such a fantastic jumper, and he was so enthusiastic about racing.

Shortly after the Cotley point-to-point, a friend offered to buy him off me for £300. I did not want to sell, but I had him vetted anyway, to insure him. The vet, Bill Martin, checked his legs in the stable, then had him out to check his heart while he was standing still. He listened for two seconds and said, 'for God's sake put the bloody thing back into the stable before he drops dead.' Then I listened, and it was the most irregular heartbeat I had ever heard. It sounded like Victor Sylvester giving a dancing lesson, slow, slow, quick-quick, slow, but it was less regular than that, it would beat very very quickly and then very very slowly. How he ever walked, let alone raced, I could not understand. But since Bill said that he was as likely to drop dead walking around the field as racing, and the old man loved racing, we decided to go on racing him. When we left Devon to come up to Wales, he was sold for a nominal price to an acquaintance who wanted a horse for his son to start point-to-pointing on, and he ran his last race only eight years later at the Cotley point-to-point, when he was seventeen years old, and came second again.

I was always at one with him. On one occasion he woke me up at three in the morning. I simply knew there was something wrong, and when I went out to have a look at him I found that he was having a violent attack of colic. And once I found I could get through to him, I started trying to get through to other horses, by concentrating all my attention on the horse I was trying to get through to – leaving myself as I put it, on an open line to the horse. And after working at it for about fifteen years I find I can get through to nearly everything, except small ponies.

Mine is not a unique experience. After all, as we have seen, the bond between man and horse goes back to antiquity, and stories about this bond go back beyond the history of the written word. The story I like best, which seems to express the essence of all the legends about the faithful steed, is that told about a French soldier, during one of Napoleon's battles against the Austrians. He was wounded and lying in a field, when suddenly his horse, which he had not been riding that day because it was lame, appeared beside him, having broken away from the horse lines. The soldier pulled himself up on to its back, and the horse carried him back to his unit, where he was received by his comrades unconscious across the horse's bare back, without bridle, halter or saddle.

Man's ability to be at one with the horse is also well illustrated by the story of the American slave who used to catch wild mustangs by going naked into the district where the herd of horses roamed, and live and move as a member of the herd. He would start off by approaching within two or three hundred yards of the herd and just staying there. When the horses moved, he moved with them. When they went to water, he went to water. When they grazed he would lie down beside the grazing herd. He would fetch his own food from a tree a mile or so away from the herd, where it was left for him. Within a fortnight or so he would be moving in amongst the wild horses and be accepted as a member of the herd. Then, when he had established his position he would half-drive, half-lead the mustangs into an already prepared corral. Simply by acting as a horse acted, thinking as a horse thought, behaving as a horse behaved, and having no contact with man, he gained the horses' trust and could single-handedly catch a complete herd of wild horses.

8: *On Gentling Horses*

It seems incredible to me that, apart from my own work, no research has been done into communication between horses, of any type, and very little into the central problem of controlling horses: that is, into what is the best form of communication between man and horse. The state of our knowledge of how to communicate even with the horses we ride is very poor indeed: we know that if you hit an animal it will run away; if you pull its mouth it will tend to stop; if you pull its head left it will tend to go left, and if you pull its head right it will tend to go right. Modern-day horsemanship is a development of these four facts, together with the refinement that you can teach your horse to respond to a verbal command, if that command is repeated again and again. This is essentially the procedure known as 'training' a horse. The fact that the early form of training is known as 'breaking' just about sums up man's attitude towards the horse.

Breaking a horse is based upon three principles:

(a) That if a horse responds wrongly to a stimulus, he should be punished;

(b) That if he responds correctly to a stimulus he should be rewarded; and

(c) That basically he must be made to do what you want him to do, by force if necessary.

A comparatively few horses have had a considerable amount of time spent on them, using this method of training; and the method, confined as it must be to the few and expensive has been written about at length. But even today the bulk of horses are trained by cruder and cheaper application of the same principles – a brave and hardy boy sits the horse until he is bucked off again, and the horse is forced

96

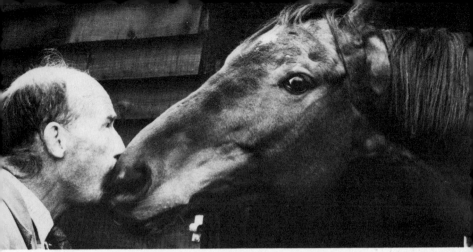

Above: 'Welcome': the author's
greeting from his horses

Right: 'I love you'

'I'm boss': the grey tries to overtake the herd leader

'Go back': the herd leader gives the grey a nip to send him back into line

'Go away, I'll pulverize you'

'I'm hungry': foal approaches mother

'Mummy loves you, you'll be quite safe'

'Come and drink'

'Go away, I'm a good girl': the mare refuses the stallion

'I like you': he approaches another mare

'Let's make love'

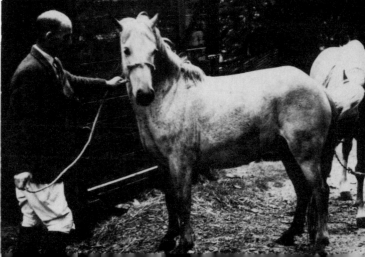

'You'll be quite safe with me': he reassures her

And she complies: 'Come on then!'

Above and Right: 'Empathic pairs'

The author's 'gentling' method of training

Catching a horse by making him come to you: the author leads the horse with a bucket of food

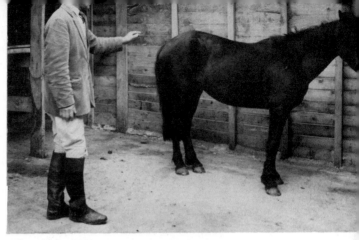

Calming a frightened or hostile horse, first by gentling with the voice: the author approaches, talking quietly to the horse in a sing-song voice

Using finger-tips he gets near enough to caress the horse with the tips of the fingers, simulating the mother's muzzle reassuring a foal

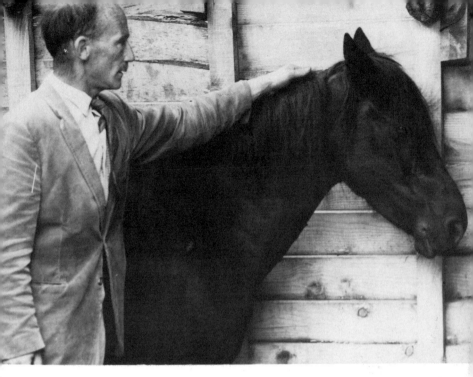

Above: Now he uses the palm of the hand to suggest the pressure of another horse's head

Below: Then he leans over the pony's neck, imitating the reassurance of the presence of another horse

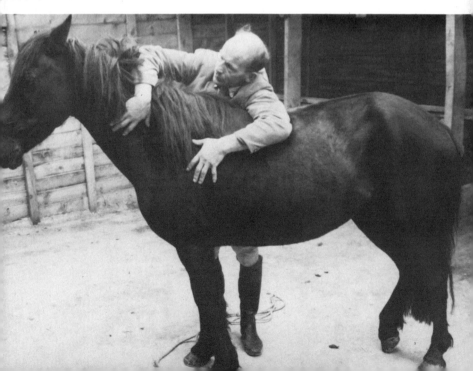

The author's wife, Leslie, takes a cross-country fence on 'Rostellan'

The author on 'Irefais Comet'

'Where's my bloody
breakfast?'

to do what it is told to do until, by trial and error and various rewards and punishments, it has been trained to be ridden or to work in a cart. This system is to my mind entirely without logic, since it is generally assumed that the horse is less intelligent than man (though I admit that at times I doubt this). It seems to me to be obvious that it would be quicker and more efficient for a man to learn the form of communication the horse understands best, rather than to try to teach the less intelligent being the form of communication man knows best.

Our own experience has taught us that it is infinitely easier to train a horse, and you can get some very startling results, when you use equine communication methods. For the past thirty years, first with my father and later on with my wife and daughter, I have been handling and retraining horses that other people had given up as unbreakable and unmanageable. Many of these would otherwise have ended up in tins of cats' meat, or on the slabs of the continental butchers. These have been, generally, of two types. The first type are very intelligent horses who have been frightened and brutalized by ill-treatment. In the early days these were much the largest group that we got. Today, most of the horses we get are in the second group – strong horses spoiled by weak handling, often by women for whom the horses are too powerful and too strong. These horses have been re-trained by using two qualities, patience and understanding.

All our reserves of patience were demanded to handle a horse we had not long ago, who could not be haltered or bridled because as soon as you tried to halter or bridle him, he would rear up on his hind legs. There were two problems we had to deal with. First, the rearing had to be cured. And second, the original cause of his trouble had to be identified and remedied. It seemed that at some time or other he had been hurt by someone putting his hands behind his ears, for this was the thing he refused to let you do. You could put a bit into his mouth sometimes, but you could never get the bridle over his head. We could simply have used a leather bridle and put it on from his neck, but this would not have cured the basic trouble, so I simply took him into a loose-box and began running my hand up his shoulder and over his neck. As I got near his head he went up on his hind legs. As soon as he came down again, I put my hand on his shoulder and went up his neck again, then up he went on his hind legs again. After about forty-five minutes I could run my hand up his neck as far as his head, stopping short of his ears. So I began running my hand up the crest of his mane, until I got behind his ears – up on his hind legs he went. But I persisted, and after about twenty minutes I could run my hand up his neck, over his ears and down his nose. When I got to this stage, my hand went from his nose, rubbing his head, up to his eyes, and as soon as I got near his ears he was up on his hind legs again. But after another five or ten minutes I could actually run my hand up his nose, over his ears and down his neck.

Then came the next stage. I got a rope halter, put it on over his nose, then ran my hand up his nose and over his ears as if I were trying to put the halter on. He reared again so I took the halter off and tried to put it on again. As soon as I had the nose piece on I once more ran my hand up his head and over his ears. After a further five minutes of this I could slip the halter on and off. When he went up on his hind legs I took very little notice. I just went on talking to him all the time in a soft sing-song voice, and in a very short time, he was beginning to settle. He had ceased to be worried about my hand running over his ears; but at the same time he was damned if he was going to let me do it easily, because he had never let anyone do it. When I could get the halter on and off without any difficulty, which took about twenty minutes from doing it the first time, I went and got a bridle, put the bit in his mouth with some difficulty, took the bit out of his mouth and put it in again, in and out, in and out until I could slip the bit into his mouth whenever I wanted to. Then I ran the reins up his head and over his ears. Up he went on his hind legs, off with the reins once more, then back on with the reins. Then I put the bit back in his mouth, put the reins over his head and began to put the bridle over his ears. Up he went on his hind legs, so off with the reins and out with the bit, then on with the reins, in with the bit, and up with the bridle. I went on doing this for about ten minutes until I could put that bridle on and off whenever I liked. I had been at him for about four hours then, so I gave him a drink and his dinner and went to have my own. It was a very light dinner, it always is when I am handling difficult horses, then I went out again and started all over again. After about an hour going at him a second time, I could put the bridle on and off whenever I wanted to. So I left him for the day.

The next day I had him in again and went through the same procedure, which took me an hour and a half in the morning, half-an-hour in the afternoon and ten minutes in the evening. Within a week he took no notice at all of the bridle being put on and I could do it whenever I liked. It was patience that did the trick, and of course basic understanding of what the problem was. At the same time I had to be confident that I was going to succeed, and never get worried or excited. My attitude the whole time was calm, so that while dealing with his stubbornness I did not have to deal also with a frightened or worried horse.

It must always be remembered of course that if you have a very strong powerful horse, or a very intelligent horse, he will never be a ride for an inexperienced beginner, unless he is well and truly 'broken' – that is to say, unless his spirit is broken entirely. Since there is an endless supply of horses which are neither big and strong nor extremely intelligent, it is surely much better for the inexperienced or the weak rider to get a horse that suits his temperament, rather than to try to break a horse of a temperament unsuitable for his purpose. By the same reasoning, when we are expecting a horse to do cross-country work, we select a horse which naturally enjoys jumping and wants to go across country, since it is

infinitely easier to get him jumping and going across country
than the horse that wants neither to jump nor to go out for
a walk. Similarly someone who does not want to go out for
a walk should get a horse that is the same way inclined, not
one that wants to go as soon as its feet touch the grass.

One example of how understanding comes into play when
we are retraining a difficult horse is our experience with
Jimmy, who came to us very recently. Jimmy had got on top
of his owner, and there were a number of things that she
could not do with him. To teach Jimmy who was boss, we
used pure animal communication. Now if you see a bunch
of horses going down the road, the boss horse will be in
front. If one of the others in the herd tries to pass the boss,
he will say 'go back' by swinging his head round and
punching the offender with his teeth. It looks as though he
is biting him, but in nine times out of ten he will merely be
punching him with his teeth – he will only bite if the horse
persists in trying to pass. So I took Jimmy out on a halter
and every time Jimmy tried to pass me, I swung my fist round
as if to punch him. I never actually connected, but I threatened
to punch his teeth in if he tried to pass me.

After three or four days of this Jimmy very clearly
understood that he could not pass me no matter how much
he wanted to, so he would walk behind me quietly and
obediently. A very difficult and strong horse, who previously
dominated his owner, thus learnt that I was boss and not
he. Jimmy had been taught to obey the orders of the boss of
the herd, and because I had used a communication method
that he understood he was neither frightened nor cowed by it.

It seems to me that the whole essence of getting the maximum of which he is capable out of the horse is communication. It is essential for the rider to be able to convey his
wishes explicitly to the horse, and for the horse to respond
to those wishes, so it is only logical that those wishes should
be conveyed in a manner that the horse most easily understands, that is, in the form of communication that the horse
uses himself. This is where e.s.p. is so important, for by this

method the horse can quickly and readily understand your desires rather than your commands. For example, a horse should respond when the owner is excited, and he should relax when you are relaxed. When the horse is a sounding board for your own emotions, then that horse will respond in competition or in an emergency instantaneously, and in a far more enthusiastic and willing way than if he is merely responding to a command. Similarly, a guard sergeant-major can teach a squad of eleven men to play football on command; but that team of footballers would never in this world beat a team of people who play together for the love of doing so, and respect each others wishes.

This is where I think that the modern method of horse-training is wrong, since it is angled towards the dressage arena where anticipation of the rider's wishes is counted as a disobedience. I believe that if you are to get the maximum from a horse, that horse should be trying to anticipate your wishes, to do what you want it to do before you actually ask it. All you have to do is be empathic with your horse, and he will anticipate your wishes, since he will know what you want him to do before you ask him.

Yet the whole art of modern training is to teach the horse to answer commands. The basic commands that you will want to teach him will take up to six months, and the more advanced work two or three years. We on the other hand have found that with gentling we can get a horse to respond within hours. It is extremely easy to get your horse to do what you want him to do when you are trying to get him to *want* to do what you want him to. And the short-cut to this is via e.s.p.. As we have already seen, ever since primitive man first made the discovery that Eohippus had other uses than that of filling an empty belly, man has been using e.s.p. to ride and control his horses, to a greater or lesser extent depending upon the rider and his methods of training; and yet nobody has written about e.s.p. with horses, and there has been no research into the subject whatever. We indeed had been carrying out research into e.s.p. for over ten years before I dared mention it to anybody. And then it happened quite by chance.

My wife wanted to visit her family in Ireland, and since as usual my car had broken down, I asked my friend and neighbour Charles Thurlow Craig to drive her to the station. After seeing her off, we stopped for a drink on the way home. One drink led to another and after the fourth or fifth drink, I happened to mention to Thurlow, who is a very receptive person, that I could communicate mentally with horses and control them by telepathy. I expected him to laugh at me and say I was too drunk to know what I was saying. Instead of which he said 'that's nothing, I can too,' and we discovered that while he could communicate mentally with Welsh cobs, and not with any other kind of horse, I could get through best to thoroughbreds and near-thoroughbreds. After an hour-and-a-half we went home.

The following morning I was troubled by two things: first, by a rather bad hangover, and second, by a somewhat hazy recollection that I had been fool enough to tell Thurlow that I could communicate mentally with horses. So I went up to see him and after we had had one or two hairs of the dog, he confirmed that he too could communicate mentally with horses and that he had been doing it for a very long time, but had never mentioned it to anybody until the previous evening. Since he was somewhat unconventional anyway, he did not want to be classed as a raving lunatic.

For the next six or eight months, Thurlow and I talked off and on about mental communication with horses, but I did not mention it to anybody else until I went to the hunt ball that year. And hunt balls being hunt balls, by midnight I was not as sober as I might have been. By this time I happened to be dancing with a very knowledgeable horsewoman I knew, and I mentioned to her this ability to communicate mentally with horses, and she thought about it and said 'Do you know I can do it with Poodle,' (that was the name of her horse). In the course of the next two or three dances, she came to the conclusion that she had had this ability with three of the horses she had ridden over the previous thirty or forty years.

The point of this story is that the first two horsey people I mentioned the matter to, realized after some thought that they could communicate with horses. Yet the idea that there could be mental communication between man and horse was on the face of it so completely outrageous that I had to be slightly oiled before I could even mention it, and that after ten years of research. After this I mentioned my discoveries to one or two close friends, then slowly to a much wider circle of acquaintances, and I found to my amazement that very nearly without exception they could all communicate mentally with their horses – not with all their horses, but with some of them. This has been going on for some two thousand years, but it has never been written about and there has been no research into the subject whatever.

E.s.p. is the ability to perceive by means other than sight, sound, touch, smell or taste. In actual fact this simply means that you can sense moods and emotions, rather than see or hear them – we know that e.s.p. mainly concerns conveying and receiving moods, emotions, feelings and limited ideas. A horse instinctively knows the moods and emotions of its companions. It does not matter whether they are human or animal, they can be animals of the same species or animals of another species. He can of course to a certain extent use his sight and hearing as well, when he senses whether they are angry or frightened, settled or excited. But we know that he can also feel their mood instinctively because we know that he will respond to his companions even if they are out of sight and out of sound.

That there is e.s.p. between animals of different species is difficult to prove, but our own observations tend to confirm it. We once, for instance, had a bull and a gander who were absolutely inseparable. Even if the gander was out of sight of the bull, when the bull moved from one field to the next the gander would leave what he was doing immediately, and go straight to where the bull was. He always knew where the bull had gone, even though he could not see him. The bull was running out with the cows and would come in and out with them night and morning, lying down in the yard while the cows were being milked. Sometimes the gander would sit on top of him or beside him, and sometimes he would go off and mind his own business. On one occasion he got shut into the feeding house, and when the cattle were turned out he was left behind. It so happened on this occasion the cattle were turned into a different field, about a quarter of a mile from where they had been grazing previously. When the gander was let out we thought that he would go straight to the normal field. Instead he ran out of the feeding house and took wing and flew straight to the new field where the cattle were grazing. This could have been coincidence. The explanation could have been that the gander flew at sufficient height to see where the cattle were. But it is within the boundary of probability that some sense told him that things were different, that there was some form of mental communication between the bull and the gander.

In another case there was a very close friendship between a cow and a pony. The odd thing about this was that the cow would know when the pony mare was horseing, and would mount the pony as one cow would mount another when she was bulling. Now there could have been no sexual smell from the pony that the cow would understand, and it is probable that there were no signs. Normally one pony mare will not mount another, so the behaviour pattern was strange to the pony and accordingly no sign would be likely to be given. Yet the cow would know instinctively when the pony was horseing. We believe that this very strong affinity between the cow and the pony caused a behaviour response that was natural to the cow and not to the pony.

Cork Beg had a very great attachment to a Friesian bull that we had, and they would stand together for hours on end. When the bull lay down Cork Beg would stand over him, and when the flies were bad they would stand head-to-tail flicking each other. The bull would use his rough tongue to scratch Cork Beg. At times they would play together: Cork Beg would stand on his back legs and strike out at the bull with his forelegs, then the bull would charge him, appearing to be hooking him with his horns. The first time we saw this, we fully expected Cork Beg to be damaged, but the bull each time he charged, would stop far enough from Cork Beg not to touch him. They would go on like this for ten minutes or a quarter of an hour at a time, Cork Beg pretending to strike the bull with his front legs and the bull pretending to hook Cork Beg's intestines out with his horns, until one or the other would get tired. Either the bull would roar, as if he were going to charge, and Cork Beg would gallop away with the bull in pursuit; or Cork Beg would dodge the bull as he charged and land two well-shod heels in his ribs, though without really hurting him. Then after five or ten minutes they would make it up and stand flicking flies off each other again. Now the curious thing about this was that the bull would know where Cork Beg was itching. If Cork Beg had an itch above his hip bone, the bull would lick there. If Cork Beg had an itch behind his ear, the bull would lick behind his ears. There was no way that we could see that Cork Beg could make the bull lick him. Further, this behaviour pattern was normal neither to Cork Beg nor to the bull, since it is unusual for cattle to lick one another, except for a cow to lick a calf, and certainly it is not usual for a bull to lick a cow except as a sexual stimulus. Equally it is unusual for one horse to lick another, though he may nip, or bite another horse to relieve an itch. Again we think that the two animals must have been communicating by e.s.p. But I would emphasize that this belief is based on observation and not on any real proof.

Two horses may or may not be emotionally or mentally in communication. We say that horses can think in different or similar thought patterns, and to some extent patterns tend to go with breeds. A thoroughbred will tend to have a thought pattern different from that of a Welsh Cob, and a Welsh Cob will have a different thought pattern from that of a pony, but there are Welsh Cobs who think as ponies, and thorough-breds who think as Welsh Cobs. Of course these thought and emotional patterns are not static. If two horses have thought patterns that are mainly unalike but have certain similari-ties, close companionship will tend to increase the similarities, so that they will become closer and closer to each other mentally. We say that the thought patterns change and become similar. Again among a group of horses, those with similar thought patterns will tend to associate with each other, and their patterns will become increasingly alike. Hence in a bunch of horses, including, let us say, Welsh Cobs and cross-bred thoroughbreds, the Welsh Cobs will tend to associate together and the thoroughbreds will tend to form a separate group. But they would also learn the thought patterns of each other. If a thoroughbred and a small pony are kept together, out of contact with other horses, they will have no emotional contact to begin with, but after a period of time, the two horses will develop an affinity and their thought patterns will become more similar. If, however, after a period of time other thoroughbreds and ponies are introduced to the original pair, the pony will tend to go back to its original thought pattern and the thoroughbred to his thoroughbred thought pattern. Thus horses of different breeds can learn by asso-ciation to communicate with horses of different breeds, and with horses and animals of different thought patterns; but they will still be able to communicate most easily with animals who think in the same thought pattern as they do them-selves.

This difference in thought patterns between horse and horse explains why a human being can get through to one horse and not another. It explains why one particular horse will do anything for you and you get an automatic response to any request, while another horse, even occasionally of the same breed, type and temperament will do the exact opposite no matter what you ask him to do.

Last spring I had two Cob-cross Welsh pony brothers to gentle. They were both by a Welsh Cob stallion called

Rhysted Prince, and a pony mare, and they were about twelve hands high, three and four years old, and strawberry roans. They looked almost identical, but one of those ponies, no matter what I asked him to do, would fight and fight me; while the other pony did whatever I asked him to do as if he were an old horse and had been ridden all his life. Yet when those two ponies went back to their owners, the one I could do anything with had the owner's son off as often as he liked to get on; but his brother with whom I had had such a lot of trouble, never put a foot wrong. It is the same with human beings; you meet some people with whom you are immediately in sympathy, and others who make the hairs on the back of your neck stand up as soon as you meet them. The French have a term for this: they say that two people are *sympatique* or not *sympatique*.

In our field of work on horses, the horses with which we have an affinity are those from whom we can get the greatest response. But we can on the other hand sometimes build and develop affinities by working at it when we are doing experiments between horse and man. I, for instance, have always been able to get through to thoroughbreds and near-thoroughbreds. No matter how difficult or awkward they are, they will always go sweetly for me, and I can very often get more out of them in a race than anybody else. But for a very long time, until seven or eight years ago in fact, I had no feeling at all for other breeds of horses, and my ability to ride or handle them would depend entirely upon my horsemanship and not on the horse. Over the years however I have developed an ability to switch wavelength to that of the horse I am riding. Even now I have no empathy at all with small ponies, and this I see as a weakness on my part, which I am hoping to overcome with perseverance and time. If you cannot get through to a particular breed of horse, you may find by working at it that you will be able to get through to one member of that breed, then to two, then three and so on, until with time you will be able to get through to most horses.

Over the last four years I have had the use, off and on, of a fourteen-two Welsh Cob, Trefais Comet, some of whose exploits I have already described. Now he is the most wayward bloody-minded little individual in the world at times. But I can get through to him, and he will always go for me, and if I am competing he gives every ounce of his ability and he is keener to win than I am. In fact he is probably the only Welsh Cob living who has consistently beaten thoroughbreds in cross-country competitions. He was second in a one-day event last autumn, beaten because he did a diabolical dressage with a score of a hundred and nine penalty points; but the cross-country course was extremely stiff and he was one of only three horses that went round clear, half-a-minute faster than the next horse and a minute-and-a-half faster than the rest of the field.

Being mentally in tune with a horse can have its drawbacks at times, however. I bought a grey thoroughbred gelding called Costa Clyde because I got through to him, and he was being outrageously cocky as he went round the ring : 'I am the best horse here, there is nothing else that can compare with me.' He turned out to be the most shameless liar in the world. Only after I bought him did I discover that he was always full of himself and his own importance, but he never made a racehorse and never won a race. But I was very fond of him and I used to love riding him, because of his supreme self-assurance and confidence. Even when he came back from a race, trailing in last, he would still be full of himself, and always have frightful stories to tell about why he had not won.

But it must also be remembered that by human standards the horse is of comparatively low intellect – its range of understanding is probably roughly comparable with that of a child of about eight. And it is the super-intelligent horses that are the most difficult to handle : they are the ones that often become unbreakable through mishandling, and get on top of their owners. On the race course they quickly learn that there is no profit in racing, especially in the tight finish, when they will get a hiding, and so they pack in racing and become dogs. But these are the horses we like, and these are the horses we get most response from with our gentling treatment.

9: *Proving E.S.P. among Horses*

Extra-sensory perception, as experienced among horses, and between horses and human beings, seems to have four different functions, which may be used separately or together. The first is to convey mood, which may be agitated and excited, or peaceful and relaxed. Now part of this message the receiver will perceive consciously, that is to say, he may see the horse's relaxed and peaceful swishing of his tail in the shade; but he will also feel his peace and serenity within himself. If the receiver is another horse he can be observed being made peaceful and serene by the first horse. But if something intrudes to disturb the peace – such as hounds going across the skyline or the sound of horses galloping – the horse becomes excited, and the second horse will become excited too, even if he cannot see the first horse and cannot see or hear what is exciting him. An observer will be able to see the second horse become agitated, looking around to see what is causing the excitement, *even if he cannot see what is happening to the first horse.*

The second function of e.s.p. is to convey emotions: anger, affection and so on. Anger is probably the strongest of the e.s.p. feelings: it is something you can feel mounting within yourself, knotting your stomach muscles, making you tenser and tenser until you feel you could explode.

I had evidence recently of just how powerful a message of anger can be. A friend had brought me an Arab-cross Welsh six-year-old for gentling, who had been used as a stallion for three years and then castrated in the spring. As soon as his wounds had healed, he was brought over to me, and I was especially interested because we had two of his sons at our place at that time. We named him Ieuan. I had an immediate affinity with him, which was rather unusual, since

I normally have great difficulty in getting through to anything with Arab blood. We worked him for about a fortnight, riding him every day and gentling him, and about Easter he was going so well and quietly we decided to put him into the trekking string. He went very well for three or four days, until a friend came to stay with us for Easter. He rode him on Easter Friday, and then on Easter Saturday she rode him again. My wife and daughter had taken them out, and they had been gone only about twenty minutes, when I could feel my stomach muscles knotting and getting tighter and tighter and I knew that I was getting a message from Ieuan. How I was so sure of that I do not quite know. So I jumped into my car and rushed after them, and when I caught up with them after a couple of miles I could see straight away that Ieuan was all over the place, just ready to explode. So I whipped Bill off his back and put my daughter on and they went off quite happily. That afternoon, however, Paddy had a young horse she wanted to ride, so I put Brian, another friend, on Ieuan and again away they went. And again after about half-an-hour I could feel my stomach muscles knotting, and off in the car I went and again Ieuan was ready to explode. As I caught up with them he started putting in a buck, but as soon as I got there he settled down and this time I put one of the girls on his back, and after that he settled quite happily.

On this second occasion I had felt the horse's anger mounting over a distance of three or four miles : a very remarkable event, since e.s.p. normally works only over comparatively short distances. This time there was in addition the unusual circumstances of a large number of witnesses to the actual working of e.s.p.

Physical sensations, such as hunger, thirst and pain are also conveyed by the horse through e.s.p., and the capacity to pick up such messages is something that all good vets seem to have. They can sense just where the horse is distressed and uncomfortable, and they use this ability in their diagnosis of illness or injury – a capacity which is clearly very important to a vet. For example, if a horse has a lame hind leg, it may be because he has injured his foot, his pastern, his fetlock or his hock; he may have pulled one of the leg muscles; he may have damaged his stifle or his hip joint; he may have pulled one of his thigh or back muscles or he may have damaged his vertebrae. And there may be no visible sign whatever as to where precisely the injury is. Of course the vet's previous experience will help him to guess where the injury is likely to be; but I have watched Bill Martin our horse vet in the West Country literally sensing out an injury. He would stand for five or ten minutes looking at a horse, maybe talking, maybe saying absolutely nothing, just looking and feeling. Then he would go, very nearly invariably, straight to the seat of the injury. I can remember him once saying to me, 'use your eyes and ears Henry, but also use your feelings.' He told me that he had a sixth sense that told him what was the matter, and I always regret that at the time I knew him well we were only in the very early stages of our communication work and I never talked to him about it.

E.s.p. can finally be used to convey very limited ideas, such as 'here is food,' 'let's go away,' and use is quite often made of it among horses. This function is probably really an extension of the capacity to convey mood and feeling, since, for example, the idea 'here is food,' does not come over in e.s.p. as a *message*, though it would come over as a message if telepathy were being used. What in actual fact the receiving horse feels is a sense that the hunger of his companion is diminished and from this he knows that the other horse is eating. Similarly behind the idea 'let's go away' is the simple fact that in flight the feeling of fear is being diminished. For practical purposes, however, I have found it useful to say that a function of e.s.p. is to convey limited ideas. The distinction is particularly useful when some form of reaction to emotion or sensation is involved; for two or three of these e.s.p. functions will often be used together. The phrases 'I am hungry,' 'here is good grass,' used together, come through as hunger and hunger diminished. The phrases

'I am frightened,' 'let us run,' come through as fear, and then the automatic reaction of flight, which is fear diminished.

This message-carrying aspect of e.s.p. has been vital for the survival of the species, since in the wild a herd of horses may often be scattered, with some members out of sight and sound of each other. But if one part of the herd should be frightened by the appearance of man, wolf or some other predator, the rest of the herd, maybe amongst the trees, can be alerted by e.s.p. even though they can neither see nor hear their fellows. Horses thus alerted will become first disturbed, then prick up their ears and snort, and start to move away from the area.

The horse will also feel the aggressive intention of another species, and this too has been vital for the survival of the horse. When for instance a wolf, man or other carnivore tries to stalk a horse to make an attack, even though he cannot see, hear or smell the enemy, the horse will become restless and disturbed. And funnily enough this is one of the abilities that has survived in man. If you try to shadow a man, you will often find that after you have been following him for a very short time he will start looking around, even though he doesn't know you are there, because he can feel you with a sixth sense. This is easy to prove for yourself. All you have to do is to pick on some unsuspecting individual in the street and follow him for ten minutes or a quarter of an hour. This sensitivity is one of the few elements that man still retains of his primitive self.

Over the last five years we have carried out a number of experiments into e.s.p. among horses. To do this we have used horses which were empathic, that is to say, pairs of horses which were at one with each other, who were close companions and who thought on the same wavelength and acted as one horse. They would graze together, walk together, and stand together and if you were trying to catch them, either both would come or neither would come. We used only horses which we knew came from the same source and had been together for two or three years at least, and, though this was not always possible, we tried for preference to select brothers or sisters, since we found that two brothers or two sisters brought up together tend to think on exactly the same wavelength. Before starting work with them we would observe them over a period of a month to six weeks to make sure that they always grazed together, and never palled up with another horse, even for a short period. This being established, and my own experience confirming that they were on the same wavelength, we were ready to select them for experiment. I sometimes found it rather difficult to be absolutely certain, from the e.s.p. messages that I was getting, that the horses were thinking on the same wavelength, since I tend to switch my wavelength of e.s.p. to the horse I am handling; but from among the forty or fifty horses we have through our hands each year, we tried to select two pairs of horses each year. After five years, we had selected eleven pairs : that is, we found the proportion of suitable horses to be about ten per cent. Of these, two pairs were eliminated because we discovered that the attraction between them was physical rather than mental – each of these pairs was a mare and a gelding, and they were sexually attracted to each other. (We deduced this from the fact that when the mare was horseing they were much closer to each other, and also much closer together in the ten days to a fortnight between her horseing periods.) The third pair we had to eliminate was an eight-year-old mare and a rather immature three-year-old gelding who came from the same farm, and had been to-gether since the gelding was a six-month-old foal. They appeared to be an ideal pair, until we actually started the experiments. I ran the five experiments on the gelding to begin with, and had a positive result in every case; but when I started handling the mare and not the gelding, we had a fifty-fifty result. Actually the pair of them came out higher than the average – 75 per cent positive, or 7–8 per cent above average – but after considerable thought I came to the conclusion that the mare was in mental contact with

myself and not with the gelding – her affinity with the gelding
was maternal rather than mental.

We were extremely fortunate from the outset in that the
layout of the farm lent itself to the experiments. We had a
loose-box next to the house, and fifty yards away, the other
side of a range of buildings, we had a railway hut by the front
gate: that is, we had two boxes out of sight and out of
hearing of each other. Since when we were working on one
horse, the other could not see or hear what we were doing,
any response recorded had to be the result of e.s.p. and not of
sight or sound. It was also possible from two points in the
intervening building to observe the second horse without being
observed; and provided we worked from the loose-box in
the yard, the horse in the railway hut did not even know that
we were in the yard, let alone handling or feeding the other
horse. In the second experiment we had to leave the yard
for a period of time, so we used the railway hut by the front
gate to saddle and bridle the horse and take him out of the
yard, and the first horse could not even see us leaving,
though it was possible for him to hear our footsteps as we went
down the road.

There were five experiments involved, and over a period
of three days we carried out each experiment three times,
varying the horses we were working on and the horse we
were expecting a response from. On the first day we would
use horse A, on the second horse B, and on the third horse
A in experiment one. For experiment two the first day we
would use horse B, the second day A, the third day B.
On experiment three we would use A, B, A. On Experiment
four we would use B, A, B, and on experiment five A, B, A.
In this way we made absolutely certain that there was a fair
spread of the primary and secondary response of both
horses.

In the first experiment one of each pair was fed in the
plastic container. For us to record a positive reaction his
empathic pair had to indicate that he wanted food at the
same time; and to make quite sure that there was no question

of habit coming into this experiment, the horses were not fed
at the same time each day, nor were they fed at their regular
feeding times, so that any response had to be from e.s.p.
On twenty-one of the twenty-four tests we had a positive
response, which was better than we dared hope for: that is to
say, on twenty-one out of the twenty-four occasions, when we
were feeding one horse, the second horse, even though he
could not see or hear us in any way, knew that we were feeding the first horse and demanded food. (Of course, before we
carried out this experiment, we had to find out how each
horse said 'where is my bloody breakfast.' Some of them
bang their feeding bins, others whicker, two of them would
walk from the door to the feeding bin and back to the door.
One particular horse would stand with his head out of the
doorway and shake his head up and down, up and down,
until he was fed, and if you were a long time feeding him he
would pull horrible faces.) This was the easiest experiment to
do and to set up, since in the first place it is quite simple to
eliminate signs, sounds and habit, and in the second place
there is no question of personal opinion coming into it whatever. Your responding horse either says 'where is my bloody
breakfast,' or he does not. There are no two ways about it.
So to my mind this experiment is absolutely conclusive proof
of the existence of e.s.p.

In the second experiment one of each pair was taken out
of the yard and into a field, then excited by cantering and
jumping and generally getting him hotted up. Positive results
were recorded if, when the excited horse returned to the yard,
the second one of the pair – who had remained in his box
– became excited. This again is an experiment where it is
comparatively easy to tell whether you have a positive result
or not: if a horse is standing still, half asleep, and he suddenly
pricks his ears and starts walking or dancing round his box,
you may be absolutely certain that something has disturbed
and excited him. Two of the horses became agitated and
started whickering: in two cases the horse in the box became
excited when the exercised horse was well over a quarter of a

mile away. But with another two – that is to say in three tests, since one of the horses was used twice – we got no conclusive results since the horse in question was a restless horse anyway and tended on occasion to become excited for no obvious reason. Nevertheless in this experiment nineteen out of the twenty-four results were positive, with three further results in which the second horse did become excited, but we could not be sure that he was excited purely because his empathic pair was excited.

Experiment three was a more-or-less complete failure, because the positive results left too much room for human error. This experiment followed on from the second experiment. After the excited horse had been brought back to the yard and we had observed the effect on his companion, we took his saddle and bridle off and went to his *companion* and started gentling him and relaxing him. A positive result was recorded, if the exercised horse relaxed considerably sooner than normal. The difficulty here was in deciding how long it would normally have taken the horse to relax. We had also to shorten the series of experiments because one of the horses we were exciting over-reached and cut himself, so instead of gentling his companion we had to spend the next twenty minutes cleaning up the wound and stopping the bleeding. So we only had twenty-three experiments instead of twenty-four. Out of the twenty-three cases we had eight positive and seven marginal results, that is to say, in eight cases we thought it probable that the horse had relaxed more quickly than usual, and in seven cases we thought it was possible that he had done so. I have included this rather unconvincing experiment in the series because I feel that with a certain amount of scientific equipment, and considerable time to set it up, it could prove one of the most definite and important experiments of the series.

The fourth experiment was quite simple. I would talk and make a fuss of one of the pair, usually the one that I liked least, and a positive result was recorded if the other showed signs of jealousy. Jealousy is shown in various ways : the horse might become disturbed and start walking around the box: she might (as happened with one of them) start banging at the door; or, like another lean upon the door, shaking her head up and down; and a third, as soon as I talked to her companion, started banging her dish. We took all these to be positive results, though they were not quite the results I expected. The curious thing about this experiment was that nearly half the horses showed a positive result by saying 'where is my bloody breakfast,' which possibly indicates that the e.s.p. message sent out was one of pleasure, which nearly half the horses took to mean that the first horse was being fed. Again we could get no definite result from the three horses which were naturally restless and excitable, because it was impossible to say their response was from e.s.p. and not from natural restlessness. But one of these was a mare who showed impatience by shaking her head up and down in the doorway, which was not the normal way that she showed her restlessness (which was walking around her box and then looking out of the door), but was the way she normally said 'where is my bloody breakfast.' We included this as a probable, not as a positive result. So in this experiment we had seventeen positive results out of the twenty-four.

The fifth experiment was a most unpleasant one, and I do not think I want to repeat it, because it involved really frightening one of the horses, and this is not a thing I like to do. I also think that it is possible to prove e.s.p. without fear. But since fear is a primary emotion, we thought it important to prove that it can be transmitted from one animal to another. I frightened the horse by rushing towards him, clenching my fists and chasing him round and round the box until he was frantic. A positive result was recorded if his companion became disturbed too. This happened in sixteen out of the twenty-four cases, plus of course the three excitable horses who could give us no positive result.

Out of one hundred and nineteen experiments we carried out in all, we thus had positive results in eighty-one cases; a marginal result in twelve more; and a possible result in eleven cases, which gave us an overall success rate of 67.5 per cent. When you consider that the only alternative to e.s.p. in explanation of these results is pure chance, it seems more than scientifically probable that there is a sense of communication between horses other than sight and sound.

We also ran a control experiment for our own interest. For this we used a mare and a gelding who were very hostile to each other, and among fifteen experiments we had a positive result in only one case. For this series of experiments we made absolutely certain there was no means of communication between myself and either of the horses – I did not like them and they did not like each other, and we were a very hostile trio! Thus, since in the control we had a positive result in 16.66 per cent of cases and in the experiment we had a positive result of 67.5 per cent, we again conclude that it is probable that e.s.p. between horses does exist.

It should be noted that the five experiments were designed to show the transfer by e.s.p. of the messages: 'hunger diminished', 'excitement', 'excitement diminished', 'jealousy', and 'fear'. What we have satisfied ourselves in the series of experiments is that it can be proved scientifically that e.s.p. exists. In fact if in our results you eliminate the excitable horses, and the failed third experiment, we have an overall success of nearly 80 per cent and not 67.5 per cent.

What interested us most in this series of experiments was not the results, which were slightly better than we expected, but the fact that they indicated the ability of horses to switch to other wavelengths. Some of the horses we used were horses of different breeds, who normally think on different thought patterns and on different wavelengths; and three pairs among the eight, what is more, were mares and geldings, whose thought patterns, because they are of different sexes, would again tend to be different. To prove that wavelengths vary between breeds and types, and that individual horses could communicate on varying wavelengths and in different thought patterns, we ran another series of experiments with four horses: a Welsh Cob, a thoroughbred mare, a half-thoroughbred thirteen-two pony and a Welsh Section B-cross stallion. The Welsh Cob was in communication with the thoroughbred mare and they were very close companions. The thoroughbred mare was in communication with both the Welsh Cob and the half-bred pony; and the Section B was on the same wavelength as the pony, but not in communication with either the Welsh Cob or the thoroughbred mare. After a very long series of experiments, we discovered that if we fed the Welsh Cob the other three all asked for food. If we fed the Welsh Cob and the thoroughbred mare was not there, neither the half-thoroughbred pony nor the Section B stallion would ask for food. When we put the thoroughbred mare back and removed the half-thoroughbred pony, the Section B did not ask for food. If we fed the Section B and they were all there, the other three horses would all ask for food. If we removed the half-thoroughbred pony at feeding time, neither the thoroughbred mare nor the Welsh Cob would ask for food. Again in this series of experiments we always fed at odd times so that there was no question of habit entering into the experiment, and we proved absolutely conclusively that the Welsh Cob, when he had food, was sending out an e.s.p. message which was received by the thoroughbred mare; who passed it on to the half-thoroughbred pony; who passed it on to the Section B. If we remove the thoroughbred mare there was no one to receive the message from the Welsh Cob, and so the other two did not know there was food about. If we remove the pony when the mare was there, she would know because the Welsh Cob would have told her he had received food, but there was no one to receive her message and tell the Section B. Conversely if, when the pony was not there, we fed the Section B, neither the mare nor the Welsh Cob knew anything about it. Put the pony back, the pony would be told by the Section B; but without the thoroughbred the Welsh Cob was completely in ignorance.

These horses were Rostellan, Iantella, Marie and Starlight. And Starlight's relationship with Marie made an interesting story. We had bought him in a horse sale as an eight-year-old stallion. We had him home and gelded him, then turned him out with the other horses three or four days later, and he immediately chummed up with Marie and proceeded to pulverize any other gelding in sight. Rostellan was petrified by him after he had been clobbered by him the first time they met. But apart from noting this affection for Marie, we did not think any more about it. However eleven months later Marie produced a lovely chestnut foal, which to us was rather confounding since he must have fathered the foal when he had already been gelded!

This experiment is a difficult one to set up, since you need a number of horses which are not all in close communication with each other. In our case Rostellan could get through to Iantella and Iantella could get through to Marie and Marie could get through to Iantella and Starlight; but it is very rare in a group of four horses for one to have no communication whatever with two of the others. It is much easier to find straight-forward empathic pairs. All these experiments however have been designed so that they can be reproduced anywhere by other people who have horses, and with very careful selection of the subjects anyone should be able to get a high proportion of definite results. Given a sufficient number of horses to select from, and adequate time to make your selection, these results can be reproduced time and time again, and we hope and believe that these six experiments will in time be standard experiments for people who are interested in proving e.s.p. amongst horses. We know that we are pioneers in the field of equine communication, and being pioneers we have to be very careful that all the work we do can be reproduced by other people in other places at a later date. We also know that the work we do now will be pulled to pieces, and fully expect that in ten, twenty or thirty years' time people will be saying 'Oh, Blake was all right, he started early, but he was wrong here or he was wrong there.' It is quite possible that in parts of this very extensive subject, we *are* wrong. But in the field of equine research in general and in e.s.p. in particular, we know that our work has been on the right lines because we know that we can, and do, communicate all the time vocally, orally and mentally with our horses. We can understand what they are saying at all times and they can understand what we are saying. We are in fact in the position of an Englishman who can speak French and can understand French. But at times he will be wrong in the elements of French grammar, and so it is quite possible that at times we are going to be wrong in the elements of equine grammar.

10: *Telepathy in Horse Language*

Most people treat telepathy simply as one of the forms of
e.s.p. But in this we feel that they are wrong, because telepathy is different from e.s.p. in that it deals with the transfer
of mental pictures, and uses the intellectual process, while
e.s.p. deals with the transfer of moods, emotions, feelings and
only limited ideas. It is a purely emotional thing and its
response is automatic. For telepathy to function it is usual,
but not necessary, for the animals to be of the same species.
And for human beings it is usual for transmitter and receiver
to be in mental and emotional, preferably also physical,
contact with each other. But telepathy in everyday life, while
it is comparatively common, is extremely hard to prove. It is
a spontaneous reaction. For example two people may think
of the same thing at the same time; but there is no method of
proving whether this is telepathy or coincidence. You may find
that you start visualizing a place you know quite well, only to
find at a later date that a relative or friend was at that place
at the very same time; but unless you actually recorded the
time, and exactly what happened at that time – what you
visualized, what you were thinking about – it is almost impossible to prove it. And even if you can prove the synchron-
icity, it is extremely difficult to prove that it was not a coincidence. Indeed, if you were to keep such records, you
would probably find the sheer number of coincidences – anything up to two hundred or three hundred in the course of
your life – puts the problem beyond the realm of coincidence.
But hard proof of telepathic communication remains extremely
hard to come by.

It is quite a common thing for someone to say 'I must
prepare food for the dog,' and the dog to appear almost
simultaneously by their side. With people who are very

123

close to their animals, this will happen almost every day. An acquaintance of mine came to live with her mother, and after she had been there for three or four months she began to wonder why the tea was always ready when she got home. The kettle had either boiled or it was about to boil. There was no question of a regular time, because my acquaintance was a nurse and the time she returned home from the hospital depended entirely on which shift she was on. Mystified, she asked her mother how she did it. Her mother said, 'Oh it is quite simple. I know that ten minutes before you get home Jojo will get up and start getting excited. She will go from her basket to the window and she will stand at the window until you get home. When Jojo goes to the window I always get the tea.' She worked out eventually that Jojo knew when she was going down a particular tree-lined avenue, about ten minutes from home. Of course sight and sound could be eliminated completely in this case, since she was still well over a mile away from home, so the dog could have known only by telepathy. This sort of occurrence is much more common than we are aware.

The Russians, who have carried out a great deal of serious research on telepathy, have conducted a very large number of experiments, one of the standard ones involving a pair of people in two different rooms, each with two tables in it. On the first table is a number of different-shaped and coloured objects. The 'transmitter' picks up the objects and puts them on the second table one after another. Then his companion, the 'receiver', in the second room will try to pick up the objects in exactly the same order and place them on his second table. In this experiment, with trained pairs, the Russians achieve about sixty per cent success.

Telepathy has fallen into disrepute in the West largely because it was the purported basis of thought-reading acts in music halls, and though no doubt some of these were genuine, most of them were fakes. But there has been increasing scientific interest in the field. The best-known people to conduct a telepathy experiment in recent years were an

Australian couple, the Piddingtons. Piddington discovered he had this facility when he was a prisoner of war held by the Japanese, and to entertain his fellow prisoners in the evening he used to demonstrate his ability with Russell Braddon, the author. After the war he and his wife travelled the world demonstrating their ability to transmit mentally over varying distances the shapes and colours of objects. On one occasion they apparently transmitted mental pictures of various shapes from a B.B.C. studio to an aeroplane.

Modern man appears almost completely to have lost the ability to transmit mental pictures, probably because this was the first skill he ceased to use when he gained the ability to speak. If you could describe with your voice what you were seeing, you did not need to transfer a mental picture. But some primitive tribes still retain the skill and we have seen that Laurens van der Post in his travels among the South African bushmen observed a witch doctor gaze at the cave drawing of an antelope, throw himself into a trance, and then so accurately describe the location where the antelope was grazing that the hunters could go out and kill it.

The ability does however seem sometimes to survive in civilized man at times of stress. I know of five cases where telepathy apparently occurred at the time of a motor accident, though in three of these it is not clear whether it was telepathy or e.s.p. that was involved. It is very hard to be absolutely certain, when asking someone about it afterwards, whether he actually visualized the motor accident at the time, or whether he was simply subject to unusual emotional stress. But there were two cases where the accident was described to me *before* the person knew that it had happened: in one case my wife knew that her parents had had a motor accident at least eight hours before she heard about it; in the other a friend of mine was told by an acquaintance that the acquaintance's parents had had a motor accident at the very time that the accident took place, some twenty miles away.

This then is what telepathy is all about: the transfer of

mental pictures. I have already told the story of how I discovered that I could direct Weeping Roger where I wanted to go just by thinking it. I would steer him to the left or right or straight ahead simply by visualizing the road. This was the first time I had consciously experienced telepathy with a horse. Since I used to exercise him for an hour-and-a-half to two hours a day, feed him, clean his box out, and groom him twice a day, I was in his company for three or four hours daily, to say nothing of passing his loose-box thirty or forty times as I went to and from the cow-yard. All this proximity strengthened the great affinity I already sensed with him. After this experience I discovered that with other horses too I could stop them from shying by telepathy: if I thought the horse was going to shy at something I would gaze intently at it and the horse would see it for what it was – a stone as a stone and not as a tiger about to spring, a piece of paper as a piece of paper and not as an eagle about to swoop. This is quite a simple trick, for a horse does not always see an object properly, especially if he sees it only out of the corner of his eye, and his natural instinct is to avoid anything that looks unusual or dangerous. But if the person on his back or leading him is extremely close to him mentally, the person can see the object *for* him, and the horse will also see it for what it is and take on the ride's confidence about it.

About the time I was working with Roger I was sent a grey gelding that was more or less unridable because he shied very badly and his owner could not do anything about it. After picking him up off the train at Axminster, where he had been sent from Ascot, I rode him home and to my surprise he did not shy at all. I kept him for about two months, during which time he always went absolutely perfectly quietly and never shied. I sent him back to his owner, who was delighted with him; but after about two months he was on the telephone to me again, to say that while the horse still did not shy and was absolutely perfect to ride, his blacksmith found it impossible to pick his feet up and shoe him. The point is that he was a very strong-willed horse, owned by a rather weak and nervous person, so the horse was working one trick after another to get on top of him. Once he found that if he shied he frightened the daylights out of his owner, he started shying as a habit. But since when I collected him from Axminster station I knew he was a shyer, and took very great care that he saw everything, he did not worry me at all, and by the time I got him home he had forgotten about shying at anything. When he went back to his owner he was completely cured; but he started the difficulty about having his feet picked up when he found that if he waved his leg in the air he frightened his owner. He was rather like a naughty schoolboy who jumps out behind a rather nervous person and says 'boo'. He just had a rather juvenile sense of humour.

Cork Beg provides further evidence of the horse's facility for thinking in pictures, for he could be kept in his stable simply by putting a thin piece of string across the door, and since he looked upon it as a barrier and could see the barrier, he would not come out, and very often we did not bother to put the piece of string up at all. On one famous occasion Cork Beg, who like all our horses was intensely curious, was in the railway hut with the door open. My wife was talking to someone on the road, and Cork Beg could not see them. He wanted to see them, so he stuck his head out. But he still could not see them. He leant out further. Still he could not see them, so he leant out further still. Now if he had not thought there was a barrier there, he could have walked right out, because the door was wide open. But he thought there was a barrier, so he leant further and further out until he overbalanced and fell on his nose and I had to put him back in! He could not come past the barrier in his imagination until my wife went and put a halter on, thus removing his mental barrier, and led him out through the stable door.

Horses in the wild use the telepathic facility to direct their companions to food and water, or to direct one horse to another from quite considerable distances. It may also be used to split a herd of horses in times of danger; you will find this

easily demonstrated if you corner two ponies that are difficult to catch, in the corner of the field. You will find that
one will invariably go to the left and the other to the right
of you, and they will try to go the same way only if you leave
them no room to go either side of you.

On a number of occasions we have had this ability to
transfer pictures rather dramatically demonstrated to us.
Cork Beg, who was in the field nearest the house, could see
us when we went to the feeding house and he would whicker
and say 'where is my bloody breakfast.' We would then feed
him. If about five or ten minutes later we went down to
where we could see the other horses, a quarter of a mile or so
away, we would be almost certain to find them all standing
by the gate shouting for their breakfast, even though they
could not have seen us or Cork Beg. We cannot be absolutely
certain that this was a demonstration of telepathy, though we
think it probably was, because it could have been a case of
e.s.p., so we did not use it as a demonstration experiment.
But one of the earliest experiments we carried out with
e.s.p. was with two small ponies who were particularly difficult
to catch. We used to corner them in a field and record which
went right and which went left, because we thought it quite
possible that one always went right and the other always
went left from habit, but there was absolutely no set pattern
as to which pony went in which direction. The one thing we
did find of interest in this experiment was that if we managed
to stop the ponies, when they tried again to shoot past us they
would change sides: the horse that went left would try to go
right and the horse that went right would try to go left. We did
not at the time attach any particular significance to this,
but it is quite possible that there is a telepathic element here
and a subject for future research.

Up to 1964 in any case we thought of telepathy as more or
less the same thing as e.s.p. Then the difference was demonstrated to us by Charles Thurlow Craig, who told us how he
woke up one night feeling uneasy and apprehensive, got
dressed and went downstairs, picked up his wire cutters and a

torch, put on his wellingtons and went out into a very black, dark and stormy night directly to the very spot, about half a mile from the house, where his favourite mare was caught up in barbed wire in a bog. He told me next day that as he went downstairs he 'knew exactly where the mare was and exactly what had happened' because he 'could see it in his mind's eye.' I made a note of the precise words he used.

I had a similar sort of experience myself the year before last. I had a thoroughbred two-year-old gelding called Royal Boy. Unfortunately he was extremely musical, and would stand all day by the window listening to the wireless and if the wireless was not loud enough, he would walk up to a pig netting fence and hit it with one of his front feet and listen to the tinkling it made. He would do this for anything up to an hour at a time, completely fascinated. We used to say he was playing the piano, and of course every now and then he would put his foot through the pig netting by mistake and not be able to get it back out again. After his first try he would stand still and wait for me, and each time I could see his foot stuck in the pig netting in my mind's eye and would get the wire cutters to get him out of his predicament. He always waited for me, and I am quite sure he could see me coming in his mind's eye. (Normally of course if a thoroughbred gets caught in this way he will thrash about trying to get himself free and probably cut himself badly.)

Once we started work on telepathy, we found we had to prove not only that it exists, but that it is different from other forms of extra-sensory perception. Thus we could, for instance, show one animal an object, usually a feed of corn, and record the response from a second horse outside of sight and hearing. If there was a positive response, we concluded that some form of e.s.p. was operating. But we could not conclude that it was telepathy. The mental picture of food in a bucket *may* be being transmitted from one animal to another, and if such a mental picture were being transmitted, there would be a response from the second animal, which would ask for food. But there is no proof that the communication is telepathic. As you may remember, we used this experiment to prove the existence of e.s.p., where no more than the communication of the feeling of hunger was involved. So we devised what we called the kit-e-kat experiment, inspired by one of the cat food advertisements on television. This was the first telepathy experiment we ever carried out and we used old Cork Beg as the subject.

Basically it was quite simple: he was offered two containers, each containing equal quantities of food, and I was to direct him to whichever bucket I wanted, merely by using telepathy. But the experiment itself took considerable preparation, because there were so many factors to be eliminated. Sight and smell were easily eliminated by using two exactly similar containers, with the same food in each of them. What was more difficult to deal with was the fact that most horses when free are left- or right-handed, usually left-handed: that is over a straight line they will veer to the left when walking freely. Cork Beg's deviation over ten yards was approximately eighteen inches to the left. So we took a line at right angles to the middle of his doorway, ten yards long, and the end of this line we took as the centre point. We placed one bucket six yards to the left of the centre point, and the other four yards to the right of it, so that when Cork Beg came out of his stable there was no bias to go over to either bucket, and without interference he did go to them on a roughly fifty-fifty basis. Now we were ready to train him to answer my telepathic commands, and this proved comparatively easy to do, if somewhat time-consuming. Each morning when I fed him, I would fill one or the other of the buckets, then I would wait until I was absolutely sure I was in telepathic communication with him, and mentally visualize the bucket that contained the food. Having done this I would let him out. Within a few days he was going straight to the bucket I directed him to, and I persevered with this for a fortnight. Cork Beg, being a very intelligent animal, quickly learnt that the bucket I was telling him to go to was the one that contained his breakfast.

Of course this experiment also involved a certain amount of training for me, since I had to train myself to use my will to focus my whole mind on the mental picture of the bucket, allowing nothing to distract me. And I also had to make quite sure that when he came out in the morning I was entirely in tune with him. But having made these preparations the experiment itself was extremely simple. For the first five mornings I directed him alternately to the left and the right. On the sixth morning, to make absolutely certain that he was not taking them turn and turn about by habit, I directed him again to the container on the left. On the seventh morning I directed him to the container on the left, and on the eighth morning I directed him to the container on the left. That is for four mornings I directed him to the container to which he had a natural bias. The ninth morning brought the most difficult experiment of all. For four mornings running he had taken his breakfast from the container on the left, and on the ninth I wanted to change him to the container on the right. Much to my relief he went straight to it. Having come out of that successfully, he had to take it again from the right-hand container on the tenth morning, from the left on the eleventh and on the twelfth morning from the right. Each morning he went directly to the correct container.

The whole of this preparation and training took approximately one month, and the experiment itself lasted twelve days. To operate this experiment correctly complete concentration is needed, the picture of the feed lying at the bottom of the particular container must be very vivid in your mind's eye, and above all you must feel the mental communication between you and the horse. The least little thing can distract you. A bird flying across your vision for just one second can break your concentration for another five minutes. But provided you get the conditions entirely correct, and provided you are in complete telepathic communication with your subject, the experiment itself is extremely easy to do. We had a hundred per cent success, when normally we would accept sixty or seventy per cent success as a positive result.

All the experiments we have carried out are in themselves extremely simple things to do. They have been designed to be simple, and inexpensive. Any research we have carried out has had to be paid for from our own pockets, so we have chosen experiments for which we can use the animals we already have about the place, and the buildings and existing layout of the farm. We have not been able to afford to put up special buildings, nor to buy the expensive electronic equipment which might have made our work easier. But this very simplicity has meant that we have had to be extremely thorough in our preparations, and extremely careful in our selection of the horses.

The research into communication by signs and sounds has been done through the very elementary means of making use of our powers of observation. We would see a certain signal and try to interpret the message; then when we saw the same message used again, it has either verified our interpretation or led to a new interpretation of the message. And so over a period of time, our observations have made us completely conversant with the signs and sounds used by that horse. And in our own communication with the horse we have tried to simulate the signs and sounds that the horse has used.

In our work on e.s.p. the experiments themselves are simple, the important and difficult thing has been selecting the empathic pair. With telepathy, however, the difficulty lies in devising the experiments. For though spontaneous telepathy is comparatively common, the difficulty is in getting any proof of it. Since telepathic communication is spontaneous, it is not repeatable under controlled conditions, and accurate records are extremely difficult to assemble.

We have been able to overcome the problem in the following manner. We verify telepathic communication by recording the time of the occurrence to within a quarter of an hour: a mental picture received must be recorded at the time it is received, and the horse you receive it from must be identified by the person who is receiving it. I usually keep most of my records on the back of cigarette packets, since I have always got a cigarette packet in my pocket, and I have not very often got a notebook. To give one example of a recorded incident, at one forty-five on the nineteenth of January 1972, I was sitting in my car in the car park in Llandeilo. It was a very cold but clear day, if somewhat overcast, and suddenly in my mind's eye I could see my wife and the two labradors walking down the road to a field in a snowstorm. I could also see my grey hunter Iantella, and my wife's second hunter Rostellan standing in the field. I could not see old Cork Beg, therefore I knew that I was receiving telepathic communication from Cork Beg, and I made a record of it. On returning home an hour and a half later, I established from my wife that the weather had looked bad, and she had decided to get the horses in. On her way down to the field it had started to snow, and she confirmed that she had had both dogs with her. She had also noted the time as oneforty when she left the house, since she had to get to the library by two o'clock. Since I had recorded this incident on paper, I knew I was receiving telepathic communication from Cork Beg. But the problem, as you can see, is first to record the incident yourself as soon as you receive the communication, and second – which is far more difficult – to make sure that you have someone else involved who has noted the time that the incident happened. Probably no more than ten per cent of telepathic communications will really be verifiable in this way, even when you are master of your subject.

We have recorded three occurrences over distances varying from fifteen to eighteen miles – the longest distance over which we have had any telepathic communication is approximately two hundred and forty miles, but we could not list this one as verified since the person with the horse at the other end knew only that the incident happened 'late in the afternoon' so we had no accurate time check. (It involved the serving of a mare. The owner of the mare 'saw' the stallion some time between four forty-five and five o'clock. When she rang up that evening to find out if the mare had been served, she was told only that it had happened 'after tea'.) We also know of three incidents, for instance, of people knowing that their horses were dying. In the first, a friend of mine owned an old horse, and while he was away on holiday his wife decided to have the old horse put down. He was having an afternoon snooze when he was woken by his whole head exploding in a flash of light. When he returned home the next day he learned that the horse had died at about that time. He told me afterwards that it had been a very weird and odd experience. The second example was last October, when Cork Beg was very ill. We knew that he was dying, and at half past two in the morning my wife woke me and said 'The old man is going'. She had been woken from her sleep by seeing him in a very green field, completely at peace and grazing. We put on our dressing gowns and went down, and the old horse was just breathing his last when we got there. On the third occasion a woman I know fainted at the precise time that her horse was being put down five miles away.

We are still not certain of the extent of telepathy between horses, since it is extremely difficult to differentiate, in communication between horses, between telepathy and e.s.p. We are not ourselves complete masters of the subject. But even so, we can say with almost complete certainty that we can interpret what our horses are saying to us and to each other, and we can make our horses understand what we are saying to them. Since I am a practical horseman, any knowledge I get is put to use in my handling and training of horses, so I use e.s.p. and telepathy when I am point-to-pointing, or hunter trialing, or taking part in a one-day event. And becaue I use these things and I understand them, I can get my horses to do more in competitions than anyone would think possible. For example, last summer I took, for a bet, an untouched and unhaltered sixteen-hand five-year-old, and in thirty-two days, between August sixteenth and September seventeenth, I had him competing in a show class. I hunted him, I competed on him in hunter trials and on the thirtieth day I won a riding club novice one-day event. In this event he was within eight points of the highest points in the dressage, and he had a clear round in the cross-country and a clear round in the show-jumping. He was of course an extremely good horse, very receptive and an easy horse to handle, and I got through to him straight away – it was because I was aware of this that I took the bet in the first place!

11: *Putting our Knowledge to Work*

Probably the best illustration of how we make use of our ability to understand and communicate with our horses is the gentling system of training horses, which we have devised for handling and training unbroken and untouched horses. We call gentling the 'easy way' to train a horse, since it is easy for the human being to train a horse if that horse understands what you want from the outset. It is also easy for the horse, since you are using a method of communication which he understands. It is not easy in the sense that it takes less time, nor in the sense that it involves less work – it takes just as long to produce the finished product, and just as much work as the conventional methods. But it is easier than they are in that there is a lot less trouble and there is a lot less argument between horse and rider, and we like to think that it is much more enjoyable for the horse. Instead of saying 'you damn well have got to do what I tell you to do,' we say 'let's do this,' or 'let's do that.' To give you a human parallel, the difference is between a Guard Sergeant Major drilling a squad of recruits, and someone taking a bunch of children for a walk.

When we are gentling we do things only in the way a horse understands naturally. For example if you walk up behind a wild horse, he will go away from you forwards, but if you approach his head, he will go away from you backwards. Now this is quite simple and logical, and on this principle we have devised the natural response to very nearly any action, and since we use equine communication the whole time, the horse understands what we want him to do.

During the course of a year we will probably gentle between thirty and forty horses. Some of these are horses that have been handled from birth, others may be six-, seven- or eight-year-old mares or stallions that have never been touched or haltered in their lives, and others again will be horses that other people have tried to break themselves and have failed with. We also get a number of really bad and unmanageable horses whom no one else can handle.

Perhaps the true merit of gentling and of the way we understand and teach horses is best revealed in our dealing with the horses we catch off the open mountain. Most of these have never been handled in their lives and are completely wild. And we get most of ours from our own mountain, which stretches for two or three thousand acres with another couple of thousand acres of forestry adjoining it, which means that the horses have a free range of about five thousand acres.

To most people it would seem almost impossible to catch an untouched wild horse off an open mountain where he has a run of five thousand acres. But in actual fact it is comparatively simple. Any one herd of horses will graze only over an area of two or three hundred acres. The horses will have their set paths and grazing procedures, places where they usually spend the night, places where they go to in bad weather and others where they graze and normally drink. If the herd is frightened, the horses will usually go in the same direction, ending up in the same place, and then they will go round in a circle and come back again. So the first thing we do, over a period of two or three weeks, is to observe the habits of the herd to which the horse we want belongs. We watch where he grazes, where he drinks, where he rests and where he spends the night, and particularly we note where he goes in bad weather, since in rough windy weather the horses will not be grazing on the top of the open mountain. Normally the herd will be grazing in an area of twenty or thirty acres, but in rough and wet weather they will all shelter together in one particular spot, usually on the edge of the mountain or in a corner by the forest. Once we have established the spot where the horses go, we wait for a very wild and wet night, and then early in the morning go to the spot, and slowly walk the horses into the nearest farmyard.

This is simpler to do than it sounds, since the horses will be rather cold and miserable, and they will naturally keep together. We do not approach very near to them. As soon as they see us they start to walk away. We walk slowly after them, keeping away but edging them slowly in the direction we want them to go. When catching wild horses, we never run, we never get excited, we never raise our voices. We are relaxed, calm and slow in our movements, talking to the horses all the time, so that the horses are relaxed and calm. We never get too near them and we never allow them to trot. Slowly and carefully we edge them down a convenient road or lane and into the farmyard. The horses will walk into the yard quite quietly and happily, and then we slowly drive them into a building. This can sometimes be a time-consuming process, but you must be patient. First an old mare will look into the building – she will be the herd leader – and then she will go in, and then her foal will follow her, and the others will all go in very quickly. The whole time we will have been talking to them in a sing-song voice, gently and slowly. We can see the bunch of horses, who have become a little bit excited and apprehensive when they get into the building, visibly relax. When they are sufficiently relaxed, we start easing the horses we do not want – in a herd of maybe five, ten, fifteen or in very exceptional cases twenty-five or thirty horses – out of the shed by ones and twos, until we are left only with the ones we need for gentling. When the other horses have been turned back to the mountain, the horses we are left with will be very agitated, because they are alone, and probably for the first time in their lives. If there is only one horse finally left alone he will be belting round the boxes, screaming at the top of his voice 'where are you, where are you, where have you got to.' And when I re-enter the box he will be absolutely terror-stricken. He will dash round the box, pounding into the corners, anything to get away from me. All his previous experience with man has been frightening, and he has been accustomed all his life to putting as much distance between him and man as possible. I ease myself into one corner, lean against the wall and light a cigarette, talking to him quietly and gently all the time, compelling myself to relax, and by degrees I will establish a thread of sympathy with him as I begin thinking on the same wavelength as he does. I shall be using e.s.p. to relax and settle him. After a very short while he will stop in the opposite corner of the box for a while, and I let him stand there looking at me, breathing fire.

The Spaniards, when they are talking about bull-fighting, say that the bull always goes back to take up his position in one particular section of the arena, and they call that the bull's quarter. We find exactly the same thing is true of a horse. When a horse is in a confined space, he will make his territory in one particular part of that space, and we call it the horse's quarter of the box. It is usually the corner of the box opposite to the one I take, and after a very short time, he will establish that as his territory and he will tend to return there whenever he is frightened or in trouble. When he has settled in his corner of the box, he will start blowing through his nostrils at me. What he will be saying is 'who the hell are you,' and I will blow back at him, pitching the tone of the blow two or three notes below his, so in reply to his 'who the hell are you' I shall be saying 'who are you.' And by degrees he will soften the tone of his blow, and I will drop mine lower still, until he is saying 'who are you' and I will have changed from 'who are you' to 'hello'. When he too comes down to say 'hello' to me I start to advance slowly and gently towards him. His range of messages is always the basic message, 'hello', but the greeting can vary from the very aggressive 'who the hell are you' down to just the plain 'hello'.

When the horse has accepted me enough to greet me as he would any casual acquaintance, I can start moving to the next stage of the gentling. I walk slowly towards him, one step at a time, after each step waiting for him to relax again, until I get right up to him. In between blowing through my mouth I am smoking my cigarette and talking to him all the time: 'there's a clever boy, there's a clever boy, there's a clever little fellow.' I also aim to approach him at his neutral point, that is the point from which he has no impetus to go forward or back. If I go towards his head he will go back, if I come up behind he will go forward, but somewhere between these two points, usually approximately two-thirds the way along the body from his tail, will be his neutral point. I may frighten him or something else may frighten him as I approach him, so that he starts racing round the box again, and if this happens I return to my corner and we start again from the beginning. But it will not take as long for him to settle this time, and eventually I will get close enough just to touch his side with the tips of my fingers, and then slowly I work my fingers in a circular motion. This is a very basic thing with horses. When a foal is frightened he will run back to his mother, and she will caress him with her nose. To simulate this movement is very reassuring to the horse: in effect I am saying 'it is quite all right, nothing will hurt you.' Also when two horses approach each other they will stick their heads out and just touch each other with their noses. Sometimes they will touch nose to nose, and sometimes they will do it on the side. At the same time they will be blowing at each other. Or one will blow whilst the other touches with his nose. They will be saying 'who are you, where do you come from.' Then, provided there is no hostile movement, they will approach closer, and this is what I do. From caressing the horse with the tips of my fingers on his coat, I start caressing him with my hands, slowly working myself closer to him and talking to him in an even voice until I have got my body right up against him. Then I very slowly work my arm over his back until it is over the other side of him, putting considerable pressure and weight upon my arm. What I am saying to him now is 'you are quite safe, I am here.' When two horses are frightened, or when a lot of horses are frightened, they will bunch together, pushing against each other, and pushing their necks and heads across each other. They do this to reassure each other. They are saying 'do not worry, you are quite safe, I am here,' the more frightened and nervous horses getting reassurance from the steadier and quieter horses. Now since our necks are only six inches long, it is impossible for me to lean across and put my head and neck across the horse, as a horse would do. So instead I use my arm and hand to simulate the movement of the horse's head and neck. I use the tips of my fingers as a horse would use his nose, and I use the rest of my hand as he would use his head, and I use my arm as he would use his neck, so that at this stage the horse is understanding what I am saying completely.

Up to this point, I have used three of the four methods of communication. I have used my voice to reassure the horse, I have used signs and I have used e.s.p.. But the whole time the horse has understood what I was saying and exactly what I was doing, since I have used the language another horse would use, and my actions have been actions that he is accustomed to. At no time have I forced the horse to do anything, because he has always been free to move away from me. At no time, apart from the first time I went into the box, has he been frightened, and I have not done anything to antagonize him. At this stage I would normally leave the horse alone for two or three hours, give him something to eat and go and have my own lunch. I would then come back to him after lunch and go through the same process again. At the end of two or three days he would then accept me as another horse. The whole key to the method is getting the horse to want to do what I want him to. A young horse always tends to be nervous and curious and wanting reassurance. A foal will get this from his mother, who will nuzzle him, as I use my fingers. The mare will be telling her foal it is quite all right. When I use my fingers in a similar way, I too am reassuring him. If flight is impossible for a horse, he will seek reassurance by physical contact with his fellow horses by bunching together, and I give him the reassurance of my body. When I get on to him at a later date, I will ease my body across him. Thus I will be increasing his confidence by giving him a feeling much the same as he will get from another horse leaning his head and neck across him. Each time and with each movement I am saying 'it is quite all right, do not worry.'

For the next week or ten days, I will follow a pretty set routine. First when feeding and watering the horse I will gentle him three times a day. Each time I feed him I spend ten minutes gentling him until he looks upon me as another horse, and treats me as he would treat another horse, and during this time I will be making a mental note of the sounds and signs he uses to convey each of the forty-seven messages – though in the normal everyday he will be using only about thirty of them. I will know I have finished this stage of gentling when I go out in the morning and he sticks his head out of the door and shouts 'where is my bloody breakfast.' If then, when I take the feed in, he pushes me out of the way to get at his feed saying 'get out of my way you stupid fool, I am starving,' I know he looks upon me as another horse, and understands and trusts me completely. I will also know by this time the temperament and character of the horse. I will know whether he is a nervous timid animal who needs to be coaxed and reassured all the time, or a placid easy-going horse that will do anything for a quiet life, or a very domi-nant and strong character. What I would do at the next stage of the gentling depends upon the disposition. If the horse is nervous and constantly needs reassuring we go on very gently and slowly, always moving quietly and always reassuring, telling the horse how clever and intelligent he or she is. The easy-going horse is also very simple to deal with. But about one in five or one in eight of the horses we get is a very strong, dominant character, and he needs a certain amount of discipline. Above all such a horse needs telling that I am the boss of the herd, I am the one that controls the herd, and not him. This message takes a little time to sink in, since that horse probably has been the boss of the herd where he comes from, and been accustomed to giving orders and not to taking them. But it is really quite simple, with a little time and patience, and by using the language the horse knows, to establish discipline in the method that the horse understands.

The way discipline is imposed within the herd is perfectly straightforward and is most easily seen in a bunch of horses loose going down a road together. The boss horse (often a mare) will establish itself in the front, and if anything tries to pass or comes too close, the boss will swing her head round, threatening to punch the offender with her teeth. At the same time she puts her ears back and says 'go back you horrible little squirt.' If the offender still tries to pass, the boss will then punch with her teeth. If the offender persists she will then bite him as he goes by. Thus if anyone offends the code of behaviour of the herd retribution is instant, and the incident is usually over in a few seconds. Even if the offender does eventually get by, the horses will settle down again quite happily walking one after another. So if I find myself with a very strong character, who when I am feeding her in the morning tries to push me out of the way and says 'get away you horrible little man,' I retaliate immediately by swinging my fist at her in exactly the same manner as she would swing her head at an inferior horse. As soon as I swing my fist, she will jump back to her corner in the box, raising her head and looking at me, saying 'what the hell did you do that for.' Then she will come forward quite happily when I put the feed in the manger. This will go on for two or three days. When I go out in the morning she will say 'where is my bloody breakfast,' I will take it in to her, she will try to push me away and I will swing my fist saying 'go back I am boss.' Within three or four days, without any real fight and certainly without frightening her, I have established that I am the boss of the herd, and she has to do what I tell her. It is most unlikely that at any time when I swung my fist at her I would actually make contact with any part of her body : I am only miming the threatening gesture. Then, once I have established my herd dominance, we are ready to go on to the next stage and for me to start mounting and riding her.

Horses come to us for gentling from all over the country, but mainly they come from within an area of fifteen or twenty miles. When they arrive it is not always convenient for us to gentle them straight away, so we turn the initial part of the work over to one of the other horses. We let the horses do an awful lot of the gentling for us. This is not quite as odd as it sounds, because all it involves is turning the new horse out into a nearby field with one of the steadiest and most established of the horses we have, who then plays schoolmaster. We will start feeding both of them every day. The first day when we take the feed down to them, the young horse will go hell for leather towards the far end of the field, while of course the old horse as soon as he sees the feed will come trotting over. Then we will put the feed down in two buckets about twenty yards apart, and talk to the old horse while he eats his feed, but not take any notice of the horse we are gentling. The horse we are gentling after a bit may come over to see what the old horse is eating, but he will not come within less than about twenty yards of us. When Jack or Tabby or Iantella or Rostellan, whoever it is, has finished his or her feed, we go away and leave them. Of course Jack will then go and see if there is anything in the other bucket, and proceed to eat that, but we go away and leave him to it. Then the young horse will come over, first sniff what Jack was eating before and then go over and see what he is eating now. After a day or two the young horse will start eating out of the bucket, and as soon as he is doing this, we start talking to him as well as Jack. He may or may not rush off to the far corner of the field, but if he does he will come back to his bucket. Within a week or ten days I will be able to go straight up to the bucket, talking to him in a gentle voice, blowing at him through my mouth, and possibly even get a hand on him. By this time I will be an established member of his particular herd, and he will accept me as a normal member of the establishment.

After he has been eating for about a week, we will start bringing the two horses into the yard for the bulk of their feed. This again is really very easy. My wife or someone else will put a halter on to the schoolmaster and lead him in, and I will get the pupil eating out of the bucket, and I will pick up the bucket and walk to the yard. Since there is still food in the bucket, the pupil will rush after me. Within a very short time, he will just put his head in the bucket, I will lift it up and he will follow me anywhere, and in this way I have taught him to be led even though I have never put a halter on him. After two or three days, instead of holding the bucket behind me when I am leading him in, I will hold the bucket in front of me, so that he is walking beside me. Then it is only a very small step to having him walking beside me with my arm over his neck. When I have got him used to this stage, I can lead him in by simply putting my arm over his neck, and he will walk up with his head under my arm, and then it is just one straight step to putting a piece of string round his neck and leading him in. At this stage, by putting the bucket on the ground, and letting him put his head into the bucket, through the nose of the halter, I can put the halter on him. Again, at no time has there ever been a battle. Always when I have been working with him, I have been talking to him in a gentle voice, and as soon as I can get my hand on to him, I have been gentling him with my hand simulating the movement of the mare's nuzzle with my fingers and hand and giving him reassurance by leaning against him and putting my arm the other side of his body, the way another horse would put his neck.

After about a week of this treatment he will know that the bulk of his feed is in the stable. When I open the gate he will try to push past me to get to his food more quickly. Again I will walk up the road in front of him, and as he tries to pass me I will swing my fist at him, using the sign he knows says 'go back you horrible little animal.' He will throw his head up and put his brakes on and say 'what the bloody hell is the matter with you,' and so we will proceed up the road. But in a day or two I will once more have established that I am the boss of the herd and not him, and when we go in he walks in behind me, and is not allowed to push past. Again at no time has he been frightened nor been made nervous or angry.

One of the most outstanding of our gentling successes was with a little mare called Spitfire. I first saw Spitfire as a twelve-three mare in Llanybyther market. She had a foal at foot and was supposed to be in foal again, and when she was driven into the ring with her foal, she went straight out over the crowd at the end. After a lot of trouble she was brought back in again, and a friend of mine bought her. I saw her from time to time over the next five or six months, until the following May my friend asked me to swop her for one of my horses. He confessed that he could do nothing with the bitch. It seemed he could not catch her, that she was not in foal, and he could not even get her to the stallion – he threatened to sell her at once for dog meat if I would not take her. I went up to have another look at her. She was a twelve-three thirteen-hand, very dark chestnut mare with a silver mane and tail and she was eight years old. She had had two or three foals, but she was now apparently barren. I could not see a strong healthy pony being shot like that, so we did the deal, and I went up at six o'clock that night to get her.

This was a mistake, because if you are going to do anything with a horse which you know is difficult, you should never do it in the evening. You should do it in the morning, so that you have all the day in front of you. She was in the field by the yard with a number of other ponies, and we made a lane into the yard with gates, and there were three or four people around with sticks, which I did not like, but I could not say anything because it was not my farm. They all got to the other side of the gates, ready for what they expected to be a performance. But we did not have much trouble. We drove her into the yard with half a dozen other horses and then, after some trouble, into a loose-box. She did try to jump a six-foot wall, but fortunately when she got her legs on top of it, there was someone the other side who caught her a clout and she had to go back. I discovered afterwards that she had previously jumped that six-foot wall five times. She had also jumped the iron gates which were over four-foot-six high, and later I was to see her jump a three-foot-six post and rails with a ten-foot drop the other side. My friend assured me that they had tried to get her into the loose-box many times before, but that this was the first time they had managed it. This was probably because we had taken the horses into the yard very slowly and very carefully, and instead of trying to chase them in, we had opened the yard gate, and let the other ponies of the herd walk in slowly. Since we were not trying to drive Spitfire in, she had followed the others. We were never within twenty yards of her. And once we got them all into the yard she could not jump out over the gates. Then we got them from the big yard into the small yard. To get these horses a matter of fifty yards took us nearly half an hour, but we never hurried them, just edging them the way we wanted them to go.

Having got the whole herd into the big stable, we then proceeded to let them out one by one. Three times Spitfire came to the door and tried to get through it, and three times the door was slammed in her face, but eventually we were left with Spitfire in a box about eighteen feet by fourteen. Now came the moment of truth, the time to halter her. So I went into the box with the halter and approached her, and of course she went round the box at a hell of a speed. When she steadied down I approached her again, and this went on for about half an hour, but gradually she slowed down until I could get my fingers on her, and as soon as I touched her, she swung round at me with her teeth and her front feet. So I punched her in the face and she retired to her corner of the box and I retired to mine, and we started again. Again after about twenty minutes I got my fingers on her, and she came at me again. I punched her on the nose again, and the two of us retired to our respective corners. This went on for well over two hours, and I could see we were getting nowhere. Each time I touched her, she attacked me, I punched her on the nose and we retired to our corners. And since it was getting dark I had to do something quickly. So the only thing I could do was to get a fourteen foot gate and put it across the box. Then I slowly edged her up to the wall. I got her about half way up towards the wall, when Spitfire went back on her hocks and come straight over the gate. So I started again. After about twenty minutes I finally got her right up against the wall, so that I could get my hand on her. I eased my hand up her neck, she managed to swing her head round and take a piece out of my arm, so again I went back. And as I went back a little bit, she came out under the gate, lifting it with her head, so I started again. Always talking to her quietly, gently and peacefully, again I got her up against the wall of the loose-box and got my hand on her and eventually I managed to slip the halter over her head and tighten it up.

Once I got it tightened and knotted under the chin, however, came the problem of leading her out. But this was not as difficult as it seemed. I put a second halter rope on the one I had, and then let her out from behind the gate, removed the gate from the loose-box, and I let her go round the shed past me. As she went past me I began shortening the halter rope. As I got nearer to her she came at me with her teeth and her feet, but I swung her past me and got into her shoulder so that I was beside her. I managed to catch hold of the halter right up under her chin. As soon as I had done this, once I got my body beside her, she started to settle down. And she quietened slowly until she was walking round and round with me leaning on her. Then I led her out into the yard and managed to get her up into the trailer without very much trouble, tying her up short in the trailer so that I could release her easily. Fortunately for me, while she would come at me with her teeth and her front feet, she would not kick. Then I took her home and tied her up in the stable for the night.

It is necessary here to explain exactly what the mare and I had been saying to each other. Once I got her into the loose-box I could concentrate on her and I followed the normal procedure of settling her with my voice and e.s.p.. When I got my fingers on her, she responded by attacking me: she had obviously been badly ill-treated in the past, and found that the only way of escape was to attack anybody who tried to touch her. So she attacked me, saying 'go back, go back, go back, or I will pulverise you,' in answer to which I punched her on the nose and said 'if you do not go back I will pulverise you,' until we both retreated to our own corners and we started again. Now given time, if I had started with her in the morning, as I should have done, we would have gone on like that for maybe four or five hours until I got my hand on her, and then I could have haltered her quite simply; but since we were running short of time and daylight, and the worst thing in the world would have been to have gone away and left her for the night and come back again next day, I had to resort to other methods to get her haltered, methods I do not normally use.

For the next week, three times a day, I fed her and watered her and led her around and gentled her and handled her, until she was relaxing and trusting me. What is more she stopped trying to make a meal of me instead of the corn I was bringing her. After that came the next stage: to try to halter her. But since I had her in the big building, where she had been tied up in one particular stall, I let her loose in the building and of course she went round me hell for leather until she finally went into the stall again. I left her standing there for two or three minutes. I walked up to her, getting her to relax, using my voice, and being relaxed myself so that I could use e.s.p. on her. Then I managed to get my fingers on her side, and slowly get my arm over her neck and put a halter on her. After this I started turning her out with the other horses by night, but of course getting her in was somewhat time-consuming, since even if you had a lot of people standing right round the outside of the yard she would jump the smallest to get back out again. But over the course of the next two months she gradually got better, until it was only a question of opening the gate when the horses came in, and she would walk up the road and into the stable. I never had any trouble riding her and from the first time I got on her, I could direct and control her entirely by using e.s.p., and she turned out to be a wonderful ride – and a fantastic jumper of course. But it took a very long time before she was coming in happily and it took me nearly nine months before I could shoe her without difficulty. It was because I always talked to her in a language she understood that she very slowly recovered from her hatred of mankind, and eventually became very fond of me.

The following winter she was turned out with the other horses, and by about Christmas she would come up to me in the field and take a feed out of the bucket, and I used to lead her into the stable with her nose in the bucket without any difficulty. By the end of June, she had settled down and was absolutely quiet, though she remained a very hot, keen little ride and was not suitable for a beginner. So I sold her to a young couple down in Glamorgan and they were very pleased with her, until the woman started a baby and the husband decided the mare was a bit too much for her. So they brought her up to Llanybyther once more to sell her. As soon as I got into the market I knew she was there. I could feel it. I went straight to the big stable, and there was my beloved Spitfire. I had regretted selling her, and could not let her go again, so I bought her back and she is now in foal to an Anglo-Arab stallion. I hope she will have a foal half as good as she is. She was a case for which gentling was the only system that could possibly have done anything. If we had not had her, she would have been shot.

Of course I much prefer handling a very difficult horse to one that is easy and straightforward. It gives me enormous pleasure when a horse which is completely impossible to handle or ride starts enjoying his work and wanting to do well.

It is only after I have got a horse going steadily and quietly that it is time to start riding her. I do this quite simply. When I go to the box on the morning I am going to start riding a horse, I always go through the same routine. First I start gentling for about five minutes. When she stands still I get my fingers on to her just where the barrel begins to narrow to the girth. She will twitch her skin, standing with one ear forward and one back, while I go round and round with my fingers. 'There's a clever girl.' Now the second set of fingers, both hands flat into her body. Bigger circles, lean on her, working forward and over the back, both sides of the neck. She takes one step forward, so work back a little until she settles, and stands well with both ears forward. Now her muscles are relaxing, tension is going out of her, mentally we are in tune. Work forward, up the neck. She has an itch under her chin, so scratch it. Ready now for the halter, work back, get the halter, work forward, halter on from far side of the neck, over the ears. I tighten the very loose chin rope and I give her to my wife to hold, get the saddle with girth and stirrups flapping, put the saddle over her and on to her. She tenses and walks forward. My wife, who has been holding her and gentling her, keeps gentling her, walks with her. I lift the saddle off, she stands still. On with the saddle again, gently with one hand under the tummy catching hold of the girth, buckle one strap loosely, talking, talking all the time. Buckle the second strap tighter. Tighten the first strap, now get the girth as tight as possible. She will object and walk round the box, but my wife is still with her, talking, gentling. She stands still. Tighten some more, get the bridle, a soft egg-butt snaffle – ease it on. Into her body, gentling her on her shoulder, on her flank, lift my left leg. My wife eases me on to her, I lie across her. She walks forward, I slide off, and walk with her, until she stands. Ease on again, leg over, slowly upright, still talking, still gentling, feet into the stirrups. She walks round the box, she stands, my wife ties the halter rope round her neck, and opens the door and goes out. She follows, looks out of the gate to the road up to the mountain. Click my tongue, we will walk through the door, out of the gate, and up the road, my wife walking four or five yards in front. Forty or fifty yards up the road I say 'whoa-a-a', and pull the reins gently. My wife stops, and so does the mare. I click my tongue, my wife goes forward, and the mare follows. Forty yards, 'Whoa', and we all stop. Click my tongue and we start. After doing this three or four times, she will be stopping and starting on command, and so we turn round and go home, still talking, talking, still stopping and starting every thirty or forty yards. But my wife is now fifty yards behind us. Into the yard, and into the stable, slide off quickly and quietly.

When you are catching a young horse either in a field or a stable, or putting your hand on him, prior to gentling him, never approach his head, never from behind, always approach at a right angle, to the middle of the body. Get yourself mentally relaxed and in tune with your horse. If you and your horse are in tune, and thinking on the same wavelength, you can get away with an awful lot of mistakes. But if you are at odds with each other, you are in trouble from the start, and you will be fighting all the time. We always try to work our horses in a confined space, approximately ten foot by ten foot, because we find this gives maximum physical and mental contact, and at the same time gives the horse enough room to get away from us. Up to the time you leave the loose-box, you are using e.s.p., sounds and signs to relax and settle your horse, but to get movement and direction you must use telepathy as well. You visualize where you want to go, so that the horse wants to go there as well. The whole time you are trying to get the horse to want to do what you want him to do. In the early stages your assistant either walks in front of you or leads you. But you will find that the horse very quickly learns the words of command to which he naturally responds : a slowly drawn-out 'whoa' to stop, and a clicking of the tongue to start. He does not understand naturally words like 'walk on', 'trot on', though he will learn them later. The bit is hardly used at all, and you ride always with a slack rein. You settle well down in the saddle with your feet well home, to give you greater control if anything does go wrong. (The idea that there is only one correct way to ride a horse is wrong: you adapt your technique to the occasion. Terry Biddlecombe's steeple-chasing seat would win few show-jumping contests. Mr Laurence's dressage seat would not win Lester Piggot many races. And as was clear on television, Harvey Smith's show-jumping seat is a little insecure when riding round Aintree. So when riding a young horse, you require a seat adapted for that purpose: one that gives you maximum security, not one in which you have your bust and backside stuck out and your toes balanced precariously on the edge of the stirrup.)

The most important thing to remember is that the whole time you are talking to the horse, you are being entirely and completely natural. As far as the horse is concerned he is enjoying what he is doing and you should be enjoying it as well. You should be in tune with the horse mentally and understand exactly what he is saying to you. You understand what he is saying when he tenses his muscles, you watch the angle of his ears and any sounds or signs he makes. But most of all you can sense what he is thinking and he can sense your relaxation and your happiness.

The simplest way to back a horse is one we very often use, especially if we have a horse out in the field and bring it in every day. After we have been bringing it in for a fortnight or three weeks, I pull him in to the bank just outside the field and let him eat the grass on the bank. I lean across him and let him carry me to the yard. After a few days of doing this, I simply put a leg across him and ride him in and out in a halter. He takes it all as a matter of course. This is part of the natural habit of his life, and he is beginning to learn the signs and sounds that he will associate with his conversations with human beings. When he is quite accustomed to me riding him in and out of the field, it is only a very short step from taking him and his companion out for half an hour. I may do this riding him bareback in a halter, or I may put a bridle and saddle on him. When I start doing this I start teaching him to stop and start, but only in spells of three or four minutes at a time. I take the horse out with his companion every day for twenty minutes to half an hour, with two or three schooling spells of three or four minutes each.

Sometimes, for demonstration purposes, we can and do take a wild horse from the mountain and have him riding quite quietly within half an hour or an hour, simply by using signs and sounds the horse understands. But of course normally e.s.p. and telepathy are used on a horse that has been handled and is quite tame, and it is merely a question of getting in tune with him straight away and getting him to do what you want him to do. In getting a horse to do what you want him to do by our methods, you do not have to train him to answer any set words of command: there is no reason at all why he should know the words 'walk on' or 'trot'.

There is a story of a poacher who was stopped by the local policeman and accused of using his dog for poaching. He told the constable that his dog would not hunt rabbits, to which he got a rude answer, so he said 'well I will show you.' So he took the dog and the policeman into a field where there were plenty of rabbits, and said 'go on boy, catch one.' The dog stood where he was. The more he said 'go on and catch one' the more the dog stood where he was, so the policeman gave up in disgust, and went away. As soon as he had gone out of sight, the poacher turned to his dog and said 'get to heel,' and the dog straight away shot out and caught a rabbit. Human words of command, in short, mean nothing to an animal in themselves, and have to be taught. But if you use signs, sounds and signals that the horse understands then you will get a natural response, and it makes the training of your horse infinitely easier.

12: *Making the Most of Your Horse*

There are only three things necessary if you are to learn to comprehend what your horse is trying to say, and make him comprehend what you want him to do: patience, understanding and unlimited time. You will need patience to spend endless hours watching and memorizing the signs and sounds he uses in communicating with you and with other horses; understanding to appreciate that a horse does not think or respond as a human being does; and unlimited time to complete your task, because a task it is, one that has taken us twenty years to complete. Understanding is the most important requirement to begin with. If you look upon your horse as another human being, you will never be able to understand him and make yourself clearly understood by him. You have only to watch a bunch of wild horses in the field together to see that their reactions and behaviour are completely alien to those of the human being. You may see one horse approach another and the first horse turn on him and attack him with his teeth and feet. But you would make a mistake if you concluded that they were enemies. Horses, no matter how friendly, will often kick and bite each other, as human beings will argue with each other, but it is always an instantaneous reaction and it is over in a minute or two. A horse is not human and the greatest barrier to the understanding of any animal is anthropomorphism, that is to say, attributing human personality and behaviour to animals.

It must also be remembered that no animal will react to exactly the same stimuli as another animal. Bearing this in mind, if you wish to understand what your horse is saying, it is probably best to begin by trying to make some semblance of order out of the signs and sounds he uses that you understand already – you will be surprised at how many signs and sounds you do know. If you are in close contact with a large number of horses, it is best to begin by concentrating on one horse, the horse that you feel closest to. When you have discovered how much you already understand of what he is saying, you will be able to start adding to the list. You will find it a very slow process, but after six months, if you have really put your mind to the subject, you should be able to understand most of what he says. You should have between twenty-five and thirty basic messages.

You can now start trying to understand signs and sounds used by other horses you are in contact with, and to find out how they convey the same basic message. For example, if you are in contact with twenty horses, and you take a basic message such as 'welcome', you will probably find eight to a dozen different variations in the way that it is said, so you will add the variations to your vocabulary.

When you have your list of basic messages (forty-seven in all), you can start extending your vocabulary when speaking to the horse. You will of course use your voice, but it does not matter what words you use since it is the tone of the voice that matters to the animal. Alex Kerr, Bertram Mills' lion tamer, used to describe how when he was training a lion or a tiger, he had to work the animal for a very long time indeed, and to get one animal to perform one action might take five or six hours. The whole time he would be talking to the animal he was training, and he found the only way he could relieve his own tension was to swear. So he learnt to swear in as many languages as he could. He would use the foulest oaths under the sun in a soft, caressing, gentle tone – he swore at his lions and tigers to stop himself getting angry with them.

Then when you are using signs, you must remember that your hands and arms cease to be hands and arms, but become neck and head, so that when you stroke the horse it will feel to him that he is being caressed with the head and nose of another horse, and when you slap him it will tingle for him in the same way as a bite from another horse. Other movements you use are very similar to that of a horse: your legs are similar in action to his hind legs, so if for example he kicks at you, it will be exactly the same movement that you use to kick him back.

And if he does kick at you, it is important for you to kick back at him straight away, since if you do not, he will think that he has dominated you by his anger. It is no use whatever if you wait until you come out of hospital, six weeks later. In a herd, you will notice that if an inferior horse kicks at the boss horse, the boss horse will kick back much harder and much more firmly; but if a boss horse kicks at an inferior horse, the inferior horse will get out of the way. So if when your horse kicks at you, you get out of the way, he will immediately assume that you are inferior to him in the social hierarchy of the herd. Only if you attack him back will he accept that you are the boss.

When you can interpret all the signs and sounds that your horses use, and they can interpret what you are saying to them, you can start using your feelings and instincts to interpret his e.s.p. messages. This is not as revolutionary as it sounds. What you are trying to do is to extend an ability that you are using already, for once you can get that feeling of oneness with your horse, it is only a small step to interpreting his moods and feelings.

In the early stages you ought to be able to tell if he is relaxed or excited even before you see him; and the more you handle him, provided that you are thinking on approximately the some wavelength, the more you will understand. The most difficult part of e.s.p., and the danger that has to be guarded against, is the fact that everyone wants to believe he can do it, and that he is indeed getting through to his horse, or whatever animal he is handling. We have found with many people that, while there is a certain amount of e.s.p. response, there is even more imagination. When you really are getting through to a horse, you will know what he is feeling and you will know what he is going to do next, and the certainty of your knowledge will be such that there is no room for doubt whatever – it is impossible to be mistaken. Part of your knowledge is bound to come from using your eyes and ears, and from your knowledge of the horse and the horse's reactions : if a horse puts his ears back and arches his back, you will know that he is going to buck. But when you are getting through to the horse, you will feel the tension increasing and the knots growing in your belly long before there is any visible sign. You will feel his hunger and impatience as you go towards the feeding house, even when you cannot see him and long before he knocks his basin and whickers.

One of the ways to extend your extra-sensory relation with your horse is to ride him without using your reins, guiding him and controlling him entirely with your thoughts. You will find this very difficult at first, but it will improve with time. You should however always remember that you are using a method of communication that leaves the free will of the individual full play. The horse may disagree with you, and if he does, you have no control over him, but can only rely on his good nature. You may say 'let's go left,' and he may say 'no, I am going right.' You may say 'let's trot,' and he may answer by saying 'why should I bother.' But when there is a complete two-way play of e.s.p. and telepathy, you will find this does not occur very often, since you will both want to go the same way.

I have occasional trouble myself with free will. When I let the horses out, I let them free in the yard and they walk down the road or up the hill, directed to the field I want by a mixture of their habit, and my telepathic messages. But sometimes they say 'we are damned if we are going there, we want to go somewhere else,' and when this happens I have to run like the devil to get in front of them. But this sort of conflict is inevitable. When you are controlling a horse with your mind, he must have the freedom to reject your suggestions or accept them at will. The more you are getting through to the horse, the more he will get through to you, and the less often this will occur.

But if you are a weak character, a word of warning in

using my methods. Don't whatever you do allow yourself to become a zombie, your mind and actions controlled by some lazy quadruped, for whom you work sixty hours a week in order to earn enough to keep *him* in the comfort to which he has become accustomed!

Appendix: Some Practical Advice to Horse-owners

The most serious difficulties that arise between horse and owner are those that stem from the plain fact that the two are simply not suited to each other. Either the temperament of the horse is wrong for the owner, or the horse is unsuitable for the purpose for which it is required : for example a nervous person should not have a horse that is any way excitable, and a person who really wants to go should never have a horse that wants only to stand around looking at the horizon.

This is why the purchase of a horse is so important and deserves a deal more thought and preparation than it normally receives.

First of all, where should you buy it? In certain areas horses are much cheaper than in others : broadly speaking, in the belt stretching from London to the Midlands, horses are dearer than they are in other parts of the country. Obviously they are going to be cheaper in those areas which produce horses – the West of England, Wales, Yorkshire and parts of Scotland – and it is much better to go to one of these areas to select the horse to suit you, rather than to some plush dealer's yard in the suburbs. In either case you will probably end up with a very similar horse, the difference being that since the dealer had taken the trouble to go to the West Country or Wales or Ireland to buy that horse and take it back to his yard, you will have to pay fifty to one hundred pounds more than he paid for it. There are of course advantages in buying from a reputable dealer since (a) he is almost certainly a first-class judge of a horse and (b) if the horse you buy is unsuitable he will probably change it for another one. But you will have to pay him very handsomely for his expertise.

On the other hand I would not advise an inexperienced buyer to buy from a private individual, since in my experience private individuals have a grossly inflated idea of their horse's value, and tend to be totally blind to his faults. If you have a very long purse you can buy privately a well-known and well proven horse; but very few of us have long purses and we have to buy the horse we want for as little as possible, which brings us to the place where I buy most of mine, which is at public auction.

To buy a horse at public auction, however, you need to be a reasonable judge of a horse yourself, or to have the advice of someone who is a reasonable judge. The best adviser without any doubt at all is a veterinary surgeon, but since it is extremely difficult to get a veterinary surgeon to come with you to an auction sale, a riding school proprietor who keeps the type of horse you have in mind is a good person to take along – provided of course he has not got a horse he wants to sell you himself! If you are going to an auction, it is important to go to one of the auctions in the horse-producing areas. The ones I know best, being a West-Country man and living in Wales, are Exeter, Abergavenny, Llanybyther (which is my own auction), Hay-on-Wye, Hereford, and Stow-on-the-Wold. At an auction in a horse-producing area a high proportion of the horses are being sold by people who breed horses commercially for sale, on their farms; whereas at the urban auctions you get a large number of throwouts from other people's stables, and so a much higher proportion of unsound horses than at the rural auction.

But of course the rural auctions are usually held in distant places, so you do have the problem and cost of transporting the horses to your home. There are three ways this can be done. You can go to the auction and contact someone there who expects to have an empty lorry going home. This is a little bit chancy. Or you can hire a Land-Rover and trailer yourself; or, ideally, persuade someone else to go down with you to buy a horse, and bring yours back in his Land-Rover and trailer. This will give you the additional advantage of an adviser on tap!

The type of horse to aim to buy at an auction is in fact something looking a little bit rough and thin, since this horse will increase in value. If you buy a horse already looking smart and polished it will cost you a lot more money, and at the same time there is always a chance that the spit and polish has been put there to hide some of his more glaring faults.

It is worth remembering, too, when you buy at a public auction, that you have four days to test out any warranty on that horse, and it is most important that you do this. If you buy a horse that is warranted as sound, as soon as you get it home you must have it thoroughly vetted. If you get a horse that is said to be quiet to ride in traffic, ride him in heavy traffic at once. It is also advisable to understand the various claims made about the horse in a catalogue. If it says that the horse is quiet to ride, it means in law just that. If it says he is a good jumper, check that he is a good jumper. If it says he is suitable for a beginner, find the biggest beginner you know and put him on the horse and see how he gets on. Mind you, I have my own interpretations of the sales catalogue descriptions. They go something like this: 'quiet to ride' means, roughly, 'has not bucked or bolted with anyone for a week and the vendor hopes it will not buck you off before the four days run out'. 'Recently broken' means that the vendor was hoping to sell it as a quiet ride, but the horse bucked his son off the day before yesterday and so he cannot give him that warranty. 'Has been backed' means the owner's son was put on and bucked off immediately. 'Will make a one-day-eventer' means that he will not make a show-jumper, point-to-pointer or a dressage horse. 'Good hunter' means 'will go out hunting provided you do not go too near the hounds and do not leave the road'. But this is just my rather humorous way of expressing a necessary scepticism. Never, never, never believe anything anybody tells you about a horse he is trying to sell. He probably believes it himself, but horse owners are rather like mothers, they cannot see any faults in their children, though they can see all their virtues. When you are buying a horse it is the faults you want to know about, not the virtues.

But do not let the foregoing discourage you. Provided you go to a rural auction, you should get a horse much cheaper than you will get it anywhere else, and you have the chance of buying a very good horse that has not done very much work. Always remember that ponies up to about fourteen-two are much cheaper in autumn than in the spring, and that hunters are much cheaper in the spring than in the autumn.

The type of horse you buy is of course of vital importance. First of all think honestly about your own personality. If you are in any way nervous or if you are worried about riding in heavy traffic you must get a quiet horse. It is no good buying a thoroughbred or an Arab because they tend to be excitable. If on the other hand you are a keen person and want to go in for competition work this type of horse is extremely suitable. If the horse has to be out all winter you must get one of the mountain or moorland types, since they winter out very well, whilst the thoroughbreds and Arabs need to be in. Again, one of the advantages of buying at an auction sale is that you will have a large number of horses to choose from, while even at the biggest dealer's yards there will be only a few of the type you want.

When you are at the auction buying the horse, the key to his personality can very often be seen in his behaviour as he stands in the stable, and as he stands outside the ring walking in and out amongst the crowd. The crowd will worry some horses, but it will not worry others. Some will be irritable and some will be placid. This will tell you something. But above all, the important thing is to pick the horse that you click with mentally : the horse that seems to be talking to you and not to anybody else. Buying a horse, I often think, is far more important than picking a wife. After all when you pick a wife it is only going to cost you a seven-and-sixpence licence, and if you are a little bit careful about your choice

---

you can make her go out to work and keep you in the manner
to which you would like to become accustomed. But if you
are picking a horse it is going to cost you a hell of a lot
of money in the first place and on top of this it is going to
cost you six or seven pounds a week to keep it, which makes
it a very different proposition. If you have got the right
horse it is worth while, if you have got the wrong horse it is
hell.

You have now bought your horse, for better or for worse,
and you have managed to get it home and all the local horse
pundits have been round to look at it and said nice things
about it to your face and nasty things about it behind your
back. This is absolutely inevitable, it does not matter what
horse you buy they will always criticize it behind your back.
But having got that over, and having tried it out thoroughly to
see that its warranty is true, it is time to start working on him.
If he is out, it is vital, to begin with anyway, that you see
and handle and talk to him every day. This means quite
simply whether you are riding him or not, that you must go
out and spend half-an-hour to an hour talking to him in a
field. And it is no good standing at the top of the field and
carrying on a shouted conversation with him down at the far
end. You want to fill your pockets with horse- and pony-nuts
and go down and feed him one or two at a time, talk to him
and watch him and thoroughly get to know him. Get to
know him as a person. You will know you are beginning to
get through to him when he does two things: first, when he
gives you a whicker of welcome and comes over to talk to
you; and second, when you see him start driving any other
horses in the field away when they try to come to talk to
you. This last will show you that you have become his, you
belong to him, and he will look after you and do anything for
you.

The next thing you will have to do is to catch your
horse, and strangely enough I have found that there is a
greater ignorance about catching horses than about anything

else to do with them. Why this is I do not quite know – probably because most horses are extremely easy to catch – but if you have a horse that is in any way difficult, there is a standard procedure for catching him. First of all you have to get him to come to the bucket, and when he comes to eat out of a bucket quite happily and quietly, you can set about teaching him to be caught. You very slowly get him eating out of the bucket until he walks past you. Most horses, no matter how difficult, will come and pick out of a bucket at arm's length. Once they have really started eating you bring the bucket closer to you and then you bring it past you, until you are standing by the shoulder of the horse. Then you can slip your arm over the neck and make a fuss of him. Having done this you put the halter rope round his neck. If he tries to break away, let him go. Do not hang on, this is the worst thing you can do. He is much stronger than you and the chances are three to one that he will get away anyway. All you do is let him go and start again. Again you lead him past your body, put your arm over his neck, and slip the rope over his neck. Having done that you put the halter on from the far side, *not* the near side. If you try to put the halter on from the near side, he will swing away from the halter and away from you and get away. But if you put the halter on the far side of his head, the side away from you, if he swings away from the halter, he swings towards you, which means that if you go on quietly you can slip the halter on quite easily. Again, if you have a difficult horse to catch, it is usually far simpler to lead him into the stable following a bucket (provided the stable is reasonably near the field and there are no busy main roads to cross), than it is to halter him in the field and lead him in with the halter.

I had to use this technique only a short time ago. Four of our horses got out on to Llanybyther mountain, and it so happened that two of them were young horses who had never been haltered and the other two were very difficult to catch anyway. But I had been feeding them in the field, and when I went up to talk to them they would come up and eat out of the bucket. After about two hours looking, we managed to find them about three miles away across the mountain. So, I just stood there, about three or four hundred yards away from them, rattled the bucket and shouted, and they came hell for leather. As soon as they each had a mouthful out of the bucket, I started to walk home, and all four of them followed me the three miles home, taking a mouthful every now and then, without any trouble at all. If I had tried to catch and halter those horses, I would have spent hours at it. Possibly it would have been better if I had spent the time teaching them to be caught, but two thousand acres of open mountain is not an ideal situation for teaching a horse to be caught. That is something you want to do in a reasonably confined space, in our experience a yard about twenty yards by thirty yards.

You will of course at times have your horse in the stable. He may be in the stable all the time or you may just bring him in to saddle and bridle him. But it is here that the really important work is done. You must get your horse understanding you, get him to understand what you want him to do quite clearly, and at the same time you must be consistent. It is no good teaching him one day to eat out of your pocket and the next day hitting him on the nose for doing just that. It is here that you teach him that he is a subordinate member of the herd to you, and that you are boss. You must not let him push you about, and if he bites or kicks you, bite or kick him back. There are no two ways about this. Just as he must trust you in every way, you must be able to trust him absolutely, and you have no hope whatsoever of being able to control him riding, if you cannot control him on the ground. If you are afraid of him on the ground you will be afraid of him on his back, and it is on the ground and in the stable that you develop trust with your horse. If you are unable to do this it is far better to sell him at once to someone who can handle him, rather than keep him yourself. This is perhaps not important as far as you are concerned, but what does concern me is that your horse will not be happy.

It is a piece of supreme arrogance to think that you will look after your horse better than anyone else and that you will love him more than anyone else will. Most people love their horses or they would not keep them, and most people look after them to the best of their ability, so it is important for the horse that he should be owned by someone who can handle and understand him, rather than be owned by someone who is a little bit afraid of him. A spoilt horse is rather like a spoilt child : he is unhappy, discontented and he tends to be ill-treated. Today in my opinion there is far more ill-treatment of horses and dogs through over-indulgence and lack of discipline than there is through outright cruelty.

The whole time you are in the field with the horse and in the stable with the horse, as well as when you are riding him, you should be talking to him and trying to observe and understand the signs and sounds he uses to you. This will lead to a better understanding between you and the horse and to a much better performance.

Feeding is quite simple. A horse should be well fed but not over-fed. There has been a great deal written in countless books about feeding, so I am not going into it in detail here, but the most important thing to remember about grazing is that the horse is a selective feeder and a field that to the layman's eye may have an awful lot of grass in it, may be starvation conditions for a horse, as a horse likes short sweet grass and will not eat tough grass. Long rank grass is not suitable grazing for a horse or a pony.

I have dealt with discipline on the ground, and discipline when you are riding is very similar. We aim to have all our horses enjoying what they are doing as much as possible, but there are times when the horse has to do things that he does not enjoy doing. But it does not matter what we ask a horse to do, he must do just that. I always say that if I asked a horse to climb Mount Everest the horse would have to climb Mount Everest, but of course you must never ask a horse to do something he is not capable of doing. If you have asked him to do something, you must persevere until he does it.

Before now I have spent four hours trying to get a horse to walk over a low bank when there was an open gateway twenty yards further down. I had turned him over the low bank before I got to the gate because it seemed quicker, to save myself half a minute; but the horse said he would not go over, so I just stayed there, and kept walking him into the bank until he walked over and it took me four hours to do it. First I asked Winberto to walk over the bank, and Winberto said 'no', so having said 'please will you walk over the bank' and had the reply 'no I will not', I then insisted 'you have damned well got to.' When we are handling our horses we always say 'please will you", but at the back of that 'please' is the determination that the horse will have to do it anyway. You do the basic work on this on the ground, if you walk into him when he is standing in your way, you ask him 'please will you get out of my way,' and if he still stands there you catch him a slap so that he knows he must get out of the way because you are boss. But you can only do this with a horse when you know and understand him, so that when you smack him, he will stand back and say 'what the hell was that for?' And two minutes later he is all over you again. We always say that when you have a row with a horse you have to make it up with him afterwards. After having had a fight with a difficult horse we go and make a terrific fuss of him. I would not like you to think that I spend a lot of my time hitting my horses, because I do not, I very rarely hit or clout a horse and when I am riding it is the exception when I carry a stick with me. But there is no point in my giving advice on how to deal with a horse who behaves perfectly, so I have picked on the exceptional cases when discipline is necessary. I always say I only have to hit a horse once if he is being a little bit difficult. I pick a situation where he is going to say 'no I will not,' and then I hit him hard and when I hit a horse I hit him hard. I do not tap, tap with a stick, I really lace him on both sides so that afterwards he will always remember being hit and I do not have to hit him again. There is nothing that annoys me more, when I am watching people riding, than to see them tap, tap, tap with the stick. It is not doing the horse any good, it only annoys him. It is far better if you are going to use a stick to really use it. But of course you must never on any occasion hit a horse unless he is doing something that is very wrong.

You should be able to get the maximum amount of scolding into your voice. I always aim to be able, when I have had a horse for about three weeks, to go into a field and shout 'come on my darlings' and have all the horses come galloping over to me. When I am handling or riding a horse, after two or three months a horse should do anything I want him to, without my actually asking him. I like my horses to anticipate what I want. As soon as I show a horse a jump, he should be tearing to get over it. When you take your horse out for a ride, it is important that you are enjoying what you are going to do, but it is equally important that your horse should enjoy it, since if both your horse and you are enjoying what you are doing you will add to each other's enjoyment. I hate watching the German riders on television, because they tend towards a type of precision and discipline that treats the horse as a robot and not as another person. The rider dominates and demands obedience. Even for a horse that is handled only at week-ends a certain amount of schooling is important, since it will increase the horse's ability and enjoyment and so increase your own enjoyment; but the type of schooling you give him depends on what you want to do. The dressage type of schooling is very fashionable at the moment, though I far prefer the polo type. Dressage schooling involves doing everything on an even stride and all your movements have to be even and smooth, whereas the polo type of schooling involves far more abrupt movements and teaches the horse to work off an uneven stride. It is fine preparation for cross country work, steeple-chasing and hunting, since in any of these pursuits you will tend to get situations where you have to jump on an uneven stride, or turn very sharply, and a horse that will change legs at a mere shift of your body and can jump and turn at the same time, and put himself right and shorten and extend his stride automatically, has a very great advantage. I find dressage work uncongenial also because anticipation is very much discouraged, whereas I like my horses to anticipate what I am going to ask them to do and do it before they have been asked.

But whatever form of schooling you decide upon, it is extremely important that you should never have a fight with your horse during a schooling session. He should look on your schooling area as a place where he is going to enjoy himself, and not associate it with an unpleasant experience. You should start teaching your horse the basic things you want to school him in during a normal ride: for example if you want to teach your horse to back, you should get him backing before you take him into the schooling area, which should be the place where you put polish on to the movements the horse is already doing. When you want to teach your horse to jump, the simple way to do it is when you are out riding normally. You get three or four horses cantering along in front of you, and just pop over a tree trunk lying on the ground – anything small, about one foot to eighteen inches high, just so that the horse has to take off – and you will find that instead of having to teach the horse to jump he will come to jumping quite naturally. It is best if you can find a fence without a lot of daylight on either side of it. With nine horses out of ten, if three or four horses are cantering along in front of him, and he is tearing along to catch up with them, just as they pop over the tree trunk he will jump over quite naturally. After that, whenever you see a small obstacle you can jump, you just pop over it, and slowly by degrees the jumps that you take him over will rise in height.

This comes back to the basic principle of teaching a horse to do anything: if he sees other horses doing it and enjoying it, and you are looking forward to doing it and enjoying it yourself, the horse will also want to do it.

A classic example of this interaction happened to me about twenty years ago. I had a young chestnut thoroughbred which I had just started riding, and I had only been riding him about ten days when the hounds met nearby. I took him out to have a look, mainly to give him an interest and he enjoyed it and found time went quite quickly. I was with a friend of mine, Bill Manfield, and we cantered down the lane and came round the corner and there was a three-foot-six-inch gate right across the lane. Bill was on his very good hunter, Melody, and he as a matter of course went straight on over it and before I knew anything the three-year-old had followed the mare. He had never jumped anything in his life, and the first thing he jumped was a three-foot-six-inch gate. This just shows what can be done, provided you take something as it arises in its natural course, and do not make a great issue of doing anything. If you treat the young horse as if he had been doing it all his life, he will do it, but if you go into it wondering 'will he or won't he, can he or can't he,' the horse is sure to stop. If you enjoy jumping your horse will enjoy jumping and will jump well. If you do not like jumping, your horse will not, and if neither of you likes jumping, do not jump. This is the key to the whole thing.

Finally, here are some do's and don'ts when you are handling your horse. Do get a horse that suits your temperament, do not get one that is beyond your abilities. Do remember that beauty is only skin deep and do not be taken in by spit and polish. Do remember that a horse who looks rough and thin can always be improved, whereas one who is fat, glossy and finished can only lose in value. Do be boss and do not be dominated by your horse. Do what you enjoy doing, do not do something just because your friends do it. Do observe his signs and sounds, but do not let your imagination run away with you. Back everything up with sound observations. Do say 'please will you' before you ask a horse to do anything, and be sure to back it up with determination to enforce your wishes. But above all do not ask a horse to perform beyond his capabilities. Do school regularly but do not fight in the schooling arena. Do think like a horse but do not endow him with human qualities, feelings and responses, because he is not a human being – fortunately for the horse! Do observe his natural wishes and desires, but do not spoil him. Do enforce discipline but do not be a martinet. Do teach him to jump naturally, but do not over-jump him: about twelve to fifteen fences a day is enough for most horses. Last of all please remember that it is important for the horse to enjoy himself, to be happy and to be comfortable, but that this cannot be achieved without firmness and discipline.

PART II

THINKING WITH HORSES

1: *Early Guesses About Horse Psychology*

As a Rugby player I had more enthusiasm than skill. But nevertheless, I managed to get my first fifteen cap, and on 20th October 1945 I played for my school against Wells. By a piece of good fortune the ball was kicked ahead and I tore up the field to find myself on the twenty-five-yard line with the ball at my feet and no one between me and the line. So I trapped the ball with my knees, controlled it, and dribbled like hell. Unfortunately the opposing fullback who had been left standing came tearing up behind me and tried to fall on the ball. But he fell on my leg instead, and smashed my knee to smithereens. I spent the next three months on my back in plaster, and then nine months on crutches. This at the age of sixteen, was a shattering blow. And for a healthy young animal, who was fit and used to running about, being confined to bed was the worst punishment imaginable. But it gave me a very, very great advantage over my fellows, because for the first time in my life I had nothing to do but think or read. And since you can only read so many books a day, I had to do quite a lot of thinking. An unusual pastime at sixteen.

I had a very nice three-year-old mare that I was working just before my accident. But unfortunately she had two very bad curbs on her hocks, so the decision was made that she had to be fired. This was done at the end of February, just after I was beginning to hobble around on crutches. Nothing could steady the mare enough to allow her to have the operation done. Time and time again the vet and the assistants came out of the stable door in a bundle, and eventually I could stand it no longer. I pegged in on my crutches and talked to her for a couple of minutes, and then went and leant against her hindquarters. The vet, who was a man of quick decision and action, walked straight in, carried out the operation, and the mare didn't move. I made a great fuss of her, collected my crutches and went out into the sunlight feeling very pleased with myself.

Unfortunately a couple of days later, trying to do more than I should have done on my crutches, I went head over heels, smashed my plaster and was banished to my bed again. Lying on my back gazing at the same blue wall, the same cracks in the ceiling, and the same hole in my counterpane I had studied for the previous three months, I began to wonder why the mare had behaved quietly when I was leaning against her, and not before. I had always known that I had what might be termed the 'green finger' with horses: unrideable horses would go calmly and easily for me, when they deposited my brothers and sister unceremoniously on the ground. I had accepted this as just one of those things. But the firing operation on the filly made me think. Why had she been so compliant for me? It can't have been maternal instinct that made her protect me: three-year-old fillies don't have much maternal instinct, since they have never been mothers. And I was honest enough with myself to know that I hadn't given her all that much cause to love me. I had ridden her hard, and made her jump when she didn't want to jump. Admittedly I had made a fuss of her when she had done the right thing, and I fed and looked after her. But as an unpleasant, bad mannered, bad tempered sixteen-year-old, I hadn't given anybody or anything much cause to love me. So why had it been more important to the filly to accept a certain discomfort herself from the operation, rather than risk hurting my injured leg? How had she even known that I was injured? I decided that she had sensed my injury. But the only possible reason for her to protect me, was that I belonged to her. That I was hers. I had already noticed that when I was with a group of other horses she would try to keep herself between me and the other animals. And it came as rather a shock to a young man who had looked upon himself as the Lord of Creation that he actually belonged to an unsound three-year-old filly.

When I was allowed out of bed and started hobbling around on my crutches again, I began watching the other horses as well.

To try and see what made them tick. I noticed that when the horses were being turned out of the yard, always the same horses led the way, and the others kept more or less at the back. It wasn't the fastest horse in the front, and it wasn't the first one out of the stable that went away in front. It was always old Fearless who led the others out of the yard. And it was always Champion who shepherded them along from behind.

What made Caravan, who was three times as fast as Fearless, and a much faster walker, walk slowly behind her? And when the horses were in the field I noticed that if something alarmed them, it was usually Chester who would go and investigate. Why if an object was frightening enough to scare Firefly into trotting away, did Chester trot over to see what the trouble was?

All these problems, and hundreds of others, started to interest me. And one of the advantages of studying horses is that they are such sympathetic animals, that they very quickly let you know whether you are right or wrong. They let you know the food they like or don't like, by either eating it greedily, or spitting it out. They let you know how much food they want by the way they eat it, or by the way their condition responds. If you do something they like, they'll show their pleasure. If you do something they don't like, they'll kick your flaming teeth in. If you ride them in the right way, they'll go beautifully for you. But if you do the wrong things, they'll tell you by going badly for you.

These reflections set me thinking a great deal about what lay behind the behaviour of horses, and I learned to verify my guesses by devising tests of their reactions.

For example, I decided that Caravan was so excitable and unpredictable in harness because nobody trusted him. And so methodically for the next week I made a great show of trusting Caravan implicitly – at the same time making damned sure that I was near enough to grab his head if he looked like going off with the cart. And Caravan acted like an angel. So one gloriously sunny June day I was sent down to the river with Caravan, plus four forty-gallon drums, to haul water for the cattle. We went out of the gate and stopped to chat to the stonemason who was busy facing the stone gate post which Caravan had demolished in one of his previous escapades. And he said, 'Don't knock this down again.' And I said, 'Oh no! I've got this horse right now, he is going absolutely beautifully. He won't do it again.' So very carefully and sedately Caravan and I jogged gently down the road with the four forty-gallon drums clanking and banging in the float. We got down to the bottom, and it was absolutely glorious, the river was beautiful, the willows were breathtaking with their delicate green and the sound of the water was extremely enticing. So I decided that when I had filled the drums, I'd have a quick swim. Dreaming of this I got out of the float and went to open the gate into the long meadow. And as I got the gate open I heard a rattle, and I was just quick enough to see Caravan turn the float in the road and go hell for leather back the half-mile to the farm yard. I followed in fear and trembling. And as I came around the corner, there in front of me was the new gate post, scattered over an area of about twenty yards. Caravan had proved to me that I was wrong. He wasn't untrustworthy because he wasn't trusted, but just because he got bored pulling a cart.

At that time we had a particularly savage bull, and moving him and the heifers from one field to another was extremely difficult and dangerous, since he would charge very nearly anyone, mounted or on foot. But I said I thought Caravan would enjoy the excitement of doing it, and I'd do the job myself. This wasn't bravery or stupidity as everyone thought. The fact was that I had the choice of doing that, (and I thought if I was crafty I could take most of the day over it) or picking early potatoes. And anyway I decided that if the bull did have a go at us, Caravan was quick enough on his feet to get me out of trouble.

My father was reluctant to agree. But it was either that or having everyone stop picking potatoes for half a day to move the stock, and anyway I had been courting death for sixteen years and survived it, so Caravan and I set off to our task. With the potato digger clanking away behind us, it wasn't a job to be hurried. I rode down to the field, and sat on Caravan studying the problem for half an hour. The cattle had to be moved out of the field into a lane, down the lane a quarter of a mile and then into one of the river fields. The main problems were first to get the bull out of the field, second to stop the cattle taking the wrong turning at the end of the lane, and third to make sure they didn't go past the open gateway into the river field. After half an hour or so the answer came to me. We had always driven them out before, and although the heifers always moved towards the gateway, sometimes slowly, sometimes going hell for leather, when we came to move the bull, he charged whoever went towards him. The answer to the problem suddenly became obvious: to make the bull charge. So I opened the two gates into the field and rode towards the bull. When he saw me coming, he put his head down and started roaring, bellowing, and pawing the ground. I rode towards him at a slight angle, shouting at him, he bellowed louder and started coming towards me with his head down. So I turned Caravan away slightly, still shouting at the bull, and eventually his rage got too much for him and he charged. I put my heels to Caravan and went flat out for the gate. The bull hurled himself after us for the best part of a hundred yards, and slowed down. So I went back and did the same thing again. This time the bull's charge carried him right out into the lane. I cantered a further hundred yards down the lane, popped Caravan over the fence into the next field, and left the bull to its own devices. With no one to annoy him he set to work raking the bank with his horns, but I didn't mind about that. I'd got him out of the field.

Caravan thought this was wonderful fun. He was dancing and cavorting all over the place. We popped over the fence back into the field where the heifers were, making quick work of rounding them up and driving them out after the bull. Some had already followed, but the rest of them went out in a bunch at a rush, and the poor bull didn't know what was happening as they charged by him. As soon as I had seen the last of the heifers out of the field, I jumped the two or three hedges parallel to the lane, and dropped off the bank down into the road just in front of the heifers so that they shot down the lane, with the bull going willy nilly in the middle of the mob. As soon as they were all in the road, again I set Caravan alight and we went flat-out down the verge to pass the bunch before they shot past the field. I pulled up just past the gate in a clatter of sliding hoofs, and swung Caravan round just in time to turn the leading heifers into the field. The whole mob wheeled in like a squad of soldiers. Caravan stood watching them with his head and tail raised, and nostrils cracking. His pleasure in a job well done was clear to see. In actual fact we had taken less than a quarter of an hour on a task that would normally have taken seven or eight people half a day. I shut the gate, and rode Caravan the couple of hundred yards on to my favourite bathing pool, where I took his saddle and bridle off and turned him loose to graze and roll, while I spent the next two-and-a-half hours alternately bathing in the cold stinging river water, and lying in the sun in my birthday suit letting the sun warm me. The stolen pleasure was enhanced by the occasional sounds of the digger, reminding us that everyone else, men and horses, were doing a hard dirty task.

This story is told as an illustration of the fact that if your guess about what motivates animal behaviour is right, the rewards can be very great. If your guess is wrong of course, you have to pay the penalty, but the more you study what makes a horse tick, the better you get to know it, the more likely you are to be right.

This escapade with Caravan started me thinking again. If the understanding of a horse's motives could help me escape a morning's potato digging, I might be able to turn it to financial advantage as well. One of my principal sources of income during the summer months was from gymkhanas. I had quite a useful gymkhana pony that I took to two or three gymkhanas a week, and which made me a reasonable income already. But if I could understand what made Chester a good gymkhana pony, and what made her win, could I not make her win more often, and so increase our winnings? Could I not increase her *will* to win?

Now I knew one of the reasons why Chester was a good gymkhana pony was that *I* worked extremely hard at it, and put in an awful lot of schooling. And I thought there lazing on the river bank that it was quite possible that I had been over-schooling her: that I had been working her so hard that the work was becoming monotonous, and her enthusiasm was dwindling. So to see if my theory was right, I didn't work her for the next couple of days. When I took her to the gymkhana on the Saturday she was jumping out of her skin. She went extremely well and won more than her usual share of the prize money.

I also worked out that one of her motives for winning was that she wanted to please me, so that if I could make her want to please me more, she would want to win more. And so over the next three weeks I made a great point of making a great fuss of her when she won, and ignoring her when she didn't. It certainly seemed to improve her performance, though it was difficult to be absolutely certain how much of the improved performance was due to the fact that she wanted to please me and how much to the fact that she wasn't being worked quite so hard, and so was enjoying her work more. But the proof that working on her affection for me had paid off came about three weeks later, at Chinnock Gymkhana in the Gretna Green race.

The Gretna Green race at this time was quite simple: one person stood at the end of the field, while his partner, in this case a girlfriend of mine who always worked with me in this event, led the two horses down. Then the person on foot got on his own horse and they had to ride back hand in hand. On this occasion Biddy, to get a quick start, stationed herself and the two horses next to the starter. Unfortunately the starter was too enthusiastic, and he accidentally brought his flag down very hard across Chester's nose. Chester reared up, hung back, and smashed her bridle, and there was Biddy with her horse, and my bridle, but no horse on the other end of it. I saw what happened, and bellowed at the top of my voice: 'Chester.' She pricked her ears, saw me, and galloped straight down the field, with Biddy in hot pursuit. When Chester got to me she skidded to a halt. I pushed her round so that she was pointing in the right direction, jumped on her back just as Biddy came up with bridle, and her own pony, and away we went back to the finishing line, winning quite easily because Biddy had had no horse to lead.

There was some muttering afterwards about the way we had won, but it was quite legal: Biddy and both horses had come down to meet me, and the fact that on the way back my bridle was draped around Biddy on her pony and not on my pony's head was a very minor technicality. Chester's affection for me had indeed paid dividends. In fact over the last five weeks of the holidays, my income went up by nearly thirty percent, which proved to me without a shadow of doubt that the effort of trying to understand a horse's motives was extremely profitable.

Over the next two or three years I tried to increase this understanding. And other questions began to come to my mind. Exactly what for instance were the horse's physical needs? What other needs did they have? How did horses see things, and what did horses feel? And above all, what was it that made horses *different*? Horses, I was noticing increasingly, might come from the same place, with very similar parentage, and behave in completely different ways. On occasions even full brothers would react in opposite ways to a sudden noise; or a pat on the neck.

Whether I would ever have gone on to more serious research into horse psychology were it not for the death of a man called Hughes, I am not sure. But Mr Hughes died at the ripe old age of seventy-nine, and among the effects he left behind were three unbroken colts that he had bred out of the same mare by a stallion called Pollards.

I was a young man, newly married and set up on my own, when a friend of mine called John Jeffries bought these three colts from the widow, and asked me to break them. This I did, somewhat haphazardly, but I got them going nice and quietly, and he offered, instead of paying me for my work in cash, to give me an unbroken thirteen-two pony. I was agreeable, broke the pony, and took it to Exeter Market. Having sold her quite well, I stood around watching the other horses being sold with the money for the pony burning a hole in my pocket. A very nice fourteen-three skewbald gelding came into the ring which no one seemed to have a great interest in, so I bought him quite cheaply and left myself with the magnificent sum of thirty bob change. I took him back to his pen and was just putting him in, when someone came up and offered me a profit of ten pounds, which I very quickly took, and he took him home. (What I didn't know, and he didn't know of course, was that the pony was a rig. He had had him home about three days when the local riding school went past. The pony took one look at the classy filly that the owner of the riding school was riding, realised that the mare was in season, jumped the fence and chased the whole riding school right through the middle of Torquay, eventually obtaining the object of his desire in the main street. But that's another story.)

I, with seventy-one pound notes in my pocket, plus the thirty bob change I had from my previous transaction, was really on the ball looking for a horse to make a fortune out of. I went looking for Tim Horgan, who was a very old friend of mine and had been selling horses to my father for the previous thirty years. He always had a string of Irish horses at every sale, and when I got there he was busy selling a very nice four-year-old to an enthusiastic farmer. 'Sure he's a grand horse! Look at the size of him! And he's so quiet you could put your mother on him!' This went on for about ten minutes with Tim expanding on the virtues of the horse and its quietness and gentleness, until the sale was completed. The new owner went off to get a bridle and saddle.

'Is he quiet, Tim?' 'Sure enough.' 'Yes,' I said, 'but how quiet is he when you ride him?' 'Oh, we will know won't we when me laddo gets on his back,' Tim replied. When the young man returned, I assisted Tim and the new owner to saddle the horse, which may or may not have had a saddle on his back before, but he didn't appear to worry, and when the boy got on his back and rode him out of the yard he went quite quietly, though it was obvious that he didn't really know what bit and bridle were for.

After we had seen him disappear from view quite safely I told Tim what I was looking for. Most of the horses he had were too expensive for me. But he had one which looked just what I wanted. She was a well bred mare, about fifteen-three. But Tim was very cagey about her. 'Has she been ridden Tim?' 'Sure she's had a saddle on her.' 'How quiet is she?' 'That I wouldn't know.' 'But she is a six-year-old mare, Tim! She must have done a bit of work!' 'Sure she has done a bit of work!' Even in his desire to sell the horse, Tim was still being extremely cagey but eventually I bought her for sixty quid, and having had a very profitable day I took my new purchase home.

We were very fortunate that the mare was by a stallion which had been standing near my wife's home, so we 'phoned a friend of hers to make enquiries. An hour later he telephoned back. 'For God's sake, get rid of the bloody animal. She has been in every yard in Cork, and no one could ride her.' Every word Tim had said was true: she had done a lot of work. She had been long-reined, she had been lunged – in fact she had been lunged for four hours on end at times – she had had a saddle on her back. She had even had someone sitting on the saddle for up to two minutes. But she was unrideable.

This was just the sort of stimulus that I needed. The mare was a challenge. The following day we made a start on her. And this didn't mean taking her out on a lunging rein, and belting around until she was too tired to stand. Nor did it mean starving her, or keeping her short of water. Making a start on a horse like this in our book meant getting to know the horse, and getting the horse to know and trust you.

We called her Starry because she had a white star on her fore-head. For the first day or two working with Starry meant standing in the stable dodging her heels. But eventually we established some sort of truce, enough for her to allow me to go into the stable, or walk up to her and make a fuss of her. And then I got Leslie, my very pregnant wife, to give me a leg up, and I stayed there for a minute or two. Starry of course didn't have a bridle or a saddle on, just a rope head collar, and she didn't object too much. So I slipped off. On again, off. On again. The third time I eased myself up, instead of just leaning across her. I eased my leg over and sat up. And she stood quite quietly, still eating out of the bucket in the manger. So I told my wife to take the bucket out and use it to lead her out of the stable door. This she did and proceeded up the lane until Starry had finished the nuts in the bucket, at which point I very quickly stopped the mare, slid off and led her home again.

We did this for three days, riding her without a bridle or a saddle and just letting her follow the bucket with her breakfast up the road. I decided then that the mare had become quite civilized, so I put a saddle and a bridle on and got on to her. Or to be more exact I started to get on to her: I got my foot in the stirrup and was half way across the saddle before I landed in the dung heap. Since my wife's pregnancy didn't allow for much athletics and there was obviously going to be a great deal of athletics, I telephoned my father to come and give me a hand.

Since he and my stepmother were entertaining some very stuffy relatives for tea, he didn't need a second invitation, and about an hour later we made another start with Starry. This time my father held her head whilst I got on, and holding her very tight by the bridle, led her up the road to the nearest field. As soon as we got inside the gateway, he pointed her up the hill and leant against the gate post to enjoy the rodeo. And a rodeo he had. I could see then why the mare had been in every yard in Cork: she had learnt a new trick for getting people off in every one of them. She bucked in a straight line, she bucked up and down on one spot, she bucked around in a tight circle. She tried to get my legs by galloping up the fencing posts. But eventually, after a large number of falls, she and I came to a working arrangement: she wouldn't buck me off if I didn't kick her in the ribs. And since it was nearly my milking time we left it at that.

My father came over the following morning to work her again, and we had another rodeo. But it was only a third as vigorous as the first day, and on the third day, apart from two or three episodes of bucking and one of going flat-out with me straight into a hedge, she went extremely well. After about ten days I could ride her out of the yard with reasonable confidence that I'd still be in the saddle when I came back.

But there was no pleasure in riding her. She was extremely sullen, bad tempered and lethargic. If she couldn't buck and get me off she just sulked.

On the tenth day the horse that I was playing polo on went lame, which meant that I was short of something to ride that afternoon. So we took Starry instead. When we got to the polo ground I got on her, and had a very short rodeo before riding her out to play in a slow chukka of polo. For the first couple of minutes she was her sulky, miserable self. And then she suddenly began to realize what was happening, and for the first time since we had had her she cantered and galloped without bucking. I rode her in a second chukka at the end of the afternoon, and she began to go happily and willingly. At the end of a fortnight the transformation in Starry was complete. From a miserable, sullen, sulky bitch she had become a sweet, kind and happy pony. And she just loved polo.

I asked myself why a horse which people had been trying unsuccessfully to break for three years, and which I had found impossible to get working with any degree of amiability, should change in a fortnight and eight or ten chukkas of polo into a model of all that was, sweet, kind and willing? The key of course was that she enjoyed playing polo – which was not extraordinary since most polo ponies love the game. So it wasn't very difficult to reason out that she had been refusing to be ridden because her experience of being ridden had not been enjoyable, so she couldn't see any pleasure in it. But once she understood that being ridden meant that she could enjoy herself doing something that she liked doing, she was quite happy for anyone to sit on her back.

This is what started me thinking about what we knew about a horse's body, and what we could deduce about its needs and desires. We knew for example that its hearing is much the same as ours, whilst the shape of its eye means that it sees objects differently. This latter is of less consequence than it seems, since if you always saw a tree looking like a sausage, when you saw an object looking like a sausage you would know it was a tree: trees in short would always have the same appearance. So though a horse's eyesight is different from ours, we have no reason to assume that its ability to distinguish objects or categories of objects by sight is very different. We knew also that the horse's tolerance to heat and cold are much the same as man's, but that its feeding habits are different, the horse being vegetarian and man omnivorous.

As for the sexual needs of horses, we knew that the needs of the mare are less than those of the woman, since the mare comes into season only for a short period each month and hardly at all during the winter months. The heat period is only three or four days a month, compared with the twenty-four to twenty-five days a month for a woman. But the intensity of the heat when it comes is for that very reason bound to be greater, and the stress caused by that heat far more intense. As for males, we were mainly in contact with geldings, but they still have a certain amount of sexual drive, although this varies considerably from gelding to gelding.

These, as we saw them, were the horse's bodily needs. But we knew that horses had other needs as well, and that if we were to understand more of what made our horses tick, we had to discover what these needs were.

We had an example of one of them almost immediately. My hunter Honesty nearly severed her near fore tendon on a sheet of galvanized zinc, which meant that we had to have her in.

But she had a special friend, my point-to-pointer, Weeping Roger, and he at that time was out to grass, relaxing after a strenuous season of racing. We couldn't have him in as well, so we turned a pony out with him, which meant that he was reasonably happy and contented, but Honesty, in one of the loose boxes, immediately began to lose condition. She wasn't eating and her coat became dull. At first we put this down to the injury she had received, but her leg healed quickly, and still Honesty wasn't eating. We tried tempting her with bits of green from the garden – I went out cutting grass for her. But she showed her disdain for it by dunging on top of it. Still she lost condition, and still she refused to eat. We didn't find the key to the problem until one day we had to catch my daughter's pony to have it shod. Since he was a little devil to catch, we caught him the day before the blacksmith came and pushed him in Honesty's loose box for the night. I went out about ten o'clock to make sure that he wasn't bullying Honesty, and saw to my surprise that not only had she eaten her feed, but all her hay. So I put some more in, and went to bed. The following morning Honesty had eaten up all her previous night's feed, and she ate her breakfast like a starving man eating his last meal.

We shod Paddy's pony (he was extremely difficult to shoe, and since he was very small we put him down, rolled him over on his back and I sat on his chest whilst the blacksmith hammered the nails on to the legs sticking up in the air), and I turned him out again.

I put Honesty's feed in again, feeling pleased that at last she had started eating. But she didn't touch it. At last the penny dropped. So we spent the whole afternoon catching Paddy's pony again, and as soon as we put him in with her, she ate.

What had been causing the trouble, of course, was the fact that Honesty was an extremely sociable horse, and when she was deprived of companionship she had no desire to eat. She was getting into a state of depression. She didn't want to do anything. And this experience gave me a new insight into the range of drives and emotions and motives and needs that make up horse personality. This complex of feelings makes a horse what he is. And finding out exactly what these feelings were and how they inter-related was going to be long and difficult. But I realized that if I *could* understand and interpret them, I could make use of them to get better results for myself and to make my horses happy.

Another point that began to become increasingly clear was that there were a number of things that a horse wanted, and needed, which were on the face of it completely unnatural to him. For example, we knew that our horses loved jumping, that they wanted, and needed to jump. Now this is completely un-natural to the horse in the wild, so we decided that there must be a whole series of drives within the horse which arise not from nature but from conditioning, from the training *we* gave. Racing, playing polo, jumping and hunting were all examples. It was our training that made a horse want to beat other horses racing, to enjoy the scrimmage and rough and tumble of playing polo, to put in the extra little bit of effort that is needed in a good jumper. Some of our horses got so excited that they would refuse to eat on hunting mornings. None of these things was to be found in wild horses.

Then, just as we were digesting this lesson, came a time when we had a series of minor accidents among the horses. Accidents and injuries in horses come in phases. One may go for weeks, months or even years, and have no trouble at all, and then suddenly you no sooner heal one wound than you have another one, you no sooner have one lame horse sound than another is hobbling around on three legs.

This time one of the ponies banged his eye. Since there was a real risk that he would go blind, part of his treatment was to keep him in a darkened loose box. This we did for ten days or a fortnight, and after about the third day, I noticed he was becoming extremely bad tempered. After a week he was going mad every time you opened the door, trying to rush out. By the time his injured eye was healed, he seemed to be almost round the bend. But as soon as we began turning him out for an hour at dusk, he started settling down again. And gradually as the days went by, he was allowed out more and more in daylight, and after a week he was completely normal.

I attributed this behaviour at the time to the fact that he had been deprived of light, and subsequent work has verified my opinion. I also noticed that when a horse was tied up he never stood still, but changed from one leg to another, stepping forward a step, stepping backwards a step. So, as well as the need for light, he had a need for movement. And so we had to discover what might be termed the needs for mental stimulus: light, movement, a changing scene. These we saw as among the horse's inherited needs.

We eventually categorized the needs of the horse in four groups. The first comprised the bodily needs, such as food and water, warmth and sex. Next came other 'natural' needs, for movement, for light, and external stimulus. Third were what might be termed the social needs of the horse, for the company and understanding of his companions. And finally there was the fourth group, the conditioned needs that had come about from training by man.

But how could we recognize them, since we couldn't see them? And how, if we were meeting the needs right, were we to know?

We could continue with the method of trial and error, trying this and trying that. But this was very time-consuming, and at times even painful.

One spring, for example, I had a rather sour, bad-tempered horse which I was racing. After considerable thought I came to the conclusion he might be sullen because he didn't like men, and he might therefore go much better for a woman. So my ever-loving, and pregnant wife said she would try him in a gallop and see. One morning with great difficulty we hoisted her five-foot-one, and her pregnant tum, up on to the big sixteen-two horse. Once she was there, with the large spread around the middle, she was reasonably stable, so we rode the two miles up to the gallop, with Wolsey walking along apparently quite happily.

We got to the gallop and lined up, and I said 'go.' Away we went. Slowly increasing our pace on the slow gallop to three-parts speed, Wolsey settled down and lengthened his stride. But after we had gone about half a mile he decided a pregnant tum bouncing up and down on the back of his neck wasn't comfortable, so he proceeded to put in a colossal series of bucks. Leslie settled back quite happily, enjoying the transition from the pounding gallop to a rocking-horse motion, but unfortunately her stirrup leather broke in the midst of a powerful buck, and she started to slide off to one side. All should have been well: she would have slipped off, and that would have been that. But unfortunately her tummy stuck on the saddle, and she was half of her on one side, half on the other, and she couldn't go either way. I galloped alongside, shouting helpful instructions such as 'Get back on,' 'Stop him,' 'Slide off.' All of which was to no avail, and I was told so in no uncertain terms. But eventually, chance took a hand, as Wolsey stumbled over a large anthill and Leslie described a neat parabola straight into a gorse bush. And since the language that came out of the gorse bush was descriptive and very blasphemous, I took myself and my horse off to catch Wolsey, who was grazing about two hundred yards away. Wolsey had shown his opinion of lady riders in no uncertain terms. When we got back to the gorse bush, I put Leslie on to my horse, and rode the miscreant home, whilst Leslie told me what she thought of me, my race horses, and that gorse bush.

Thus it became imperative that we should improve our communication with our horses by some method other than guesses tested by trial and error.

2: *We Learn To Communicate With Horses*

We were making a rather slow beginning with our work on communication with horses,* when, after the birth of our first daughter, I bought a horse for my wife. He was a fifteen-two brown gelding, and when I bought him for twenty-six guineas at Exeter Market, he was more or less unmanageable. We called him Cork Beg, and from the very beginning we both found that we had a special affinity with him. We could understand his feelings, convey our feelings to him as it were instinctively, and anticipate his actions and reactions.

And he started us observing and trying to understand how he conveyed and received messages to and from other horses. At this stage we weren't making much headway, because we made the same mistake as everyone else looking at animal communication: we were trying to put a set meaning to each sound used by a horse.

There are a few sounds that can be made sense of in this way: for example, a mare calling her foal to her, or reassuring the foal, uses a very distinctive sound. But by and large we found that there was very little consistency between one horse's use of a sound, and another's. Shortly after we acquired Cork Beg, however, we made what I considered to be our major breakthrough in animal communication.

One night I was unable to sleep, and during the long watches I started thinking about this and that, as people do. One of the things I was turning over in my mind was whether the apparent stupidity of the *au pair* girl who was helping my wife out with the baby was really natural stupidity, bloody-mindedness, or

* For an account of this see my earlier book *Talking with Horses*, Souvenir Press, 1976.

simply inability to understand plain English. The girl had come from Italy and although she could read and write English fluently, she seemed to find it very difficult to understand us. It occurred to me that the problem really arose in interpreting the nods, the grunts and the murmurs which constitute conversation between most human beings, and which vary according to language and culture and even among families and individuals. Language, in short, was not a question of sounds only – it was a whole complex of verbal and non-verbal communication, some of it highly individual and dependent on familiarity for its comprehension. It was exactly the same problem we were facing with the horse.

So it was that I realized that each horse has his own individual language, just as each human being does. He uses sounds to convey various meanings, and anyone who knows him will be able to understand, but there is no set pattern of sound, just as there is no common pattern of sound in the vast variety of human languages.

Even among four people speaking the same language – such as English – you might find four different ways of expressing agreement, for example. One might agree with you by saying 'aye'; one might say 'yes'; one nod his head; and one just grunt 'mm, mm.' You would know they meant that they all agreed with you. But they would be using three different sounds, and one sign, to mean exactly the same thing. So it is with our horses. So we began to make a list of the messages we understood, such as 'Where's my bloody breakfast?', which is the phrase we use when a horse wants food, and to set out the various ways in which each horse conveyed that message: Cork Beg says this by a wicker, Weeping Roger says it by banging his bowl; Starlight says it by shaking her head up and down, and so on. We very quickly had a list of ways that a horse might use to communicate a single message, and we found that the variations around a particular meaning were not very great. We found by this means we could begin to make a pattern of horse vocabulary.

Over the next ten to fifteen years we discovered that the horse uses eleven distinctive notes to convey a message by sound.

These vary from a low snuffle to a scream of rage, fear or pain. But we also discovered that it was pointless to consider sound only in trying to understand horse communication for a horse uses signals and body movements just as frequently; and eventually we were to come to understand that he also uses methods more subtle than man himself: extra-sensory perception and telepathy. It was as pointless to study one of these methods in isolation, as it would be to try to understand English by studying only the verbs.

We also discovered that each horse expresses itself differently. So we started to compile a dictionary of signs and sounds used by horses, and we found that, apart from a few exceptions, it was impossible to say that a certain sound meant a certain thing. But it was possible within certain limits to say that a horse would convey a certain meaning in one of a defined number of ways. 'Welcome', for example, can be said by a low wicker; it can also be said by a gesture, such as rubbing his nose against you.

On the other hand, the welcome wicker might have a number of meanings as well as 'welcome.' Cork Beg would say 'Welcome' to my wife using his wicker, but the same wicker could mean 'Come here' to his girl friend; or, to me, an instruction to hurry with his feed. He would use exactly the same note on each occasion. It was, we discovered, the context in which the note was used that told you exactly what the horse was saying.

By raising the note of his wicker, we found that the horse could put an imperative into what he was saying. If he got impatient with his current girl friend, for instance, the wicker of 'Darling come here,' would very quickly change to a higher and more urgent note which said 'Get over here immediately you lazy little bitch'. And he did the same to me if I didn't bring him his breakfast straight away in the morning. 'Where is my breakfast,' would change to 'Where is my bloody breakfast you fool, I'm starving.'

The 'welcome' call alone had six imperatives, all of which meant approximately the same thing if used in greeting, but the higher notes used in a different context could also mean, 'Is anybody about?' A similar note would be used by a companion in reply, to say 'I'm here.'

All of this sounds very complicated at first, but once you start understanding your horses, it will be much simpler than it sounds. We also found that when a horse discovered that the messages that he was trying to convey were understood, either by another horse or by man, his range of communication could be extended considerably.

Our researches revealed that there were some thirty or so basic phrases which were used by the domestic horse; but over the course of time we discovered that there were also another seventeen which were used occasionally, or in special situations.

For example a whole series of messages applied to the love play between mare and stallion; and another set of messages were used by the mare in caring for a foal.

Different breeds of horses have slightly different ways of using sounds and signs, and in a large group of mixed horses and ponies, horses of the same breed tend to form smaller groups in a very short time. So though the way of imparting any message does vary from horse to horse, similarities may be seen in horses of the same breed.

In the same way one may trace similarities according to age, or sex – bearing in mind that there are of course three sexes in domestic horses: male, female and gelding.

The horse has, as I have mentioned, eleven different tones of voice. Two of these are made by inhaling: one is a sniff, the other a gentle breathing in. The remaining nine tones are made by exhaling: the snort, the blow through the nostrils, the wicker and the whinny use the nostrils; the neigh and the bell come from the upper nasal region; the squeals come from the nose and mouth; and finally the scream comes from the lung, in a gust of pain, fear, and rage. Each of these eleven tones can be made in a large number of keys, which again help to convey the meaning.

In the wild, the stallion has the greatest vocal range; but the mare has the ability to convey the greatest number of messages.

Among domesticated horses, however, it is a mare owned by a man, or a gelding owned by a woman, that will extend its vocabulary to the greatest degree. In some cases, in the process of understanding and response between man and beast, the vocabulary of the horse can be almost doubled.

In learning to interpret the horse's vocal sounds, the tone, note and delivery are all to be taken into account, and so are the non-verbal messages – the body signs – that accompany the sound. A message such as 'that hurt' for instance, may be communicated in several different forms: by a sharp intake of breath, a wicker, a whinny, a neigh or a scream of pain. Each of these taken by itself may sound like a dozen other messages, but taken with the body signs and the feeling you get from the horse, the meaning will be very plain.

The following story very well illustrates what I mean. Some years ago we had about fifty acres of land about twelve miles from our main farm, on which we ran some odds and ends of ponies and young horses that we weren't doing anything particular with. I would go over once or twice a week to see them, and going over was always a penance as it entailed doing about eight miles on the main Sidmouth to Seaton road which, during the summer, was a hell of roaring cars, stinking petrol, choking exhaust fumes, frustrating traffic jams and frayed tempers. But it was worth it, because once you got there – I always tried to go over in the evening – you found yourself in a valley completely secluded from the rush of the main road. It was like walking into a patch of paradise – I always felt rather like a lost soul who, having had a taste of hell, was finally allowed through the Pearly Gates.

This particular evening as I walked through the gate, the only sounds I could hear were the liquid note of a thrush and the croak of a crow. As I wandered down looking for the ponies through the towering, billowing crowds of bracken, with the sun beating down on my neck, I could almost believe in fairies – especially when I came to clearings in the bracken which had been mowed by the razor edges of a thousand rabbits' teeth.

Eventually after a very short search I found the ponies sheltering under a patch of trees. They were standing like statues, the only movement being the pendulum-like swing of their tails, ticking away the seconds to eternity.

My peace was shattered by the realization that Mousie and her foal were missing. I foresaw a very tedious search through the alder trees down the bottom, and was just turning round for a preliminary search through the bracken when I heard a sharp and imperative whinny from below me. I immediately walked down to where Mousie was standing, in obvious irritation and rage. Mousie was on one side of the bog, and her foal was on the other side of the bog, beyond the next door fence. I slipped a piece of twine over Mousie's neck and led her back down the side of the bog to where I knew there was a weak place in the fence. The foal, neighing in agitation when she saw us going away from her, immediately started to walk along the top of the bank. She fell off. Mousie wickered encouragement to her, the foal got to her feet and cantered down the other side of the fence trying to keep up. Eventually we came to the weak place, and without very much difficulty got the foal through. But now we came to another obstacle. As far as the foal was concerned, it was impossible to walk through six inches of water in the stream. I led Mousie away, Mousie called to the foal to follow, and eventually she summoned up her courage, put in a gigantic leap and cleared the water by at least two feet. Mousie started wickering reassurances to the foal, who shot her head under the milk bar, and took some well-earned nourishment.

As I walked back through the bracken to my car, and the hell of a main road, I realized that Mousie had illustrated for me a whole library of vocal messages. She had used in fact only a small range of whinny and wicker sounds, but her movements, her stance and the situation itself had given them a series of quite specific meanings, clear as much to me as to the foal itself. So my journey had been very much worth while.

As well as the forty-seven basic messages we were eventually able to identify through our researches, we discovered there were also fifty-four sub-messages. Some of these we assumed to be natural to horses in the wild, others not, but we found that even a wild horse fresh from the hills would learn the 'domesticated' vocabulary very quickly, usually from other horses.

Our best teacher without doubt was Cork Beg, who had the most extensive vocabulary of any horse we've ever had. We very quickly discovered that, as he extended his own vocabulary, he was teaching other horses as well, and we ran a series of trials over the eighteen years we had him to see how quickly he could teach other horses basic phrases.

We would put a wild and untouched pony in with Cork Beg at feeding time, for instance. Cork Beg would ask for food, and in a very short time his young companion would be whinnying in imitation. Then, when segregated again, the colt would ask for food when he was hungry. Of a hundred and twenty-two cases only three had not learned to ask for food within seven days.

All these experiments, our experience in communicating with horses and the dictionary we compiled of horse language, are treated at length in my book *Talking with Horses*. Here I propose only to remind the reader of the basic principles of horse communication, because no one can begin to study horse psychology without first learning to read the messages his animal is sending.

Anyone wishing to understand his horse should start by learning to observe the whole complex of body movements – some of them the mere flick of a muscle – with which the horse signals his messages. Horses' sign language is far more easily understood than their vocal messages, partly because the signs follow a far more definite pattern. Each sign tends to have a consistent meaning. Aggressive movements for instance are easy to interpret. The sign may be a mere flicking of the skin, or the relaxation of a set of muscles, but the message is there for anyone to see. Most horsemen anyway understand most of these signs, and all vets use the sign language when diagnosing a sick or an injured horse. In conveying messages the ears are nearly always used, but they mean far more than most people realize. Everyone knows that the ears flat back mean 'I'm going to buck.' The ears half back on the other hand simply mean, 'I'm relaxed,' or, if you have the habit of talking to your horses when you are riding as I have, 'I'm listening to the tone of your voice'. In some cases ear movements have a distinct meaning in themselves, and in others they are only part of a whole message being conveyed by body movements, voice and other means simultaneously. The neck, tail, legs, skin and all the muscles are used to give signs. But remember that interpretation can be learnt only by being patient, and observing the horse quietly.

When we came to trying to talk back to the horse, of course, we could not reproduce his signs exactly, but we could use our own bodies to convey feelings: comfort, encouragement, reproach. We found that we could use our arms to comfort, as the horse uses his neck. And our hands and fingers could make similar caressing movements to his head and nose: the feeling he got when being caressed by the tip of our fingers was very similar to the feeling he got when being caressed by the nose of another horse. In exactly the same way a slap of the hand gave a sting like that of a nip from an outraged companion.

The arrival of the Pooka, a fourteen-two three-year-old Skewbald gelding, illustrated how both signs and sounds could be put to use in horse psychology. The Pooka kicked, and kicked badly at anyone who went near him. His owner and everyone else was terrified with him. So when he arrived we turned him straight out with Cork Beg, Honesty and Wolsey. Cork Beg jogged over to investigate him. As soon as Cork Beg got near enough to him, the Pooka whipped around and lashed out. Cork Beg, as boss of the herd, wasn't having this. He quickly switched ends so that his well shod heels were pointing towards Pooka, and belted hell out of him. Pooka returned to the corner. Cork Beg followed and again kicked the living daylights out of him. Ten seconds later, before I could intervene, Cork Beg trotted away, leaving Pooka cowering in terror in the ditch. Ten minutes later the Pooka very slowly and hesitantly edged towards the other three horses. When he got to within about five yards of them, Honesty, who was normally extremely mild and inoffensive, turned her head, put her ears back and raised one leg. The Pooka retreated in terror. All ideas of being the big bumptious bully had disappeared in the ten seconds' treatment meted out to him by Cork Beg.

I noted that instant and severe retribution had made an immediate change in Pooka's whole attitude. When he entered the field his one desire had been to dominate the whole group, and yet thirty seconds later, his one idea was not to offend anyone. And he even seemed quite happy with his new humbled status in the herd, though his humility receded slightly over the next day or two as his natural youth and exuberance once more asserted themselves.

This example of how the desires and habits of a horse could be changed by using the correct method of communication was not lost on me, so when I got the Pooka in two or three days later to start work on him, and he swung round and lashed out at me, I put my new knowledge to good use. I dodged his kick with a nifty piece of footwork which brought me at right angles to him, and as I landed, brought one foot back and landed the toe of my boot in his midriff. The Pooka was turned into a pillar of salt, so great was his surprise. So to drive the message home I followed my left boot with my right boot. This was too much for the Pooka, who shrivelled up in a corner like a deflated balloon. I stood still for two or three seconds, and then started talking to him quietly, walking towards him. He shrank to an even smaller size, but allowed me to get a hand on him to touch him, and then slowly, I worked my fingers round, still talking to him gently. He gradually began to reflate, until he was standing normally, though very tense. Another ten minutes' talking and gentle rhythmic movement of my fingers on his skin brought him into a relaxed and happy state.

Having got to this point, I left him alone, and went and got him something to eat. As I came in with the bucket he made a rush at the doorway. I clouted him smartly across the nose, and he retreated to his corner and stared at me. This form of treatment was completely new to him. He had been shouted at, he'd been hit before for kicking people but no one had ever slapped him across the nose and then walked over and made a fuss of him because he had done the right thing. And I could see that the communication was getting through to him very quickly. At the same time his attitude to human beings and life was being altered. He was learning that when he did the wrong thing he was instantly punished, but when he did the right thing he was made a fuss of.

The more we studied how the horses were communicating with each other and with us, however, the more we came to realize that there was more to communication than signs and sounds. We became convinced that the horses were sensing our moods and feelings and anticipating our wishes. I began to read around the subject, and my reading reinforced my suspicion that some form of communication other than sounds and signs was at work. Although nothing I read treated the subject scientifically or even explicitly, all the books on horses seemed to contain phrases like 'put your heart over a fence and your horse will follow.' We called this undefined factor in communication Extra-Sensory Perception. We knew that the fact that our horses seemed instinctively to know our moods could in part be explained by what they could see and hear, but there was more to it than this. To discover the real nature of this instinctive knowledge, we ran over the next ten years a series of experiments with pairs of horses whom we knew to be friends – what we call empathic pairs.

An empathic pair is simply two horses which are mentally and emotionally close to each other. Such horses may find themselves automatically in tune with each other from the first time they meet: these will probably be of the same breed and type. Or alternatively they may become mentally in tune with each other through close and constant companionship. A truly empathic pair is a pair of horses who literally think as one. From among the forty or fifty horses we were handling each year, over a period of five years we selected eleven pairs in all, of which we found eight pairs suitable for our experiments.

These experiments I have described in detail in *Talking with Horses*, and I shall only summarize them here. But what we learnt in these experiments about the extraordinary mental capabilities of the horse was fundamental to our future work on horse psychology.

Five experiments were involved, which we ran over a period of three days. We carried out each experiment three times, varying the horses that we were working with.

In the first experiment, the two horses were placed in separate stalls, well out of sight and hearing of each other. One of each pair was then fed in a plastic container. For us to record a positive reaction his empathic pair had at the same time to indicate that he wanted food. To make quite sure there was no question of habit coming into the experiments, the horses were not fed at the same time every day, nor were they fed at their regular feeding times. In twenty-one out of the twenty-four tests we had a positive response, which was better than we had dared hope. That is to say, on twenty-one out of the twenty-four occasions, when we were feeding one horse, the second horse, even though he couldn't see or hear us in any way, knew that we were feeding his empathic pair and demanded food.

In the second experiment, one of each pair was taken out of the yard into a field and excited by cantering, jumping, and generally getting him hotted up. For this experiment the horse pair was always in a loose box where he couldn't see his companion leaving the yard. A positive result was recorded if the horse in the loose box became excited.

Experiment three was a more or less complete failure, because the positive results left too much room for human error. It involved trying to calm an excited horse by gentling – caressing and calming by voice – not him but his companion. The difficulty lay in deciding how long it would have taken the horse to relax *without* the gentling of his pair.

But the fourth experiment was quite simple. I would talk to and make a fuss of one of the pair, usually the one I liked the least, and a positive result was recorded if the other, well out of sight and hearing, showed signs of jealousy: that is if it became unsettled and disturbed.

The fifth experiment was rather an unpleasant one and I don't think I would like to repeat it. It involved frightening one of the horses. But since one of the most basic emotions in an animal is fear, I felt that it was extremely important to prove that fear as well as excitement, jealousy, and the desire for food could be conveyed by Extra-Sensory Perception. In this case I frightened the horse by rushing toward him, clenching my fist, and chasing him round and round the box until he was extremely nervous. A positive result was recorded if his companion became nervous too. This happened in sixteen out of the twenty-four cases.

Out of the one hundred and nineteen experiments we carried out, we had positive results in eighty-one cases, a marginal result in twelve more, and a possible result in eleven cases, which gave us a definite overall success rate of 67.5 percent: well above the rate that could be predicted by pure chance. We had to conclude that some extra-sensory form of communication was indeed being used.

A point of interest that arose from this series of experiments was that we found that the horses seemed to be able to switch from one thought wave-length to another. That is, some horses who have one natural thought-pattern, according to their breed and upbringing, learnt to communicate with horses of quite different breed and thought-pattern after a long period of close companionship.

So we ran another series of experiments to test these thought-patterns. We chose four horses, each of which we knew had communication with at least one other horse in the group. For convenience we will call them horses A, B, C and D.

We discovered that if we fed horse A, horses B, C and D all indicated a desire for food. If we fed horse A, having removed horse B to some distance away, horses C and D did NOT ask for food. Similarly if we fed horse A whilst horse B was present, and horse C was absent, horse B would ask for food but horse D would not. If we fed horse D without horse C being present, neither horses B nor A would ask for food. Therefore we were able to conclude that

Horse A had communication with horse B.

    "   B   "   "   "   " A & C.

    "   C   "   "   "   " B & D.

    "   D   "   "   "   " C, and not with any of the other horses.

It would seem therefore that some horses were able to communicate only with horses of a similar thought-pattern to their own, while others – in this case horses B and C, could communicate with horses of different patterns.

We also discovered that Extra-Sensory Perception thought-patterns are not a static thing; by companionship and association horses could and did change their thought-patterns over a period of time.

This concept of thought-patterns helped to explain why a horse can get on well with one horse and not with another. And we discovered that our ability to get through to any horse was entirely dependent on our ability to think on the same wave-length, that is to learn his pattern of thought.

I discovered early on, for example, that I could get through to thoroughbreds without any difficulties. But I had a great deal of difficulty in establishing any rapport with small ponies. Over the years I have developed an ability to switch wave-lengths from one horse to another, but this took a lot of work and a lot of practice.

Extra-Sensory Perception, it emerged from our work eventually, apparently has four different functions, which may be used separately or possibly together.

The first is to convey mood: friendly or hostile, peaceful or excited.

The second is to convey emotion, such as anger or love.

The third is to convey needs, such as hunger and thirst.

And fourth, these three functions together enable the horse also to convey limited ideas: such as 'here is good grass', 'let's go away' or 'I'm hungry'. 'I'm hungry' or 'Here is good grass' would come through to another horse simply as hunger, and hunger diminished, and 'I'm frightened, let's run away', would come through as fear, and fear diminished.

We realized of course in all our work on communication that the horse is of comparatively limited intellect: we thought of it in human terms as that of a child of about eight, though a stupid horse could have the mental capacity of a dull seven-year-old and a clever horse could have the ability of an intelligent nine-year-old. And we very quickly learnt that the intelligent ones were the most difficult horses, and often unrideable if they had been mishandled. But these were the horses that I preferred, since they extended my ability to the limit.

My interest in Extra-Sensory Perception, and the work we did on it, was first triggered off by the purchase of an emaciated and neglected eight-year-old gelding named Weeping Roger. This purchase nearly led to the breakdown of our marriage. I can never resist buying an emaciated, broken-down old thoroughbred, I've got a spiritual kinship with them; but emaciated and broken-down old thoroughbreds cost a fortune to feed, and they usually mean trouble, so Leslie when she sees me after one is likely to cut up very rough indeed. But on this occasion I was a little bit too quick for her, and I bought Weeping Roger.

When I began to exercise Roger, I found that all I had to do was get on his back, slip my hands into my pockets (it was winter, and cold) and think where I wanted to go, and the pace I wanted him to go at. I could direct and control him entirely by thinking what I wanted to do next. Now how much this was due to un-conscious signals I was giving him, and how much to Roger's ability to interpret *my* thought-patterns, I can't definitely know. The only thing I know is that by working on the sub-ject consciously I could control him. Thinking I was on to a good thing, I thought I would try exactly the same thing on Wolsey.

So the following morning I got on to Wolsey, and since it was particularly cold, jammed my hands in my trouser pockets and started off. All went well for the first fifty yards. Then Wolsey, instead of walking as I wanted him to, started trotting. So with great concentration, I relaxed my body to make Wolsey relax, and thought about the muscular movements of the walk. To no avail. Wolsey's trot quickened, very shortly became a canter, and then a hard gallop. With me still thinking hard about walking, we proceeded up the track until Wolsey, finding his head free, decided to put it between his knees, throw four colossal bucks and stop suddenly to watch with great satisfaction as I turned three very neat somersaults in the air and landed on my back-side. Rubbing the painful bruise left by a large stone on my posterior, I walked back down to the yard to recapture Wolsey, who had preceded me there at the rate of knots. This gave me adequate time to realize that you cannot control every horse by Extra-Sensory Perception.

So it was a question of back to the drawing board. By pains-taking study we discovered that the limitations on the use of Extra-Sensory Perception as a means of control are as follows:

a) when you are using it the horse is entirely free to do what he wants;

b) its effectiveness is limited by your own ability to get through to that particular horse; and

c) in exactly the same way as when you are trying to control or understand a horse using signs and sounds, you have to see any single aspect of communication as only part of the whole pattern of language, and not rely on only one part of the whole.

In other words, it is impossible to communicate with the horse successfully using only signs and sounds, and it is just as impossible to communicate with a horse using Extra-Sensory Perception without using signs and sounds as well.

Our work on Extra-Sensory Perception led to the discovery of a fourth method of communication, used comparatively rarely but important all the same. We discovered between 1958 and 1964 that whole mental pictures may be transmitted from one animal to another: that horses can and do have the ability to communicate by telepathy. The two animals do not necessarily have to be of the same species, but they usually are. And, we found that we could use the horse's ability to 'read' telepathic messages in our riding by 'transmitting' mental pictures ourselves, mainly of where we wanted the horse to go. Also, when we came to an object the horse was likely to shy at, we discovered that by gazing intently at the object we could make the horse see it for what it was, a stone or a twig, not a tiger about to spring. So he didn't shy.

Early in 1958 we had a grey gelding called Iron Side sent down to us from Ascot. He was said to be unrideable because of his shying: he would refuse to pass quite simple objects, and shy into the path of oncoming traffic, which made him extremely dangerous to ride.

I guessed from the beginning that part of the trouble was in the weakness of his owner, but first I had him checked for defective vision. The vet examined his eyesight, and after exhaustive tests he decided that his vision was absolutely normal; but that due to the position of his eyes, and his very prominent cheek bones, he wasn't seeing objects behind and below him as well as a horse normally does. When loose, this didn't matter because he was constantly turning his head, but when being ridden on a tight rein he would have difficulty. Since his owner was so nervous about his shying, she was keeping him on an extremely tight rein, which of course would make him very nervous in turn.

I set out to cure this, first by riding him on a very slack rein and making him stop, look, and walk up to any object he shied at. Then I discovered that if I rode him on a slack rein and at the same time gazed intently at any likely object myself, he didn't seem to need to shy at all. And after about a fortnight riding him like this, including four hard days' hunting, he became quiet and sensible and almost completely stopped shying.

We also found that horses used telepathy among themselves to direct other horses to food and water, especially over distances when they were out of earshot and out of sight of each other; or to split the herd in time of danger.

To test our telepathy theory we devised what we called the Kit-e-Kat experiment, inspired by the television advertisements starring the white cat, Arthur. Cork Beg was offered two containers of food, and I had to try to direct him to the one out of which I wanted him to eat, using nothing but telepathy. There was considerable preparation and training before we could start, but after a fortnight's training we ran a series of twelve experiments, and in all twelve of them he chose the container to which I had directed him.

Cork Beg was a very easy subject, because he wanted to please. But nevertheless I had to learn a very intense form of concentration: the picture of the feed laying in the bottom of the bucket had to be very vivid in my mind's eye. Above all, such an experiment depends on complete communication between man and horse.

Also, over ten years, we developed the habit of recording telepathic communication whenever it seemed to have occurred. When we thought we had telepathic communication with one of our horses or with each other, we made a note of what had happened, and, most important of all, recorded the time that it had happened. In the end we had thirty or forty proven cases of telepathy: three recorded occurrences, with exact times, were across distances of over eighteen miles, and one instance was over two hundred and forty miles, although we were unable to count this as a verified account because there was no recording of the exact time, for our definition of verified telepathic communicatio: required that the time be recorded within a quarter of an hour, and that the picture received must be recorded in writing at the time it was received.

It is easy to identify what animal you are receiving the message from, since he won't be in the picture you are receiving. So if for example I received a telepathic communication from Cork Beg, I would know I was receiving it from Cork Beg and not from Iantella, if Iantella was in the picture and Cork Beg was not.

Telepathy is the most difficult form of communication to learn, though since it is used only to a very limited extent, the skill is not essential to the handling of horses.

But our work on communication was only part of our continuing work on Horse Psychology. We wanted really to understand what made our horses tick.

3: *First Lessons in Horse Behaviour*

As we began better to understand what our horses were saying to us, and to interpret it, we also began to see that we could not generalize about horses in general from the individual behaviour of any horse.

We could see for example that the things that excited Cork Beg left Wolsey completely cold, and vice-versa. Cork Beg was a very shy feeder. He'd pick a mouthful of food out of his basin, then walk over to the door and have a look to see what was going on outside. Then he might or might not go back and have another mouthful. Whereas Wolsey's whole life revolved around his belly: the only real interest he had in life, other than hunting, was to see how much he could stuff into his mouth, and how quickly. So if we wanted Wolsey to do something in particular, such as allow himself to be loaded on a lorry, we had only to rattle a bucket of nuts, and Wolsey would be ready to follow you through the gates of hell to get at them. But since Cork Beg wasn't interested in food at all it was no incentive to him to try and tempt him with a bucket of nuts, and we had to invent subtler encouragements.

The two horses' likes and dislikes were as different as they were different physically; and if their likes and dislikes were different it seemed probable that their psychological patterns would be different too.

We could not observe thought-patterns. But we could observe the way such patterns were expressed in behaviour, so we set out to study horse behaviour. Above all we were interested in the horses' reactions to us, and to our actions. But we started by studying the horses' reactions to each other. The first task was to watch our own horses, very carefully, and with open minds. One of the first things we observed was that whilst two friends would caress each other with their noses, and scratch each other with their teeth, they never patted each other. The nearest thing to a pat that one horse gave another was a bite or a kick. So we concluded that if we patted a young or a nervous horse, the horse would think that we were punishing it for something. We also saw that when a strange horse approached another, he would sniff, or blow through his nostrils at it. And that when any horse was frightened by something, it would go into the main bunch and seek bodily contact and reassurance. A mare too would reassure a frightened foal by nuzzling it. And we imitated these actions as best we could with our own bodies.

Soon we found that we were having far less trouble with difficult and nervous horses. One of our first tests came when my friend, Henry Squires of Bower Hinton Martock, brought me two unbroken colts of about fifteen-two hands, straight off Sedgemoor. They were turned into the yard, but I managed to separate them into two adjoining loose boxes with comparative ease, simply by taking Wolsey into the yard, leading him into the first of the loose boxes and driving the colts in after him. Then we took Wolsey out, and the colts of course tried to shoot out too. We let one back into the yard and quickly shut the door on the other. Then Wolsey was taken into the adjoining loose box, the second colt followed him, and was shut in in turn.

I started working with the first colt, a grey gelding that we called Tinsel. He was very wild and very nervous. His only experience of man had been being caught for castration in the spring, so it was hardly surprising.

Previously our method had been to get a halter on to the colt somehow, and leave him tied up for a while to fight the halter. Then I'd simply get on his back until he bucked himself out. Whilst this was very exciting, I was absolutely certain it wasn't the best way to quieten a nervous horse. So putting my new observation into practice, this time I just walked into the loose box and shut the door. Tinsel made a very creditable attempt at climbing up the walls, but there was no escape. So he stood in the far corner and shivered. I just blew at him, and was very agreeably surprised to see how quickly he settled down. Slowly, one inch at a time, I eased myself towards the middle of the loose box. Each time I moved, he froze like a statue ready for flight. But after about half an hour I managed to get right up to him. As chance would have it, I came not to his head but to the middle of his body and slowly and very tentatively stretched out my hand. As I touched his coat with my fingers, it was as if he had been branded with a red hot iron: he exploded into a frenzy of belting around the box. I just stood still until he came to rest again. And again I edged into him, and touched him with my fingers. This time, apart from trying to disappear through the wall of the box, he didn't move. Slowly and gently I moved my fingers round until I got the whole of my hand, and then the whole of my body up against him. After about five minutes of this treatment he relaxed completely.

Having succeeded beyond my wildest dreams, I left him for the day. I came back to him early the following morning however, and by lunch time the following day I had a halter on him without any battle at all. Very quickly he came to look upon me as an extremely friendly animal.

His companion Russet, whilst even more nervous to begin with, relaxed quicker still, and I had him riding quite quietly within about three days.

Having demonstrated to my own satisfaction the effective application of horse psychology, I went back to my work on equine behaviour with renewed zest.

I found that each piece of work was falling into three stages. First I would observe the behaviour of the horses among themselves in the field, or the response of a horse to some action of mine, and make a note of what I saw. Then I would have to think about it, to deduce what motivation might lie behind the behaviour I had observed. And having made my deduction, I would carry out an experiment to see whether I could reproduce that behaviour with other horses, in the same way.

I could see, for example, that the horses got excited if I blew the hunting horn. Now it didn't take very much intelligence to guess that it was not only my accomplishment as a musician that was sending the horses into ecstasies, but the association of the sound of the horn with the excitement of the hunt. I could verify this in two ways. First I played a variety of musical instruments to see whether the horses were interested in them – which of course they were not. Then I blew the hunting horn to horses that had no experience of hunting whatever. Again there was no response. I then felt justified in concluding that it was the association with the hunt that excited the horses when I blew the hunting horn.

One of the aspects of horse behaviour that had always interested us was the question of dominance within the herd. We observed over some ten years that certain horses, irrespective of their size, would take over the leadership of the herd, while other horses, no matter what group of horses you put them with, would take a subservient position. We also found that horses gravitated naturally to one of four groups within the herd: the boss group, the upper middle group, the lower middle group or the bottom group.

Then we had a little bit of time on our hands, and decided to run a series of tests or trials on herd behaviour. We split the main herd into three separate groups, and as each new horse arrived we would put him in with one of these groups. After about seven days we would note the position he had assumed within the herd. Then we would remove him from herd A, and put him into herd B, again note the position he assumed in that herd, and repeat the process in herd C.

Herd A was a group of seven registered Welsh Cobs, all similarly bred and from the same farm.

Herd B was a mixed group of thirteen-two and fourteen-two ponies.

And herd C was again a mixed group, of two-year-olds, three-year-olds and twelve-twos.

We found our earlier observations completely verified: it didn't matter which group the new horse entered – and as a complete stranger he would not know the other horses of course – he automatically took the same position every time. If he was a top echelon horse, he went into the top group of the herd. If he was a subservient horse he'd go to the tail of the herd. And if he belonged to one of the middle groups, he would go there.

A classical example of this behaviour was Star Light. Star Light was a twelve-two stallion which I had bought in Llanbyther. We brought him home and had him castrated the next day. I knew that after castration he would make an extremely high quality gelding.

We put him in herd C first. And after he had demolished the two leaders of that herd without any difficulty whatever, we took him out and put him straight in amongst the Welsh Cobs. Every one of the Welsh Cobs was well over fourteen-one, and they were all extremely strong, rumbustious geldings. Rostellan, who was the boss of the herd at the time, trotted over with his brother Red to investigate the intruder. Star Light just stood and watched the approach of these two seasoned campaigners. They came one from either side of him, so that whichever way he turned one of them could clobber him. Star Light just watched, and I watched Star Light. Rostellan trotted up towards his head, whilst Red circled slightly to one side so that he could put two crafty heels into Star Light's ribs. Star Light let them get just close enough, then he pivoted like a ballet dancer on his front feet and planted two hoofs hard into Rostellan's chest. As his feet touched the ground, he launched himself with his teeth and front feet straight at the unsuspecting Red, caught him with both feet, gripped his neck with his teeth, and wrenched, ending up with a mouthful of skin and hair. Red fled, with Star Light in hot pursuit. Red made a circle of the field, but as they came back past Rostellan, Star Light put the brakes on and Rostellan, who had been observing this scene, suddenly found that he was the one at the receiving end of Star Light's fury. He too disappeared for the horizon. Star Light did two circuits of the field, with head and tail up, snorting in triumph, after which he proceeded to whip the rest of the herd into a suitable state of submission.

Pound for pound he was the equivalent to a fly-weight compared with two heavy-weights, but his aggressiveness and mental dominance had far outweighed any disadvantage of weight and size.

We did another experiment on the emotional influence of one horse on another. The only thing necessary to carry out this experiment was time and patience. We repeated it time and time again with various horses, but the most clearcut case was that of Merlin and Chance. Merlin was extremely placid, easy going and rather lazy, whereas Chance was excitable and very nervous. Over a period of five months we kept them in close contact together, in adjoining loose boxes in the stable and working together the whole time. At the end of the five months the behaviour change in Chance was extremely marked: he had steadied down considerably, he would walk extremely well – before he had danced and jogged along all the time – and his jumping had become controlled where previously he had gone tearing madly into his fences. Then Merlin went back to his owner. Chance began to revert to his earlier behaviour, and if anything his excitability and nervousness became worse than before he had come under Merlin's influence.

These are just two very minor examples of what might be called observational research and experiment. But they illustrate the type of work that can be done quite simply by anyone with enough patience and care, who wants to understand the behaviour of horses. One rule, however, must be remembered: you can only prove one thing at a time.

If, for instance, your horse is sleepy and dull and you suspect he is suffering from mineral deficiency, it is no use adding oats *and* mineral supplement to his diet, because even if he regains his alertness you will never know whether it was the oats, or the minerals, or both that did the trick.

Similarly, if your horse won't jump for you, and someone else gets on carrying a stick and he then jumps, you don't know whether he is jumping because of the change of rider, or because of the stick. You must change only one factor at a time.

Having identified a factor – say a change in the way you ride him – that affects the behaviour of a particular horse, you can then try the same change with other horses, and thus establish whether your discovery applies to horses in general, or simply to one special horse.

I had been keen for some time to study the effects that changes in environment and handling could have on the performance of a horse, so when a friend asked me to buy a thoroughbred two-year-old for him at Newmarket, to run his pony mares, I persuaded my very reluctant Bank manager to allow me to purchase a horse for myself at the same time.

So one November Sunday Leslie and I departed for the wild and dangerous world of Newmarket. We arrived there on the Sunday night, and at half-past-eight on the Monday morning, determined not to miss a minute of it, we arrived at the Sale Yard. For the next hour we admired and examined the cream of the racing industry.

I always like buying horses at Newmarket. With a limited pocket like my own, when buying for myself, I can only afford to buy rubbish at a sale. But the advantage of Newmarket is that you get a much better class of rubbish there than anywhere else.

The first two or three lots in were thoroughbred two-year-old weeds, of no pedigree or racing distinction, and they were all led out unsold. But lot seven was a different sort of horse altogether: a fifteen-three chestnut by Eudaemon with a lot of bone, substance and quality. Whilst he had no racing pedigree, he was the perfect horse for a crossing stallion, so I purchased him for my friend, for a very small sum.

The next three lots again were of no interest to me, but lot eleven was the horse I wanted. He had an excellent pedigree, and had won as a two-year-old, then over the next three or four years had won three races and been placed seven times. Then as a six-year-old he had just packed it in and had never done a thing since, which is to say he hadn't troubled the judge: the judge must have had considerable difficulty in seeing him in the far distance when the rest of the field had passed the winning post. And indeed when he came into the ring, with his big head half way down between his knees, he was the picture of complete dejection. Life held nothing for him now, and the sale ring at Newmarket was just another piece of degradation in a long and tedious life.

Without any difficulty I bought him for a maiden bid of fifty quid, and having done my business I left to get home to Wales in time to do the milking that night.

The two horses arrived in the yard on the Sunday morning, and before they had been unloaded from the trailer, the purchaser of the two-year-old arrived. He asked how much? I told him what I wanted for the horse, and he said 'I'll have him', and this before he had seen more than the colour of its tail.

We transferred Broken Promise to Stan Williams' trailer, and then unloaded Argonaut. Argonaut walked into the yard, looked round, put his head back to its customary place between his knees, and trailed slowly into the stable.

Over the next three months we made strenuous efforts to penetrate Argonaut's barrier of sullen dejection and boredom with everything.

The first thing I noticed was that although he was eating plenty of food, he wasn't looking for his breakfast with any zest, so for a week or ten days I cut back his feed to practically nothing: just two or three pounds of corn three times a day. As soon as his belly was being affected, Argonaut started to take more interest, and soon enough, when I went out with his feed in the morning, he was screaming for it and telling me that I was starving him.

The next thing was to get him to take an interest in his work. So instead of doing normal exercise, I used him for shepherding, which meant not only that he had the interest of watching the dog working the sheep, he also had to shepherd the sheep himself. And very quickly, if a sheep broke, he was spinning round and going flat out after it. Whilst this wasn't very good for the sheep, it was extremely good for Argonaut.

And to replace his racing gallops and schooling over fences, I took him out hunting.

It happened at this time that in one of our best pieces of country we had a semi-tame fox. He used to live in the gorse on the other side of the road from the house by day, and during cold wet nights he'd sleep in the hay shed and he'd steal any bits of bone that the sheep dog had left behind. We always knew him because when he was a cub he had been a bit slow going out of the yard one morning, and as he jumped the fence my bull terrier made a leap and caught hold of his tail. They had a tug of war, something had to give, so the fox's tail parted in the middle, leaving him with an abbreviated brush about three inches long. After that we could always identify him. And from then on we christened him the bob tail fox, commonly known as Bob.

Bob was a great womanizer. He roamed all over the country, and two or three times a season, especially during the mating season, while we were out hunting, we'd put Bob up and he'd head straight for home.

On one of our first days hunting, Argonaut was not showing much interest. He performed adequately, but no more. There was no heart in his jumping or his galloping, until suddenly the hounds put Bob up out of the cover just above Llanybyther, and away we went. We had a couple of little fly fences, and with my wife on Cork Beg and myself on Argonaut, we took them stride for stride. And then Bob swung slightly to the left, and we had a mile straight across a whole farm with nothing to stop us. Two or three banks in the middle, and Argonaut really stretched out and Cork Beg stretched out with him. At the far end of this was a gate on to the road. Argonaut was determined that he was going to get to it first, so he sprinted a little bit and flew the gate, landing on the verge, almost slipping as he turned on the road.

We had about three quarters of a mile on the verge of a piece of forestry land and as we came to the bottom of it we could see hounds streaming up past home and into the gorse. They hunted the fox at the top end of the gorse for about ten minutes. Then as we came to the gate of the yard we saw Bob coming down on top of the bank, completely unruffled. He turned along the bottom of the gorse by the road, ran up a big gorse bush and proceeded to jump from one gorse bush to the next, until he disappeared from view.

Hounds came down the bank about a hundred yards behind him, swung along the bottom and were completely baffled by Bob's trick. I put Argonaut in and got out another horse to take the hounds back to the Huntsman, whom we met coming up the road about half a mile away. We handed over the hounds and went back to the yard to make sure Argonaut was quite comfortable. And he was walking around and around his box to relieve his pent-up excitement. From that day on he was a changed character.

Since I had done so well out of my expedition to Newmarket, my Bank manager didn't need much persuading to allow me to go back to the sales to buy another horse to help restore the Blake family fortunes.

Unfortunately on my second visit, horses were much more expensive and I couldn't see anything I wanted at a price that I could afford. So at the end of the first day I decided to stay overnight, and try again the following morning.

In the bar of the hotel after dinner I was having a well needed restorative, when I got chatting to someone else who was similarly employed. We were both looking for the same sort of horse, and we both had been frustrated by the prices.

I happened to mention to him that I had an eight-year-old for sale with a bit of form about him and who was quite a fair hunter, and before much ado we had concluded the deal at five hundred on condition that he could have the horse on a fortnight's trial. So we both turned to go to bed.

As we reached the door of the bar, he said 'By the way, what's the name of this horse?' And I told him 'Argonaut.' He stopped. 'Good God' he said. And I said, 'Why, what's the matter?' He said 'I brought Argonaut down here and sold him six weeks ago for fifty quid.' So we went back to the bar for something to calm our shattered nerves.

It turned out he had bought him as a five-year-old, and done very well with him that season, but never again. Three years later, in despair, he had brought him down to Newmarket for what he could fetch.

When I got home I continued my treatment of Argonaut. I had him sufficiently fit and happy to run him point to point at the first of the season, but he wasn't fully wound up and was beaten on the run in. I took him home and put in a bit more work on him. The next meeting being my local hunt meeting, I started the day off quite nicely, winning the hunt race by a street. Then I had what I always think to be the worst time in racing: a long hour before a race you think you stand a pretty good chance of winning. I just sat in the jockeys' tent visualizing all the things that could go wrong, and all the mistakes I could make which would make me look an even bigger fool than usual. I saddled Argonaut, and he boosted my sagging confidence because he was as fit and as well as he could possibly be. He had his head and his tail up and was really ready to go. Then came the setback: when I got back to the jockeys tent, I was told that the bookies had made him favourite. Now if the bookies make you favourite and you win, nobody gives you any credit; and if you don't win everyone who has backed you goes round telling everyone else that you shouldn't be allowed to ride a donkey on the sands, let alone a racehorse. But, I reasoned, after nearly twenty-one years of riding, I had surely ceased to worry about what people said about my abilities as a jockey.

And then finally one of the stewards' assistants came in and said 'Jockeys out', and the seven of us trooped out, making cheerful noises to each other to hide the fact that our hearts were in our boots and there was a dirty great cavity where our bellies should be. But this is normal to anyone riding a race. I tightened Argonaut's girth and vaulted into the saddle – one of the disadvantages of being the oldest jockey riding is that you have got to prove to the crowd that you are more agile than anyone else, so I do this by vaulting on myself instead of having a leg up. And down to the start.

As an old campaigner I got in on the inside, tight to the starter so that he couldn't see me, and managed to get a flying start. I led by about two lengths into the first fence. Argonaut stood back and rocketed over, and proceeded to do the same with every fence afterwards, never making a mistake, always standing well back and gaining ground in the air. And the further he went the more he was enjoying himself. I didn't see another horse until I came to the second last fence, when the second favourite, May Flower, came up on my side. We flew the fence side by side, landing neck and neck, and drove for the last fence, both of us riding for our lives. As we came into it I thought Argonaut had made a mistake. He took off a stride early, and I thought we had had it. But not a bit. He had put in an extra large jump, and we landed a length in front of May Flower. As we went up the straight, every pounding stride he took carried him just that little bit further in front. We pulled up having won by two lengths, and danced back to the unsaddling enclosure.

As we went in to the paddock, someone roused a ragged cheer, which was all Argonaut needed. He put in two colossal bucks from sheer *joie de vivre*, nearly getting me off.

Argonaut won another race that season, and he was placed every other time he ran. We also discovered he wasn't really a three-mile horse, because he didn't enjoy his racing unless he led from start to finish, and three miles, carrying twelve-seven, was that little bit too far for him. The one race that I tried him coming from behind was the only time that he wasn't in the first three (we finished fourth, with Argonaut putting in a very pedestrian effort). And since he did not enjoy racing unless he was in front, I let him bowl along the way he wanted to, because I knew if he stopped enjoying racing again I would never get him to do anything.

The story of Argonaut shows how, unless you have a horse full of joy and enthusiasm, he won't win a race. And indeed in any form of riding you are restricted by two things: first the horse's physical ability – that is the maximum he can attain with his body when he is fully fit – and second his mental fitness, for when you have a horse fit mentally he will use the absolute limits of his physical ability.

One of the things that continually amazes me is how, in buying a horse, people will pay great respect to the physical make-up of the horse, and give detailed attention to the various points of confirmation, but they take no notice whatsoever of the mental make-up of the horse – which is equally important. Parents buying a pony for their child will be influenced by its colour, and its show points, forgetting that colour and show points have no relevance whatever to its suitability as a children's pony. Dozens and dozens of letters are written to the horse papers about the evils of breeding from sub-standard ponies, yet these may be the very ponies that have the kindness and mental stability that's essential to make a good children's pony. The beautiful show ponies, stallions and mares are often much too excitable for a small child to ride.

It must be remembered too that needs of nutrition and handling will vary from horse to horse. Mental states in the horse can very often be affected by feeding: under-feeding will make a horse much lazier and easier to handle, whilst overfeeding, and underwork, can make him extremely excitable. These things are well known. But it is also true that an imbalance can upset a horse mentally.

So in looking at the psychology of any particular horse, it is essential to make sure that the feeding for that particular horse is correct – always remembering that what is correct for one horse will not necessarily be correct for another. This is particularly important during the period of training, because deficiency of protein in the diet during the time of learning, particularly in infancy (it must of course be remembered that a horse is learning from the time it is born) will retard his learning ability.

This has been experimentally proved with rats. I've done no work myself with horses on this, and I don't know of anyone who has, but a series of trials were carried out with twenty rats on a high protein diet, twenty on a normal diet, and twenty on a diet deficient in protein. And it was discovered that the group of rats on the normal diet took twenty percent less time to learn how to negotiate a maze than those on the high protein diet, who themselves learned how to negotiate the maze twice as quickly as the rats on a deficiency of protein.

Similar tests have been done on other animals, so it is probable that the same principle is true for horses. Great attention in teaching horses must therefore be paid to correct diet, which should be neither too high nor too low in protein, and balanced in mineral intake. A horse that seems to be stupid, awkward, or bloody-minded may simply be suffering from a food deficiency.

It is also true that the character and ability of the person handling a horse can considerably affect its performance. Constant weakness in handling from birth, for example, can make a horse unmanageable as a three- or four-year-old, while too much severity and brutality can terrify a horse so much that he becomes mentally unstable.

The worst example of this that we have had was a horse called Potty. He was called Potty because he was completely mad. When I traced his history back I found that, an unregistered Welsh Cob, he had been bred just above Tregaron out of a Welsh Cob mare by a Welsh Cob stallion, and he was supposed to have been castrated as a yearling. He was bought by a young girl, but in actual fact he had been only partly castrated, and was still a rig. The girl loved horses, but tended to treat them as children, and by the time he was three years old she was terrified of Potty. She sold him to someone who attempted unsuccessfully to break him, then Potty was trailed yet again to Llanybyther horse sale – this was the third time he had visited the market – and was bought by an acquaintance of mine who was quite sure that he could sort out this very handsome, but completely unmanageable, three-year-old.

First he tried to beat him into submission. And when this didn't work he starved him. After starving him of food and water for three days, he got on his back and tried to gallop him into submission. Potty got him off and attacked him when he was on the ground so he was sold again and sent to me to break.

When he arrived he was so round the bend that anyone going into the stable did so at considerable risk. He would either attack them with his front feet, and teeth, or kick them. And he had his own particular brand of trick: if he could get someone into a corner, he would back up against them and proceed to push and push.

The first thing I did was to put Strawberry, my daughter Paddy's pony, into the loose box with him for a couple of days. I went in every now and then to feed and talk to him quietly, until he began to lose a little bit of fear, and be slightly less hostile.

Then on the third day I had an early breakfast to give myself plenty of time to get Potty sorted out in the stable. The first thing I had to do of course was to put a halter on him. This was impossible by normal methods, since as soon as he saw the halter, he'd attack you. So when I went in with the halter, I was careful to keep Strawberry between myself and Potty all the time, and eventually after about an hour and a half, using Strawberry as a shield, I managed to get a halter on to him. Then I tied him up short to the partition, and still using Strawberry as a shield I got him saddled and bridled. Then I got on to him. He bucked solidly for ten minutes, but it was a comparatively easy buck to sit, and having found that this tactic had failed, he proceeded to bolt. I didn't make the mistake that most people make on a bolting horse: I didn't try to stop him, all I did was to give him slack rein and let him gallop. The only time I touched the rein was to prevent him from galloping straight into something, when I leant over and pulled him away from the object he was galloping towards. After a further ten minutes Potty had had enough, so he went quite quietly for the rest of that day.

The following day, after bucking for a couple of minutes, he went off again for two or three hundred yards, then realizing the futility of it he settled down for the next twenty minutes or so, only to go suddenly up on his hind legs, trying to come over backwards. This is a very nasty little trick, but it's quite easy to cure. All you do is slip off over his tail, and when the horse comes down again vault back into the saddle over his backside. This sounds very difficult, but in actual fact it's purely a question of timing. Again finding himself frustrated, Potty went quite happily that day.

Over the next three weeks he tried every trick I'd ever seen in a bad horse, other than laying down and rolling on top of me. But at the end of three months he was going quite nicely and quietly for me, though he wasn't yet a very safe conveyance for anyone else. Eventually he was extremely lucky in his purchaser, who, whilst being extremely firm, was also sympathetic, so Potty gradually regained his sanity and became an extremely good Welsh Cob.

Just as malnutrition and ill-treatment can break a horse both mentally and physically, so can boring, monotonous work. A good example of such lethargy is the trekking pony which does nothing but walk day after day with complete beginners on his back, at the rate of about two miles per hour. A lively, active pony can change into a bored, sulky individual in a single trekking season, and even two or three months of nothing but trekking can completely ruin a pony.

So it can be seen that handling, nutrition, breeding and the type of work that a horse has been doing are all factors that have to be taken into account when you are assessing the psychological make-up of a horse.

We know from our own experience of course that the intelligence of horses varies considerably, but no work has been done on the inheritance of intelligence in horses. Two gentlemen called Williams and Thompson however, did a considerable amount of work on intelligence in rats, in 1954. They selected the most intelligent rats and the least intelligent rats of a group, and for six generations they interbred the most intelligent rats, and the least intelligent ones. They discovered that breeding from the most intelligent rats they could increase their intelligence threefold. Among the least intelligent rats intelligence had decreased in the same ratio. Their work was of considerable assistance to us, since their description of how they assessed intelligence in rats gave us pointers as to just how we could gauge the intelligence of our horses.

Since it has been shown that intelligence in rats is inherited, and that intelligence in human beings is also inherited, it is probable that the intelligence in horses too is inherited. And if intelligence is inherited, excitability, laziness and other personality factors, we thought, may be inherited too. A foal from a dominant mare, therefore, is himself likely to be dominant, not only from example, but also partly because of his heredity. This factor is something that has been neglected by the commercial breeder, since a sober, stable disposition isn't usually a marketable factor. Indeed in some cases, bad tempered and bloodyminded mares have been put to extremely excitable and unmanageable stallions, simply because the stallion is the right colour, and has the right show points. Yet excitability, emotionality and savageness have all proved to be hereditary in rats, so it is likely that they are hereditary factors in horses.

We also know that environment has been proved scientifically to have a considerable effect on intelligence in human beings: difference in environment can affect human beings' intelligence by as much as twenty-two percent. This too tends to confirm scientifically what every horseman has known for a long time: that temperament can be affected both by heredity *and* training.

What we wanted to know now was more exactly how horse personality was formed, and what we could do to influence our own horses.

4: *Motivations of Horse Behaviour – And How To Use Them*

What makes a horse tick? What makes a horse do this rather than that? This is a fascinating question because what motivates a horse lies behind everything that it does, and when you can discover what makes a horse do something, you can apply it to your advantage, and improving the performance of your horse will give you satisfaction beyond words. But finding what motivates a horse is always frustrating, because it is like looking for a needle under a blanket: you are probing around in the dark, and you only know you have found it when it sticks into you, and makes you jump. You can never *see* the reason why the horse does something because that is hidden away somewhere in his head. You can only see the result of the reason. The best you can do is to guess what motive lies behind what he is doing, and test out your theory afterwards. That has been our work over the last twenty years.

We made one of our successful guesses with Bella. Bella came to us as an untouched four-year-old, but within six or eight weeks of being gentled, she started shying very badly. Now we worked out that she could be shying for any of five reasons. She could be shying out of boredom or fear; from habit; from a sense of insecurity, and lack of confidence; or out of sheer bloody-mindedness, trying it on with her rider; or from any combination of these things.

From observing her in the field we noticed that when she was being driven with the other horses, she hardly shied at anything, so we knew it wasn't habit, or any very serious fear. We also knew it wasn't boredom because we were trying to keep her work as varied and interesting as possible. But she was being ridden by a girl who was rather a weak rider. So we concluded it might be slight fear of strange objects, but that mainly it was a combination of lack of confidence in herself, and in her rider. She was a dominant member of her group, so we concluded also that she might be trying it on with a weak rider.

The cure was comparatively simple. First, I rode her myself for a week; then I made sure that she continued to be ridden by a strong rider, so that she not only gained increased confidence in her rider and herself, but also had no chance of trying it on. Second, since there was the possibility that fear was involved, I made quite sure by gazing at any strange object that we came across myself, and drawing her attention to it, that she saw it properly. And after a week or two she went back to riding in her normal quiet and sweet way.

All our work in horse psychology has in fact been aimed at making accessible to the ordinary horseman the skill that comes to the great horse handlers instinctively. They already know, by intuition, what makes a horse do certain things, and it is for this reason that they are top class horsemen. We who are not quite so gifted need to acquire our knowledge more laboriously. We have to deduce the motive from the action of the horse. If, for example, we know that the horse has not been fed for forty-eight hours, and he asks for food, we deduce that he is asking because he is hungry. If on the other hand the horse has been fed within the last half hour, and is still screaming for food, we know that he is just plain greedy. But of course behaviour is not always as easy to interpret as this, and a wrong deduction may simply compound the problem.

If, for instance, your horse, like Bella, is shying, you may have been able to reduce the possible reasons to two: either he is bored, and looking for something to make his life a bit more exciting; or he tends to be a bit sleepy and doesn't notice the object, so it startles him. If the reason is the first, and he is bored, then he needs to be punished to stop him shying. But if on the other hand he was fast asleep, and the object startled him, and you punish him, he will then associate pain with the object he shied at: if it is a white paper bag that startles him, and you punish him, he will then associate white paper bags with pain, and instead of curing him you will simply have made him shy at white paper bags.

Motivation is an all-inclusive term covering just about anything that makes a horse act, or respond. The term comes from the Latin word meaning to move, and if we think of motivation as the mover of the horse, the cause of the horse moving, we won't be very far wrong. But it is convenient to the study of horse behaviour to divide motivations into two separate categories: physical and emotional.

The drives to satisfy physical needs – the requirements of the body – are inborn in all horses, to a greater or lesser degree. When a horse is hungry he is driven by hunger to find food; when he is thirsty, his thirst drives him to find water; and when a mare is in season her body drives her to find a stallion. Mother Nature takes great care of her children, especially her favourite child, the horse, so she provides him with the instinct to know exactly what he needs and how to get it. If a horse is short of one particular sort of food, Nature will drive him to look for exactly that food. This instinct of course goes back to the primitive horse who ranged over enormous areas searching for various different grasses to balance his diet. For Nature has taught the horse to be a selective feeder, unlike the cow who eats everything available.

I watched this careful selectivity in a group of 'wild' horses not long ago. When we have to catch a pony out of a bunch that runs free in the mountain, I like to observe the herd for two or three days to observe their habits: where they spend the night, which line of grazing they take, where they drink, and where they shelter in bad weather. This is a labour-saving device, to enable me to pick the easiest place to drive them off the mountain to a spot where I can catch the horse I select. And since I had this time to catch two ponies out of a particular herd, I had an excuse to spend two glorious June days sitting in an assortment of sunny spots observing the ponies grazing. The only drawback was having to get up early. But the inconvenience of leaving home before dawn in June is more than compensated for by what you see when you get out on the mountain.

I knew from previous observations where the ponies had spent the night, and I was in position just before dawn. As the sun rose over the other side of the valley I could see the ponies sleeping below me. There were five or six mares and foals, half a dozen yearlings and two-year-olds, and the two three-year-olds that I wanted to catch, all sleeping in a tight group within an area of about fifty yards. Most of the mares were standing with their heads drooping over their foals, who were lying stretched out under their noses. And round the main body of the mares were a group of last year's foals, and the two-year-olds, also fast asleep. As the sun began to warm them, first one foal then another raised its head, saw it was time to get up, scrambled shakily to its feet and shook itself. Then each one stretched, first its head and neck, then its back and finally its hind legs, one at a time. Feeling hungry, without exception, they all then went and had breakfast at the milk bar. Having done this they proceeded to play, disturbing the yearlings and two-year-olds, who were sleeping a bit late.

The newly awakened herd proceeded to take the knife-edge off their appetite by cropping the short sweet grass near their sleeping place. But slowly, one by one, led by an old white mare who had long ceased to bear foals but who was still the leader of the herd, they ambled off, picking a mouthful here and there, down to the stream for a drink. The old mare drank first, as the others drifted in ones and twos down to the water. No sooner had she slaked her thirst than she climbed up the other side of the stream to a vantage point where she could observe danger, whilst the rest of the herd drank. When they had finished drinking they made their way up the hill to the mare, and she in turn set off to higher ground where the grass was more abundant. The others followed her, still picking a mouthful of heather here and there, and eventually, half a mile further on, they came to the spot the old mare had selected for their breakfast. Everyone got his or her head down and started tearing at the young grasses, as if there was never going to be another meal. Then they moved on another mile or so to a south-facing slope of a higher valley.

Here the mares took a nap, whilst the foals indulged in a bit of horse play and tag. Every now and then one of the smaller foals would be getting the worst of it, so it would flee from its bigger companions to hide behind its mother. It would stay there for a minute or two, then peep around her backside to see what the others were doing. And you could see it weighing the pleasure of playing against the chance of getting hurt again. In a state of indecision it would have a quick snack, then slowly edge back towards the playing foals, and by degrees join in the game of tag again. This ritual was repeated over and over again until about half past ten, when the mares decided they were thirsty again. So they made their way slowly down to another stream, again preceded by the old mare, who after drinking walked up to a vantage point whilst the rest of the herd drank. From here they went to another grazing spot. This time instead of the shorter grass, they were grazing a mixture of heather and coarse grass. From here they moved on to yet another resting spot. They drank and grazed in this way three times more, each time choosing a different type of grass in a completely different place. And each time they drank they chose a different stream. In all during the day they had five different grazing periods, five different sleeping periods, and the foals had five different playing periods, with journeys varying from half a mile to a mile between each. The circle eventually completed was over three miles between its two widest points. What struck me was how after each resting period the old grey mare knew exactly where she was going, she knew what type of grass they needed next. Whether they drank from five different streams because the water in each too provided something different, I don't know.

Just before the sun started setting the ponies were back in their sleeping place. And it was here I decided that I would catch the two I was after, because there was a convenient lane down to a farm nearby.

I thought a lot that day about how deliberate was the feeding

pattern I was observing: how when the horses were eating the
coarse grass and heather, they tended to take off the tips only;
how, apart from picking odd bits here and there between grazing
spots, the herd grazed where the old mare told them, and yet
how carefully she had chosen a variety of foods.

We knew from our own experience that all horses don't
necessarily have the same nutritional needs. In fact my wife and
I once had an argument as to whether or not our horses were
getting enough salt. So I conducted a series of trials.

First of all I mixed one ounce of salt with ten ounces of earth
and gave each horse a fragment of the resulting paste with his
feed. All of the twenty or so horses we had in at that time thought
this a joke in very poor taste, with the sole exception of Grayling,
who licked up all the mixture of earth and salt. So I knew Grayling needed salt very badly. The following day, I mixed four
ounces of salt with twelve ounces of soil, and that day two more
horses licked the mixture of earth and salt. I moved on from one
quarter salt in the earth, to a half, to three-quarters, and when I
finally got to pure salt only Biddy and Spitfire left it. This was
one argument I lost: we proved that of the twenty horses, one
had a desperate need for salt, and only two didn't need salt at all.
So I adjusted the salt in their feed accordingly.

Through a very simple trial such as this one, it is possible to
determine the bodily needs of any particular horse. And since
each horse is completely different from the next, it is very important to establish early on what your horse needs for his bodily
wellbeing. The need for liquid, for instance, can be measured
very simply. All you have to do is to measure the amount of water
you offer him each day, and work out the average he drinks over
a period of at least five days. This test of course must also be
related to weather conditions, and the amount of work he is
doing.

Over a period of years with a large number of horses, we have
found one horse who needed as little as three gallons of water
per day and another who drank eighteen gallons a day. Of these,
the one drinking only three gallons of water was in the stable

during a very clammy, damp period, whilst the eighteen gallons a day was drunk by a horse doing moderate work during very hot dry weather.

It is easy enough to assume, if your horse seems in general good health and happy, that you have given him all the food and water he needs. Most of us do that. But it is only by observing *exactly* how much he needs of hay, corn, water, salt and minerals, that you can get to know your horse really intimately. The results of the conscious study of the horse's basic needs in themselves may indeed be superfluous; but by making this conscious study you will be subconsciously studying him as well, and you will absorb a great deal of unconscious knowledge of his mental needs.

Rostellan is a typical case in point. His bodily need to keep him in good condition for hunting and minor competition work, is twelve to fourteen pounds of corn a day, but he is quite capable, if he gets the chance, of eating twenty-one pounds of corn a day. Once he got as fat as a pig, and was jumping out of his skin on this diet but because of the increased body weight he was putting much greater strain than usual on both his heart and his legs. So to know the upper limit of his food consumption was as important as it was to know how much he needed to keep him in good health. It helped us to measure his greed factor – Rostellan had a greed factor of fifty percent, that is he would eat fifty percent more food than he actually needed for his bodily condition, and this helped us to know Rostellan better.

Here, mixed up with bodily requirements, was a more complex need, determined by the inner life of the horse. Such needs are the need for love, the approval of his owner, and the respect of the other members of the herd. None of these needs is purely physical, but it is compelling all the same. The horse has a need for varied outlook, he needs a change from everyday things, he also needs bodily movement and a certain amount of light for his mental well-being. These are the needs we have taken great trouble to identify, because although you can force a horse to do so much with brute force and ignorance, he will do far more if he is satisfying a drive within himself.

Some of these internal needs are like smoking cigarettes: they are addictive, so the more you give him, the more he needs. When you first get a young untouched horse, for instance, he doesn't know what praise and approval are, and since he has never had them, he doesn't need them. But the more praise and approval you give a young horse, the more he will do to get more praise and approval, and constantly excel himself to get the praise he needs. In fact I use praise with my horses constantly, and of course disapproval, for mere disapproval from the owner can be a very severe punishment in itself.

At Penrice one-day event, in the spring, I used this technique on Biddy. She was horseing, and she went extremely badly, so after we had finished I didn't touch her with a stick, but I voiced my displeasure, and when I got off her I completely ignored her. Someone else groomed her, put her away, fed and watered her. I didn't go near her for five days. If I passed her box I ignored her completely – of course, someone else fed, groomed, watered and exercised her for me, under strict instruction not to praise her in any way whatever. At the end of five days, when I got on her, she was turning herself inside out to please. I took her up to our one-day event course and put her over all the stiffest fences in the most difficult possible way. They were far worse than anything that she had had to face five days previously, but she jumped them all superbly. And then of course she got her praise. My disapproval had been the most severe punishment that I could give her. So the following one-day event, even though it was only her second, she finished eleventh, having the fastest cross-country time of the day.

Rostellan on the other hand is a great deal more difficult to deal with. He is like a naughty small boy, always getting up to one sort of mischief or another. Among the tricks he has taught himself is to unbolt his stable door and let himself out. We usually have a series of barricades and bolts that he can't reach to stop him doing this. But occasionally the bars and bolts are not put properly in their place, which is what happened one morning, just after he had been groomed. There he was beautifully clean, with his mane and tail brushed out ready to take part in a showjumping competition at the Riding Club, when we left him to get changed ourselves. When I came out the first thing I saw was that Rostellan's door was open. The next thing I saw was that he had opened the front gate. And just inside the front gate was a dirty great patch of mud.

Fortunately my wife had not seen him yet, so I shouted, 'Rostellan', and he came bolting and bucking down the road, trotted up to his stable and put himself back in, knowing he had been extremely naughty. When he heard my wife coming out through the front door, he retreated cowering to the corner of his box, peering round the corner of the door to see what sort of a temper she was going to be in. When she saw the mud over his freshly brushed coat and she heard what he had done, she started to scold him. But it was no good. She couldn't go through with it. The sight of a very dirty Rostellan cowering and trying to disappear through the back wall of his loose box was too much for her, and she simply had to laugh. You can't be disapproving when you are laughing.

Rostellan immediately swaggered to the front of the box to tell everyone how clever he was, and I decided to disappear and get a bucket of hot water to wash the worst of the mud off. My wife did her best to repair the damage to his mane and tail.

A horse may also be stimulated by something outside himself, rather than by an inner drive. I was able to observe a whole series of actions and reactions in response to external stimuli when I spent an hour recently watching Spitfire's foal Spit Again, commonly known as Gain. It was early on a fine May morning, and Spitfire and Gain were fast asleep in a sunny corner of the field, Gain stretched out in his favourite posture under Spitfire's nose. He was completely relaxed, soaking up the warmth of the sun and the security generated by the presence of his mother. When he heard me coming into the field, he raised his head, looked up and then, very slowly, got to his feet. When he was more or less vertical, he started stretching: first one leg, then another, then his back, and finally he stretched his neck. He stood watching me for a minute or two, then something moved in the hedge behind him. He jumped forward startled, and then trotted twenty or thirty yards away from the noise, to which his first reaction was one of fear. When he had reached a safe distance, however, he turned to see what had startled him. It was a half-grown fox who had come out of the hedge and was trotting down it.

This stimulated his curiosity, so he trotted towards the cub to investigate. The cub quickened his pace to a canter, Gain reacted with excitement, and gave chase. But the fox cub dodged back into the hedge. Unable to follow him, Gain slid to a halt.

The hedge, in stopping him, could be called in the context a negative stimulus: for something that makes a horse do something need not necessarily be positive, it can be negative, in that it stops him doing something else, in this case moving.

He then saw a particularly succulent patch of grass, which, after the exercise he had just taken, put an edge on his hunger, so he went over and grazed for the next twenty minutes. When his hunger was satisfied he stopped grazing – again the satisfaction of his hunger being a negative stimulus to stop him grazing – and decided he was tired again so he slept standing up in the sun until about ten minutes later the sun clouded over and a shower of rain began beating into his face. This was uncomfortable, so he turned round to point his back to the rain. The shower had passed over and about five minutes later a group of trekking ponies went past the end of the field. Again his interest was aroused, so he cantered across the field, stopping only when he ran into a barbed wire fence by the road. The wire hurt, making him shy away.

From this account of a single hour in a foal's life, external stimuli provoked fear, curiosity, hunger, sleep: made him move away, move towards and stop. Indeed, each stimulus could be seen either as creating movement or stopping movement. Some of the movements were violent and some very minute, such as the

movement of the jaws as he was eating. But all had been extern-
ally provoked.

It is providing such external stimuli – the right stimuli to
provoke the reaction you require – that is important when you are
riding a horse. Horsemen tend to think that the only way to teach
a horse is by repetitive training, using a bit and heels to stop
him or to stimulate him. This of course as far as it goes is fine.
But if you can extend the number of stimuli you use to make a
horse *want* to do something, it is possible to extend the performance of the horse itself.

If you analyse the stimulus-reaction sequence in horse behaviour you will see that if the stimulus comes first, the second
phase is a desire to do something. The stimulus, whether from
inside the horse or from outside it, awakens a desire; and the
desire in turn drives it to *do* something to satisfy it. So if a horse
is thirsty (internal physical stimulus), this will awaken a desire
for water, and he will walk until he finds water. Then he will
drink to satisfy his thirst. So his thirst has made him do two
things, walk and then drink, the first being designed to achieve the
second.

Hunger and thirst and avoiding pain are all bodily needs
which can be satisfied. But the need for excitement is an emotional
need, within the horse's mind, which also demands satisfaction.
The need for excitement to alleviate boredom is perfectly illustrated in Bluebell, a three-year-old black cross Welsh Cob gelding, thirteen-three hands high, whom we had on our farm for a
while. He was in need of constant excitement, and when he was
feeling bored he used to go and tease Madam. Madam was the
herd boss – mainly because she was extremely bad tempered and
clobbered anything that came near her. Bluebell would try to
get the other young horses to play, but if they wouldn't he would
wander over to where Madam was sleeping or grazing. She would
put her ears back and raise one hind leg, and he would retreat
a pace or two. Then he would take a step forward, and stick his
head out. Madam would swing round and try to have a piece out
of him. He would turn towards her again. And saunter up again

with his head out. This time she would probably flick out with one hoof. Bluebell would dodge the kick quickly, and again edge round her. He'd keep this up for ten or fifteen minutes until Madam had finally had enough, and chased him half around the field – which is what he wanted in the first place, since he knew he had the legs of Madam.

At one time Cork Beg was friendly with a bull. We had no other horse at the time, so he was turned out with the bull and they grazed together and slept together, the bull lying down and old Cork Beg resting a leg, with his head nodding over the bull. But the old man couldn't stand still for very long and eventually he would saunter away and start grazing. Then to alleviate his boredom he would come dancing up to the bull and pretend to box him. The bull would put his head down and roar at Cork Beg and the old man would continue to tease the bull until the bull charged him. Cork Beg would swing to one side as the bull charged, the bull would go lumbering past, and Cork Beg would turn in pursuit, trying to bite at the root of the bull's tail. The bull would stop and charge again, Cork Beg would flee this time, and this game would go on for ten minutes to a quarter of an hour, until the old man had got his excitement and the bull had had enough. Whereupon the bull would really charge Cork Beg seriously and Cork Beg would kick at his face and take the best possible means of escape.

Both these examples show how, if a horse is bored, he will actively court danger to get a bit of excitement. Excitement in other words is a very real need that must be satisfied.

Hunger for food, thirst for water, the need for excitement and the need to escape from boredom, thus all provide a horse with reasons for doing something. And the third phase in the cycle is the achievement of the object: when the thirsty horse finds water, drinks and satisfies the thirst, ending the motivational cycle for the time being.

There are, then, three distinct phases in any motivational cycle. The first stage is the stimulus that initiates the movement – the stimulus of thirst, which makes the horse move. The second stage is the movement itself – walking toward the water. The third phase is the achievement of the initial object, in this case having a drink of water.

This cycle of motivation plays an integral part in success in competition and I made full use of it with Biddy in the cross-country at a recent Welsh one-day event, held at Builth Wells. Biddy, whose name is officially Esther Aeron, is an extremely good horse for a cross-country course, but unfortunately like all women she tends to be a little bit temperamental. Biddy needs love and approval. She is also very proud, and like any thorough-bred needs to expend energy, so she wants a lot of excitement – all these things are characteristic of any good competition horse. Further, the energy Biddy expends is both nervous and physical so to excel in competition she has to be extremely fit both mentally and physically. You go to a lot of trouble to build up this energy within the horse, which then needs release. And since Biddy loves jumping, she expends her pent-up nervous and physical energy by jumping and galloping.

Just before we start competitions of this sort, Biddy is usually dancing round all over the place, and it is extremely difficult to get her to stand stationary for the starter. On this occasion, just before we were due to start, I got her to walk the last two or three strides, to halt for two seconds and when the starter's hand came down we were away.

The first fence was bales with a pole on top. She tore into this, and flew it. We then had a very sharp corner with a big combination fence of two three-foot-six telegraph poles. And then two strides, and a four-foot parallel standing at the maximum three-foot-six. I steadied her with my hands and voice, 'Steady girl. Steady girl. Slowly. Slowly, gently,' and brought her well back on to her hocks. The last second was just an explosion of energy which flew her over the first section, she bounced for one stride, and I drove my heels into her just to give her extra incentive over the parallel of two poles. The next fence was a pile of tree trunks, three foot high and seven foot at the base. By now she was well into her stride, and really galloping, and I didn't need to do anything. I just sat still, and at the last second gave her her head. And she flew them like a steeple chaser.

It was about three hundred yards to the next fence and we were really going: in fact we were going so fast that I had a job steadying her. We had to go up on to a bank and jump over a low V-fence with a five-foot drop on the other side. When I finally steadied her, she dropped back to a walk and just popped over without any difficulty whatsoever. We flew over the paling fence which came next, and then we came to one of the most difficult fences on the course: a three-foot wall, one bounce stride, and then a post and rail. 'Steady girl, slowly girl, steady girl.' I managed to get her back by using only my voice. She popped on to the bank and bounced out over the rails. Almost before I was back in the saddle she was belting on at the next fence as fast as she could go. This was a gate, which she rocketed over.

We were really motoring now. Fences eight, nine and ten she took in her stride. We had to go down a steep bank to fence number eleven, which was a set of steps. As we got to the top of the bank, she skidded to a halt, went down the other side, almost sliding on her bottom, then popped over the steps. The bull pen had to be taken at an angle, one step over, one step out, and away again over the next three fences.

Biddy was really enjoying herself. In fact it was hard to decide who was enjoying it most, Biddy or myself. The speed at which she was going into the fences was incredible: great long raking strides, and taking each fence as if it were her last meal. The water trough, the log piles, the pedestrian crossing, and the ski jump all floated away beneath us. The sheep pen provided some difficulty, because Biddy was going much too fast at it and I was having a job to steady her, but she flew over the corner, and over the next brush fence too. Then we came to the coffin fence, which was a solid fence with a drop to the water, over the water and up out over a post and rails. She did this with spectacular grace and ease, and flew into the last fence as if it was the first. And we were home with nearly a minute to spare.

As that story shows, I had made use of the horse's own need to expend energy, and satisfied her need for excitement and praise, and her pride. By using my reins and heels I had used additional external stimuli to steady her and to drive her over fences. Fortunately since she is a very good free-going horse, I hadn't had to use my stick at all. But I would have used the stick, and provided the stimulus of pain to make her jump a fence, if she had been reluctant to do so. But the important ingredient of success was the fact that that underlying need Biddy has to excel and receive praise and admiration, had been satisfied.

From this it can be seen how just by harnessing the various motivational drives within the horse it is possible with a competitive horse to achieve outstanding cross-country performances.

Some of these motivational drives are positive, and where possible these are the ones we stress in dealing with horses. Others are negative – pain, for example. Or if you watch a foal you will see a whole variety of negative drives in action. A foal sees something, is frightened by it, and will run away and hide behind its mother. The drive this time is fear; but when he gets to his mother the fear will subside.

In comparing examples of positive and negative drives we note that they play completely different roles. A positive stimulus arises directly from a motive: a horse is thirsty, he searches for water, and he finds water and quenches his thirst. In the case of a negative stimulus, the stimulus *causes* the drive: the foal is frightened by something, and it runs away to escape, and to gain the protection of its mother. The easiest way to think of it is thus: the horse moves towards a positive goal, and away from a negative goal. If you think of a small boy reaching for a packet of sweets, and escaping from a kick on the backside, the sweets are the positive goal, and the kick on the backside, which is painful, is the negative goal.

Robert Louis Stevenson during his *Travels with a Donkey* got the donkey going with two sticks. On the end of one long stick, he dangled a carrot and at the end of another he had a pin. And he used to dangle the carrot in front of the donkey's nose while at the same time applying the pin to his rump. So the donkey naturally wanted to go towards the carrot and away from the pain of the pin. Here you have positive and negative stimulus used simultaneously.

It is far *easier* to set about training an animal, especially a horse, using pain and fear. The memory of pain and fear will stay with the horse far longer than the memory of a pleasant experience, and it is extremely difficult to eradicate. And the horse, after an unpleasant experience, will associate similar situations with the pain and the fear a long time afterwards. But it is not necessarily the most effective.

Jezebel illustrates this point perfectly. We got Jezebel because no one could catch her, or do anything with her. Her fear of a confined space was such that she would jump a six-foot wall, half jumping and half climbing, rather than stay in a yard. She had run wild on the Preseli Mountains as a yearling and a two-year-old, and she had been born with two things: a temper with a very low boiling point, and a fantastic jumping ability. So when her owners wanted to catch her, and she was driven into a yard for the first time, when she had never been handled in her life, her fear of man made her take the easiest way of escape, jumping out over the gate. But they needed to catch her, so she was driven back into the yard again, with some difficulty. Everyone's tempers got a bit frayed in the process, so they stationed people round the yard with sticks to make sure she didn't try and jump out again.

She took the very simple expedient of charging, and jumping out over the lowest point and the smallest man. She then got herself hit over the head, which increased her fear. This process was compounded again and again, each time they tried to catch her, so by the time we got her she was not only terrified of all human beings, but she hated them as well. Overcoming this fear and hatred was a major problem which took me a very long time to solve.

She now has her own stable, and all we need to do to get her in is to drive her down the road, and she trots straight in and stands there. Occasionally when she is feeling a bit bored she'll decide to cut up rough with the old man, but there is no real fear or enthusiasm in it. She merely does it to annoy me. It has taken me three or four hundred attempts and endless patience and understanding to achieve this – sometimes it took us three or four hours to get her in without frightening or upsetting her – all to overcome at most a dozen unpleasant early experiences.

This is why when we are gentling a horse, in the early stages we try to avoid any conflict at all, and above all we take pains not to frighten the horse.

A very difficult horse, who tested our capacity to do this to the limit, was called the Bishop, because he belonged to a Dr Dean. He was sent to us as a five-year-old, unbroken and unbreakable. Fortunately we had stipulated that he should have shoes on when he came, and he arrived about four o'clock one afternoon whilst I was milking. As soon as I had finished milking my father and I had tea, and made a start on him. We had a lot of difficulty getting a saddle on because, as soon as we tried to girth him up, he started bucking and kicking. So we took the girth and stirrups and stirrup leathers off the saddle, and for the next forty minutes we just lifted the saddle on and off his back, until instead of exploding each time the saddle came near him he was half asleep, chewing out of his manger, when we put the saddle on his back. When we could leave the saddle there without him firing it off, we attached a single girth to one side and put the saddle on and off again another dozen times. The first time the girth was put across his back, his back came up like a bow ready to fire an arrow, but there was so little difference between having the girth on the saddle and not, that after two or three times he took no further notice of it. Then we left the saddle on with the girth dangling for a couple of minutes. Then my father, being very careful not to touch him with the girth, handed the girth through to me and I buckled it on to the bottom hole. As soon as I had done this, he eased it up his side a hole. Then I eased it up my side a couple of holes, until it was just touching his chest. Immediately he stopped eating. And up came his back again. We left him a couple of minutes, and when nothing else happened, and down came his back and he started eating again, we put the second girth on in exactly the same way. Again when it touched him, up came his back, and again after a minute or so it came down again. Then I tightened up the first girth another hole. The Bish exploded. But the saddle was on firmly enough now for us to leave him to his own devices for a couple of minutes.

Eventually when the saddle was still in place and no one was taking any notice of his gyrations, he stopped bucking, went back to his manger and started eating again. And I tightened the second girth up a couple of holes. And again the Bish exploded. Each time he exploded we just left him to his own devices, until he had had enough of his blowing and bouncing, and in this way eventually we got the girth tightened and firm, put on the stirrups and bridle, and took him outside on the end of a long rope. As soon as he got out of the door he started bucking again, so again we just left him to buck with the stirrups flapping, standing at the full length of the rope. He bucked round in a circle for five minutes or so, with me pivoting as he went, but talking to him quietly and gently all the time. 'There's a bloody fool, there's a bloody fool, who's the bloody stupid fellow, who's a bloody stupid fellow. Who's a bloody fool' – repeating this over and over in a singsong voice.

Eventually since no one was worrying and no one was excited, he stopped bucking, and I went over and made a fuss of him. Then we led him down to the breaking field, which was a two-acre field, and absolutely dead flat. This was important in the case of the Bish, since I had a pretty good idea that as soon as I got on him he was going to start bucking, and the last thing that I wanted him to do with me was to buck downhill. Every few strides toward the field the Bish would start bucking again, but I let him get to the end of the rope, talking to him all the time, and whenever he had finished bucking, we went on. When at last we got to the field, my father eased me up so that I was leaning across the saddle. As expected, as soon as he felt my weight on his back the Bish exploded again. I just slid off, and allowed him to buck in his circle. He was getting a bit bored with this, and after four or five bucks he had stopped again, so my father eased me on to his back again, again he exploded, and again I slid off. This went on for about a quarter of an hour, until eventually he allowed me to lean across the saddle. I made a terrific fuss of him and he stood still, enjoying being told what a clever horse he was – for once.

Next time, I eased myself so that I was sitting upright on his back, and got my feet into the stirrups. My father undid the long rope, and led him forward. As soon as he had taken a couple of steps, he exploded. But one of the advantages in breaking a big sixteen-three thoroughbred horse is that he will usually buck in a straight line, and sitting a big strong buck in a straight line is rather like sitting on a very superior rocking horse. After three or four circuits of the field, with me showing my enjoyment, Bish decided that it wasn't worth expending all that energy for no purpose. So he slowed down to a canter. I let him canter round the field a couple of times, he slowed to a trot, and eventually I settled him down to a steady walk. Talking, talking, talking all the time. When he stopped I started him again: a couple of strides, then a couple of bucks. But by now the Bish was fairly worn out. So I slid off his back and we led him back to the stable, rubbed him down, gave him a feed and a drink, and left him for the night.

I spent the next day putting the saddle on and off, and riding him for half an hour in the afternoon. This was largely another rodeo performance, but again it ended up with a gentle walk and a trot when he had had enough bucking.

That night I phoned up the Master. I knew the hounds were meeting near Smallwood, which was about two miles away, the next day, but I wanted to find out where the first draw was. My wife and I left next morning aiming to get there just before hounds. I was on the Bishop and my wife was on Cork Beg, who had then been going for a couple of years and was considered reasonably sane. The Bishop proceeded to the Meet in a series of bucks and plunges. We were a bit earlier than we would have liked, because we had to hang about for ten minutes to a quarter of an hour before the hounds found, but we were very lucky, because the fox broke quickly, came out on our side of the cover, and crossed quite near us with hounds hard on his heels. As soon as they had gone a couple of minutes I pointed the Bishop in the direction they had gone, and drove my heels into him. Four or five bucks later we came to the bank at the side of the field. I drove my heels into him again, which stimulated the Bishop into giving an extra large buck and brought him up on top of the bank. Another buck took him off the bank. Cork Beg had jumped in front of us and was cantering across the field. The Bishop followed him in a series of bucks, and when we came in to the second bank, I used the same technique of driving my heels into him so that he bucked on to the bank and off again. But half way across the second field the Bishop was beginning to realize what it was all about, and he was enjoying himself. He stopped bucking and started galloping. When we got to the third bank, because it was the only way he knew to negotiate it, he bucked again, but towards the far side of the fourth field he passed Cork Beg, stood back and rocketed beautifully over the fourth bank.

By now the Bishop was really enjoying himself. The hounds ran for about another mile and a half before driving their fox to ground, and we were in sight of them all the time. After that I thought the Bishop had had enough for the first time, and so we went home.

From that time the Bishop stopped bucking altogether. Or rather, the only time he ever bucked after that was from *joie de vivre*, when he would put in two or three almighty bucks just to show he was really enjoying himself.

It is true that, with time and patience, we might have got him going right using almost any method. We could have broken his spirit completely using tough rough methods. Or we could have spent endless hours long-reining, and working him on the ground before riding him. But by showing him straight away that being ridden was fun, we achieved our object quickly and with the minimum of trouble. We had got a very difficult 'unbreakable' horse enjoying himself and wanting to work, and what is more we had made life easier and more enjoyable for ourselves.

My technique had been to use what I knew of the horse's motivations. For the first part of the hunt I had used his dislike of being ridden, by making him buck in the direction I wanted him to, and by driving my heels into him making him buck even higher, I had negotiated the first two banks. But after that the joy of galloping with other horses, and the desire to be as near hounds as possible, had been all the stimulus that was needed to get him going really well.

The first thing that is involved in training a horse then, is the horse's own innate desires: that is to say, those things that are born in the horse, that he does naturally without any training whatever. The first thing the foal does when it is born is to seek nourishment from his mother. And his mother will push him into her flank to suck. While he is a foal, the milk he drinks gives him both food and liquid, but as he gets older he'll imitate his mother and eat grass and drink water, and if he is in the stable he will eat a little corn as well. So we can see that the need for food and water is born in the foal. Also within the foal is the desire for movement. He will exercise himself, for all horses have to move and keep moving. He will also need a certain amount of excitement. And later on as he gets older his sexual desires will be aroused. The horse also needs air, and needs light. All these things are born in the horse. They are all necessary for his physical and mental wellbeing. If he does not get them he will either die, or become mentally unbalanced.

We can use all these things in training a horse. His desire for food, for example, can be used to tempt him to follow you. His desire for movement and excitement can be used to make him gallop and jump.

But whilst these things are all inborn, they can also be increased or decreased by handling and training. One horse's desire for movement and excitement may be greater than another's – we call the horses that have very little desire for movement and excitement 'lazy' or 'sleepy'. And those that have a very great desire for movement and excitement we call 'excitable' or 'mad fellows'. A horse may be a greedy feeder or a shy feeder. Now these things, whilst they are partly inbred, are also influenced by the treatment the animal receives. If you starve a horse or if you overfeed it, his desire for movement lessens; or if you get it very fit the desire increases. A lot of slow tedious work will make a horse lazy; a lot of very fast work, galloping and jumping, will tend to make it hot. All these things must be borne in mind when you are training a horse. In training a horse what you are basically trying to do is to ingrain habits: when training a horse to stop on command, you start by saying 'Whoa' as you put pressure on his mouth. But after a very short time the horse will stop automatically when you say 'Whoa' whether you touch the reins or not. This is because he has got into the *habit* of stopping when you say 'Whoa'!

As I have already said, with a horse you can use one of two methods of training: you can motivate him by negative goals – that is you make him do something or perform a certain task to avoid pain, discomfort or trouble; or you can train a horse by stimulating his desires, by giving him a positive goal – making him *want* to do something. You offer him a reward, a titbit or approval, for doing what you ask. Or you allow him to do something that he does want to do, as a reward for doing something he does not want to do.

As a simple example of offering a positive goal, when we are first riding a horse we always ride him with other horses, because he tends to want to follow the other horses, so he goes quietly and easily, whereas if he were being made to go by himself, he would either tend to stand still, or try to drag us all over the mountain. If he is following Rostellan, and two or three others, he regulates his pace to theirs, just because he wants to stay with his friends.

Most commonly, of course, when you are training a horse, you use a combination of negative and positive goals: you use his desire to avoid pain, and you use his desire for reward. That is, you praise him or make a fuss of him when he does right, and punish him when he does wrong. But once a horse is trained by a negative method, since he is a very intelligent animal, he will do only just enough to avoid punishment and no more. Whereas if you have used praise and rewards, he will expend far greater effort to gain greater praise and greater reward.

It is equally important that when punishment and praise are given, the animal should know what he is being punished or praised for. This is an apparently self-evident fact which in practice is often simply not recognized.

Suppose, for instance, a horse bucks you off. He is immediately rewarded by being able to gallop around free and do what he wants to do. So he is being rewarded for doing something *wrong*. And then if you catch him, and you are feeling angry with him, you give him a clout for bucking you off and galloping away. But as far as the horse is concerned you are hitting him for allowing himself to be caught! This is a very simple example of how a horse can be rewarded for doing wrong, and punished for doing right. Similarly, if a horse jumps an extra large fence, you may punish him by coming half out of the saddle and jagging his mouth as he lands. This sort of thing happens all the time with horses, and makes training extremely difficult.

It is also a very important fact that things learned by *positive* goals are usually forgotten very quickly, so you must constantly be praising and rewarding the animal to reinforce the lesson. Whereas learning by negative goals, that is the avoidance of fear and pain, lasts for a very long time. So if a horse hurts himself, or is punished for doing something that he *should* do, it will be very difficult to eradicate this fear at a later date, in spite of rewarding him when he does the right thing later on. The relevance of this is extremely important. If, for example, a horse is overfenced jumping and hurts himself, the fear of hurting himself again will remain with him, and tend to be compounded by later experience unless you adopt a very deliberate strategy to see that this does not happen.

For instance, the first time you shoe a horse you may have trouble with him, and find yourself involved in a battle royal. The horse after that will look upon shoeing as an unpleasant experience. And next time you shoe him he will immediately start getting frightened and angry, for, like a human being, when a horse gets frightened he tends to get angry as well. So the second time you have an even greater battle. And this goes on and on until the horse becomes more or less impossible to shoe. It is thus extremely important that the first time you shoe a horse it should be easy; you must never have a battle shoeing if you can possibly help it.

This factor is particularly relevant of course when you are jumping, because if you once make a mistake, and the horse hurts himself, the next time he takes a fence, he will be iffing and butting as he goes into it, so be likely to take off wrongly, which means that he will hurt himself again. And before long you will have a horse that has gone completely off jumping. This happened to me this summer with Biddy. Since Biddy had been schooled specifically for cross-country, her showjumping has always been a bit chancy, and when doing the showjumping section in an event she usually has one or two fences down.

I rode Biddy at Dauncey Park one-day event, in the open section. She adores jumping though she tries to treat the show jumps as steeplechase fences. The showjumping ring at Dauncey was rather small, very tight and twisty, and the jumps were close together. But we went off in great style, and I steadied her nicely over the first two. But we were really motoring by the time we got to the third fence, which meant that she was completely wrong at the fourth, which was a big double of upright rails, the second part of which was a four-foot spread. She went straight into the first part, but was completely wrong at it and when she came to the second part she put in an almighty effort, and caught both rails with her hocks. Somehow we completed the course, but it was a disastrous round. Then we went on to the cross-country, and put in an outstanding performance.

I made the mistake after that of not schooling her over show jumps, but letting her go on doing her cross-country which she adores, and hoping that she would forget about hurting herself showjumping. The next event we took part in was the two-day event at Osberton, and she jumped the first fence with difficulty. Then she refused to jump any more, and it took me nearly two months' careful and quiet schooling to get her showjumping again. This is a simple example of how one careless fence, and one mistake on my part, could completely undo the good work of two years. Even now she is still a little doubtful about her show jumping, though since hurting herself she has probably jumped the best part of a hundred fences successfully. And yet she remembers the one fence at which she hurt herself.

This is a clear example of how a single negative stimulus may be remembered when a hundred positive stimuli may be forgotten.

By just such a process a two- or a three-year-old that gets carved up towards the end of a tough race may never race again, or at the very best will take a very long time before he is really trying once more.

A friend of mine had a very good race horse who had a very slight breathing defect. This had not mattered for two seasons, but by the third, though my friend did not know it, the defect had got worse. The first race that season he managed to win, but because of his restricted breathing, he collapsed between the winning post and the paddock. After about twenty minutes he got up again, and appeared to be all right. But the vet, on examining him, decided that his breathing had gone, and the horse was hobdayed. The following season – twelve months later – he was fit to race again. But after the second fence he just packed it in. He refused to race, and he hasn't run a race since.

This story again illustrates how one unpleasant experience can completely destroy a horse's desire to do something that it has previously done extremely well, and enjoyed doing.

You cannot win a race unless you have the wholehearted enthusiasm and cooperation of the horse. And you can't win a jumping competition unless the horse is extending every nerve and fibre to compete and win. So if a horse that has previously raced and jumped with enthusiasm suddenly takes against racing or jumping, the best thing you can do is to take it away from jumping and racing altogether for a time, and do something else with it, and hope that eventually you can reintroduce it, with patience and training, to its former skill.

We very often buy race horses that have taken against racing, and give them a season's hunting before racing them again. And if one of our own horses suddenly takes against a particular activity, though we make him complete the task at the time, we take him away from it completely afterwards. If one of the event horses suddenly takes against jumping, we put him hacking or shepherding, then bring him back to jumping very slowly: just pop him over a few ditches or low fences to start with. Then we give him a day's hunting, where even if he doesn't jump a fence all day he will be enjoying himself. This is the important thing with all horses: they must enjoy themselves in what they are doing, to do it satisfactorily. The desire to keep with the other horses out hunting gets them galloping and jumping with enthusiasm, so with time and patience, they will again enjoy galloping and jumping by themselves. With competition jumping one of the important things is that negotiating a fence must become a reward in itself. Some horses in fact will only jump out hunting. They won't jump at home, and they won't jump in competition.

The power of the learned negative goal, so familiar to horsemen, was demonstrated some thirty years ago by an experiment involving rats (Miller 1948).

A number of white rats were placed one at a time in a white box separated by a door from a black box. In the floor of the white compartment was a grid through which a mild electric shock could be applied. The rats were given a mild shock every five seconds. Then the door of the box was opened and the shock was turned on steadily. The rats escaped by running into the adjacent black box. The sequence was repeated on ten different occasions after which the rats registered terror as soon as they were put inside the white box, even though a shock was not applied. On the five subsequent occasions that the rats were placed in a white box with the door open, the learned fear was strong enough to make them run straight into the black box; and when the door was closed they would force the door open to get out of the box, even though no shock was applied.

This experiment illustrates how pairing the shock with the white wall of the box could cause the colour white to frighten the rats enough to make them force the door. This parallels Biddy's behaviour, when she learned to be afraid not of jumping and jumps – for she continued to jump cross-country fences with enthusiasm – but coloured jumps, because it was on a coloured jump that she had hurt herself. So she associated the colour with pain. She remained quite happy jumping four-foot-six timber. She was refusing to jump two-foot and two-foot-six coloured post and rails.

Most things that a horse fears it didn't fear as a foal. It learned its fears at a later date from its experience, often from experience with man.

5: *Reward and Punishment – Positive and Negative Goals in Training*

Though the whole question of reward and punishment is much more complex than it at first appears to be, at its simplest it is merely a question of giving a horse a handful of nuts when he does the right thing, and clouting him when he does wrong. But what is reward for one animal can be punishment for another.

For example, when Rostellan has done a piece of schooling work particularly well, he is allowed to jump some fences. This is a reward for him, because he loves jumping, and really enjoys competition and performance. On the other hand, Pudding jumps extremely well, but he doesn't enjoy it, and for him to be made to jump is a chore. So what is a reward for Rostellan, is punishment for Pudding.

But the natural inclination of a horse can also be altered by the way it is handled. For animals, like people, are conditioned by their experience. An American researcher demonstrated this very dramatically with some puppies. He wired up pieces of raw meat to an electric current, then showed it to the puppies. They went for the meat, and got an electric shock. He fed the puppies on dried toasted food, and every time they went near the meat he gave them an electric shock. He then took the experiment one stage further by dropping a piece of meat into their boxes, and as he did so turning on the electric current. He eventually brought the poor puppies to such a state of terror that as soon as they saw a piece of meat they started screaming in fear.

It is clear then that the way you present your work to the horse can be very important. When we first started dressage with Biddy for instance, she hated it. She found it boring and monotonous, and her whole attitude showed this. So she did an extremely bad dressage test. We decided to present the work to her in a totally different way, and were able completely to alter her attitude.

I had up to then been doing my dressage with her before taking her out exercising, which meant that the dressage was a prelude to dull and boring work. So I changed the order by doing the dressage work *after* she had exercised, and before she was put back into her stable and fed. This in itself completely changed her attitude, because instead of being a preliminary to the dull monotony of exercising, dressage became the prelude to going in to enjoy her dinner. Her attitude changed visibly. Towards the end of her exercise, before entering the dressage arena, she would start brightening and tightening herself up, and become fully alert. She knew that her dull exercise was over, and she had only another five or ten minutes' work before her meal.

My wife does it differently with Rostellan. She does her dressage work before schooling him in jumping. Again, he knows that the dressage is a prelude to enjoying himself jumping.

Thus a simple change in the timing of your work can change your horse's whole attitude to it. What previously was a dull and boring task becomes a rewarding one for the horse, and with Biddy I have actually achieved the stage where she sees the dressage schooling as the reward for having done her exercise. A full hundred yards from the dressage arena she will draw herself together, arch her back, and bring her head up in preparation for the dressage schooling. So whereas originally the dressage was rewarded with dinner, now it has become itself the reward for exercise.

It is quite possible, in short, to make a horse look on something he has previously looked upon as hard work, or as an unpleasant task, or as punishment, as in fact a *reward*.

Another success of this kind was with a horse called Clear Reason. Clear Reason was a sixteen-two dark brown gelding by High Treason. He had been purchased for a big price as a two-year-old, and put into training. He won one race, and in the following race, when he was odds on favourite, he had had an extremely hard race and got a hiding for his pains. He was beaten into second place and after this he wouldn't race again. They kept him in training the rest of his two-year-old career, and as a three-year-old, hoping he would improve. But he just refused to race.

We bought him as a four-year-old, at a very big price for us in those days. But he was a fine horse with a lot of potential. We schooled him jumping, and had him out hunting quite regularly during the winter, until he had settled down with us, and was quite happy in himself. Then we took him racing. I rode him quietly down to the start, but he refused to start on the starting line, and the others had gone fifteen to twenty lengths before I finally got him going. I let him canter slowly into the first fence and just popped him over. And I did that for the first three fences until he discovered that no one was caning him, no one was forcing him to do anything. And I sat still on him for the rest of the race. After we had gone about two miles, his own innate ability and superior quality got him up into fifth or sixth place in a field of twelve. I let him lie there quite happily for the next half mile until, as he was beginning to tire, I pulled him up.

We didn't run him the following Saturday, but a fortnight later I had him out again. And again I ran almost exactly the same race, except this time I let him finish, and we finished very comfortably and quietly in fourth place.

The third time out was Easter Monday. He jumped off at the start so sharply that he nearly had me out of the saddle, and I had great difficulty in restraining him and keeping him in the middle of the field. We did one complete circuit in the middle of the field. And then on the second circuit I just let him go. Unfortunately he fell at the last fence but one, when in the lead, or I think he would have won. He was a most unlucky horse, because shortly afterwards he broke down in one of his fore legs, and of course never raced again. But simply by letting him take his racing easy, and enjoy his jumping and galloping, what had previously been something to fear and dread, had become a terrific game, something he really enjoyed. This is what makes handling difficult horses such a joy: by the time you have finished with them you

Horses are herd animals, so they tend to graze together, and move on together. Herd of ponies grazing loose on the mountain

The herd has a leader — often one of the older mares. If she moves, the others follow

They are sociable animals — with each other and with man. Here CARAVAN & ANDY say 'hello' to each other in the stable-yard

CUDDLES shows his affection for the author by mouthing his hands

IANTELLA saying 'I Like You'

Joined by CUDDLES

Aggression in horses: the herd leader, REES, gives a young
upstart a nip to keep him in his place

IANTELLA threatens ANDY

ANDY backs away in fear. Note the ears laid back angrily in all the pictures

Horses need movement, and stimulation. CUDDLES has been kept in the stable too long, and as soon as he is let loose, he trots down the road to get rid of excess energy

CUDDLES shows his restlessness by 'bouncing' under his rider

Horses are curious — they come up to investigate their master's prone figure — hoping he's dead, suggests author

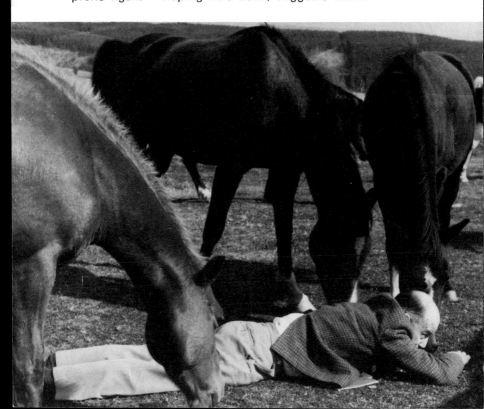

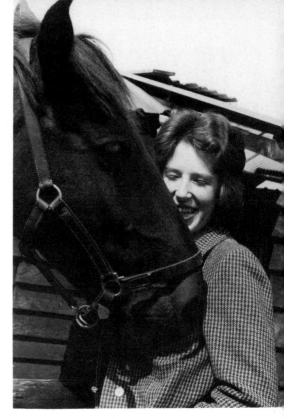

CUDDLES searches the author's daughter-in-law JUDY's pocket to see what she has in it

WATCH expressing annoyance and suppressed exuberance – note the ears twitching and muscles tense

Top Left: The author's understanding of his horses' needs and feelings can be put to good use in training. The need for food and drink suggests a reward
Top Right: Scratching fingers — another reward. WATCH shows his appreciation
Below: CUDDLES has misbehaved and flees to safety to escape retribution

The horse's need to be with other horses is here used to teach
TRABOLGAN to jump — he follows CUDDLES over small
fences

The horse's love of excitement and need for stimulation can be expressed in competitiveness with other horses — WATCH and IANTELLA racing over a fence

RIDING A HORSE FOR THE FIRST TIME

The author reassures and restrains CARAVAN

He accustoms CARAVAN to walking with a rope halter dropped round his neck, leading him at the same time with a bucket of nuts

Once CARAVAN is used to a halter, the author slips a bridle over his head

Then while CARAVAN has his nose in a bucket of feed, he leans over him, gets a leg up, and mounts

The author, on the new horse, encourages him to leave the yard by getting his wife, on another horse, to lead the way. The bucket of feed is still there, so the horse is being motivated not only by his need to please his master, but also by his need for food, and his need for the company of other horses

The horse follows the bucket of feed, allowing himself to be ridden without a companion

Henry Blake with REES

With COBBLERS and
REES (Centre)

Riding WATCH (Lower)

have completely changed their mental attitude and their outlook on life.

A further example of such a transformation took place in a horse called Ranne, sent to us one spring as unbreakable. Her owner had sent her away to the stallion and at the same time to be broken, but unfortunately the man who did it was rather rough with her, and she became completely unmanageable. When first I went into her loose box, she just stood in the corner and shook with fear.

So the first thing to do was to overcome her fear of men. My method was very simple. I didn't fuss or bother her in any way. I just left her alone, only going into her box when I fed her. The result was that within forty-eight hours she was looking for me to bring her food: she, who had been afraid of all men, was associating a man with her dinner. So she was calling for her dinner and calling me at the same time.

The next stage was also simple. When I gave her food, I stood by the basin until she was eating. And then I scratched her in an itchy place. All horses have places that itch: under the chin, on the line of the jaw; on the chest; or at the base of the neck just in front of the withers. Horses always like to be scratched in these places, so simply by scratching – in Ranne's case particularly the chest – I made her look forward to seeing me. From her chest I graduated to scratching her neck, from the wither up. And within two or three days I could run my hand up and down her neck, and scratch her behind her ears. The next stage was simply going in and out of her stable. Each time I went in I just scratched her. So within some ten days I had transformed a horse from exhibiting sheer terror at the sight of any man, into looking forward to seeing me – by doing absolutely nothing other than making the horse want me to go into her loose box, first because I fed her, then because I scratched her.

From then on her gentling went very quickly. She was an extremely sweet mare to gentle. The only thing that had to be watched was her tendency to anxiety, so each new experience had to be introduced very gradually, or she would get into a panic.

We started her off jumping low poles. She didn't really enjoy jumping them, but each time she jumped a fence I made a terrific fuss of her, and within a very short time jumping the fences became a reward in itself.

The important thing in gentling what had been an unmanageable horse was to make each task, when it was learned, the reward for doing the next task. The first task she had to learn was to accept me: then accepting me, and being made a fuss of by me, became the reward for being ridden, and jumped. And then the jumping became the reward for doing dressage work. And so it went on. If the presentation of each new thing is correct, then that will naturally become sufficient reward.

In fact, until she went back to her owner, I hunted hounds off Ranne for the first three months of the season, and she was one of the best hunters I have ever ridden. She was absolutely rock steady when I wanted her to stand still. On top of this, she was an extremely fast and willing horse, and she became a superb, but very careful, fencer.

It is fascinating to see how far this kind of learning, making each task when learned the reward for doing the next, can go from the original aim, and also to observe how long this kind of learning lasts. How can you explain why a horse should expend enormous effort on a task just because it was originally associated with praise? Most horses work just hard enough to avoid pain – that is to avoid being punished for not working. Yet a number of horses will work far beyond their limits for *no* apparent reason.

Why for example will a good steeple-chaser gallop himself to complete exhaustion? He doesn't do it from fear of pain – very often he will go on galloping and jumping long after he has lost his jockey. He doesn't do it to stay with other horses, because very often, after he has lost his jockey, he will lead by ten or twelve lengths.

Molfre was such a horse. At the third fence at the Carmarthen point-to-point, Molfre was brought down by another horse falling across him. I was knocked out for a moment or two, but when I came to, I could see Molfre pursuing the other horses. When he came into sight again out of the dip, he was ten lengths in front of the other horses. All the fences at Carmarthen on the far side of the course are island fences – that is to say they stand in the middle of the field, and the horse if he wants to can go around them. Yet Molfre, ten lengths in front of the other horses, met each fence right, and jumped it right. We eventually caught him when he had done almost a complete circuit by himself.

A horse who for no obvious reason will gallop himself completely into the ground is little Cefn Solomon. Cefn Solomon belonged to Dill Thomas of the Cefn Park Stud, and he had bought it for his daughter Bunny to hunt, and possibly to race at a later date. He asked me to ride him to begin with, so we introduced him to racing slowly. He went quite creditably, being placed in most races. Then in a very hard maiden race at the Glamorgan point-to-point I was asked to ride him again. I got a nice start and led into the first fence, to keep well out of the way of trouble, and I kept among the first two or three over the first half-mile. I eased him back to sixth or seventh place for the next two miles, and half a mile from home I was lying fifth. I could feel little Cefn Solomon was getting tired, so I just clicked my tongue, and, keeping him straight and balanced, let him go on at his own pace, encouraging him with my voice. The first two miles had been fast for most of the field, and they started dropping back past me. I still managed to keep my tiring horse straight, and placed him so that he could jump the fences with the minimum of effort. We came over the last fence in second place, about three lengths behind the tiring leader. I knew that if I touched Cefn Solomon with a stick, or shifted in any way, I would unbalance him completely, so I just sat still and kept him going with my voice. Eventually we were beaten at the winning post by only about two lengths, and I came in for some criticism from the less knowledgeable spectators, yet the little horse was so tired going back from the finish to the paddock that he could hardly walk, and when he got back to his loose box that night, he refused to eat his supper and he just lay down flat for the next twenty-four hours, refusing to get up even to eat. It is always a mystery to me, what makes a horse like this gallop himself to complete exhaustion. I hadn't hit him, or even kicked him with my heels. I just sat still. Yet he had galloped on, driven by his own indomitable spirit, and will to win.

And what is more, that extremely hard race in no way diminished little Solomon's desire to race in future, and give his best at every opportunity. Dill decided in 1975 to run him again the following season, and in the spring of 1976, he came down for a day's hunting to see what sort of a mess I was making of hunting a pack of hounds. After hunting we talked over the prospects for the coming season, and which horses he was racing, and he told me that Solomon was fitter than ever he had been. He thought that he might win a race early in the season. He never spoke a truer word in all his life.

At the Banwen Miners point-to-point on 21st February, although the weather was atrocious, we came to the second last fence. I had pegged the favourite's lead back from four lengths to two lengths. We jumped the second last fence, the favourite being so tired that he rolled very wide to one side and I went past him. Down the hill, when I was sitting absolutely still and not having to ride at all, the favourite made one despairing effort, but he was so tired he couldn't take off from the ground, and went base over apex. I went past the winning post a very easy and comfortable winner, with little Solomon as fresh as if he had hardly been out of his stable.

If I had used a stick on Solomon the previous spring, I would have had to punish him very severely to have beaten the favourite then – and even if I *had* belted the living daylights out of him, I don't think I would have won. For if he had had a very punishing race at the Glamorgan, he would probably never have run again. And he would certainly never have won a race afterwards. But by sitting still and never punishing him, I had made sure he retained his enthusiasm for racing. We hope now that he will go on and win other races in the future.

It is of course possible to win one race on a horse by beating the living daylights out of him. But there are very few horses who will take it a second time. They will simply never get themselves into a situation in which they are likely to be asked for the supreme effort.

This is why it is so important to teach a horse with patience and understanding: so that he *wants* to do what you want him to do. And this is what a learned positive goal is all about. Cefn Solomon's motivation could only have been the fact that he associated his galloping and jumping with enjoying himself. He loved the praise and appreciation he had got in his previous races, when he had given everything he had. It is only by teaching a horse in this way that you can achieve the ultimate in competition.

But learned positive goals have also to be constantly renewed. The horse has to receive praise and reward all the time, so that he learns to keep his enthusiasm. The success of little Cefn Solomon was maintained simply and solely because of the patience and understanding of his owner, Dill Thomas, and his daughter Bunny. Without these things, he would have been just another nice little lady's hunter.

To explain the fact that most horses work no harder than is required of them to avoid punishment, and others work quite happily without any obvious reward, requires however something more than the idea that they work for learned negative or positive goals. There is in fact a convergence of motives. This means simply that several reasons for doing something become involved in a single activity. To put it another way, one particular kind of work may lead to satisfaction of several needs at the same time.

Take the case of the green, untouched horse that becomes a superlative race horse or show jumper. He is like any other horse to begin with, he will learn either because he wants to do something, because he has damned well got to do it or get clobbered, or because if he does what he is told he gets praised. But as time goes on, he will begin to enjoy his work. He will begin to enjoy the burst of energy of jumping and racing. His training will keep him active and fit, and will satisfy his need for activity, excitement and movement. It will satisfy his somewhat restless nature by keeping both his body moving, and his mind alert. If he is a show-jumper the challenge and problems of jumping fences will satisfy his need to exercise his brain. He will also enjoy the praise and adulation that he gets when he wins or does well in a competition. So a whole variety of motives will converge with experience, re-inforcing each other and increasing his will to perform.

All these motives have then to be taken into account when training and handling a horse, because it is the fulfilment of as many as possible of the varying needs of the horse that makes the successful competitor. Without the right psychological make-up, physical excellence will go for nothing.

A friend of mine has for instance a very good hunter mare, with superb confirmation for a showjumper. She will jump five foot with ease but she is useless in competition. Time and time again she will do a clear round up to the last fence and then have the last fence down. In spite of her physical excellence Fred Broome had to decide that she would never make a showjumper, simply and solely because she didn't want to win in competition.

On the other hand, with the right mental approach a horse can make up for a certain amount of physical shortcoming in competition. An example of this is my wife's cob, Rostellan, or to give him his correct name, Trefaes Dafydd. As far as I know he is the only registered Welsh Cob taking part in one-day events. He is fifteen hands high, and like all Welsh cobs, his natural pace is a trot. Again like all Welsh cobs, whilst he can jump great heights, he has great difficulty in jumping spreads. So what drives him to gallop himself to exhaustion, or tackle cross-country in a one-day event? First of all my wife has had him for six years now, and he has developed such love for her that he will do any-thing to please her. And I have already described how, when he has misbehaved, he looks as crestfallen as a small boy who knows he is going to be punished for being naughty.

So the first and greatest need within him is the drive to please the person he loves most. And he achieves this by giving every-thing he has got. Then again he is very fit, and full of corn, so he has a great store of energy within him to be released by jumping and galloping. Again, like many Welsh cobs, he is a very great showman, and he enjoys the admiration he gets from what amounts to his fan club. So that whilst it is physically impossible for him ever to win a one-day event, simply and solely because no matter how much he tries he can't gallop fast enough to do so, every time he takes part he puts in an outstanding performance.

Probably the best performance he has ever put in was in spring 1976 at Penrice. After a season's hunting he was as fit as a fiddle, so, as often happens in one-day events, his very fitness meant that he didn't do a very good dressage test. But the showjumping and cross-country were both extremely stiff. All the fences in the showjumping, and most of them in the cross-country, were absolute maximum for one-day events. (In fact two of the cross-country fences had to be made smaller, as they were over the maximum). The showjumping fences also included spreads, and were on a slope, which made jumping extremely difficult. Yet Rostellan did an outstanding round. How he managed to complete some of the spreads, which in theory were completely beyond him, I do not know. And again when it came to the cross-country he performed way beyond his natural ability. It was a very long and stiff course, with plenty of ups and downs. The first three fences were comparatively easy, the third fence being a spread of bales which he made nothing of since he got over his difficulty in jumping a big spread simply by jumping on top of the bales, and off them. Fences four and five were big crossed poles, and then a fence and ditch, and another fence out over it. He got over these perfectly well. There was a long stretch into the sixth fence, and he carted my wife flat-out, steadied himself and jumped the fence immaculately. He proceeded round the course at such speed that by the time he had got to the third last fence he was very tired. But his determination and spirit carried him over the finish. By then he was exhausted, having galloped himself into the ground in a time nearly as fast as that of the thoroughbreds.

Getting a horse fit for any competition is rather like stoking up a boiler until you have got the right head of steam to be released: too much steam and the boiler explodes, or the horse becomes unmanageable, and expends too much energy early on; too little steam, that is too little fitness and mental drive, and the horse won't compete at all. At the same time you are building up tension, which he releases by expending everything he has in the competition.

Over the course of years, by careful training, the horse will have been taught to love jumping, or whatever he is doing. And that's another reason for competing well. Any competition horse is a very proud horse, and also a terrific showman, so the admiration he receives when he is competing satisfies him, and the praise and admiration he receives when he does well gives him an added incentive to excel himself.

Thus in competition as in any form of riding, the greater the number of motivations you can involve in the experience, the greater the pleasure you and the horse will get out of it. Though I tend to emphasize competition and jumping, these of course are not the whole purpose of riding, or even the major parts of it: they are with us, as with most people, only a very small part of our work with horses. Most of the time we are just hacking, and schooling. But the advantage of competition is that it provides you with a measure of whether the work you are doing on the horse is correct. If each time you compete with a horse, the horse does a little better, then you know that your schooling and basic work is correct. If on the other hand the horse is making no progress, or appears to be going backwards when you are competing, then you know that the work you are doing is wrong. So competition is a very necessary yardstick for any form of equestrianism. And of course unless your schooling and riding have some object in view, they tend to lack point and become boring. If on the other hand you are aiming for something particular – a showjumping competition or a dressage competition, a one-day event, a race or a day's hunting – your schooling and training will take on a new urgency, and stimulate the horse accordingly.

Rostellan may take part in two or three showjumping competitions, a couple of hunt trials and a couple of one-day events in the whole year, though he will also have twenty or thirty days' hunting. But we can see by each one-day event and by each showjumping competition and each hunter trial, whether Rostellan is fit and well. Because whilst he may be jumping out of his skin at home and in the box, you can really only tell whether the horse is right and well when it comes to the crunch of competition.

We like also to vary the competitions which our horses take part in, simply and solely because each competition needs a different form of schooling and work. Each small riding club competition he takes part in, because he has had special schooling for that competition, makes for a slightly better and more widely experienced horse.

In short, I tend to look at any races, hunter trials or one-day events I take part in rather as a schoolmaster looks on the end-of-term examinations: I use them as a measure of progress the horse has made in the intervening time. As well as telling me whether the horse is fit enough, and well enough, they tell me whether the form of training I have been giving him is correct.

6: *Using the Horse's Natural Drives*

If you look out of your window, you may see a tree, a motor car and a dog. You will know that they are a tree, a motor car and a dog because they are similar in appearance and behaviour to objects that you have seen before that are trees, motor cars and dogs. You will know that the tree will stay where it is, the dog will walk and bark, and the motor car will smell, make a horrible noise and, if you are lucky, get you from point A to point B. Experience has taught you to recognize objects and predict their behaviour, so you act accordingly.

The horse organizes his experience in much the same way. If you have been feeding him horse and pony nuts, and change him to race-horse nuts, or Olympic nuts, he will eat them because they are similar to the food he has been eating before. In the same way, when you are riding or jumping him, he will treat various objects and tasks according to how he can relate them to something that he has done before. He will jump a variety of objects and perform a variety of tasks quite happily and readily. provided only that each is similar to something he has done before. And most of your training makes use of this fact.

If, for example, a horse has been accustomed to jumping a single pole two feet high, and you put a second pole underneath it, he will jump it quite happily because jumping two poles is very little different from jumping one pole. If you put the second pole parallel to the first, say a foot or two away from the first, again he will jump it quite happily. He will relate anything new to something he has done previously, and provided his original experience has been pleasant, he will be quite happy to attempt the new one. But if the thing he has done before has been unpleasant, he will treat anything similar with suspicion.

For nearly two years we had Madam on the place. She was rather an antisocial horse to the rest of the herd, so much so that if any other horse went near her, she kicked its teeth in. I then bought a nice little black mare at Llanybyther horse sale because she was something similar in appearance to Madam, and the same type. Since we had done very well with Madam, I bought the little mare hoping that she would be as good. When we turned her out with the other horses, all the other horses gave her a very wide berth for four or five days – she was similar in appearance to Madam, who had kicked them, so they treated Beauty (that is what we called her) in exactly the same way. The way I guess they thought was: she is like Madam; Madam kicks; therefore she kicks. And until they found that Beauty had a much sweeter and kinder nature than Madam, they kept well away from her.

This logic by association is also illustrated by my experience with my beloved twelve-two pony Jezebel, whom I have already described. She is an extremely intelligent, active and rather nervous pony with a fantastic jump in her, but the temper of a demon. I got her as an eight-year-old. Her previous owner persuaded me by threatening that if I didn't take her he would have her shot in the field the next day, she was such a nuisance in making his other horses as impossible to catch as she was. Even after I had had her for some time, she would jump five-foot gates with ease rather than be caught. On one occasion she jumped a four-foot barbed wire fence with a ten-foot drop on the other side, without turning a hair.

Her temper and her determination not to be confined, combined with the fear learned through the ill treatment she had received, expressed itself in Jezebel in a hatred of all mankind. Men to her were unpleasant, brutal and to be escaped from. If she couldn't escape, she attacked them – not because she wanted to attack them, but because it was the only way she knew of defending herself.

It is of course impossible to change the attitudes and habits of a lifetime in five minutes. And in an eight-year-old mare of the calibre of Jezebel, you can never completely get rid of old suspicions. But what I had to try to do was gradually to replace her negative associations with the idea of man, with good ones. I had consistently to offer her kindness and gentleness, and persuade her to associate good things with me. And hard work and great patience have at last built between her and me a very great affection and a very deep trust each of the other. I still can't, and I don't ever think I will be able to, walk up to her in the field and catch her without difficulty. But when I open the gate of the field she'll trot a mile down the road and into a stable, and stand there waiting to be tied up. Funnily enough the odd time when I have come off her hunting or in competition, she has stood waiting for me to catch her and get on again.

We can't of course *know* how a horse associates one experience with another, since we can't experience what a horse experiences. The only thing we can do, is to infer that since he reacts the same way to two similar foods, to him they appear and taste the same. Or if he jumps two fences in the same way, that they appear the same to him. If a horse has been friendly with a cat and used to having it in his loose box, and when a dog walks into his box he treats the dog in the same way that he treats the cat, it is reasonably safe to assume that he is relating his experience with the cat to his attitude to the dog.

As in everything else with the psychology of a horse, we can only infer the horse's motives from his reactions. But our observation of these reactions does lead us to conclude that one of the experiences most readily generalized by the horse is that of fear.

If a horse tries very hard to please his owner or rider, he may very well be motivated by fear, if his original trainer was difficult to please and rather cruel.

A horse may jump a fence out of desire to please his owner, because he enjoys jumping fences, or because he knows if he doesn't he will have the living daylight whaled out of him. But motives may also be in conflict: the horse's desire to jump a fence and please his rider may conflict with the fear of hurting himself if he does so – or even with his tendency to pure laziness!

A horse in competition and jumping is very often subject to this conflict of motive. You might, at a fence, get four motives all in conflict: a desire to please his rider, in conflict with a desire not to hurt himself, and his wish not to expend more energy than he has to, in turn in conflict with the fear of being punished. These drives are not always in balance: if the fear of hurting himself is very great, and his desire to please his rider very small, he will refuse to jump the fence. Or if his desire not to expend energy again is very large, and his fear of being hit is very small, again he will refuse.

As an experiment, we took Madam and put her in a small dressage competition with two different riders on her, the second one going *hors du concours*. They were both judged by the same judge. The first rider had a dressage score of eighty-nine penalties; but the second rider had a score of just forty-eight penalties. The difference in the score was simply accounted for by the difference in the horse's desire to please. We chose Madam because she tends to be particularly nappy, and whilst a very active little mare has to be ridden with a minimum contact on the reins, or she throws her head about. The difference in the score was not in the competence of the riders, for both were good riders. However, Madam didn't get on with the first girl on her back, and she adored the second. So it was a pretty fair test of how desire to please can change the performance of the horse.

There are of course other environmental factors affecting a horse's performance on any particular occasion. If for example he is undernourished, his desire to conserve energy will far outweigh his fear of punishment. If on the other hand the horse is overfed, and under-exercised, he will be so bubbling with energy that he will jump a fence and gallop, whether his rider wishes to or not. We try to see that all such factors are working for us when we deal with our horses, and in particular we lay very great emphasis on our horses enjoying themselves: partly because we like our horses, but mainly because we know that if a horse wants to do something, it is so much easier to get him doing it than if he doesn't.

In our training we try to relate high levels of performance with high levels of enjoyment. At the same time we realize that over-indulgence, that is letting a horse do what he wants to, to mis-behave as he wants to, is not kindness, it's just another form of ill-treatment, even when from the best of motives. If for example you allow a horse to get away with biting you, without punching his teeth in, he will bite anybody and everyone, and he will certainly come to a stage when he is biting you so much that you have to get rid of him. And a horse that bites people has only one end: that's in a Cat's Meat tin.

Over-indulgence of a horse, and allowing him to acquire vices, in short, is not only not kindness, it can even amount to extreme cruelty. For it must always be remembered that many of the things that a horse does, he does spontaneously and uncon-sciously – it is you, the rider, who must do some of his thinking for him and decide where his best interests are.

Rostellan, for example, as I have already said, will eat whatever you put in front of him. No matter how much you give him, he will go on eating, for he is a compulsive feeder. This, in part any-way, is because he was very badly treated as a foal and as a young horse. If anything, since we have had him, he's been slightly over-fed. Yet if he is allowed to, he will eat nine or ten pounds of corn at a sitting, and no matter how much hay you give him, it will always be cleared up by the morning.

The scientists tell us, and no doubt they are right, that the horse's stomach can carry only five pounds of food. But on two measure trials, Rostellan ate first nine-and-a-half pounds of horse and pony nuts, and in the second a whole bale of hay, which weighed thirty-nine pounds: between six o'clock one evening, and eight-thirty the following morning, he had eaten all that hay, and on top of that he had eaten five-and-a-quarter pounds of horse and pony nuts! His normal day's feed was fifteen pounds of horse and pony nuts, and ten pounds of hay.

This is the sort of phenomenon that makes for difficulty in trying to understand horses! For if you were to be able to ask Rostellan why he ate so much, he would probably say because he was hungry. But of course this cannot be so, since he goes on eating long after he has been adequately fed. It is probably in his case a legacy of a certain amount of underfeeding when he was young. But compulsive eating isn't always traceable to malnutrition when a horse was young: I have seen a four-month-old foal so grossly fat that it was suffering from lamenitis; and I have also come across horses that have been almost starved, yet have been very difficult to get into condition because, in spite of being underfed, they remain very shy feeders.

A horse, like a human being, will acquire habits of which he is largely unaware. He has been conditioned by his experience, and often one can do no more than guess at that experience.

For instance, a horse may shy at a certain place on the road, for no reason that is apparent at the time. At some time in the past, let us say, he was frightened badly there. When he passed the same place the following day, the memory of being frightened there was still with him, so he shied again at the same spot. And again on the third day. Within a week or two, unless great care had been taken with him, he would have acquired the habit of shying at a certain spot. If he changed hands and went past the same spot again he would still shy there, and the new owner wouldn't know the reason why. Indeed, if a horse gets used to shying in one place, he may start shying in another, again for no apparent reason, and he acquires the bad habit of shying simply and solely because of a frightening experience that was not dealt with at the time it occurred.

One horse I had some time ago had the intriguing habit of moving his tail to one side when he dunged – he didn't raise his tail to dung as a horse normally does, he just moved it to one side. When I tried to trace this habit back, I discovered that he had been very badly fed, and got into an extremely weak condition at one period when he was a two-year-old. The effort of lifting his tail to dung had been just too much for him, so he had learned merely to move his tail to one side. Even when he got stronger – he was jumping out of his skin when we had him – he still retained the habit of moving his tail in this way.

Thus, since the horse is a creature of habit, it is extremely important to stop him acquiring bad habits, and to make sure that he acquires good ones.

I have a friend who hunts a lot, and when out hunting she always trots up to a fence to make sure that it is jumpable. As a result, all her horses have acquired the habit of refusing once at every fence: solely because she does the very sensible thing of making sure that each fence is free of wire before jumping it. It means that none of her horses will jump in competition.

Kerry, when he came to us, had the reputation of striking out with his front feet. He didn't. What he did was bounce up and down on his front feet, and this had terrorized his previous owner so much that as soon as Kerry bounced she jumped to one side. So he had got into the habit of 'bouncing' whenever he wanted to get past anyone – a very threatening habit indeed. When he came to us, we cured him of this very quickly. But what he did was simply transfer the habit to his jumping. When we were hunting, just before he started into a fence, he would bounce up and down on his front feet. Just as he had bounced when trying to pass his owner, who was a barrier, he bounced in front of a fence because this was another barrier. This is a perfect example of how a habit once acquired can be transferred to a completely different situation, long after the original reason has been forgotten.

This brings up the question of measuring motives. When you have discovered what makes a horse do something, it is often important to know just how strong the motive for doing it is. But you can't measure it with a tape measure, nor put it on a scale and conclude that this motive is two feet high, and weighs three and a half pounds. It is possible however to measure a motive, or rather to measure its strength. This can be done in four ways.

First we can measure certain drives according to what the horse *consumes* as a result of his drive: you can measure the strength of his thirst by the amount of water he will drink, or the amount of food a horse will eat will measure his hunger. You can also measure the greed of a horse using this method.

This you do, having fed the horse sufficient corn for his needs, by measuring the amount of food he will eat on top of that. This is the way we measured Rostellan's greed. His normal feed was five pounds, but in our first test he ate nine-and-a-half pounds of corn at a single feed.

Biddy, on the other hand, whose normal feed is six pounds three times a day, would not only not eat seven pounds when we offered it, but she wouldn't eat her next feed either. So we can say that Biddy's greed is nil, whilst Rostellan's is ninety percent.

Another method of measuring a need is to deprive the horse. This is a good method for measuring such factors as the amount of movement or the amount of light a horse requires.

The need for movement and light, which are vitally necessary for a horse's mental and physical wellbeing – if he is deprived of either he will not only become mentally unbalanced, but he will also lose condition physically as quickly as if he were dying of starvation – cannot be measured directly. But they can be measured indirectly by measuring the effect of withdrawal of either. Measuring the effect of withdrawal of movement is best done with a horse that is being stabled at night and out by day. A reasonably active and alert horse, if you turn him out into a field after being in at night, will canter round a couple of times and then settle down and graze. This particular trial, to eliminate a build-up effect, we normally carry out once a week for three or four weeks. It is quite simple to do: you measure the time it takes the horse to settle down and graze after being turned out over a period of days. And then one night, instead of putting him into a loose box, you tie him up in a very narrow stall to restrict his movements, for twelve hours, then you turn him out the following day and measure the time it takes for him to settle down and graze. By subtracting the average time it takes him normally to settle down to graze, from the average of three or four occasions when he has been allowed only minimal movement at night, you can measure the effect the restriction of movement has had on him. If the average time it takes him to settle down grazing normally on being turned out is four and a half minutes, but on the four occasions when he had been restricted in movement it was seven and a half minutes, the difference would be a hundred and eighty seconds. We simply call this a movement factor of a hundred and eighty. And by doing this with three or four horses, we can compare the different amounts of movement and exercise various horses need.

These figures, when it comes to applying them in training, are usually in *inverse* ratio to the amount of exercising a horse requires. That is, a horse that takes a relatively long time to settle down after a night of restricted movement, is likely to have taken more exercise in his loose box than one who takes a short time to settle down after a night of restricted movement. So it is the horse that moves little in his loose box during the night that in fact needs most exercising by day.

Another way to measure the strength of a horse's drive is to test exactly what he will do, or how far he will go, in order to satisfy it. If, for instance, a horse will perform very highly for praise, and you know that he will improve his performance through praise, you know that his desire for praise is very strong. If on the other hand a horse will improve after a clout with a stick, then you know that his fear of punishment is strong. By a series of small trials you can test which form of stimulus will make your horse perform most willingly, and which are his strongest drives.

The fourth way of measuring, a variation on the last which is extremely important in training a horse, is to test just what a horse will learn to do in order to attain a particular object.

For example, when we are schooling a horse to jump, we plan the routine so that the last thing the horse does before going home is to jump. He thus very quickly associates going home to his dinner with jumping. And of course we jump towards home. So the horse very quickly learns that if he jumps the fence that he is pointed at, then he goes home. Whereas if he messes about, refuses, and knocks the fence all over the place, he has another half hour to forty minutes work before him. We measure the strength of his wish to go home by the way he jumps the fences when he knows that he is going home, compared with his performance, say, before he goes out to work.

The fascination about horses of course is that no two of them are the same, and their personalities vary even from day to day. Indeed the whole character of a horse can alter once his personality is allowed to develop, and one of my greatest joys is to watch the change in a sullen and rather bad tempered horse when his personality starts to grow.

Few horses have given me more pleasure in this way than Charlie. We had bought Charlie at Ascot in the autumn, with three possible aims in view: to put him in one-day eventing, to ride him point-to-pointing, or to put him into training for hurdling. What I had not intended with Charlie was that he would do very much hunting. His breeding makes him a six-furlong flat-race horse, and I didn't think that he would stand up to very much hunting, though we used him hunting a little, simply to get him interested in his work.

But unfortunately for me, Ranne's owner came back from America and naturally wanted Ranne back to hunt herself, so Charlie was pressed into service as my second horse, which meant that two days a month I had to hunt hounds off him. And this Charlie didn't enjoy to start with.

First, he didn't like the hounds. Second, he hated being by himself. And third, he didn't like the work involved because it meant galloping down hills, which he thought was extremely dangerous. So he was a bad hunter. But very slowly, in spite of himself, he developed a liking for the job. Once he discovered that the hounds weren't going to bite him or eat him alive, he stopped taking umbrage every time my hounds came near me. And then he began to enjoy hunting, with my daughter Paddy riding him on the days he needed a day's hunting, and I didn't need him. Next he began to enjoy jumping. He realized that scrambling fences and pig netting and banks, which are the greater part of the obstacles we jump out hunting here, were quite fun to jump. He also began to enjoy showing himself off at the Meet, leading all the horses all the time. This development of his pride was easy to see in the way he began to hold his head up, and stick his tail out at an angle of sixty degrees like an Arab stallion. He absolutely swaggered out of town after a Meet. But he still wasn't enjoying the hard work involved in drawing, and he certainly didn't like being by himself when galloping with running hounds.

But suddenly all this changed. We had an extremely good hunt. It started off with a very sharp point of about a mile and a half in which he was being his usual Bolshie self, then, when the fox left the second cover, he got away a bit in front of hounds, and as we often do I went one way and my wife went the other – in case we got stopped by an unjumpable barbed wire fence. I hunted hounds slowly for about half a mile on Charlie. Charlie was still going forwards backwards, and eventually we came to a boundary fence that was impossible. So, I got off my horse, left him standing by the fence, and went on hunting hounds on foot. Shortly after, my wife came up. I took her horse off her, and she had to take Charlie the long way round and catch up with me again. This took about half an hour, and Charlie was absolutely furious. He has got a very nasty habit, when he is very angry, of doing little fly kicks, which are uncomfortable to ride, and he had done this the whole time my wife was on him. When she caught us up again the fox was in a patch of kale, and we were trying to get him out. So I changed back on to Charlie, and she took her horse. Charlie was completely different: he was suddenly putting his heart into his work. His whole attitude had changed, from that of a reluctant partner to that of someone who was doing his best in what he thought were impossible circumstances.

Hounds came out of the kale like rockets, and as they went over a wire boundary fence and disappeared from view, we lost them completely. And so the first whip, my wife and I went looking for them. We all made wrong guesses at the direction in which they had gone, and spent the next hour going round in ever increasing circles, until Grayling, the horse my wife was riding, could go no further. And Charlie too was extremely tired. But poor Charlie had to go on, because I had to find the hounds, and we had another ten miles to go. I was expecting ten miles of hell, because Charlie would be by himself which he hated. But not a bit of it. Charlie gave everything he had and went happily and willingly. Even when we eventually found hounds, we had a six-mile hack back to the Meet with them, yet although Charlie was as tired as he possibly could be, he went home with his ears pricked and his tail up. When at last he saw the trailer he let out a wicker of delight, and couldn't get into it fast enough – a horse who in the past had been somewhat awkward to load.

After that Charlie put all he could into his hunting. I think what had happened was first, that he had suddenly seen *why* he was supposed to be doing the things that I was asking him to do, and second, when I changed on to my wife's horse, that he thought he had been demoted and was in disgrace, so he was extremely relieved when I got back on him and he discovered that he had been promoted again – though why he should think he was being demoted when my wife got on him, I don't know, because she is much kinder and sympathetic a rider than I am when I am hunting hounds. My horse has to go, whether he is tired or not, simply because you have to stay with hounds when you are hunting them. She nurses her horse, and looks after him, whereas anything I'm hunting has to look after itself and me.

Charlie, in effect, wanted status and approval, and by offering him both we had changed his whole attitude to hunting. His story shows how important it is to know what a horse's needs and desires are, and how strong they are, so that we can know how far we can go in using his existing desires to make him want to do something new.

I've seen a very nervous filly walk up and down next to a rail six inches high, rather than step over it to get to her food, which was a mere two yards the other side of the rail. Later on the same filly was tearing at her bit to jump three-foot-six fences. The only difference in the filly, other than a certain amount of fitness, was that she had learned to *want* to jump fences.

Hunger and thirst are controlled by factors from within the body. But other factors also have a great influence on needs as primary as these, and we have already seen that they vary from one horse to another.

A horse, for example, will often drink water that it doesn't need. If when you are out riding, you allow him, he will sip at a pool of water, then fifty or a hundred yards further on stop and sip at another pool of water. A horse that has been recently fed will still eat a handful of nuts, and pick at the grass in the hedgerow if allowed to. This is partly because most horses have a natural instinct to consume as much as possible to store up body fat against a time of need, and partly because eating can relieve nervous tension. We have discovered that after a race, a horse will cool down and relax more quickly if allowed to stop every few yards and take a mouthful of grass while he is being walked.

Sexual and maternal drives too are no more constant in horses than in man. During her natural cycle the hormone balance in a mare's blood alters completely, so the very nature of the horse alters. This may have a considerable bearing upon her performance: it is well established that a mare in season usually races well below her normal level of ability. On the other hand there are some mares who will win races only when they are in season. And since hormone balance has a bearing upon a mare's racing performance, it is probable that it will also affect her performance at showjumping, or eventing, and any other form of competition:

in fact, that a mare's performance and ability will vary right through the twenty-one-day cycle. If you drew a graph of her performance at competition through a period of weeks, it would almost certainly bear a direct relation to a graph of her sexual cycle. In some mares the highest point of performance is at the mid-point between the two heat periods.

Towards the end of a mare's pregnancy other hormones come into play. The presence of the foetus in the uterus stimulates production of prolactin in the pituitary glands. And though no experimental work has been done on this phenomenon in mares, some experiments on rats are extremely interesting. Virgin female rats put in contact with baby rats, even though they had not bred themselves, displayed typical maternal behaviour. And *the level of prolactin in their blood* at the end of a week was treble the normal level. If exposing mares to foals alters the hormones in their bodies too, it explains why one mare will act as a foster mother or an aunt to a foal: the sight of the foal actually induces changes in the hormones of the blood. Equally a mare will mother and protect an immature yearling, or a two- or three-year-old. She may even take a weak gelding under her wing. It also explains why some mares will look after their owners with maternal care, be the owner male or female; pony mares will often seem to look on their young owners as rather badly brought up foals!

The sexual drive in geldings varies quite considerably: from nil to a drive comparable with that of an uncastrated stallion. Pudding, who had served mares when he was young, before he was castrated, will even now serve a mare in season. A gelding's sex drive is affected by the age of castration, and the degree of sexual development at castration. The sexual drive in a gelding is very often expressed in extreme protectiveness towards his owner, if the owner is a woman. And the gelding tends to retain the protective instinct of a stallion for his mares.

Stallions themselves vary considerably in sexual drive: we actually had one stallion sent to us who wouldn't bother at all to serve mares that were in season. And we cured him. First, we changed his diet. Then we allowed him to run with single mares as they came into season, turning the mare out with him at least a week before she was due. His interest in mares gradually returned, and he is now serving very successfully.

7: *Sensory Stimulation*

If you observe horses carefully you can hardly escape the conclusion that, although some of their behaviour springs from their
primary physical needs – for food, drink and sex – most is
caused by something else altogether. You have only to watch a
horse in his loose-box with the top part of the door open, standing
most of the day with his head leaning out, watching what goes on
outside, to realize that he has a great need for sensory stimulation: in other words that the horse needs to use his sight, his
hearing, and his senses of touch, smell and taste. Leaning out
of his stall, he can see us going to and from the house doing our
daily chores, hear the sounds of what is going on in the countryside, smell the galaxy of odours that pervade the yard – of the
dung heap, the hounds, the hay in the feeding house.

Without this stimulation for his senses, the horse is mentally
deprived. We know from our own observations that if in a stall
a horse is unable to see and hear what is going on outside, he
will become depressed, will go off his food, and begin to deterior-
ate physically.

We have done two small experiments on this kind of deprivation. The first was on Molfre. He lived in the end loose box of
the stable block where he could see and hear everything that
was going on, and he spent his day, no matter what the weather,
with his head out over the door, watching our comings and
goings from the house, noting when we went out in the car, in
which direction we went, and how long we were gone. When we
came back he would welcome me back with a wicker of welcome.
And each time I went past his stable door he would nudge me
on the arm to say hello.

However, that January the weather was so terrible – there was
a strong south-east wind, a mixture of Arctic gale, rain and sleet,

all blowing into the front of the stable – that to stop Molfre getting frostbite in his ears I kept the top half of his door shut for three days. At the end of those three days he had changed dramatically. From his normal cheerful self, he had become morose and dejected, and his food consumption had dropped by over two pounds of corn per day. Yet as soon as we opened the door again, within twenty-four hours he was back to normal and his food consumption had risen again.

The horse also seems to have an emotional drive to take risks. He needs excitement, and this need is linked with his curiosity. You can see it for yourself if you keep a horse shut in a darkened stable for twenty-four hours, completely deprived of excitement and interest. When he comes out he will react to all sorts of objects, which normally he would ignore in passing, and exhibit alarm where in normal circumstances he would show none. This suggests a need for excitement, for fear as a stimulation, whether actual or imaginary. A horse will look for danger and excitement even when there is none there – which is what we have called the need for risk. And what we term boredom in horses is actually a deprivation, a failure to satisfy its need for stimulation and excitement.

This also we found with Molfre. When I took him out on the fourth day after he had been shut in, instead of just putting his head down and walking, as he does normally, he was jumping out of his skin. He shied six times on a five-hundred-yard stretch. It was a simple matter of reasoning to deduce that some change was affecting him, and the obvious change was the closed stable door. To check this theory, I had only to count the number of times the other horses shied in similar circumstances.

We found that over a stretch of road about five hundred yards, four horses between them shied twenty-one times – that is, an average of five times each. We then worked them for three days. Then over the next week we kept count of the number of times they shied on the same stretch of road – which they had been going up and down on for the previous twelve months – and we discovered that on an average they were shying half a time each: that is, over a week, the four horses between them shied sixteen times. After being shut up without any mental stimulation for four days, in other words, they had shied ten times as often as their average when being worked normally. This is a simple piece of research that could be carried out by anyone.

We concluded from our experiment that depriving the horses of any interest or excitement for four days caused them to look for interest and excitement, to manufacture things to be frightened of, in order to feed a need that had been building up within them.

The second experiment was in part also an involuntary one. Due to the bad summer of 1974, we were very short of good quality hay for the winter, and unable to get any more, so just before Christmas we changed over from corn and hay to complete horse food. The horses did extremely well physically – in fact they were fitter and better than they had ever been – but the effect on them mentally was quite unforeseen. Within twenty-four hours, they all became slightly edgy in temper and almost simultaneously they started eating the wooden stable partitions and doors. Their tempers were in a state very similar to my own when I am deprived of cigarettes for any length of time.

To satisfy their obvious need for something to chew, we eventually collected fir branches and gorse which we hung in their stables. These they could chew to their hearts' content while they were getting all the nutrients they needed in the complete horse food. But before we solved the problem this way, we did a little test. To measure their need for chewing, we creosoted all the wooden edges that the horses could chew. After one creosoting, two of the six horses stopped chewing altogether. Three of them stopped eating wood after two creosotings. But Biddy, who was having more food than any of the others (she was getting twenty-one pounds of complete horse food a day), was still chewing at the edge of the doors and partitions, after three coatings of creosote. I had to stop here, because she was beginning to get blisters on her mouth.

When we came to analyze these results, we found that although

Biddy, who had the greatest need to chew, was the horse receiving the most horse nuts per day, she was however the one receiving least hay – only five to six pounds. And we also found that the most placid horses were the ones who stopped chewing the partitions first. Biddy was the most irritable and temperamental of them all, and the one who kept chewing longest. Once we had supplied them with the fir tree tops and gorse to chew at, all the horses' temperaments went back to normal.

I encountered the most extreme case I have seen of the effects of sensory deprivation on a horse some twenty-five years ago in Ireland. I was asked to take on a fifteen-three thoroughbred gelding called Danny Boy, apparently completely unmanageable and unbreakable, to try to break him. In his attempt to master him, his owner had first deprived him of water. When this hadn't worked he had tried shutting him in a darkened stable, and when I was brought in he had been in a dark stable without light or much fresh air for nearly a month. He had almost gone round the bend. There he was, standing with his head near the ground, shaking it, waving it from side to side for hours on end. His coat was dull, he was extremely thin, and his staring eyes gave him the appearance of being completely insane. When anyone opened the stable door, he came at them with his teeth and his front legs.

It took me nearly two and a half hours to get a halter on. Eventually I managed it, attached a longer rope to the halter rope, and opened the door and let him out into the cow yard. Once he was outside, he galloped round and round for nearly half an hour before finally he slowed to a trot. I had great difficulty in making him change direction every five or ten minutes, since I didn't want him galloping in the same direction for too long. When he finally settled down to a walk, I managed to get him into a much larger box, out of which he could see, and then for the next forty-eight hours, I spent as much time as I could talking to him and making friends. Every day for the next fortnight, I led him out for an hour or so, letting him wander at my side as he wanted to, picking the grass. All the time I was talking to

him, and getting him settled. And after that it was quite simple.
I lived at that time about fifteen miles from where he was stabled,
and to save the long journey backward and forward I decided to
shift him nearer to where I was living. I led him the first mile
and a half of the journey, then I just popped on his back and rode
the last thirteen and a half miles bareback, on a halter.

His advance from here was quite dramatic. He was never
mad, of course, he had merely been handled roughly and been
terrified. And the combination of rough handling, starvation,
water-deprivation and being confined to a darkened stable, had
temporarily unbalanced him. But once the need to have his
senses stimulated had been satisfied, and he had been induced to
relax in the company of human beings, he became an extremely
easy and willing horse.

However, ten days after I got him near home, I had still not
yet managed to get a saddle on his back. It was still one of the
things of which he was terrified. So I was riding him without a
saddle, with only a bridle, when one morning, to make a change in
his work, I thought it might be a good idea to let him see hounds.
I rode him towards where I knew hounds were hunting, and as
I rode along the road, heard them find in a piece of gorse just
above me. Then suddenly, without any warning, the fox popped
out about five yards in front of me, followed hard by the whole
pack. I turned Danny Boy into the bank, and he went over it
like a stag: the first fence he had ever jumped in his life. Then
ensued what was probably one of the best hunts I have ever had.
Hounds ran absolutely straight for about fifteen miles, and we
were stopped by wire only once during the day. Towards the
end Danny was going so well that twice I jumped off a bank over
barbed wire. We were very, very fortunate. Hounds were not
going so fast that we couldn't stay with them, but on the other
hand they never stopped hunting, eventually killing about fifteen
miles from home. Danny, who until the start of the hunt had
never jumped a fence, was within four or five fields of hounds
all the time.

And then followed the most uncomfortable three hours I can

remember. After riding fifteen miles of cross-country without a
saddle, my backside was like a piece of raw beef. And I was faced
with a fifteen-mile hack home! I was so sore that it was absolutely
agony even to walk, so for most of the way home I rode leaning
across him on my stomach, until I had taken all the skin off my
belly as well, and then I alternated between lying on my stomach
and sitting on my backside for the last four miles. After I had
groomed and watered Danny, I went home and had a bath, and
spent the next forty-eight hours swathed in bandages trying to
find the least agonizing place to lie on. But it was a fantastic hunt
and worth every twinge of pain I suffered afterwards. And Danny
Boy from that day on became a really wonderful hunter, and
only two days after that first hunt I put a saddle on him without
any trouble whatsoever.

There has been very little scientific work done, as far as I
know, on deprivation in horses. But considerable work has been
done on sensory deprivation in man and ape.

Twenty-odd years ago an American researcher named Buxton
did an experiment on depriving human beings of all sensory
stimulation. College students were paid twenty dollars a day
– then quite a large amount of money – to lie on a comfortable
bed, confined in a small, darkened and totally silent cubicle. To
reduce visual stimulation to the minimum, all the students wore
opaque goggles, and to reduce tactile stimulation they wore gloves
on their hands and socks on their feet. At the beginning it seemed
to the students that this was a very easy way to make money.
But very quickly most of them found it intolerable. After two
or three days they wanted nothing more than to get out. They
began to have hallucinations, became disorientated in time and
space, and lost their ability to think clearly, or to concentrate on
anything for very long. Some of the symptoms lasted for a considerable time after they had been released.

This is only a single illustration of the evidence that *all* animals
need to have their senses stimulated. And the need for stimulation
also implies the need for *change*. The horse is always looking
for something new – a horse that can see out and see things

happening is far happier and far more alert than one that is gazing at a blank wall all day. He needs changing sounds, changing scenery, tastes and smells. Unlike the dog, the horse has in fact a somewhat limited sense of smell, but he still needs variation in the things he smells and tastes. The horse is naturally inquisitive and curious, and he needs to experience new things all the time.

Some years ago another American researcher corralled a group of wild mustangs, straight in off the Prairie, then drove each in turn singly into a smaller corral, in the middle of which was a blanket. Without exception each horse proceeded to walk round and round the blanket, in quite a short time to touch and smell it. Then, having done so, it ignores it – walking over it, dunging on it and taking no notice of it whatever.

Then in a further experiment, a slight change was made. Half of the subjects were left in the corral with the plain blanket, which they continued to ignore. The other half were herded into another corral where an inflatable bladder had been put under a blanket, which from time to time was inflated by remote control so that the centre of the blanket rose up in the air. When this happened the horses immediately retreated from the blanket, then began to investigate it again very cautiously. When this was continued for up to forty-eight hours these horses retained an interest in the moving blanket, where with the settled blanket they had come to ignore it within half an hour.

A horse is interested and intrigued by anything new. But he tends to get bored quickly once he has investigated an object and found that it is not dangerous or in any other way interesting. Only if it is moving, or appears different from time to time, will it retain his interest. We know from our own experience, both with stationary and moving objects, that single coloured objects will retain the horse's interest for less time than a multi-coloured or moving object. (That is not to say that a horse necessarily sees colours – even if he is colour blind, he will see different shades of grey, and varying shades are of greater interest than a plain grey). We also know that if an object makes a noise, it will be

more interesting and of course more frightening, than an object
which makes none.

Rostellan once gave us a good example of how a horse likes
to change the pattern of noise around it. We had put up a block
of five new loose boxes, and so that the horses could see out
better we put in glass windows. The glass windows stayed intact
for nearly a year. Then one day Rostellan accidentally broke a
pane of glass. The noise of the glass falling on the concrete outside at first frightened him, then fascinated him. He put his head
out through the window to see what had caused it. A piece of
glass balancing on the edge fell to the ground with a tinkling
noise, so he drew back and pushed out another. After that, whenever he was feeling a bit bored, he would use his nose to push out
another piece of glass from the edge of the window, just to hear
it shatter on the ground outside. Each time he pushed out a
piece of glass, he would take half a step back and listen to the
tinkle as it fell. Within four months he had managed to break
every window on the place. He would break most of the glass at
the first push, then proceed to push out all the fragments from
the edge of the window one at a time, with his nose. After the
first window we ceased to worry, since he never scratched or cut
himself on the broken edge of the glass. And it didn't matter
what I did to try and protect the windows: he somehow managed to break them every time. I even put wooden bars across
them, and he caught hold of them one by one with his teeth,
leant back and wrenched them off. After this I gave it up as a
bad job, and just let him get on with it. Eventually I took out
the windows, and blocked up the place where the windows had
been, since I was not going to go on for ever putting in new panes
of glass for Rostellan to break.

Just before this series of incidents, we had done a short trial
with metal feed containers, but very quickly had to abandon it
since the horses kept us awake all night with the noise the metal
containers made all over the floor. I thought at first that the
containers were being pushed round because there were stray bits
of food on the edges or underneath and in the corners; or that

they were being moved by chance. Then for a week I measured the distance that the metal containers had been shifted from their original spot in the corner, and this averaged out at just over five feet. This did not mean of course that the container had only been moved five feet in the night – from the row that was going on the horses seemed to be playing football with them. It only meant that in the morning the average distance of each container from where it had been left the previous night was five feet – it could have gone twenty times round the stable first for all we knew. We then changed the metal containers for plastic buckets, and discovered that though these were much easier and lighter to move than the metal ones, in the morning they were only a matter of a few inches from their original position. Since the feeding pattern in each case was exactly the same, and the food in the containers was exactly the same, we deduced that the heavy metal feed containers had been moved about to provide more noise stimulation for the horses.

We did make deliberate efforts to provide this stimulation. Because I thought they would enjoy it, I hung metal chains from their hay racks, so that they could entertain themselves during the night. But after forty-eight hours I had to take them out, because nobody could sleep for the ghostly clanking of chains. And since it was a question of depriving the horses of a plaything or the whole family of sleep, the horses lost their toys. But then I am a very hard, cruel and selfish man.

The conclusion to be drawn from all this, when you are training a horse, is that, if you can make what he is doing fun, and a game – in other words a source of constant excitement – the horse will enter into each new thing with a whole-hearted enthusiasm that at times is quite staggering.

If ever there was a horse who responded to excitement, it was Passing Cloud. He belonged to a friend of mine, Martin, who one hunt meeting managed to have a fall in an early race, and before he was carted off to hospital asked me to ride his grey in subsequent hunts, and school him a bit. He left me with the parting injunction not to do too much with him because he had only jumped a few hurdles and didn't know anything about point-to-point fences. So at the next race I lined up a bit behind the other horses at the start because I didn't want to get too involved with the field. But unfortunately I got a flier, and found myself leading into the first fence between two other horses. The young horse almost skidded to a halt trying to refuse, but we were going too fast so he shot straight up into the air as the best way out of his problem, and somehow or other we landed the other side, more or less together. And away we went again, with him really taking hold and enjoying himself. He was determined to catch up with everybody else, because the time it had taken us to negotiate the first fence had meant that we had fallen back from second or third place to last. This didn't deter him. He tore into the next fence, and since he had negotiated one obstacle by going straight up in the air, he went straight up in the air again, and again landed on the other side. By the time we had jumped the third fence he was beginning to get the hang of things and we didn't lose very much ground. I was quite happily keeping my place at the rear of the field, and so we completed the first circuit. By the time we passed the crowd for the first time, he had jumped seven or eight fences, and was taking off immaculately.

The first circuit had been very fast indeed, so as we went into the second, tired and beaten horses began to drop back past us. I didn't take any notice of these. I kept Passing Cloud going comfortably, and not pushing him. As we jumped the third last fence, however, I suddenly realized that I was lying in third place with a double handful under me. So I touched him with my heels, and the result was electric. He quickly caught up with the two leaders and met the second last fence absolutely perfectly. Between the second last and the last I passed the horse that was lying second. And went up to George Small who was riding a mare called Skittles. Both of us raced into the last fence, but Passing Cloud's inexperience was no match for Skittles' speed and jumping. He caught it an almighty clout, which almost brought him to a standstill, but we finished a comfortable second.

That was on Easter Sunday. And since Passing Cloud was none the worse for wear, Martin decided to run him again on Easter Monday, at the Taunton Vale, where we won the Maiden race by a distance.

The point is that to Passing Cloud at this stage of his career racing was a new and enjoyable game, so he put everything that he had into galloping and jumping. Whereas if he had been taught that galloping and racing was a chore, he would never have raced with the same success.

Of all the horse's sensory needs, perhaps the most striking to the observer is that for movement. Indeed a horse is almost *never* still. As the reader probably knows a horse never really goes to sleep: he merely dozes. And if you watch him at rest, you will see that he is constantly moving a leg, twitching an ear, moving his head slightly from side to side or up and down. First he will move one foot slightly, then put his weight on another one. When the horse is stabled, exactly the same thing happens. He spends most of the day and a large part of the night moving round the stable or shifting his muscles from time to time. If a door is open, he will stand looking out, but he will not be still: his head will be moving from side to side, and he will be moving his feet even when he is resting his body. He will be using and moving his muscles.

Now the point arises, is this movement simply a physical end in itself, or is there a psychological reason for it? As we saw earlier there was a psychological need for the horse to chew, and it seems more than probable that there is an equally in-built need for a horse's body to be moving at all times.

I had the opportunity to observe the extraordinary restlessness of a group of horses one morning last spring. Our cross-country course was in some need of repair after the bashing it had received during the previous winter, so choosing a nice sunny day I went up to carry out the necessary repairs.

In the field there was a herd of five horses: Rostellan, Bluebell,

Grayling, Flash and Madam. And when I got there they were all over in one corner. But as soon as I started work on the first of the fences, they drifted over to investigate, led by Rostellan. They stood watching me, no doubt to make sure that I didn't skimp my work. Rostellan then decided that I must have something to eat in my pocket, since it was bulging, so he started investigating with his prehensile lip and before I knew what he had done, he had my handkerchief between his teeth. The white flapping object was just the excuse he needed. He stood up on his hind legs, spun round, and galloped round in a circle shaking the thing.

Since he got no reaction from me – he was hoping that I would pursue him to get my handkerchief back – he went next to annoy Madam. Madam wasn't interested in off-white handkerchiefs, so she put back one ear and lazily waved a leg in his direction. Knowing what that meant, Rostellan decided to leave her alone. And since no one was interested in his game, he dropped my handkerchief and went over and started teasing Grayling. But Grayling wasn't interested in playing either and he was thirsty anyway, so he set off towards the stream to drink. The others came awake one by one, and in single file, with gaps of twenty to thirty yards between them, wandered slowly down to the water with him. Bluebell, once he had finished drinking, then took it into his head to strike the water with one fore-foot, and since this produced a nice splash, he did it again and again. Then he tried with the other one, and for the next five minutes proceeded to strike the water first with one foot and then with the other, soaking himself in the process, and everybody else, and making the water extremely muddy and unfit to drink.

Madam, who is not of a frivolous nature, drew her skirts about her like the angry Duchess she is, and stalked away from the coarse yobbos who were making all this splashing – the other horses having joined in the game with Bluebell – and with a reluctant look at the others, Flash, who was enjoying himself, followed his beloved Madam. And they wandered up from the stream, picking a bit of grass from here and there. Madam came across a nice bit of clover and started grazing seriously. Flash joined her. And the others drifted one by one up from the stream and started grazing too.

I had meanwhile finished repairing the second of the fences and felt that I had earned a rest. So I went and sat under the sunny side of the bank to smoke a cigarette. The horses saw me sitting down, and decided to come over and see what I was doing. After all it might have been their lucky day, and I could have been dead. First Flash and Madam came up and talked to me for a minute or two before going back to their grazing. Then Rostellan came up, quite sure that I was dangerous. He stopped five yards from me, put his nose out and sniffed. I didn't move. He took a couple of steps forward, and sniffed again. Still I didn't move. He came right up to me, and blew in my face. So I blew a mouthful of smoke back at him. And he drew back, thoroughly offended, which left the way open for Bluebell to come and chat. Bluebell is quite a favourite of mine – he's got a certain amount of character and an extremely nice temperament – so I managed to find him a couple of nuts, and this was too much for Rostellan, who came and shoved him to one side and demanded nuts as well. Which of course he got. Both of them then made a nuisance of themselves trying to persuade me to give them more, and since my restful cigarette had ceased to be restful I went back to mending my fences.

Without me to annoy, Rostellan and Bluebell had nothing to do but tease each other. Rostellan started nibbling Bluebell's front legs, and Bluebell retaliated by squealing and then taking a piece out of Rostellan's side. Rostellan swung his backside round at Bluebell and kicked vaguely in his direction. Bluebell shoved at Rostellan hitting him in the side with his shoulder. Rostellan pivoted on his hind legs, and for the next few minutes they both stood on their hind legs boxing each other. Then, tiring of their game of stallions, they decided to race, and half-way round one circuit of the field Grayling joined in. Then they were all extremely tired and went to sleep again, and they slept for the best part of an hour. But at no time did any of the four stay completely still.

One or another was always flicking an ear, moving a muscle. Rostellan was flapping his lips.

I had by then had the horses under reasonably close observation over a period of four hours, yet none of them had been completely still during that time even for a couple of minutes. There was no necessity for them to move at all, other than to graze or to go for water. Yet there was this need within them for constant movement.

When a mare is in season, Nature makes her even more restive, to satisfy her sexual need. In the wild this extra need to move about of course increased her chance of mating.

The fitter the horse is, too, the greater its need for movement. A horse that is over-fat, or in some way under-nourished, will move less, simply because Nature conserves what energy she can. But a fit, well horse needs movement all the time. No matter how long a horse has been domesticated, and how well bred it is, it still retains the impulses of the wild horse. And the fit wild horse that moved a lot had a much greater selection of grazing, and a much better balanced diet. This meant that by natural selection the horse that had the greatest need for activity and movement was most likely to survive. And the stallion that was constantly on the move was not only fitter and stronger, but was also more likely to sire a large number of foals than the lazy stallion who, like a Sultan in his harem, stayed in the same place waiting for the women to come to him. And in the same way the horse that even at rest was alert all the time, was far more likely to be able to escape a predator such as a wild dog, or wolf, than the horse who relaxed completely and slept deeply. So by natural selection, Nature ensured that those horses with the greatest need for activity and movement were those that survived and reproduced, and the horses which had very little drive for movement were the ones that didn't breed or died of starvation, or were eaten by other animals.

The constant movement of horses, on the other hand, rarely involves galloping about like cowboys chasing Indians. It usually means simply a slow walk, grazing and moving, and drinking.

In our observations of mountain ponies, we have seen them leave good grazing, just moving on, picking a bit here and a bit there, to quite poor grazing, and then staying there for an hour or two, then moving slowly back towards the good grazing. The urge to move from place to place is usually over a defined but quite large area – the natural grazing area of any herd of horses may be anything from two to five thousand acres – and they will naturally stay within that area, though of course they will change their grazing area according to the season. An active stallion on the other hand will cover an area grazed by four or five different herds.

This need for movement is not confined to horses: it applies to most animals. For example, even tame rats need to be constantly on the move. In some experimental work, tame rats were confined in a very small place, which restricted their movements, and then allowed to run on a wheel. It was discovered that the length of time the rat was confined in a small space was in direct relation to the length of time he ran in the wheel: in other words, a rat that had been confined for four hours ran twice as long as one that had been confined for two hours.

We have found this principle holds true in our own work with horses: a horse that is confined in a stable that restricts his movement to the absolute minimum for twelve hours, when released in a field, will canter round twice as long as the same horse when he is confined in a stable for only six hours.

8: *Social Behaviour – The Horse and the Herd*

All horses have a very great need for the company of other horses. This applies even to the loner, the horse that will almost always graze away from the other horses by himself. You may think from casual observations of him in the field that he has no need for the other horses, and yet if you move the main herd of horses from one field to another leaving him behind, he will try to follow, and if you leave him shut in the field by himself, he will soon be belting round, shouting to the others, 'Where the hell have you got to?'. He needs at least to be near a group of other horses.

And very closely linked with this need for company, is the need of some horses for real affection. Such a horse will make a particular friend of another horse, and the two will become inseparable. If you move his particular friend from the herd, that horse will be as upset as if you had moved the whole herd away. If on the other hand you move the herd leaving the pair behind, they will both try and follow the main body of the herd.

This of course is one of the first of the natural habits that has to be modified when you are training a horse, since a horse is no use at all if he won't go away from other horses. And a close friendship link, though it may be used in the education of a young or difficult horse, may well be a nuisance if it prevents him from doing anything by himself. We had an example of such a close friendship between Flash and Madam, both of whom were sent to us for gentling two years ago.

Madam, as the reader will remember, is a bad-tempered mare whom not everyone has cause to love. But, in spite of her awkwardness, Flash adored her. And where Madam went, Flash went too. Flash, being part Arab, wasn't a natural jumper, but

Madam was, and since Flash wanted to stay near Madam he had to jump to keep up with her. And he turned into a superb jumper, and an extremely good cross-country horse.

The summer of 1974 was extremely wet and cold, and Flash with the Arab strain in him began to lose condition, so we decided to keep him in all the time. Madam, being of much hardier New Forest stock, was thriving under the same conditions, so we kept on turning her out at night. But we very quickly had to turn Flash out again too. He totally and absolutely refused to eat in the stable, unless Madam was there as well. We tried feeding him when she was there, but he was still not getting enough food in him to last him through the twenty-four hours – especially since the rest of the time he was pacing in his box screaming his head off, and wasn't relaxing and sleeping at all.

The closest ties between horses are usually between mare and gelding, particularly between a strong-charactered mare and a rather weak-charactered gelding: rather in the same way as among human beings you may find an exceptional bond between a very big strong-charactered woman and a weak rather insignificant little man.

This need for affection has its roots in an old response to fear. When a foal is frightened, it will return to its mother for affection and protection, and only once it has received the expected signs of affection from its mother will it begin to show its curiosity again. If something frightens a foal, it will gallop back to its mother, who will nuzzle it and say 'It's quite safe, mother is here'. Then when the foal has been reassured, it will go first to look at, and then to investigate, the object that alarmed it.

This need for reassurance/affection is hard to test in laboratory conditions with horses, because the foal is rather a large and difficult animal for laboratory conditions. But an animal that has been tested in this way is the monkey. Within two to ten days of birth a baby monkey moves round on its own, and manipulates objects, so scientists can measure what it does and does not do, and what it responds to. It can suckle a bottle and be reared in artificial conditions which can be chosen at will.

Monkeys were used in an interesting series of experiments on affection, in one of which monkeys were raised singly in cages providing a comfortable environment and adequate care of their bodily needs. In each cage two artificial mothers were put: one was a wire mesh cylinder with a block of wood where the head would be – this was called the wire mother; the other was an artificial mother made from sponge rubber, and sheath towelling – this was called the cloth mother. Behind each mother was put a light bulb which provided radiant heat for the baby monkey, and either mother could be fitted with a bottle where her breast would be. The purpose of the experiment was to see how much time the infant monkey spent with each mother, when that mother had the bottle.

The experiment was designed to test the theory that love was learned through rewarding the baby monkey's hunger motive, and the results showed that the monkeys strongly preferred the cloth mother, regardless of where the bottle was. They spent fifteen hours more per day with the cloth mother than with the wire mother, even though not more than one hour was spent feeding. At twenty-one to twenty-five days, when the wire mother had the bottle, the baby monkeys still spent at least eighteen hours with the cloth mother and when the cloth mother had the bottle they spent twenty-three hours a day with the cloth mother, and only one with the wire mother.

Two conclusions can be drawn from this experiment: first that the monkey has an unlearned tendency to be near mother; and second that this tendency was one of seeking contact and reassurance from the mother – that is, it was not exclusively related to the taking of food.

The only work of this nature that has been done with foals was with artificially reared thoroughbreds who were fed by an automatic feeder near, or at a distance from, a source of heat, i.e., a heating lamp. The foals did considerably better, up to fifteen percent in body weight at five months, when the artificial feeder was near the heat lamp, than when it was at some distance from it: the most important factor was found to be the heat.

Also, the foals spent at least two hours a day more near the heat lamp when it was against straw bales than when it was placed next to a wooden partition, or a stone wall: the best result was obtained with a block of bales two feet long and three feet high, next to the artificial feeder with the heat at the end nearest the feeder. In these conditions, the foals fed more readily and easily, and made considerably more body weight, and it was thought – though no methodical observation was taken – that they were taking more exercise and were more venturesome than the foals that had to walk from the heat lamp to the feeder.

Emotional and temperamental qualities will of course vary from horse to horse even more than directly physical ones. The need for movement, for example, is very slight in some horses, who will be quite happy to stand around flicking an ear, or moving from leg to leg and doing absolutely nothing else, while other horses will spend the whole day walking round and round in their box. This need for movement in some horses is so great that they need hardly be *exercised* at all – they keep themselves fit wherever they are.

Old Cork Beg, for example, was never still in his loose box. He would stand at the door looking out for a couple of minutes, then walk to the back of the box and take a mouthful of hay, or a sip of water, or just walk round the box, then go back and look out of the door again. He did this so much that it was extremely difficult to get any condition on him. But once you got him fit, he needed very little exercise.

At the other extreme is Royalty, who will stand in one corner of her box all day, positioned so that she can look out through the door and if she feels like it take a mouthful of hay, just moving from one foot to another – with her head slightly to one side so that she can see out better. There is hardly any other movement at all. This makes her an easy horse to have in the stable, because there is only one corner of the box to clean out. But she has to be exercised regularly, to prevent her from becoming sluggish and fat.

The same variation is to be found in the degree of curiosity exhibited by one horse and another. Some horses are very curious and some horses couldn't care less. Equally, when it comes to competitiveness, some horses are good competitors, and others don't mind whether they are beaten or not.

In fact many of these motives seem to be linked together in a type of horse personality: the lively active horse tends to be the one that is also curious and a good competitor. The lazy sleepy horse is much less likely to be curious, and if he is very lazy he can't be bothered to compete. These are examples of what might be termed linked motives. Greed and laziness too go together; and high sexuality in a mare tends to be linked with irritableness. It is worthwhile remembering that very often these needs and motives can be linked together, and that certain motives may be linked with certain vices.

For example, a very sociable horse will tend to be nappy. Laziness in a horse will also mean that he tends to refuse a jump if he can, and laziness of course, like everything, is a motive. The reason for the horse's laziness is the negative desire to do anything. Motives of course can be negative, as well as positive. The desire to be with other horses can be termed what we call a social motive. Social motives are the reasons for the horse's behaviour with other horses, and of course with his owner and rider. Some of these will be learned and others are born in the horse, and even those that are born within the horse can be modified by his handling, and what he has learned.

Because of their size and habits, there has been very little laboratory research into these motives in horses. Most of it has been carried out on animals that fit into the hygienic white-coated environment of the laboratory better – such as human beings, monkeys, rats and dogs. But most of this research can be applied to the horse and has been verified by our observations of the horse.

The supreme competitor was Molfre. Molfre at home is an absolutely superb jumper, and will place himself at a jump and jump four foot of fixed timber with no difficulty at all. It is obvious when you are riding him that he enjoys the challenge of jumping timber, and he also enjoys placing himself correctly at a fence and jumping it perfectly. He will give a little flick of his tail each time he has cleared a fence. If he makes a very slight mistake, his annoyance is obvious. But when he is racing, it is a different cup of tea altogether. The excitement of the race and his competitive urge completely override his desire to jump perfectly and he is a very chancey fencer indeed. He will jump most of the fences superbly but if he is wrong, it's a question of just bash on regardless, and hope for the best. At times Molfre and I land up on the ground and, at other times, we end up with me clasping him in a loving embrace around his neck, desperately trying to find out where the hell my saddle has got to.

I rode Molfre in the Players Gold Leaf Point-to-Point Championship qualifier at Ludlow in 1974. The field went off like bats out of hell and I managed to drop him in at the back of the field. Without very much difficulty we completed the first circuit more or less in the rear of the field, and he jumped every fence absolutely superbly, meeting it right, placing himself, and gaining lengths on each jump. At the beginning of the second circuit, I started moving up through the field, mainly because the other horses were tiring fast, and partly because of Molfre's fantastic jumping. He was standing right back and rocketing over the fences, and gaining lengths each time. There was a fairish run from the fourth last to the third last fence, and by the time we had jumped the fourth last fence, I had moved up to sixth place. When we got to the third last, I moved up into fourth place, going infinitely better than any of the other horses. I was sitting on a double handful and was beginning to wonder by how many lengths I would win. I could see Knightsbridge, who was just in front of me, rolling from side to side with fatigue, and the two other horses in front of him were also tiring rapidly. But my luck was out. Knightsbridge, who was just in front of me, fell and this distracted Molfre's attention at the crucial moment. He took off a stride too far back and we hit the fence going fast, and we both slid twenty yards the other side. His sheer competitive nature when he came to racing and jumping had overridden his desire to jump properly, and the result was that we ended flat on our faces in the mud!

One of the first things we notice about our horses is their very great need for the company of other horses. This can be observed in foals from the very beginning. The foal at first will stay entirely by its mother's side. Over the course of the next three or four months, it will start venturing away a few steps at a time. Then it will meet and play with other foals. And at approximately a year old in its natural state, it will leave its mother entirely and choose other companions for which it shows a great affection. Horses don't like being by themselves. And though this desire for company may be stronger in some horses than others, the herding instinct always survives.

This need for companionship reflects a number of separate but closely linked needs. One is the need to give and receive affection – which it expresses with its owner, its close companions or its offspring. A second is its more general need to be with other horses, be they friendly or not; this is an inherited need, with its roots in the wild when the chances of survival were considerably greater for a horse in a large herd than for one grazing by himself. In times of stress horses will always group together in a bunch, receiving bodily contact and reassurance from other members of the group. And a third, and related, need is the horse's urge to know his own particular place in the hierarchy of the herd.

It is the ancient herding instinct that makes a horse that loses his rider head for the nearest group of horses. I've seen a horse travel three miles to get to a herd when he was turned loose on the mountain. The nearest group of horses in sight was on the other side of the valley, which was nearly three miles away, so as soon as he was set free, he stood for a few moments looking round, saw the group of horses on the skyline, called to them, and proceeded to take the shortest and most direct route to reach them. When he finally got there, the herd leader came out and kicked his teeth in for intruding within the group. The strange horse stayed on the fringes of the group for two or three days before he was absorbed and accepted by the group.

One of the mysterious things about this need to join the herd is that the horse always seems compelled to take the most direct route, even if it means surmounting quite difficult obstacles in order to do so. We saw this peculiarity in Jezebel when we wanted to keep her in for the stallion. When we turned the horses out that night, instead of letting Jezebel loose with them, we left her shut in her loose box, but as soon as she realized that the other horses were going out without her, she jumped the three-foot-six lower half of her door, on to the concrete. And then, instead of turning right to go down to the front gate as she did three times a day at least, she jumped the railing in front of the stables – which again stands at three-foot-six high – crossed to the other side of the railings, dropped another six feet from the bank on to the drive to the house, then over a two-foot-six wire fence which drops away a further six feet to the road below. The further the horses went away from her, the stronger seemed her need to join them. But it would still have been just as quick and considerably easier for her to have trotted down to the front gate than to take those three very difficult jumps, fantastic jumper though she is. She seemed compelled to go in a straight line. I have also seen a horse that normally wouldn't take off from the ground if an atom bomb was set off under its backside jumping sheep netting with barbed wire on top to get to a strange group of horses, when he had been turned out by himself. Then when the rest of his own herd were turned out after him, he jumped the fence the other way to get back.

A bunch of four unbroken Welsh Cobs we once kept had the run of three fields. They were accustomed to going from one field to another through the opened gateways. But one day, for some reason, Phoenix got left behind when his companions moved on to the adjoining field. All he had to do to join them was to go down to the gateway. Yet what he did was to canter up to the wire fence, and jump it. Like Jezebel, he took the more difficult but direct, route in order to reach the herd.

This very deep inherent need to be with its companions can be used very effectively when breaking and gentling a horse. The thing to do is to work him together with a group of other, broken, horses. First he will try to behave as the big boys are behaving, which will make him better behaved; and second, he will receive reassurance from the group, and so will go much more happily. Riding a young horse, after all, is making him do something that is strange and repugnant to him, at the same time as trying to break a behaviour pattern which has been his for the previous three or four years, so the presence of other horses can be very reassuring – though it also has its risks.

At one time we were breaking large groups of horses together, and riding them together, and this worked extremely well. Most of the time they all behaved perfectly – you could see them competing to show how well they could perform. But just occasionally one of them would explode. And then they would all explode, one after another, like a series of fire crackers, and you would have people falling off, and bodies scattered all over the mountain.

My father used to have an extremely good method of teaching foals to accept a halter. He used to put a halter on to a foal, then tie the halter rope to its mother's tail. The foal, when it felt the strangeness and the strain of the halter, would fight a little bit. But then he would automatically go to his mother for reassurance, which meant that the rope went slack. This would go on for ten minutes to a quarter of an hour. Compared with the normal method of tying the foal up and leaving him to fight it out, this was a remarkably quick and peaceful way of accustoming the foal to a halter. The foal was taught to lead in exactly the same way. With the foal still tied to her tail, the mare would lead and as soon as the foal saw its mother going away, he would try to follow her. So he very quickly learned that the tug from the halter meant that he had to go forward.

A similar method was also used by the Mohawk Indians when

they were training a horse. When a horse was to be backed, he would be tied extremely tightly to an old horse for a day or two, and led round with his head on the old horse's shoulder. When he was used to this, and going quite happily, a rider would get on him. This method made it impossible for the horse to buck, since he couldn't get his head down. And since he was already accustomed to walking beside the old horse, he very quickly learned to go quietly when he was ridden.

Both these methods illustrate how what can very often be a frightening experience to a young horse, and an awkward time for his handler, can be made simple and easy by using one horse's natural desire to be near another.

Within the herd the horse also needs an assured place within the seniority pattern of the herd. And the place he finds is a fair indication of his temperament and ability. The dominant, the independent, the bloody-minded and bad-tempered will be at the top of the social structure; while the lazy and weak-charactered will be at the bottom. But each horse within the group needs the approval and acceptance of the group as a whole. And this need for approval applies equally to horses which are being handled by man. The horse will perform quite exceptionally for the person for whom he has special respect and affection. And both of these are needed: affection without respect is useless, just as respect without affection will severely limit the amount the horse will do for its rider. Yet within the herd the need for respect does not have anything to do with the need to be liked – it is quite simply a need to have an established and recognized position in society.

In our own herd, at the top of the social scale are Madam and Jack. Madam is very much a loner, and except by Flash, who dogs her heels and adores her, she is liked by none of the other horses. When I go into the field with a bucket of nuts to feed them, she'll attack and kick anything who approaches me, other than Flash. When the horses are driven in from the field, Madam will refuse to allow anything else to pass her, either by driving at the other horse backwards with her teeth, or by kicking as it comes up to her. So she may be liked by none of the other horses, but they do respect her. She's got an established position as the herd boss, and woe betide anything that threatens her authority. Jack has an equal position with Madam at the top of the herd, a situation they are able to maintain because they tend to avoid each other so that they don't clash. When I go into the field with the bucket of nuts, Jack will approach from the opposite side to Madam, so that I am between them, and there can be no conflict. When they are coming in from the field, Jack does not contest Madam's place at the head. He will punch anyone who infringes his dignity, but he doesn't hammer anything unless it is misbehaving. He is a very sociable animal, is well liked by the herd and will always be found in the middle of the group.

Flash being under Madam's protection neither is hammered, nor hammers, since he is a very sweet kind horse. And he has his own secure position within the herd. Jezebel and Biddy, being my special horses, and Rostellan, being my wife's horse, have each a very strong social position within the herd, because they are under our protection for a lot of the time. When they are out in the field the other horses will tend to leave them alone, and provided they don't invade their special preserves, neither Madam nor Jack will bother them.

At the bottom end of the social scale come Swallow, Grayling, Zoom and Gypo, who tend to stick to a group by themselves, and keep away from the herd bosses because they are automatically hammered. But at the same time, should any strange horse intrude, that is a new horse be turned out with them, they would be protected by the strength of the herd bosses, so they feel safe within the group.

The social acceptance necessary for each horse within a herd is, as I have said, very similar to the approval the horse needs from its rider, or the person who is handling it. And when a horse goes to a new owner a battle ensues very like the battle that takes place within the horse herd to decide who is boss, and whether the new member is going to be in the top, the middle, or the bottom end of the social spectrum. And your horse is likely to relate to you in a way not unlike the way he relates to other horses.

If you get a horse that has been at the bottom end of the herd, he will be comparatively easy to handle, at least to begin with, because he is accustomed to being bossed around by other horses, and will accept the authority of a new owner quite readily. If, on the other hand, you get a horse who has a dominant personality, and has thus been accustomed to being the boss of the herd, he will try and dominate his new owner. He will be probing for weak spots in his rider, testing whether his owner has a strong or a weak personality, whether he is a good horseman or a bad one. And he will very quickly make use of any weakness. At this stage it is extremely important to be firm but kind with a new horse, and to punish any infringement of discipline instantly – and punishment is not necessarily, of course, flaying the skin off his backside with a hunting crop. It can be a quiet 'stop it', or if the horse persists, a slap on the nose, or the nearest offending portion, is usually enough. What is necessary is to establish yourself as herd boss, *not* the horse.

However, in addition to the security of being a member of a group, it is also essential for a horse's wellbeing to be able to think well of itself. (This is relevant to its position within the herd too, because the horse that thinks well of itself will naturally be high in the social hierarchy). And if he has a high opinion of his own abilities, he will constantly strive to do his best, while other horses who have a low opinon of themselves will do only the minimum to avoid punishment. This need for some horses to assert themselves regardless of what the rest of the herd may think, this need for self-esteem, is shown in a variety of ways. The horse, in asserting itself over other horses to obtain power within the herd, may need to beat the other horses when it is galloping with them, or to jump fences better than the other horses. So this ambition can be channelled to get the horse to succeed in competition: in fact we go to great lengths to build up a horse's self-esteem when we want it to compete.

For example, when I am training my horses for point-to-pointing or hunter-chasing, I make quite sure that I don't gallop them with horses that they cannot beat quite easily. I want them to get used to winning, so that their self-esteem will be built up, and at the same time they will feel an increasing need to win.

If, over a period, one observes horses in competitive work – showjumping, eventing or racing for example – it is difficult to avoid the conclusion that there is a natural drive within some horses to do something well, simply to achieve a competence for its own sake alone. Some horses have this need to excel, to do something better than any other horse. Even when they are not competing such horses have this need to be supreme. This need must not be confused with the need to compete – for the same thing can be seen in a super beginner's pony who takes terrific pride in taking care of his young rider well.

Jack is an example of what I mean. He is an extremely good and very fast pony, and at times he takes great pleasure in depositing a rider who gets too presumptuous firmly on the ground. But when he has a very nervous person or a complete beginner on his back, he will take great pride in looking after him, and giving him as much confidence as possible. You will see him pacing forward with his ears pricked and his neck arched, putting one foot carefully in front of another, making sure that his young rider is absolutely secure. There is nothing competitive about this: it is purely Jack's desire to do whatever he is doing as well as he possibly can.

Not all horses have this quality – there are others who seem to take a perverse pride in doing as little as possible without punishment. But many have, and in training it is invaluable.

This urge to excel again is something that has come down from the primitive horse, since the horse that was the biggest, strongest, fastest, and most mentally dominant was the one that had the best grazing, and was the best able to escape from any predators. He was also the one, if he was a stallion, who had the greatest number of mares, and sired most of the next generation of foals. Similarly a mare who was mentally dominant, and physically the strongest, and fastest, was much more likely to live through the rigours of the winter than her weaker-willed sisters.

If you remove pride from a horse, you will remove his will to win and his will to succeed. This is why a horse that has been broken and cowed will never be so good a horse as one who has been allowed to develop slowly and naturally.

You can destroy a horse's pride by allowing him repeatedly to be beaten in a race. Or you can equally do so by over-racing him. For example, if your horse is successfully jumping three-foot, and jumping spreads of three-foot-six or four-foot, you can build up his pride and his self-confidence, so that if you face him at a four-foot fence with a five-foot spread, he will indeed attempt to jump it. But if he fails, and fails the next time he tries to jump a big fence, you will completely have destroyed his pride and his self-confidence so that even when you put him back to the three-foot fences he will refuse to jump them. Self-esteem is a very fragile thing and you will have to go back to fences two-foot and two-foot-six high, that he can step over, to build up his pride again over a considerable period of time. Pride and self-esteem can only be built with patience, and gradually, and no horse should be pushed too far too fast. Even the toughest and most obstinate horse is vulnerable.

We once had a very dominant yearling. He was a rather un-pleasant horse, and a terrific bully, who hunted and chivvied the other young horses relentlessly. So to cure him of this we put him in with three or four very strong, tough horses. And for the next week or so, they hammered the living daylights out of him. Then we put him back with his companions, whom he had pre-viously been bullying to distraction, and instead of being the boss of the herd, he was right at the bottom end of it. His pride had been shattered, and for a considerable time until he had built up some self-respect again, the youngsters that he had previously bullied, were bullying him.

A horse however has an inbuilt need to be aggressive. This is part of his survival equipment. Without this aggression, he would always be driven away from the best grazing, be the last one to get water, and at the back of the line the one most exposed to danger. But how much the aggression is innate and how much learned, it is very difficult to say: as always, it is hard to separate genetically inherited characteristics from those conditioned by environment and by training.

Early environment is extremely important. The size and strength of the foal when he first meets other foals will, for instance, condition his future attitude to other horses: if the other foals are bigger and stronger than him, he will tend to be bullied, and subservient; whereas if he is bigger and stronger than they, he will boss them. And if he is big and strong when he is weaned from his mother in the autumn, his ability to convert food will be good, he will winter well, and be stronger and more robust than his companions in the spring. So his early environment will play a considerable part in deciding how he copes with the hurly burly of herd life.

Then the inherited characters will come into play. At times the boss of the herd will not be the biggest, strongest foal or yearling. He may be a very aggressive smaller foal, bred from dominant parents.

On the other hand, training in aggression will start from the time he is born. If he is accustomed to his mother bossing the other horses, he will imitate her in his behaviour towards the other foals, but if his mother is in a subordinate position in the herd the foal will be trained by its mother to move away from the herd bosses when confronted by them.

Early handling by the human species is influential too. If from its earliest weeks the foal is allowed to misbehave, and get its own way, it will be extremely difficult to handle later on. It will lack respect for human beings, and consequently also affection, since an animal tends to be less affectionate towards those whom it doesn't respect. It is thus important to dominate a foal, that is make it do what it is told, from the beginning, so that when you come to handle and ride it, it will be disposed to co-operate.

When we are talking about boss horses, of course, we are really talking only about some ten percent of the herd: that is, in a group of ten horses one will probably be very strong-charactered; one very weak-charactered, bullied by everything else; a couple more may be fairly strong-charactered or weak-charactered, but the sixty or seventy percent of the horses in the middle of the herd will tend to be easy-going and easily handled. It is the ten percent strong-charactered horses, however, that I am interested in, since they provide the greatest challenge to the rider, and the greatest reward – for they are the ones with the strength of character to make use of every ounce of their ability.

9: *Emotion In Horses*

Emotion is a very powerful force in the behaviour of a horse. Fear, anger and excitement can all make a horse act in a way quite different from his normal pattern.

But what is emotion? It means several things. One of them is a physical state: a change in the chemical balance in the body, or in muscular tension; and another is the feeling arising out of the physical state. This feeling may be pleasant or unpleasant, but it cannot be seen or heard. It can be recognized only by the signs and sounds that the horse makes. You can see if a horse is frightened, if he is angry or if he is excited by the way he behaves. And you also can see their opposites – all emotions including fear, anger and excitement, have their opposites. As we want to avoid strong emotion in horses, it is the opposite states we are seeking: confidence, co-operation, calm. Thus it is important to understand what causes emotional changes, particularly extreme changes, so that the causes can be avoided.

A horse may do something because he is excited, or he may do something to become excited, because a horse enjoys excitement. The very sight of a jump may send some horses into a tizzy of excitement; and other horses are made excited by jumping. So a horse may jump because he is excited. Or he may jump to become excited. And he easily gets into a state where the more he feeds his excitement, the more excited he becomes. In a similar way, if you are shoeing a horse he may get angry because you are picking up, pulling about, and banging his feet. He kicks because he is angry, and the more he kicks, the angrier he becomes.

What happens is that any kind of emotion, anger, fear or excitement, arouses the horse. Intense emotion is a state of being highly aroused. And when the horse is highly aroused, he is more likely to react to situations with strong emotion, so a spiral of intensifying emotion quickly develops which can get beyond your or his control. If a horse becomes excited at the thought of jumping fences, he will be even more excited after he has jumped the fence. So he will tear into the next one, more than likely making a complete mess of it and go flat on his face. The more excited a horse becomes, the more likely he is to make mistakes. In the same way, if you clobber a nervous horse he will become more frightened of you and all future attempts to catch him will make him even more frightened.

Emotion thus feeds upon emotion. The only cure is quietness on your part. If you are relaxed you can make the horse relax. Or you can put him with another horse who is relaxed and quiet, and this will steady him down. When a horse becomes aroused emotionally the muscles of his body tighten, his adrenal glands work overtime, his rate of breathing tends to increase, and his heart speeds up slightly. And though, when we are competing, we want the old adrenalin pumping, we don't want too much of it.

In competition of course a certain amount of excitement is inevitable. The difficulty is in keeping the level under control. The level of arousal that is required to stimulate an emotional response varies from horse to horse, depending on how the horse is bred, and how he has been handled. And the difference in temperament between one horse and another may be considerable.

If you set off a bomb behind a horse like Pudding, he would stay relaxed. I've seen Pudding grazing in a field, and two low-flying aircraft go past within fifty feet of him, one of which broke the sound barrier just as it passed him. And Pudding didn't even lift his head to look at them. Admittedly we are in an air force training area, and he is reasonably accustomed to low-flying air-craft. But so am I, and on this particular occasion they made me jump out of my skin. But Pudding just went on grazing as if nothing had happened. Pudding is a very placid horse. Nothing ever excites him, fusses him, frightens him, or makes him angry. He just goes on in his own quiet, sweet way.

At the other extreme is Royalty who had been mishandled in an attempt to break her as a three-year-old, as I shall later describe. When I got her, she wasn't particularly difficult to gentle, but she remained very nervous, and anything strange upsets her. She needs a lot of sympathy and understanding.

When we first had her the rustle of a paper bag in the next stable would send her into a near panic. On one occasion, shortly after she arrived, instead of carrying her feed in to her in the bucket I left it in the paper feed bag and emptied it from the feed bag into the bucket. And of course to get all the food out of the feed bag, I had to shake the bag. I did this unthinkingly. The next thing I knew, Royalty was climbing up the wall in a state of sheer frenzy, and it took me nearly an hour to get her to settle down and eat her feed. I couldn't of course allow Royalty to get into a state every time anyone rustled a paper bag, so I got her over it quite simply, once I got her settled down. I shook the paper feed bag gently, but nearer and nearer her until she took no notice of it. But still anything strange or un-expected sends her into a near panic. She is a horse, as we all recognize, with a very low arousal point indeed.

I have been hunting hounds off her this winter. The first time I got her hunting with the hounds, they worried her considerably. And if I berated the hounds, or waved my hunting crop, she became very upset indeed. But after four or five days she accepted the hounds, and even the hunting crop, though I still had only to curse the hounds to get her nervous again. She couldn't under-stand that I was not swearing at her – she thought that whatever it was was her fault. But eventually she settled down completely, and became one of the best hunters I have ever ridden.

These are two extremes of course. But even horses that have been brought up together, and handled by the same people all their lives, will vary in their emotional level. One may have two horses in neighbouring loose boxes, one of which will sleep all day and the other spend the whole day wandering round and round his box in a mild state of excitement, all the time alert to anything that is happening outside. The point at which he becomes aroused is simply much lower than that of his companion, so he will need to walk around more. He will eat less, he will dance about all over the road when you are riding him, and he will be a much better jumper than his companion whose one ambition is to stand still and go to sleep, and a much better race horse. The adrenalin in his blood will be pumping so fast that he just has to tear into the fence, and jump it, he just has to reach that winning post first. The size of his adrenal glands will be large, and his muscular development will be completely different from that of his sleepy friend because he has used his muscles in a completely different way.

One emotion can also change very easily into another: fear can change to excitement, and excitement to anger at the drop of a hat.

About four years ago I had a very excitable horse, a big sixteen-two thoroughbred called Sally Boy. We used to call him Boyo, and he really was a Boyo. He was an infuriating horse to exercise because he never walked in a straight line, he would dance from one side of the road to another, and since I had to work him for an hour-and-a-half to two hours a day, I found him very tiring. One day I had had enough, so I decided for the last half mile home I would make him walk every step. Every time he came out of a walk, I would stop, back him a stride, and then make him walk forward again. On an average, for every two strides he walked, he was going back one. And it took me two-and-a-half hours to cover that last half mile. In actual fact I never quite got him there. After about five hundred yards his excitement had changed to anger and he was in a tearing rage. We had been having a battle on the same spot for a solid ten minutes, when he finally went up on his hind legs and came back on top of me on the bank. I managed to stay in the saddle, and he scrambled to his feet. But I had lost my stirrups and my reins, and before I could retrieve them we were going back up the mountain flat out, with Boyo in complete charge. Three miles further on I managed to stop him, having weaved past four or five cars, petrifying the drivers and nearly killing myself and Boyo.

I stopped him by turning him straight into a solid wall of young fir trees, which he crashed into. But they made him lose his balance and he came down. Always making the most of my opportunities, I very quickly sat on his head, got out my cigarettes and matches and proceeded to have a smoke, while he simmered down, and I simmered down. After my second cigarette I let him get up. A two-and-a-half-hour battle and a three-mile gallop to end up with had taken most of the fizz out of Boyo, so when I got on him and set him off for home, he walked, he didn't jog. Two or three times he started dancing, and I turned him round and made him walk away until he had settled down again. And eventually, very, very late for my dinner, which I had to eat in the doghouse, we got home in one piece with a few scratches but otherwise no damage done.

Fear, as I have said, can be mixed with pleasure. And so can anger. Some horses positively enjoy being slightly frightened. If there is nothing startling in the hedge, and they are feeling a bit bored, they will imagine things to shy at and frighten themselves. Others will get great pleasure from the surge of anger they get out of a battle with their rider. In fact, fear, pleasure and anger can all be mixed together.

The overall aim of all our work might be said to be to give the horses pleasure. This is not a piece of altruism: it is very practical. If your aim is to give your horse pleasure, your horse is going to enjoy what he is doing, and if he is enjoying what he is doing he will put everything he has got into it. And you are bound to enjoy yourself more. This is what all horse psychology is about. It is about finding the easiest way to make a horse *want* to do something. There are many things that give a horse pleasure. A horse will get pleasure when he has done what he has wanted to do, and he will get pleasure from eating his dinner. This is a fact we know, so we make use of it. We put a little bit of his dinner in our pockets, for instance, and when he has done something well, we give him a tit-bit.

Similarly, we know a horse enjoys affection. So we give him plenty of affection and make a great fuss of him when he jumps or does something else well for us. Then he will not only get pleasure from jumping the fences, he will also get pleasure because you are pleased with him. And he will probably get more pleasure from the admiration and applause of the crowd. And one pleasure will reinforce another, all combining to make him excel in performance.

Biddy, for example, loves jumping cross-country fences. She will show her pleasure by the way she tears into the fences. But even if someone else is riding her, she will come back to me for praise when she has completed her round. And if I don't give her any she will nudge with her nose to remind me that I have not told her what a clever girl she is.

The things that give a horse pleasure will change with his training and his development. If you put your hand on an untouched foal of two or three weeks, he will be so badly frightened that he will run back to his mother in sheer terror. But the same foal, a month or two later, after he has known you and been handled by you, will come to be touched and stroked, and will show his pleasure. Similarly, an untouched horse off the mountain, if you put him into a loose box with a bucket of corn, will be terrified by the bucket and the corn. But a week or so later, when he has discovered what corn is, and that the bucket won't hurt him, will be bellowing 'where is my bloody breakfast?' when you appear with the bucket.

So with training – and everything you do with a horse is training – a horse's idea of what is pleasant will change considerably. In the case of the foal, fear has been transformed by affection. To start with, you were strange to the foal, and when you touched him he was frightened and ran back to his mother for reassurance. But when he got to know you, the touch of your hand did not arouse fear, so much as curiosity.

Fear on the other hand can be induced by training. I was called out last summer to a farm near Lampeter, to deal with a foal who was completely unmanageable and terrified. She had been teased by a horde of small boys from the neighbourhood, who had made great sport of chasing and running after her. By the time I was sent for the creature was so completely terrified of human beings that no one could get near her, or touch her, she was in such a state of terror. The foal was a registered cob filly, but the owner had decided he would have to sell her because he could not do anything with her.

I quickly realized what had caused the original trouble, but the problem now was how to undo the damage. With a lot of time and patience we eventually got the mare and foal out of the field and into the farm yard. Using an old pony, Topsy, as 'schoolmaster', we managed to get the mare and foal into a loose box and from then on it was all plain sailing. We just left the old pony in with the mare and foal for a couple of hours. Then I went back in. The foal tried to climb the walls of the loose box in absolute terror. But I kept old Topsy between me and her all the time, so that the foal began to feel that I wasn't threatening her in any way. After a minute or two, she stopped by her mother's side. I pushed Topsy until she went over by the foal, then I got the tips of my fingers on the foal, very, very gently. She shot round, but after four or five attempts, when I touched the foal again, she shook with terror but didn't move away. Then very, very gently I worked my hand all over her body. Old Topsy got bored about half way through and went from underneath my arm, so that I was standing right next to the foal. But by this time she was beginning to realize that I wasn't going to hurt her, and stood still, and after four or five sessions like this she began to look forward to seeing me, and settled down quite happily.

This is an example of how early experiences can first arouse fear of an object, in this case the human being, and then dispel that fear.

The difference between fear and anxiety is important, especially when we start to study the personality of a horse. Fear is aroused when the horse can recognize what causes that fear, and know what it is afraid of. Anxiety on the other hand is a vague fear that a horse will experience without knowing what causes it: a horse can be made uneasy and anxious by the memory of something that happened a long time ago, or by an alteration in the routine or pattern of his life.

I had an example of this distinction last summer. During the summer the pack of hounds I hunt are kennelled at the knacker's yard. This is for convenience, since the food supply there is on the spot. During the early part of the cub-hunting season we hunt hounds from there, in the surrounding area, so that any hounds that are missing can find their way back without any difficulty. It happened that I had borrowed a pony to ride cub-hunting, and the first day I rode up to the knacker's yard, the pony flatly refused to enter it. There was no apparent reason for this: there was a slightly unpleasant smell, but not a strong one, and it wasn't the noise that the hounds were making that was frightening, since the pony had already been hunted for two seasons. But it simply and flatly refused to go in. When I tried to make it do so, it shook with fear. Now I could have overcome this fear with a bit of a battle, but there was very little point in doing so, so I simply left the pony outside the yard while I got the hounds out, and we went off and had quite a pleasant day's hunting.

Then towards the end of the day, one of the perennial curses of this area, a low-flying aircraft, came over the trees and thoroughly frightened the pony. It carted me for about a hundred yards before I could stop it and quieten it.

These two incidents clearly demonstrate the difference between anxiety and fear: the first case, when there was no apparent reason for the pony's state of nerves, was anxiety. The second, when the source of the fear was easily identifiable – that is, the low-flying aeroplane – was fear.

Anxiety too can be induced. A classic experiment might be simultaneously to blow a whistle and hit a horse, or administer a mild electric shock, and to do that over a period of two or three weeks, four or five times a day. Two, three or even four years later you would produce anxiety in the horse simply by blowing the whistle. Needless to say we have not carried out this experiment ourselves, but it has been carried out on dogs, and the dogs retained the memory of an unpleasant experience associated with the whistle after a period of four years. In this case the dogs were trained to jump a fence when a whistle was blown and an electric shock administered at the same time. After five or six lessons, the dogs jumped the fence when the whistle was blown whether or not an electric shock was administered. And when the experiment was repeated four years later, one dog still jumped an imaginary fence at the sound of a whistle. And when he was confined in a pen where he was unable to jump, he showed signs of extreme anxiety at the sound of the whistle.

Now whilst we do not want to induce anxiety in our horses, it is important to know how it is induced, so that if we do come across any inexplicable fear or anxiety in a horse, we can attempt to trace it back to the unpleasant experience that caused it; and set out, taking time and patience, to retrain the animal until he no longer associates that particular thing with fear or pain.

Some time ago we carried out an experiment ourselves to test this process of association in horses, though we did not in this case induce fear, but hunger. We blew a whistle two minutes beforehand, every time we fed the horses. And within seven days, the horses were saying 'where's my bloody breakfast' as soon as the whistle was blown. It didn't matter what time of the day the whistle was blown, the horses still asked for food. And one horse continued to ask for food in response to the whistle after he had been turned out for three weeks.

The unconscious memory explains a lot of bad habits that can be found in horses: the horse may have forgotten the original situation that caused his fear, but the fear will still be there, and a similar situation years later may cause him great anxiety.

We had Jasmine as a two-year-old, and then later as a three-year-old. She was a sweet kind pony, but she used to wander around the yard a bit, getting in everyone's way, and stealing food where she could. Eventually she discovered that if the door of the feeding house was open, she could have a quick breakfast out of the feed barrel, which was a forty-gallon oil drum, before anyone discovered her.

On one particular occasion, she saw the door of the feeding house open, shot in, and dived into the feed barrel to have a quick breakfast. What she didn't know was that there was a hen in there already, also having a quick breakfast, and the hen, badly frightened, tried to fly out, and when it found the way barred, pecked Jasmine hard about the face and head. After that Jasmine never went into the feeding house again.

Jasmine was sold soon after that, but two years later, as a five-year-old, she was back with us. She came back rather late at night, and we put her into a loose box, where the manger was an oil drum three parts full of concrete. When I went out the next morning, however, I discovered that, though she was obviously hungry, she hadn't touched her feed. So I changed the feed, thinking that there was something wrong with it. She still wouldn't go near it, but I left her while I went in to have my breakfast. When I came out again and she still hadn't been near the feed, I just couldn't understand it. Then I remembered the incident of Jasmine and the hen. So I put the feed in the bucket, and she immediately ate it up. For the next three days I fed her in the bucket. At the end of the third day, I put the bucket into the drum for convenience, and again she wouldn't go anywhere near it: her one unpleasant experience with the hen, even after two years, still made her anxious about oil drums.

This is a typical example of how, once an animal has been badly frightened, behaviour can be affected over a period of years, and the damage once done can be very difficult to undo.

A horse that is apparently unreasonably nervous or frightened may also be generalizing from a different, but similar, situation he has encountered in the past: when a horse has learned a certain response to one situation, he may respond to all similar situations in the same way. Thus if a horse has had a pleasant experience when being ridden, he will look upon being ridden as a pleasant pastime; but if on the other hand he has been frightened when being ridden, he will tend to be nervous and upset whenever anyone gets on his back. And his current owner may be quite unaware of the reason.

Sometimes, if a horse has been badly treated by a man, he will be quite easy to handle by a woman, and go quietly and gently for her. But if he is ridden and handled by another man, even a gentle and sensitive rider, he may show signs of nervousness and anxiety, because he is associating men with pain.

The point to remember when training a horse, as I have already insisted, is that anything that frightens and upsets him, or is painful in any way, will be remembered for a very long time. And I can't stress enough how important it is that a horse should never be frightened or upset in his own particular stable: that he must have a place where he feels absolutely secure and safe. So if you have anything unpleasant to do with a horse, shoeing him, for instance, if he is difficult to shoe, never do it in his own loose box. Move him into another one. If you have to do something that is either painful to the horse, or likely to frighten him, always move him into a different stable so that he never associates pain or fear with his own stall.

If we are to keep our relations with our horses friendly and co-operative, it is also of course important to be able to recognize other emotional states than fear and anger. A horse doesn't feel the same all the time: from day to day, from hour to hour, his emotions will change. He may be happy, depressed, as well as afraid or angry. For the horse, like us, is affected by a large number of experiences, and it is extremely important that we should be able to identify each emotion as it shows, because it will affect the behaviour of the horse.

The classical reaction of a horse is what might be called the 'startle' pattern. You can observe this for yourself by tiptoeing up behind a horse, and clapping your hands. The reaction you will get is a startle: he will look towards the sound, open his mouth slightly, thrust his head and neck forward, and as his legs bend ever so slightly, his muscles will become tense. The uniformity of this response from one horse to another suggests that it is an inborn response, modified very little by learning or training.

Another stereotype response more regularly seen in animals than in people is the orientating response. This is a term that is applied to a horse that is orientating itself to a new stimulus or stimulus change. It involves tensing the muscles, and changing the position of the head, which in a horse is very similar to the startle pattern, except that the muscle tensing typically raises the head and tail, and draws the feet together. You can see this if you walk into a horse's loose box at night and turn the light on suddenly. The main difference from the startle pattern is that the startle pattern will prepare the horse for flight, whereas the orientating response does not prepare it for flight.

Other emotional responses vary from one horse to another. Each individual has his own way of expressing himself, but once you know your horses you will be able to interpret what emotions they are showing from their postures, gestures, and possibly also the sounds they make. Reading these signs comes into the field of equine communication, which I have dealt with in my book *Talking with Horses*, and it is a skill that anyone can learn.

In the horse there are only a few instinctive automatic responses that are inherited, and therefore universal: blinking the eye in response to change of light, flinching in response to pain, a salivary response to food it shares with human beings. And we all know the movement of the ear in response to variation in sound. But if you are trying to interpret a particular horse's emotions, you will have to get to know it as an individual, for its behaviour will be its own.

For example, Biddy shows affection by rubbing me with her nose, while Rostellan shows affection to my wife by catching hold of her sleeve between his lips. Rostellan shows fear by pricking his ears, and looking at the object, but Biddy shows fear by turning her head slightly to one side, putting her ears back, and raising one hind leg. Each horse says 'I am angry,' 'I am frightened,' or 'I am pleased' in his own particular way.

Some horses have extremely quick reactions. Jezebel's anger

for example explodes like a bomb into an aggressive movement, and it happens in a twinkling of an eye. While other more placid animals react slowly, giving you warning signs as the emotion builds up. The easiest way to interpret a horse's emotions is to observe him over a period of time in basic situations, and you will very quickly be able to discover how a horse shows his emotion, and exactly what emotion he is showing. Once you know whether he is pleased, enjoying himself or angry and frightened, you will know how to proceed in teaching him. For instance, if a horse when you pop him at a fence shows he is enjoying it, you can proceed quite happily. But if he is a little bit nervous and frightened you have to proceed slowly and very carefully, and build him up until he is enjoying what he is doing. If he is sullen and hostile, you must use patience and understanding to remove the hostility before you can hope to get him to enjoy himself.

It is of course the horses of strong emotion, and strong but nervous character, that can be most rewarding. They are a challenge, like Jezebel.

She, it will be remembered, was at one time considered to be completely unrideable and unmanageable. I had not had her very long when I decided to take her into a cross-country and dressage competition. This was a little ambitious since Jezebel had never done any dressage in her life, and her only schooling was conducted in the half-hour before we were due into the arena, at a canter. Already Jezebel was quite sure we were going to race and jump – she could feel that I was keyed up inside. So she either stood still, or set off at a strong canter when what I was trying to do was to get her to walk. At one time I thought I might risk a trot, and she responded by going absolutely flat-out in a circle. So the state of my nerves must be imagined when the time came for us to go into the dressage arena. We came up to the entrance of the arena at a brisk canter, with me expecting to do the fastest dressage test ever accomplished: I thought we might do most of it in about thirty seconds flat. Yet as we approached the entrance she changed her deportment completely. Instead of holding her head at an angle of forty-five degrees, looking straight up at the sky, she carried it straight with her neck in the perfect arch. And she dropped back into a trot. We came to the centre of the arena, and she halted at the exact spot, whilst I saluted the judge, then went off at a very nice working trot and completed the test superbly: trotting when she should, walking when she should, cantering when she should, and ending up with only thirty-five penalties. This put her into fourth position.

We had a fair wait until the cross-country sections, and I had the opportunity to walk the course, and observe that most of the fences were young tree trunks which had been fastened to substantial gate-posts. This didn't do anything for my self-confidence. Expecting a twelve-two pony to carry twelve stone a mile and a half over three-foot-six fences, some of which had a four-foot spread, was asking a little bit much. But, since I had entered, I thought we had better make an attempt at least. So I got Jezebel down to the start in very good time and walked her round slowly. Her earlier desire to gallop when I wanted her steady had completely disappeared, and she walked round in what was for her such a civilized manner that I was able to light a cigarette, which helped me relax a little bit. We went up to the starting line: ten, nine, eight, seven, six, five, four, three, two, one, and we were away.

Jezebel went off like a bullet, and I had strong fears of disappearing over her tail. When I managed to get back into the saddle we were over the first fence, which was an easy one. Straight over a bank into fence two, a three-foot sharks teeth. And fence three, a gate. Jezebel was sailing. I knew that when riding Jezebel, like many very strong, very keen horses, it was a mistake to try and steady her, because she just takes hold and goes faster. So, I gave her all the rein she wanted and all the time she wanted. And this had the effect of steadying her a little bit. After that I didn't touch the reins at all, just calming her with my voice, and she jumped every fence immaculately. We finished up with the third fastest time of the day – which put me up into third place.

The only two horses to beat me were both sixteen-two thoroughbreds, and established eventers. The point is that I had complete empathy with Jezebel. All I had to do was to point her at the next fence, helping her with my weight all I could, but leaving it entirely to her to judge her distances, and her speed. I just talked to her all the time: 'Steady darling, steady darling, steady my beautiful. Now take it easy. Here we are going up-hill . . .' encouraging her all the time with my voice. When we pulled up, she had given everything. As soon as I got over the finishing line I got off her, and she stood and she panted and heaved for a good five minutes before she was able to walk away.

Ten minutes later she was as fresh as a daisy again. I got someone else to walk her round because I was too exhausted, and after a while I wandered over to tell her how clever and how good she was. She showed her affection by rubbing her head up and down to scratch her ears against my shoulder, so I caught hold of one ear and pulled it affectionately – thus abusing my privilege, because she took a sharp nip out of my arm and told me to behave myself.

10: *Dealing With Conflict*

Conflict arises within the horse who has two or more simultaneous needs, both of which cannot be satisfied at the same time. This causes one of the motives to be frustrated. And if one of the things that is frustrated is fear, this will make the horse anxious.

Of course the number of possible conflicts of motives that a horse can meet is enormous. The best and most common example of conflict, perhaps, arises in the horse that is reluctant to be caught. If you take a bucket of nuts into the field with you, the horse knows that you have food in the bucket. But he also knows that you want to catch him. And immediately a conflict arises between his greed for the nuts, on the one hand, and his reluctance to be caught on the other. If he satisfies his hunger, he is caught. If he stays free, he stays hungry.

Eventually of course, if you go about it the right way, he will come over to eat out of the bucket, and you will catch him. So you have frustrated his desire to be free. Now this is quite simple and straightforward if, once he is caught, the horse quite enjoys his work anyway. But if when you ride him he is frightened, or hurts himself jumping, next time you go to catch him you will have conflict not between two motives – greed and a wish to remain free – but three. You will have to contend also with the anxiety and nervousness caused by being frightened last time he was caught and ridden.

This sort of minor conflict arises very often in working with horses. But at times you may come across a major conflict between two powerful fears. If a horse is afraid of hurting himself jumping, and there is someone standing behind him with a dirty great hunting crop, the conflict of fears will be between hurting himself jumping and getting belted with the hunting crop. If the fear of hurting himself jumping is not very great, and his fear of the hunting crop is enormous, then he will jump the fence. But if on the other hand he is equally afraid of both, he is going to make a mess of jumping the fence, and so hurt himself more, so that the next time, in spite of the hunting crop, he will refuse to jump altogether. This is a conflict of two very great fears, and it can be very damaging.

If on the other hand he bundled over the fence somehow, hurting himself only a little, he will jump it again next time because he must. But as soon as the hunting crop is taken away, he will refuse to jump. And after that he will look upon jumping as something that is unpleasant and frightening. He is likely to display a complete revulsion against crossing any form of obstacle, and it is only by resolving this fear with sympathy and understanding that he will be encouraged to jump again willingly.

In a situation like this, the first and most important thing to do is to get the horse to enjoy jumping again. The best way to do this is to let him follow other horses over a series of low obstacles, two-foot or two-foot-three are high enough. When he is enjoying galloping and jumping with the other horses, you can send the other horses on in front, and when they are at the other end of the jumps he will be tearing to get at them so he will actually enjoy jumping the fences.

Similarly you can pop over a few low fences when he is going home to his dinner. Then when he is jumping low obstacles happily to get to other horses, or on his way home, you can take him out by himself and let him jump the same obstacles alone. You do not want to change the height of the jumps until he is jumping the low fences every day with enthusiasm and pleasure. You will know when this is because when he comes to the first fence he will be reaching for the bit and saying 'come let's get going'. You can then raise the fences two or three inches. Or you can introduce a new jump, always making sure that anything he jumps he is going to enjoy jumping. It's a very long and slow process. Depending upon how frightened and upset he was originally, it can take anything from six months to three years before you get back to jumping really big strong fences in competition. As in all things with horses, and especially in retraining, there is no quick way, there is no short cut. At the same time it must be remembered that boredom is something that will cut right across his training programme – this again will involve a conflict of emotions, the feeling of dull monotony conflicting with his desire to do what you want.

The art of handling any conflict between one set of desires in a horse and another, is to eliminate the cause: for example, if the conflict is between his boredom with his work and his desire to please you, varying the work so that he is no longer bored will eliminate the conflict altogether. Since when a horse says that he won't or can't do something, you have to stay there until he does it happily and willingly for you – if you ever hope to work successfully with that horse again – as the horse is bigger and stronger than you are, this is often the *only* way of dealing with conflict.

An example of such a technique arose in our work with a yearling sent to us because, among other things, he was impossible to load into a trailer or a lorry. So the first thing we did was slowly, patiently and determinedly to train him to accept the lorry. This involved, first, coaxing him with some nuts, second, moving his legs forward one at a time, and finally two people pushing him hard from behind.

When we eventually got him on to the lorry – it took us about forty minutes – we made a tremendous fuss of him, gave him a few nuts and took him out again. Then we put him back on the lorry again, which this time took us a quarter of an hour or twenty minutes. When he was in, he had a few nuts, was brought out again, and loaded straight back in again. This time the process took only about five minutes. By the time we had finished, we were leading him in and out of the lorry with no trouble whatever.

This problem had arisen from sheer bloody-mindedness on his part, which made his owner a little bit frightened of him, and angry. So he got walloped and this compounded his fear, until he was impossible to load. Such a conflict could be resolved only by:

(a) removing his fear of being loaded – at no time when we were doing this did anyone raise a voice, and at no time was he hit;

(b) making him realize that when he got into the lorry he would be made a fuss of, and fed;

(c) impressing on him that whether he was difficult or easy, he had to go into the lorry anyway.

For the next week, he was fed only when he was in the lorry. And at the end of the week, you only had to drop the tail board of the lorry and he was straight into it shouting 'where is my bloody breakfast'.

We had thus changed his attitude completely within a week. From flatly refusing to go near the lorry at all, he was so anxious to do so that the one thing he wanted in the world was to get into the lorry and have a feed.

This epitomizes the whole essence of training a horse, which is not getting a horse to do a thing because he has to, though you may have to do this to start with. It is getting a horse to do a thing because he *wants* to – changing his wishes and desires so that by allowing him to do what *he* wants, you will be getting him to do what you want. The bond he has with you will be all the greater, as jumping a fence or exercising or schooling becomes a reward in itself because he enjoys doing it. And you are increasing his enjoyment each time you do it.

Two forms of behaviour are typical of the problems that arise from conflict in the motivations of the horse. One is what might be termed avoidance behaviour, manifested for example in the horse who goes into a fence 'will I,' 'won't I,' 'can I,' and at the last moment refuses to jump, or attempts to jump and makes a mess of it. This avoidance will be far worse the next time and every succeeding time he tries, unless tackled immediately. Another type of avoidance involves bucking the rider off, bolting, or refusing to go near the fence altogether.

Such a conflict problem faced me three years ago, and caused great mirth locally. A friend who has hunting hounds had a nice little fourteen-two chestnut mare named Robbie that he wanted to hunt hounds off, and he offered to lend her to me for a few days to get her going quietly before he hunted her himself. I'd had the mare for some time, and she was going quietly and gently – she was an extremely good and willing jumper – when we attended a very big lawn meet. I got on her, and hounds were unloaded, and I noticed she was going a little bit crab-like, and had her back up. But I thought this was because she hadn't done much work recently, and was just feeling full of herself. We proceeded on to the lawn of the house, and as I attended to the hounds, keeping them under control, I noticed that she was flicking her ears, swishing her tail, and half threatening to kick. I got myself set in the saddle ready for trouble, but I wasn't quite quick enough. She exploded into three gigantic bucks, and I did a neat parabola in the air, landing on my backside in the middle of the hounds.

I got back on her and managed to keep her from bucking for the next ten minutes, keeping her head well up and my backside well down in the saddle. But while everyone else was drinking and speechifying, the hounds moved off to the first draw. As soon as she felt grass under her feet, I was on the ground again. I mounted a third time and we went on to draw following a sheep path alongside the mountain on a very steep slope. We hadn't gone fifty or a hundred yards before she suddenly turned straight down the hill, bucking as she went, and I didn't stand a chance. Again I executed three somersaults, disappearing from view into a patch of bracken whilst Robbie proceeded bucking on her way. Whipping into hounds isn't the time to have a battle with a horse. Fortunately I had lent my own horse to a friend of mine for the day, so I gave him Robbie and took my horse back, and proceeded to have a very good day's hunting.

Apart from having to listen to my various so-called friends making suggestions that I should take riding lessons, and asking when I was going to put on another rodeo performance, I was not much damaged so I arranged with the owner of Robbie to have her delivered to me the next day. As soon as I had had my Sunday lunch, I went out and put saddle and bridle on her and took her out. She had one minor go at bucking, but that was all. She didn't make another mistake. After that I had her out every day, working her gently, cantering, jumping and no trouble at all. A month later I thought she was going so sweetly and kindly, I would amaze everyone with the transformation in her, and took her hunting again. But to make quite sure, we stopped the Land Rover and trailer a couple of miles from the Meet and rode the last two miles, Robbie going very sweetly. Unfortunately the Huntsman had had trouble starting his Land Rover that morning, so he was half-an-hour late, and I sat on Robbie, talking to various people at the Meet about how quiet and easy she was.

The Huntsman arrived eventually, got his horse out of the trailer, and let hounds go. Immediately Robbie exploded into a buck. I rode her for the next hour keeping a very tight rein on her, but the whole time she was attempting to buck, and every time hounds came near her her ears started flicking, and her tail started swishing.

Otherwise a completely sweet and easy horse to ride, it seemed Robbie would become a devil incarnate when she saw hounds. I don't know why – she may have been a member of the League against Cruel Sports. To this day I am completely mystified. She is the only horse that I have ever come across who didn't love hunting.

A further avoidance technique a horse will use, apart from bucking, bolting, and refusing to go near the obstacle, is rearing. This is caused either by fear of a particular object or experience, or by bad handling on the part of her rider.

All vices can be overcome with time and patience provided of course that the vice you are trying to eliminate is worth the time and patience involved in tackling it. If, for example, I had persevered for two or three months hunting Robbie, I could eventually have got her hunting, in a reasonable manner if somewhat reluctantly. And in time no doubt she would have come to enjoy it, since she was an extremely good ride, and a very good little jumper. But it was much simpler to hunt something else that wanted to hunt – it is much more fun hunting a horse that's mad to get after hounds than the one that isn't particularly enthusiastic. And in Robbie's case, she was a superb little hack, very quiet and gentle, and it was thought it would be a very great pity to get into a major conflict with her, and possibly sour her very sweet nature, merely to turn her into a reluctant hunter. Other than in the hunting field she never thought about bucking or misbehaving.

Anger and hostility in a horse is almost always caused by interference. A horse that is by himself in a field cannot get angry or hostile. Even a subordinate horse within a herd will never show anger or hostility to one of the herd leaders, and similarly the herd leader will not show anger or hostility – until he is interfered with by another horse. But as soon as something interferes with him, anger, fear, or hostility can be aroused. The whole essence of our training must be to avoid anger and hostility. We go to a lot of trouble to do so.

This can be done in two ways: either by training the horse in such a way that we give him so much pleasure and excitement that the question of rebellion does not arise; or by repeating a controversial action so often that habit replaces anger and hostility.

We use such techniques when we are gentling a horse. We take him out with other horses so that he is so much enjoying being with other horses that he forgets to resent being ridden: equates being ridden with enjoying himself. He will very quickly look on the sight of his bridle and saddle with pleasure, because he expects that when they are on he will enjoy himself. On the other hand, when we have to make a horse pick up his feet, which he finds it very hard to do willingly, we use the other strategy, of simple repetition to create a habit. All horses have a firm idea that their four feet are meant to be kept on the ground, and they get annoyed to a greater or a lesser extent as soon as you try to pick them up. But if you constantly pick up the horse's feet, he becomes accustomed to having his feet picked up, and the more often you do it the less notice he will take. You will eventually get to the stage where as soon as you touch his fetlock he will lift it up himself. Repetition in fact has reduced the original anger and hostility at having his feet picked up to nil.

Few people welcome anger and hostility in their horses, even when they sympathize with their fear and frustrations. They recognize that anger produces a cycle of action and reaction that is very difficult to escape from: when a horse gets angry, people tend to feel threatened by them. This makes them frightened, and to hide this fear they will probably stimulate more anger by shouting, or threatening with a stick. This of course increases the fear within the horse, so that the horse himself will feel threatened, and so the cycle continues.

In actual fact the easiest way to extinguish anger and fear in a horse is by calmness and determination. If you are calm and quiet with a horse, no matter how frightened and angry it is, the horse will tend to become less frightened, and less angry. The last thing on earth to do is to shout and brandish a stick, or to try to punish him in any way for his fear.

Just after Christmas I was called in to handle a difficult and unmanageable horse. She kicked very badly. As soon as you went into her stable, she would go into the far corner and present you with her backside, and if you went near her she would kick out at you with one leg. Even when you got to her head she would kick forward, something I have seen only once in a horse before. She caught me with her hind leg when I was standing by her front leg. But I just talked to her quietly and gave her a few oats every time she turned her head towards me. In about half an hour I could walk up to her and put my hand over her neck, without her kicking me. Then I put a saddle on her. As soon as I went to fasten up the girth, she kicked again. But again talking quietly and slowly, I eventually got her so that I could fasten the girth without too much trouble. Her previous experience of course was that every time she presented her backside she had got hit, which started her kicking, which in turn made her owner more and more frightened of her. This meant that in effect she was getting away with kicking her owner, and getting her own way. But by quiet determination I taught her in a very short time that I was going to catch her, that I wasn't afraid of her, and that when she did come round she would get rewarded with a few oats. The motive behind her behaviour was thus changed very quickly from a desire not to be caught to a desire to get caught in order to be made a fuss of, and have a few oats.

However, if I had been aggressive with her, indeed if I had raised my voice above the quiet sing-song note, she would immediately have been frightened and terrified, presented her hind-quarters to me again, and no doubt kicked me hard in a tender spot to teach me to behave better next time.

We must thus always suppress the anger within ourselves when reacting with horses. We know that it will only evoke the expression of more anger, and more fear in our horses. We must stay cool and quiet. This state of affairs is no doubt extremely frustrating to the horse: anger is a momentary and very immediate emotion in a horse, that needs to be vented immediately, so when he is all set for a battle, he must feel extremely frustrated if he is causing no response in you. But in due course he will calm down. On the other hand if you punish anger in a horse, you are only giving him another cause to be angry, and increasing his fear – which is usually the initial cause of the anger – and he will react until he is beyond your control, and his own.

If a horse is frightened by something in a hedge, and you, his rider, punish him, instead of curing the vice of shying you may be increasing his fear of the object. You are in effect justifying his fear: he shied at a paper bag, and he got hurt at the same time, so he will equate being hurt with the paper bag. His rider could quite conceivably be making the vice worse by increasing his fear and nervousness. The best that suppressing the anger in a horse by punishment can achieve is to teach the horse not to *show* his anger, and you end up with a sullen, bad tempered and un-willing horse who is by countless means avoiding doing what you want.

Some people find themselves at odds with their horse because they are trying to force him into a mould that the horse is un-suited for, either temperamentally or physically. Or it may be that weakness in the rider allows the horse to misbehave. A horse may go quite sweetly for one person and be nearly unrideable by another.

Fear and anger and frustration are the causes of most of the vices that develop in horses. And anger is the thing that most people are least able to deal with. When the anger within the horse is suppressed it is the frustration of the anger that causes the awkwardness and bloody-mindedness. If a horse has been accustomed to doing something, and you stop him, his automatic reaction is bound to be 'Why the bloody hell shouldn't I? I have always done it.' And if you respond to this by saying, 'You aren't doing it because I damned well say you aren't', you im-mediately land yourself in the classical situation of conflict. If the horse then does what he originally wanted to do, and you let him do it, he has established a position of dominance over you by a display of anger, and will be encouraged to display anger on future occasions when he wants his own way. If on the other hand you stop him doing what he wants to do, and establish your position of dominance over him, you are going to be little better off, because he is just going to be sullen and bad-tempered over the whole incident. And if you punish him severely in the process of stopping him doing what he wanted to do, he is going to be not only angry and sullen: he is also going to be frightened.

If on the other hand your reaction to his 'Why the hell shouldn't I?' is 'Because we are going to do so-and-so instead, and you are going to enjoy it', then he will accept the change quite willingly and happily.

Imagine, for example, that a horse has refused to take off from the ground with his previous owner. You present him with a three-foot-six fence, going away from home. You can make him jump the fence by flogging him over it with a hunting crop, but he will end up afterwards disliking jumping, disliking you, and a little bit frightened of you as well. Or you can allow him not to jump the fence, and he will have established his dominance over you.

On the other hand, you could put up a small fence on your way home. And when you come to the fence, when he says, 'Oh, I don't jump fences. I can't jump fences,' you could say to him 'You are going to jump the fence because this is the way we go home to dinner.' He will scramble over the fence, and find he gets home to dinner. And the next day when you come to the same fence, he will scramble over it a little bit more easily. At the end of the week when you come up to it on your way home, he will pop over it quite happily.

It must be remembered that there is a great deal of difference between allowing a horse to do what he wants, and getting the horse to want to do what you want him to. They are two completely different things, as diametrically opposite as getting a horse to do what you want him to do and making him do something that he has bloody well got to.

Most people when training a horse tend to concentrate on the *suppression* of his anger. But the real skill, especially in the early stages, is to avoid any situation that would lead to anger. So in our work we lay the emphasis on getting the horse to enjoy himself. But of course, when we are riding a horse constantly, we are bound at some time to come across a situation where the horse refuses to do what we ask him to. And then we must make our stand, with patience, and if necessary with a smack, but not too much of the smack, we insist that the horse do what we tell him to. And then when he does that, we tell him what a clever horse he is.

Teaching Jack to jump was a challenge that might well have been mishandled if we had ever decided to confront it head-on. We had Jack for four or five years, and he solidly refused to jump. But since he was a fantastic riding pony, we didn't bother to teach him – we had plenty of horses who wanted to jump anyway, and for us it is seldom worth spending time on making a horse jump who doesn't want to. Then one day we were out riding and there was a tree laying across the track. As soon as they saw it all the other horses pricked their ears, cantered into it, and popped over. It was only about eighteen inches high. Jack in his hurry to catch up with the other horses forsook the principles of a lifetime, and took off, all feet off the ground at the same time. We made such a fuss of him that he must have felt he had jumped a fence at least twice as big as Beechers Brook. And after that, whenever there was an obstacle in the way on the ride, instead of going round it Jack jumped over it. And within about six weeks Jack was jumping everything quite happily and well.

Of course we could have *made* Jack jump much earlier, but it would have entailed a battle. Our work involves teaching people who have never jumped, to jump, so we have to have horses who jump willingly and well, and basically this means horses whose one desire in life is to jump, not horses that have been taught to jump reluctantly. A sullen and frustrated horse is not a good and happy companion. In general, then, the rule is that it is much better to avoid conflict where possible.

I always try to avoid head-on battles with horses, except on grounds of my own choosing. For example, if I have a horse sent to me that is a very bad bucker, I will do all I can to avoid doing anything that makes him buck until I come to the bottom of a steep hill. Then I point him up the hill, driving my heels in, and saying: 'Right, go on you beggar, buck!' And every time he lands, I drive my heels in and say: 'Go on, good boy, buck again.' By the time he has gone half way up a steep hill, the effort of bucking and failing to dislodge me from the saddle seems more and more pointless, so he stops bucking. I find, if I do this four or five times, all desire to buck vanishes, and in future that horse will buck only out of *joie de vivre*. Just occasionally, however, you start something, as I did with Boyo, not realizing that you are going to have a pitched battle, but then, having started, you must finish what you are doing. You must finish it, or you don't go home.

Most, if not all, shades of emotion are a combination of feelings: fear is often mixed with anger, just as it can also be mixed with pleasure. And if a horse is frightened, and you make him do something he doesn't want to do, his fear will change to anger at you for trying to make him do it.

Twenty years ago, when we first had the Bishop and he had just recently been gentled, I took him out exercising one day. It was about two hours' ride, going in a circle from the yard, and I intended to get back to the yard just before dinner. Twenty yards from the stable was a ford across a small stream however, which we had to cross to get back into the yard. What I didn't know when I chose the route was that the Bishop had never crossed water in his life. So when we got to the stream, he stopped dead. I tried to coax him forward and he took two steps to one side. I coaxed him again and he took two steps to the other side. So we went on, with me getting more forceful, and his reaction to my forcefulness increasingly acrobatic: he reared and bucked, plunged, did everything except go forward across that stream. His initial fear of crossing the water had combined with anger at being asked to do something that he had never done before, and which he thought dangerous, if not impossible. As a result I didn't get my dinner that day until half-past three.

I had to stay there, coaxing and talking, until I had eventually calmed him down. Then he put one foot in the water, quite by accident, and when he had discovered that the foot hadn't disappeared, and it wasn't painful, I coaxed him forward again, and he put it in again. Again it didn't disappear and so with great courage he put another foot in the water. He stood like that for at least five minutes. Then I managed to coax him forward half a step, then another half a step, until eventually he had all four feet in the water. This was too much for the Bishop. He stood there trembling for a couple of minutes, then he spun round and was flat out back up the way we had come. I steadied him and walked him back down to the river. This time he walked in with two front feet, and finding it quite pleasant, decided to take a big stride forward. But as the next foot hit the water a drop splashed up and hit him on the nose. This again was altogether too much, so he he decided to get rid of me, and he arched his back and went into a terrific buck.

Fortunately it was in the right direction. He landed with all four feet in the water, the shock of the splash sent him into another buck, and this took us out and up the other side. I rode up to the yard to collect my wife, who jumped on Cork Beg, and we rode back down to the stream. Cork Beg was being asked to act as schoolmaster, so he splashed through the water. The Bishop, seeing Cork Beg go across without thinking anything of it, tried to jump the stream in one, but landed in the middle again and splashed his tummy. However, when we got to the other side, Cork Beg turned round and went back across the river, and the Bishop very gently followed. Thus we walked back and forward twenty or thirty times, until the Bishop had finally accepted the fact that crossing the river was neither dangerous nor impossible. Then with great thankfulness we went back up to the stables, unsaddled the Bishop, and gave him and Cork Beg a feed. And I went to my very dry and very tasteless dinner.

From these two instances it must not be thought that I am perpetually having battles with my horses at the wrong time. I am not. I have remarkably few battles with my horses. But when a battle is forced on you, you have to go through with it. And those are the battles that always stand out in your mind. Not only do you remember the battle, you remember your empty stomach as well!

Of course, if I had realized that the Bishop had never crossed water, or that he was afraid of water, I should have led him across the water, following two or three other horses, in the first place. And I would have avoided a battle. After seeing the other horses cross the water, the Bishop would have crossed without any difficulty at all. We are perpetually looking for ways round conflict, for a battle is of little use to anybody. All it does is upset

you and upset your time schedule – and if you are as busy as I
am, you have a very tight time schedule. And they set back the
work you have been doing on the horse by days, weeks and sometimes even months.

11: *Practical Applications of Horse Psychology*

Pure knowledge to the scientist may be an end in itself, but to the practical horseman it is pointless unless use can be made of it. And it is only of use with horses if it does one of four things:

first, if it increases the wellbeing of the horse;

second, if it makes the horse's work easier for it to perform;

third, if it improves its performance, not only in competition but in quite simple hacking and riding;

and last, if it increases the owner's enjoyment of the horse, and improves his riding ability.

These four conditions are like a pyramid. The horse's wellbeing makes it possible for his work to become easier, because unless he is strong and fit his work is bound to be hard and tedious. And if you have a fit well horse it is important to make the most of him, which in turn is bound to improve his performance, and of course if the horse's performance improves, his rider's enjoyment will increase automatically.

The first task, then, is to make sure of the horse's physical wellbeing. The most important thing is to know what its basic needs are. The experts tend to lay down rules: they say that a horse of certain such a size, doing such and such work, needs X pounds of food. And I can state quite categorically that this is wrong. Each horse is an individual with his own individual likes and dislikes, and his own individual needs. It may well be that the average horse, say of fourteen-two to fifteen hands, doing a reasonable amount of work, needs on an average twelve pounds of corn and twenty pounds of hay a day. But unfortunately I have never come across an average horse, just as I have never met an average man – who no doubt would be a mixture of black, white, yellow and various shades of khaki, but I wouldn't know him if I saw him anyway. I've only come across individuals, and there is no way I know of assessing an individual's needs except to get to know him.

Let us start by finding out how much water he needs. This isn't just a question of finding out what his total requirement of water is, but of how also he likes to drink it: a small or large amount of water at what time of the day. For example, Rostellan normally drinks about six gallons of water a day, but when he comes back from hunting or show-jumping he will drink six gallons of water in the space of about three or four hours. This isn't just because he has been sweating: he requires water to relax him physically and mentally.

I know from my own experience that when I am riding in a race my mouth goes dry, and after a race I am always thirsty, even if I have fallen off at the first fence, and taken very little out of myself. I've probably passed a great deal of urine before racing, from excitement, and this water has to be replaced. And it is exactly the same thing with Rostellan. If we know what his increased requirement of water is after hunting, we can meet the requirement. If on the other hand we don't know that he has an increased need for water after being out, we could quite happily put his normal ration of water in his stall, leaving him thirsty.

The same principle – familiarity with individual needs – applies to the feeding of a horse. The first thing you need to know is the amount of food he requires to maintain his bodyweight, given the work he is doing. This may be the average amount of food prescribed by the text book, or it may be two or three pounds more, or two or three pounds less, depending upon his abilities as a food converter. But on top of this it is also necessary to know exactly what his greed factor is: just how much more food he will eat given a chance. This information can be of use in two or three ways.

If he is an extremely greedy horse, and has a greed factor that will make him eat eight, ten, or twelve pounds more than his ration, you can then of course use his greed to make him perform better, that is, you can use food as a powerful reward. But it is far more important to know that he is a shy or difficult feeder, or if he tends to refuse to eat after competition, because this knowledge not only helps you in feeding him, it also tells you something about his degree of nervous tension, the build-up within him if he is hunting or competing. It may then be necessary to resort to all sorts of subterfuges before competing to get the best out of him.

Molfre was a typical example of this. The day before racing, if he knew he was going to race, he would tend to eat only half his feed, and he would sweat. The build-up of tension also meant that he was sweating up long before you got to the race course. We overcame this tension within him in two ways. First, we made no preparation the day before racing. We didn't give him any extra grooming or tidying up, or trim his mane or tail. Second, I would load him into the trailer just in his night rug; and on non-racing days I'd take him out for a drive in the trailer in exactly the same way – just drive round the mountain for half an hour, bring him back and unload him. By this strategy he never knew whether he was going racing until he actually got on to the race course. We had relieved his tension and he hadn't taken a lot out of himself before he got to the meeting.

To show the variation in the needs of different horses for food, I have only to look at the three horses that we have been hunting this winter: Rostellan, Clancy and Charlie. All three have been having the equivalent of fifteen pounds of corn per day, although Rostellan and Clancy have been hunting on an average three days a fortnight, and Charlie has been hunting only about three days a month. At the beginning of winter they were all approximately of the same bodyweight, Charlie being an inch taller than Clancy, and Clancy an inch taller than Rostellan. So in theory they all needed approximately the same amount of food. Yet Rostellan has been putting on condition slowly all winter as he built up and muscled up; Clancy has maintained his bodyweight, certainly hasn't lost any condition, and has put on an awful lot of muscle; whilst Charlie has been losing weight all winter. This has proved very difficult to correct, because whilst both Rostellan and Clancy would have eaten half as much again as we were feeding them, we were feeding Charlie right up to the limit of his consumption, right through the winter. The real reason for his loss of bodyweight, we concluded, was that it was taking him a very long time to settle down psychologically after five years in training. For not only had we disrupted what were for him the habits of a lifetime, we were demanding new and different things of him, which brought new and different needs and drives into play. He didn't relax, and was still not happy until we had had him nearly six weeks. But once he had relaxed and started realizing what was required of him, and enjoying the work that he was doing, he stopped losing bodyweight, and over two or three weeks he started putting on condition again.

I can even put a date on the day he started putting on condition. He hadn't been going at all well out hunting, being surly and bad tempered. That day, January 7th, we had an extremely long run from Drefach and it took me a very long time to find hounds. Then about half-way through the day Charlie suddenly settled down and started working well, and by the time I had found hounds and got back, and I met the Land Rover and trailer coming to look for me, Charlie was so tired he could hardly lift one foot after another. But he seemed contented with himself. Of course after a hard day's hunting like that, he went back to looking an absolute skeleton and he hardly touched his feed that night, or the following morning. Yet the following evening he ate up well. On the Friday morning after that I opened the stable doors, went back up the line of boxes to fetch the feeds, and I passed Charlie who put his head out and caught hold of the sleeve of my coat, and stopped me. I rubbed him between his ears, and scratched his chin. And he reciprocated by rubbing up and down on my shoulder nearly knocking me off my feet.

From that moment on, slowly and certainly, his attitude to his work became more and more cheerful. He became happier within himself, and he stopped losing condition. About a fortnight later he had quite clearly started improving.

This is an example where all the feeding charts in the world could be of no help at all, because the crucial factor was a psychological one. Emotional tensions can affect digestion and health. This can be verified by your own observations of your own horse: if you take him out and get him excited, you will immediately see him evacuating dung, and while he is under the stress of the excitement or nervousness, you will see the texture of his dung change. He will evacuate it much sooner. This is nature's way of accelerating his digestion preparatory to emptying his stomach for flight in the wild. Mental stress in fact can change the digestive processes of the horse completely, so that he is converting his food less efficiently – his food is shooting through his body like a moonshot through outer space. But once he becomes mentally relaxed, the whole digestive process will be slowed down so that he digests his food more thoroughly. So if you want a horse to digest his food efficiently, you have to get him mentally relaxed and well: to get your horse physically at the peak of his form, in other words, you must first get him mentally fit.

In particular he must be mentally and physically relaxed in his stable, because not only will this promote his digestion, it will also help him to recharge himself mentally and physically for further endeavour.

After the needs for food and water, the next thing we must discover about our horses is the extent and nature of their sexual drives. These can have a considerable influence on their performance.

For the time being, anyway, we can ignore the sex drive of the stallion, since most of us don't ride stallions, and certainly most of us don't use one in competition. We ride geldings, or mares, and the drives of geldings, as I have already mentioned, will vary from horse to horse. Some geldings can be considerably affected by the presence of mares in season, to the extent of being distracted by them, which makes them either nappy or excitable and of course impairs performance. So it is extremely necessary to know what your horse's reactions are likely to be. Nothing is more annoying, after taking a horse fifty miles to a competition, than finding your gelding, instead of dazzling everyone with his ability, and leaving the crowd dumbfounded with admiration at yours, spending all his time shrieking at the top of his voice to a lady love; or when you come up to jump a fence he is so distracted by some seductive beauty that he goes straight through, and you land flat on your face.

Equally, a mare's performance will rise and fall with her sexual activity, usually reaching a peak midway between the times she becomes in season, and a trough when she is actually in season.

You will also be observing how much exercise your horse is taking in his stable, and how much movement his temperament requires, movement and light being as necessary for a horse as food and water. We explained earlier how you can measure the amount of movement a horse needs. The fat lazy horse is quite easily managed. Apart from the fact that you know that he needs a large amount of exercise to keep his spare tyre at a reasonable size, you don't have to worry very much about giving him mental activity. Stimulating him mentally is probably as difficult as stimulating him physically, and he may require an atom bomb to wake him up.

The horse that is walking round the stable like a caged lion, however, needs more careful handling. In the first place, it must be remembered that although he will not need very much exercise, he is also walking off the condition you are trying to put on him at great expense – mainly because he needs the mental stimulation that the movement is giving him. However, if you accept the fact that he is pacing round his stable either because his nerves are tense and the movement relieves the tension – in exactly the same way as when my nerves are on edge I like a glass of Guinness and a cigarette to relieve my tension – or because he is bored, you can begin to take remedial action.

Miracle cures for a horse of course do not exist. But it is possible to steady his nerves and to reduce his boredom. One remedy that has had some good results is playing music.

It is an established fact that milking cows let their milk down far more readily in the milking parlour if music is being played while they are milked. And we have observed with our own horses that some of them do enjoy listening to music, so if you could, you might put an expensive transistor into every box. But then some of your horses will be lovers of Brahms, and others will like pop music, and when the radio changed from Brahms to pop or vice versa, they may smash the radio. They are quite likely to smash the radio anyway, out of curiosity and boredom.

A far simpler way of providing mental stimulation for the horse is to make absolutely certain that at all times throughout daylight hours, he can see out of his loose box; not only to see out, but put his head out so that he can look to the left, look to the right, and gaze up at the sky at the aeroplanes if he wants to. Since all horses, like the Elephant's Child, are full of satiable curiosity, they will tend to spend a large part of the day looking out in case they miss something interesting. And if they are standing at the doorway looking out, they are not walking round their boxes and losing condition.

Once you have got to know something of your horse's physical needs and his temperament, you can set out to discover whether or not he is a free natural jumper, whether he does a good dressage test, whether he is a good hack, whether he's fast, whether he's competitive, whether he enjoys doing something for its own sake or whether he's an equine hippy with one desire in life – to live on Social Security and loaf around all day doing nothing.

It has always amazed me that while nobody would dream of trying to turn a tone-deaf individual like myself into an opera singer or a pianist, people will spend countless hours and endless energy trying to turn non-jumping horses into show jumpers, non-galloping horses into race horses, and shambling lazy individuals into dressage horses.

I must admit however that I'm in no position to throw stones, since I live in a glass house myself, spending a large amount of time trying to train horses that aren't fast enough to catch a cold to win point-to-points for me. And just occasionally I am very lucky with them – just often enough to make me keep on trying.

I had a typical example of this sort of luck at the East Devon point-to-point eighteen or nineteen years ago. I'd been asked to ride a very slow and ponderous hunter in the Cotley hunt race, and since I'd been booked to ride in every other race on the card that day, the only race I could ride Sandyboy in was the open. But whichever race he was in he was going to come last anyway, we reasoned, so we didn't let the fact that every other horse in the race was a very good point-to-pointer worry us.

The start of the East Devon in those days was just beyond the finishing post. And after the starter, who had the nickname among jockeys of Blind Bertie, had called the roll there were five minutes to wait for the start. A couple of the jockeys, to keep their mounts moving, rode back up into the crowd, whilst the others walked their horses round in a circle. Since my horse was going to need all the energy he could summon in the race, I stood by the starter and did not move. Suddenly Blind Bertie called the runners into line and, without bothering to see if everyone or even anyone, was there, he dropped his flag and away we went. The jockeys who weren't ready, including the two up in the crowd, spent the next two or three minutes arguing with Blind Bertie about whether or not he could start the race when they weren't ready, and by the time they realized that the race was on I had already jumped three fences.

Sandyboy was putting his best foot forward and going at least twice as fast as he had ever gone before in his life. We proceeded in this manner for two circuits and led the field all the way until just after the last fence. Unfortunately I was caught twenty yards from the winning post, beaten into second place mainly because Sandyboy had already given everything he had got and galloped himself into the ground. He could hardly totter over the winning line. But to get within two lengths of Gay Peri, in an open point-to-point, was no mean performance.

Some horses are lucky just as some people are. They simply seem to be born that way. On another occasion at the South

Dorset point-to-point, I rode another non-galloping horse who seemed to have the luck of the devil. Two very good horses had been brought down from the Mendip Hunt, and since nothing else was going in the open race, we slipped my horse in on the grounds that he was at least guaranteed third place.

The other two went off at a hell of a pace, while Rory and I went round in a very sedate manner, knowing we were getting a fiver for our pains, and enjoying a grandstand view of some beautiful riding and fencing by the two cracks. After we had gone two miles it wouldn't have been true to say that I couldn't see the others, but they were at least a fence in front of me. As we came round the Flagstaff, which was the corner into the straight, I saw them going hell for leather into the last fence and disappearing the other side. Then as we took off at our leisure at the last fence, I was rather surprised to see a somewhat silent crowd in front of me and no sign of the other two. Only when we came down and landed on the other side could I see why. One of the jockeys was sitting on the ground hammering it with his whip, and the other was lying recumbent with two ambulance men leaning over him trying to decide whether he was dead or only unconscious. I proceeded in solitary magnificence past a dumbfounded and silent crowd to a very welcome and unexpected winning reception.

Lucky occasions like this however are very few and far between, and it is infinitely better not to try and train a horse that doesn't want to jump for competition, or to make a dressage horse out of something that would be far happier pulling a plough.

So the first task is to find out the things a horse does well naturally and the things he wants to do. After that you start creating new things for him to want to do, and trying to extend his natural abilities. It is most important at this time to decide two things:

(a) whether you are mentally compatible with your horse – whether you have that essential empathy that is necessary to get the fullest enjoyment out of him; and

(b) whether the horse is suitable for your purpose.

What your desires are only you know; this is something you have to be honest about with yourself. Just because your friends are all dreaming of becoming Ann Moores and Marion Moulds, doesn't mean that you have to showjump. And because your grandfather's second cousin once rode round Aintree, doesn't mean that you have to ride point-to-pointing. It is what you want to do yourself that is important – what you enjoy doing.

If for example you feel the need to have a priest give you the last rites every time you have to jump a fence, don't jump. If you think that riding and racing is a very inefficient form of suicide, don't race. And if you think that dressage is something that should be confined to the circus ring, don't attempt to do dressage. You don't even have to ride the blasted things: some people get great pleasure out of keeping a horse just for its company – looking after him, grooming him, wandering out at night to chat with him when no one else will listen. But do make sure that the horse you have is one that naturally does the things that you want to do, and if it doesn't, get rid of it and get one that does. I'm not thinking of your wellbeing when I recommend this, but the horse's. There is nothing so frustrating for a good free jumper than being ridden by someone who is scared stiff going into a fence; and there is nothing so frustrating for a free active horse than being ridden by someone who wants to amble round the countryside, admiring the view. So if you want to jump, get a horse that jumps naturally. If on the other hand you want to sit on top of the hill admiring mother nature, get a horse that is quite happy to go to sleep while you do so.

Once having got a horse that wants to do the same things as you do, you have to start to extend his abilities. The basic component of all riding is hacking. It doesn't matter what form of equestrianism you are going in for, three-quarters of the time at least you will be doing nothing but walking and trotting on the road. And it doesn't matter whether you have a race horse, a dressage horse, a showjumper or an eventer, the basis of all this work is fitness Fitness is achieved by exercise, by walking and trotting, and this is the thing that you will be doing most. It is essential that the horse should do it well; so you school him.

Now schooling has two aspects:

first, you are trying to accustom him to good habits so that he does the right thing naturally; and

second, you are trying to make him *want* to do those things in the correct way.

It is of course impossible to force a horse to do anything. All you can do is to apply so much physical and moral pressure on him that eventually he will accede to your wishes. But first you have to make sure the horse is physically fit and well, since a half starved dejected animal is physically incapable of working freely and well. When you have him fit, he should naturally want to go forward, his head will come up, and he will be ready to start his schooling at the basic pace, the walk. The fitter he is the higher he will carry his head. If on the other hand he is being overfed, with too much corn, he will tend to refuse to walk at all; he will be dancing along, trying to get rid of the surplus energy that he has stored up. So by adjusting his feeding you can increase or decrease his energy. If he is slopping along with his head and tail down, it means that there isn't enough steam in the boiler, so the boiler needs stoking with more corn.

When you have got him walking at the pace you want, you can start thinking about improving his head carriage. Now the height of the head can be quite simply controlled by the height that you hold the reins. If you raise your hands, the horse's head will come up; if you lower your hands, his head will come down. If the horse's head is being carried too low, you have to raise his head slightly higher than you will want it eventually, because when his head is up, you can easily bring it down and in – always remembering that the horse's mouth is a very, very delicate thing and any pressure on it should be very gentle. If when you are riding you imagine you have an egg in your hand, and remember that if you squeeze too hard you will break the shell, you will have about the right pressure on the horse's mouth. When the neck is arched and the head has come down into the desired position, you will find that his quarters have also come under him. With good feeding you have increased his natural desire to go forward, so his hind quarters have gone forward, then by getting his head into the right position you have brought the head and the tail nearer to each other, so the horse will be carrying himself well. You will not of course be at his head and mouth all the time. To start with you will be quite happy if you can get him going correctly for fifteen or twenty yards. Then you let him relax again for half an hour. Afterwards you school him for another fifteen or twenty yards. By degrees, as his muscles develop, you will be able to extend the distance that he can happily and naturally carry himself.

Schooling is absolutely essential because it improves your riding. It is no good saying 'Oh! I don't need a schooled horse, I only want to hack round a bit.' It is always more enjoyable to ride a well schooled horse, even if you are just going down once a day for the paper. But it is essential to remember that the age of miracles is dead, and you must always be quite satisfied if he is going a bit better this week than last week.

Once you have improved the walk, you will find that the improvement follows quite easily into the trot, and the canter. And at the same time that you are improving the walk, you can also be changing any other annoying habits, such as not standing still when you get on, or taking a mile and a half before you can get him to halt.

Standing still for you to get on is a very easy habit to instil in a horse. You simply make him want to stand still. Again there are two or three ways you can make him do this. One of them is to put a bucket with a few nuts in it in the corner, and let him eat the nuts as you get on. Or you can get someone to hold him still in a corner when you mount. This is one of the things that you cannot deal with by having a battle with the horse, because if you do have a battle he will be dancing around so much that it will be *impossible* for you to make him stand still.

One of the tricks I use myself is to get a restive horse to stand with his head over a gate. Then I open the gate from his back and away I go. The advantage of this system is that the horse very quickly gets used to standing still in the gateway, and later he will stand still out of habit even when the gate is open, and eventually even when there is no gate there at all.

Teaching a horse to stop you use very much the same method. If you have a horse that refuses to stop when you tell him, it is quite simple to pull him round to that he is facing a fence or a solid object, so that he has to stop. This of course is a manoeuvre that you do at a walk: it is no damned good careering into a fence at a good long gallop and hoping he is going to stop for you to get off. He is just as likely to jump it, as I know from personal experience.

One of the tricks I used to employ in my youth to ensure that I was allowed to go where I wanted when out hunting, was to specialize in opening the gate for the Huntsman. This meant going flat-out up to the gate, skidding to a halt, jumping off and opening the gate for the Huntsman to go through. The Huntsman was thus quite pleased to see me going in front of him. I had a horse that was extremely good at this. I would gallop her flat-out at the gate, she would skid to a halt, I'd swing off and have the gate open and be away long before the Huntsman got to the gateway. This worked very well except on one day when my father had bought a new horse, and I took her out hunting the next day. At the first gate, as I tried to do my trick and started to swing off, Evette took off to jump the gate, and I went flying, ending up with my head between the bars of the gate, looking round like a prisoner in the stocks.

Having got your basic habits and the basic paces going well, you can proceed to get your horse jumping, and jumping well. The basic rules for teaching a horse to jump are these:

first, either the fence must be facing towards home, or several other horses must have jumped it in front of you;

second, the fence must look solid, and not over two foot high;

third, it must be made more or less impossible for the horse to run round it – which means it should be very wide, or in a gateway;

fourth, the horse must not be allowed to refuse.

As with schooling your horse walking, you will get the best results going towards home, simply because the horse knows that when it has done whatever you have asked of him he is going home to his dinner; or in company with other horses – by having a horse jump towards a group of horses, or following a group of horses over jumps. Both techniques give the horse an added wish to do what you want him to.

In all his early training, the horse must never be allowed to refuse. If he stops at a fence, he must not be allowed to turn his head from the fence. You can if necessary back two or three strides, for most horses can jump three-foot quite simply in three strides, and in the early stages you are not going to try more than eighteen inches to two feet, so that if necessary he can step over it. Once you allow a horse to turn his head away from a fence, you are encouraging him to refuse. When he is jumping two or three fences eighteen inches high one after another happily and well, you can start putting them up a couple of inches every three or four days. But make quite certain that if he makes a mistake, or is starting to get worried by the increase in height, you immediately drop the fence three or four inches and start again.

The whole time you are training your horse you should be increasing his desire to please you by giving him titbits and making a fuss of him every time he does something right. By this I don't mean he should be constantly rewarded when he is walking – you would expect him to do that perfectly before you praise him. But when he shows a certain amount of improvement, and you tell him what a clever fellow he is, you are developing his need for praise, and his need to excel, in order to earn that praise. And since you should be developing what he does all the time, a very great improvement can be seen quite quickly: a matter of weeks rather than months.

When you are jumping and cantering with other horses you should also be developing his desire to compete. For example when you jump him alone you should try to persuade him to do better each time; and when you jump him with other horses, you should be comparing his performance yourself with the other horses, competing against them all the time. In this way you will not only be developing the competitive side of his character, but your own competitive urge as well. And it is important to go into competition as often as you can, because this is the only way to measure how your training programme is proceeding. At the same time open competition will give an impetus and add a zest to your training.

12: *Royalty – A Short Case History*

We have now covered, through this book, the general principles of understanding what makes a horse tick, what makes him want to do some things and not others, and how these needs and desires can be used in the training of a particular horse so that he comes to want to do the things his rider wants. In this last chapter I am going to describe in detail my experience through one summer with Royalty, as the best demonstration I can offer of how I work from day to day with horses, and how I try with an individual horse to enter into his thinking – his psychology – in order to gain his goodwill and cooperation.

Royalty, whom I have already mentioned, came to us in the middle of June 1975 as an unbreakable and unmanageable four-year-old. And in the three months from the middle of June to the end of September, she progressed from being completely unmanageable to being able to take part in a small one-day event down in Pembrokeshire. We achieved this by using a combination of communication and psychology, both disciplines being seen as equally important halves of a whole. It doesn't matter how good your psychology is if the horse does not understand what you want him to do, and you do not understand without any ambiguity the horse's wishes and desires and feelings!

Royalty arrived while I was away, and the first time I went into her loose box she cowered in the corner saying, 'Oh! My God! here comes another horrible human. What's he going to do to me?' And as I went towards her she prevented me with her backside and told me in no uncertain terms that if I came near her she would kick me from here to Kingdom come. From this it was no feat of intuition to deduce that she had an antipathy for the human race. So the first thing to do was to reverse this, to transform her dislike and fear of human beings into a desire for my company.

At this time she was very restless in her box, and we realized that she had a great store of nervous energy, a need for movement, and a dislike of being confined.

Over the next forty-eight hours we also discovered that she would only eat about eight pounds of corn a day, and very little hay. Since she was pig fat we knew that she wasn't naturally a shy feeder, so it was obvious that the move and being shut in a stable had upset her digestion.

All these problems had to be overcome before we could get on to more serious work.

The feeding wasn't any problem at all, since we were reasonably certain that this would be overcome as she became more settled. Her dislike of a confined space we tackled by trying to make sure she felt safe in her stable, and making absolutely certain that anything likely to upset her was done elsewhere. For example when we shod her a week or ten days after she arrived, we did it in another stable. When we saddled her, we took her out of her own loose box, and the same when we groomed her, the first two or three times, until she began to enjoy being groomed. By this means, within a matter of days, her loose box, instead of being something that confined her, became a safe place for her to retreat to, and the far corner of the loose box became her own particular territory which was not invaded by me when she was in it.

It was obviously important that she should come to me and not me to her. So I put her food in that first night, but didn't give her any water. The following morning, before I put her food in, I went in with a bucket of water and put it on the floor, about three or four feet inside the stable door. Then I just stood outside the stable door, which I shut. Since she was thirsty she immediately moved towards the bucket, but then, seeing me, she stopped. Because I had the door shut, and I stood absolutely still, after two or three minutes she walked over and started to drink. As soon as she started to drink, I opened the stable door.

She retreated three or four steps and watched me. Again I stood quite still in the open stable door. She came over to the bucket after a bit and took three or four mouthfuls of water. Then I eased myself forward one stride; then two strides. Each time I moved she stopped drinking and retreated, but she always came back to the bucket of water. When she had finished, I took the empty bucket out, and put a small feed just inside the door. Again I shut the door. She watched me for a few seconds, then came over and ate the feed. So I left her to enjoy her breakfast, and went about my work.

I did the same thing again at dinner time. But this time as soon as I opened the stable door, she went back to her corner, and refused to come near the bucket of water. So I took it out and put her feed in, shut the door, and she came over and ate. By the evening of course she was very thirsty again, so I put the bucket of water just inside and stood outside with the door shut. After a minute or two she came over to the stable door, I opened it and she retreated a few steps. Then she came back and finished her bucket of water with me standing by it. I gave her more water, and she drank about half of the second bucket. When she had finished drinking, I took the water out, put her feed in again, put some hay in the rack and left her for the night, very pleased with the progress I had made in twenty-four hours.

The following morning when I put the bucket inside the stable door, she walked straight over to drink before I could even shut the door. As soon as she had drunk I gave her some more water, half of which she drank. Then I took the bucket out and put her feed in, and since she was very hungry for her breakfast, and she hadn't been hurt, and I hadn't done anything to frighten her other than stand in the doorway, she came over and ate her breakfast from the bucket, with me standing by her head. And all the time she was eating or drinking I talked to her in a sing-song voice, helping her to relax.

The third morning, when I went out first thing, she had joined in the chorus of the other horses and they all shouted 'Where's my bloody breakfast' together. So, in order to make the most of the progress that I was making, I varied the pattern very slightly. When I fed and watered her, instead of standing in the doorway, I stood just inside the door so that when she was drinking and feeding I would be standing just behind her shoulder. By now she had realized that I wasn't going to hurt her, and without any qualms at all on the third morning she went straight over to the bucket. First she drank and then she ate, then she alternated two or three mouthfuls with a sip of water to help wash the feed down. I did the same thing at lunch time, and when she was eating, I just let my fingers touch her body behind the shoulder. As soon as I touched her she jumped as if she had been branded with a red hot iron, but she didn't move back from the bucket, and after a second or two she put her head back down and I caressed her with the tips of my fingers, on her barrel, and on her shoulder. By the time she had finished eating I had my hand on her neck, and half-way up her neck along the ridge of mane, and was scratching her there in an itchy spot.

A couple of days more and I could go into her and handle her as and when I wanted, and I thought that I could start grooming her. So I led her out of her box into another, though still leaving her loose.

With a nervous horse like this, the first time I groomed her I would not use a brush. I used the method used by the Indian *sais*: he grooms a horse entirely by using his hands and his forearms, rather like a Swedish masseur. I always like to groom a young horse for the first two or three times in this way, though of course I don't put as much power and vigour into the movement as the *sais*, partly because I am too damned lazy, and partly because if I really pummelled the horse I should frighten the living daylights out of him. But on the other hand most horses quite like the rhythmic movement of my hands and arms going all over his body, and once they are liking this it is only a very slight change to having a body brush in my hands when I am doing it, and then to progress to using the body brush and brushing in the normal way, and finally to using a dandy.

By the end of a week Royalty's food consumption had gone back to normal, her restlessness had decreased considerably, and, provided no sudden movements were made, her nervousness had almost disappeared. Since she now liked and trusted me, I could go very quickly on to the next and more important stage.

So one day after lunch I moved her into the adjoining loose box and put a saddle and bridle on her. I did this without any difficulty, except that she arched her back when we tightened the girth, which about fifty percent of horses do when saddled for the first time. Then with the reins behind the stirrup leathers, and the stirrups flapping, we put her back into her own stall for the rest of the afternoon.

When we had had tea, we got out Rostellan and Irish Clancy – these are both big cobs with very fat, broad backsides – and Paddy and Mark, who were staying with us, got on the two cobs while I led Royalty into a very tight corner of the yard, which is where we like to mount horses the first time. She was actually in a passage six feet wide, with her head facing one building, another building on one side and railings on the other. In such a space a horse has no choice but to stand still when you are getting on to him, so someone held Royalty's head, and my wife gave me a leg up, easing me quietly up so that I was leaning across the saddle. Whilst I was doing so, I was talking to Royalty, and as soon as I got my arms over the other side of her I caressed her neck and flank with my hands. Her immediate reaction was something like 'My God, what the hell is he doing now.' But when she realized that I wasn't going to murder her, her natural trust of me reasserted itself and she relaxed. So I eased a leg over to the other side, sat up and put my feet in the stirrup. 'My God, what's happening,' she said, but I just talked to her and caressed her. My wife turned her round so that she was facing the other way, but still with the barrier of Rostellan's and Clancy's backsides blocking her path. We stood for a second, and I said 'Okay.' Paddy and Mark started their horses forward and Royalty followed them, half a length behind.

Paddy and Mark went out of the front gate and up the road towards the field where we have the horses running during the summer months.

All the time I was sitting relaxed, talking to Royalty and scratching her mane with my finger nail, which she liked. A couple of hundred yards up the road I said 'Stop.' Rostellan and Clancy halted, I said 'Whoa Royalty,' and gently squeezed the reins. Since there was no way past the two mountainous backsides in front of her, she had to stop. I said, 'Okay' again, the other two horses started forward, so I clicked my tongue and said 'Go on girl.' And of course she followed Rostellan and Clancy, going extremely sedately. A hundred yards or so more and I said 'Whoa' and touched the reins. The other two stopped and Royalty stopped. And we progressed in this manner the mile or so up to the field. By the last three or four times I said 'Whoa,' Royalty was stopping as soon as I touched the reins, before Paddy and Mark had stopped the other two horses.

A hundred yards from the field we stopped once more. Paddy jumped off Rostellan, gave her reins to Mark and came round and led Royalty the last hundred yards into the gateway, so that her head was over the gate. As soon as she was standing still, I gently slipped my feet out of the stirrups, and slipped to the ground. I unsaddled Royalty and held her while Paddy and Mark unsaddled their two horses and turned them into the field, and then I turned Royalty in after them.

The next couple of mornings Royalty came in quite happily with the other horses. And in the afternoon, after tea, before turning the others out, I rode Royalty to the field behind Clancy and Rostellan. On the second day for the last half-mile we alternated stopping and starting with walking and trotting. By the third day Royalty knew so well what was happening, that she gave a little bit of a wriggle and squeal as I turned round to go out to the field, and she did everything perfectly, stopping and starting when she was asked, and walking and trotting when told to do so. In fact about a quarter of a mile before we got there, she managed to get past the gigantic bottoms of Rostellan and Clancy and trotted down to the field by herself, stopping once without any difficulty. And when she got to the gate of the field, she jogged up to the gateway, stopped with her head over, and waited for me to get off and turn her out.

So within a single week we had changed a frightened, untouchable and unmanageable horse into one that was actually enjoying walking and trotting with someone on her back. And we had been able to do so because the task to be performed had been presented throughout in a natural progression and as a normal piece of equine experience. When we got on her for the first time, for example, and rode her, she could see the other horses being ridden and enjoying it, so she immediately realized that being ridden was a pleasurable activity, and not something to be frightened of.

The following morning – that is when we had had Royalty no more than a week – I decided to take her out when we were working the other horses. Quite by chance the direction we took went past the jumping lane, and since everyone else wanted to go up the jumping lane I asked them to come back to me on Royalty as soon as they had finished. But Royalty had other ideas. As soon as she saw the other horses disappearing up the jumping lane, she indicated that she wanted to follow and as I didn't want a battle, I decided I might as well let her. She belted into the first fence on Rostellan's tail, since he was at the back of the line. Rostellan popped over the fence, which was made of loose brush and about two foot high, and as he jumped Royalty was suddenly presented with what no doubt appeared to her to be a gigantic obstacle. Anyway, she put in a jump to match, shooting me several feet in the air – she went straight up and down again almost in the same place, and the heavy thump of me landing on her back was too much for her, so she put in two gigantic bucks, and this brought her to the next fence. Then, without thinking, she put in a third buck, which took her over the second fence, but this time I was ready for it. I didn't come down with a thump on her back, so she cantered quite nicely into the third fence, passing Rostellan on the way, and jumping the fence as to the manner born.

Since everybody, both human and equine, had thoroughly enjoyed the jumping lane, by unanimous decision we decided to go up it again. This time I decided to let her follow Biddy, since they were much of a size and pace, and Biddy went away with her customary dash and enthusiasm. Royalty followed, putting her best foot forward. She jumped the first fence perfectly, misjudged the second, sending loose brush flying all over the place, and went over the third with immaculate timing.

I decided that Royalty had done enough jumping for her fourth day mounted, so we continued our ride for an hour and a half, getting home in good time for dinner, elated that simply by allowing Royalty to use her natural talents we had got her jumping so happily within so short a time.

The following day the blacksmith was due to come, and since Royalty was getting a bit footsore, we decided we would have to shoe her. Shoeing a horse for the first time is always extremely important. If he gets hurt or frightened, or a battle is allowed to develop, bad habits can arise which persist for the rest of his life. So the following morning I took out a set of partly worn shoes that were just about Royalty's size. When Bryn came he took one look at her foot, altered the shape of the shoes slightly, and when he tried them they fitted her perfectly. Then without any fuss or bother he very quickly tacked them on, only putting five nails into each shoe. When he had nailed the four shoes on roughly, I held up one front foot whilst he clinched the other three shoes with Royalty's feet on the ground, the whole operation taking less than twenty minutes.

Whilst the shoes were reasonably firmly on, this technique did of course mean that she would have to be shod again in a couple of weeks. But when we shod her a fortnight later, we shod her hot, and since she had already been shod she knew what it was all about and there was no bother at all.

Over that fortnight, Royalty's education proceeded slowly but surely. I started doing a little bit of schooling on her, which meant that she was going out with the other horses for about two hours a day. As I rode I collected her by squeezing the reins so that her head had to come in. Since she wanted to keep up with the other horses, she collected her hind quarters under her. I did this every ten minutes or a quarter of an hour for a space of fifteen or twenty yards. At the end of about ten days the fifteen or twenty yards had been extended to forty or fifty, and by the end of about a month she was holding her head high and her body composed for a couple of hundred yards during every ride without any difficulty. Once she was walking collectedly for short periods, I got her trotting correctly too, which was very simple, and then cantering in the same collected way. Each time we used the impetus of her desire to stay with the other horses. I didn't need to use my heels or any other form of compulsion because the natural inclination was there, provided by the other horses. And all the time she was doing this she was also jumping fifteen or twenty small fences a day. By degrees the fences got bigger, and the type of obstacle changed slowly from a low brush fence to an even lower rail, then when she was jumping two or three low rails in succession we started raising them slightly.

At this stage Royalty was never asked to jump a fence by herself. She was always allowed to follow the other horses over it. But after about six weeks we began jumping her by herself. She had been jumping about three foot, but when we asked her to jump by herself we dropped the fences back to eighteen inches or two feet, and to make doubly certain we always jumped her towards a group of other horses. This we accomplished by letting the other horses jump the fences first, and then getting her to jump towards them a couple of minutes later. The next step was to get her jumping the line of fences away from the other horses, and when she had done this the other horses followed her. After that we had her jumping a dozen or fifteen fences in a circle, so that she went round in a circle away from the other horses, and then jumped back towards them. While she was doing this we very quickly got the fences back to about three foot, then increased them more slowly, until some of the fences were one-day event standard.

We had brought her to this standard rather more quickly than we would have normally. This was partly because we found we were merely developing her own very considerable natural desire to jump, and partly because we wanted to get her up to standard for a small cross-country competition we always ran at the end of August. The last fortnight or so my daughter Paddy took her over completely, riding and schooling her herself. And she rode her in the cross-country competition, doing extremely well with only a couple of stops at one of the bigger fences. Whilst this put her out for the prize money, we were delighted with her overall performance since she had done quite a good dressage test and a very good cross-country round.

Three weeks later Paddy took Royalty down to a one-day event in Pembrokeshire, finishing fifth out of twelve against some quite good horses. She did an extremely good dressage, had one stop at cross-country and one stop showjumping. This was absolutely fantastic when you remember that the first coloured fence she had ever seen she saw when she entered the arena to do her showjumping round. Paddy had asked my opinion of her prospects beforehand, and I had told her 'You will get round the cross-country, and do a passable dressage, but you are bound to get eliminated showjumping since Royalty has never seen a coloured jump in her life.' So for a very green four-year-old that was an excellent performance and we were extremely pleased with her.

The impetus her training had already given her had been reinforced by the two small competitions, neither of which had been of a particularly high standard but they had meant that the mare had to be ready to do a certain thing by a certain date. The standard she had reached was a little above average for the time, but it is this standard that is needed as a basis for any work. In the three months she had become an extremely good ride, going nicely and collectedly. And she could jump three-foot-six of solid timber, and small showjumps. Any horse following this routine and getting to this standard can go from there in any direction necessary. In Royalty's case I hunted hounds off her up until Christmas, and the sound groundwork of her basic training made her a superb hunter. She can now go one-day eventing in the summer, again building on the groundwork of her basic training. If she had been a thoroughbred she would have gone point-to-pointing in the spring, and because she had been properly schooled in the early stages she would have taken to it like a duck to water. And if I had been inclined to go show-jumping again the basic groundwork she had had would have been exactly right for showjumping. Biddy, who had gone through exactly the same regime of training, one-day evented last spring and last autumn extremely successfully.

The successful training of Royalty is typical of the use of good basic communication, and making the most of the horse's natural ability and desires (which is what equine psychology is about) to make training easy and satisfying for both horse and rider. And it shows, further, how a horse can be induced to achieve quite exceptional levels in competition in a remarkably short time. I hope that this book will have shown that by learning to 'think with' the horse, it is within the reach of any sympathetic horse-man or woman to gain new enjoyment and exceptional standards of performance.

PART III

HORSE SENSE

How To Develop Your Horse's Intelligence

1 : *Beginnings of Horse Sense*

Back to my very earliest memories, my life has been preoccupied with nothing but horses. By the time I was four I was riding a pony to school and I started hunting at the age of five. I used to hunt on a little black pony called Black Beauty who would go anywhere and jump anything. In the early days this meant that I was on the ground as often as I was on Black Beauty, but by the time I was eight, Beauty and I would think nothing of jumping a five-bar gate out hunting. A year or two later, if hounds were near on a Monday or Thursday, I would develop a convenient sick headache at school, before break, so that I could be sent home and have a good day's hunting. This for a season and a half worked wonderfully well – it was simply a question of riding Beauty to school, being taken sick (usually by ramming two fingers down my throat), being sent 'home' and going hunting instead. But after a couple of seasons, I inevitably got found out, had my backside well and truly tanned and after that my hunting was confined to Saturdays.

One day I remember we were hunting at Barrington, and Barrington Park was divided neatly by iron railings, each of them only about three feet six high, but considered more or less unjumpable because the horses failed to see the top rail. Hounds found a fox and away they went. I was on the corner of the cover where the fox went away, so giving the hounds plenty of room I set off at a good long gallop, which was Beauty's best speed. It wasn't particularly fast, but adequate for keeping up with hounds.

As we approached the first set of railings Beauty looked at them, sized them up and, deciding that this was a most unpleasant obstacle, dropped back to a trot. I banged her hard with my hunting crop and she trotted to within two strides, cantered

371

the last two strides and just popped over, putting in a hell of a big jump.

She jumped the three foot six, clearing the railings by a good six inches. I, unfortunately, cleared them by a good four or five feet. I went head over heels, landing in front of Beauty, who stopped and looked at me and asked me what on earth I was doing lying on the ground when hounds were running. I scrambled back into the saddle and away we went.

The huntsman – Oliver Moss, who, apart from being an outstanding huntsman, was an excellent horseman – had also jumped the railing but no one else had dared to try, so I put Beauty on the tail of his horse, a famous hunter called West End, and he and I had five or six sets of railings by ourselves, which took us completely away from the field.

This was the first time in my life that I had ever been more or less alone with hounds. The pleasure was such that I have never forgotten it, and whenever I've been hunting since I've done my best to leave the chattering mob behind and enjoy the bliss of riding across country after hounds by myself.

I shall always remember Oliver Moss with great fondness as an extremely kind man who indulged a small boy by allowing me to follow where he went. I can only have been a great nuisance to him, but he put up with it and encouraged me in every way. In 1939 he went back into the air force – he was an ex-airman – as one of the test pilots of the first of the Gloucester Meteors. He was killed on a test flight in 1943 or 1944.

As well as playing truant for the odd day's hunting, I was also riding to school every day. My father was doing a little bit of horse dealing on the side, buying the odd pony which might or might not make a show pony or a show jumper or a gymkhana pony, and I was usually the first to be put on top. My elder brother Charles, though a much better horseman than I, preferred to stick to his own ponies which he was showing and show jumping, rather than try some impossible animal that my father had bought cheap off the gypsies or in Exeter market.

These odds and ends of ponies taught me some things very quickly; that there must be an easier way of teaching a horse to be ridden than hitting the ground with a bump over and over again until the pony got tired of depositing you; there must be an easier way of teaching it to turn left or right than catching hold of one rein with both hands and heaving it round; that there had to be an easier way of catching a horse than chasing it round and round a field until he lay down from fatigue; there was surely an easier way of teaching it to jump than pointing it at an obstacle, saying the General Confession and the Lord's Prayer and hoping for the best. I discovered that if I could get the horse to want to do what I was trying to get him to do, he would do it.

For example, it was much easier to teach a horse to go from a walk to a trot going home than going away from home; and it was easier to teach him to turn to the left or right if he first learned to respond to the rein and the heel by following another horse. I also discovered that the most important thing of all was to make my wishes clear to the horse without annoying, frightening or upsetting him. If I was relaxed, happy and comfortable the pony would be relaxed, happy and comfortable.

This was the beginning of my study, which developed over a period of thirty-odd years, of how horses communicate. Because to get him to do what I wanted him to do, it was necessary to communicate my ideas to him, it was important to know how he thought and what made him want to do certain things and dislike doing others. Also as we went on I could see that some horses liked doing one thing and hated doing another.

It became very quickly obvious, in short, that horses are as different from each other as chalk is from cheese. Whilst they may look something alike, their thoughts, their desires, their abilities vary with their temperament and experience.

At this time in 1939, one of the best show jumping ponies we had was a little thirteen-hand Exmoor mare called Susan, who was kind, sweet and rather sleepy. You could put any fool on her and she would walk and jog along quite happily without putting a foot wrong. If you took her out hunting you had to work like hell to keep anywhere near hounds at all. Yet the same pony, as soon as she got into a show ring, altered completely –

she became alive, alert and jumped superbly. Beauty, on the other hand, would deposit you on the ground with absolute regularity once or twice a week, just to tell you to mind your manners. Out hunting she was a marvellous ride. As I've already described, she would jump anything, and provided she was in sight and sound of hounds she was happy. But take her into the show ring and canter into the first fence, she would prick her ears, lengthen her stride, and just as you got ready to take off she would stop. You would end up, to the delight of the crowd, on one side of the fence while she would stay firmly on the other. If you let go of the reins she would go back to the collecting ring and say 'Well, that's it for the day' – and it was.

Beauty didn't mind hunter trials so much, although she was not very reliable. She liked working in pairs, with my brother's horse Bill the Baby, because the pair of them used to enjoy racing each other. So we did quite well with her in the hunter trialing in the pairs events.

Here you have the perfect example of one pony who was something of a sluggard at home and a superb show jumper, and the other a superb pony at home or out hunting who wouldn't have anything to do with show jumping. This was my first experience of how horses vary in thought, character and what makes them want to do a certain thing – in other words, motivation.

The more horses I handled, the more I learned to take account of these widely varying characteristics. And I also learnt that, whilst you may be able to improve a horse's particular abilities with training, and you may also change the things he wants to do by handling him, and teaching him to do something else, in the correct way, you only have to make a single mistake by teaching him in the wrong way, to end up with a bloody-minded creature as stubborn as a mule.

I also found that there are certain horses who want to do something but are physically incapable of doing so. Old Fearless was such an example. She was an extremely bad jumper and not particularly good looking, but we found that she really enjoyed the showing.

We took her to one very small show and gymkhana, tarted her

up, plaited her mane, groomed her and she got a third in the show class. But she had every fence down in the show jumping and was hopeless at gymkhana work. The following week I noticed that she went about her work with an enthusiasm that she hadn't shown before. Then came the following Saturday, when we were off to another gymkhana, but on the basis of Fearless' failure the previous week we left her behind.

On Sunday morning I took her out to pull the dung up to the field. When I went to harness her up, the first thing she did was take a swipe at me with her hind leg, and when I tried to put the collar on she fastened her teeth round my shoulder and shook me like a rat. Eventually I got her harnessed in the dung putt and started to haul the dung up to the field. She wouldn't pull at all, and she was awkward the whole of the following week.

So, come Saturday and gymkhana day, I groomed her and got her ready again, and rode her leading a string of other horses to the gymkhana. I left her tied to the fence, just putting her in for the show class, where again she got a second or third. Then we rode home again. Her behaviour that week was transformed. She did everything with enthusiasm and, apart from the odd nip when I annoyed her, her behaviour was angelic. I very quickly came to realize that she looked upon her Saturday off, going to a show and mincing around in the show class like a pimp in Piccadilly, as a reward for a hard week's work. If she didn't get her reward, God help anyone who tried to handle her.

She wasn't a very good hunter, either, but I had to hunt her occasionally to keep life and limb intact. Shortly after this I smashed my leg playing rugger, and, as soon as I was capable of doing so, I went hunting in a dog cart with Fearless between the shafts. This was the thing which really suited her because I wasn't trying to change the habits of a lifetime; so Fearless and the dog cart were near the front of the field, and when hounds went we went, hell for leather across country, from gate to gate and gap to gap, with the cart bouncing up and down like a jack-in-the-box.

Although I smashed my plaster regularly, Fearless and I really enjoyed ourselves. It was not, however, a pleasure necessarily appreciated by the odd-bod who asked for a lift. I remember one occasion when hounds went away while I was giving a friend a lift in the trap. We galloped up the headland and across a ploughed field, with the cart bouncing from side to side, through a gateway, only to find that hounds had gone away through a small hedge into the next field. I had the alternatives of going back or jumping the hedge, cart and all. So I caught Fearless one across the backside with the loose end of the reins, and we went into the low bank, which was about a foot high with a two-foot fence on top. We hit the low bank at a rate of knots, bouncing up into the air and landing on the other side – fortunately with the two wheels still on the cart and the two people still inside it. We cantered down the field and got to the road, where there was a crowd in the gateway. My passenger scrambled out without even having the good manners to say 'thank you' for the lift!

After about two months of this there wasn't much left of the cart, and my leg hadn't got much better. But Fearless's work rate had gone up fifty per cent. The intelligence of the mare was such that if she walked into the yard before lunch and saw me washing the mud from the previous week's hunting off the trap, she knew that we would be going hunting on the following day. And after lunch the person who was working Fearless was going at a rattling rate, with no hope of stopping her.

She was also one of the many horses I've had who actually enjoyed being tarted up and made pretty. Normally when you wanted to groom her and brush the mud off, she'd be trying to catch you a sly one with her heels when you were at the back end, and having lumps of backside for breakfast if you were near the front. But when you were preparing her to go hunting or to a show she'd stand like a rock and you could groom her any-where and do anything with her and she'd never move. When you plaited her mane she'd put her head down to the ground so you could plait in the easiest position.

Another of the things I noticed was the way that some of the horses enjoyed doing certain tasks. For example, Champion the cart horse adored horse-hoeing. This entailed pulling the horse-hoe, which was an implement something like a plough with two blades set at an angle sixteen inches apart, between two rows of mangels or kale planted eighteen inches apart. If the horse deviated, instead of hoeing out weeds you hoed out a neat line of kale leaving a horrible gaping hole. Usually when doing this you needed somebody to lead the horse and another person to guide the hoe. Not so with Champion. The precision of the work so fascinated him that he would lift each foot, placing it precisely in position, so that the person guiding the hoe had neither to steer the hoe nor Champion. Champion's pleasure in doing a difficult job precisely was a pleasure to see, and his motivation to complete the work perfectly was so great that if you attempted to steer him out of line he would ignore the reins completely.

In direct contrast was Caravan. On the one occasion we tried him I led him for the first two rows and he danced about all over the place, leaving more gaps than kale. Then my father decided that he would lead him. Caravan was very angry by this time, and after doing half a row – during which he flattened my father's feet with his own – the old man called over my sister, Olive, who had come to watch the fun. She was set to lead on one side and I on the other. We got ready to start, my father took a firm grip of the reins and the horse-hoe and told Caravan to hold fast, which he did by plunging forward, throwing Olive and me aside like wisps of hay, and at the same time jerking the horse-hoe and reins out of my father's hands. He proceeded around the field at a good long gallop, dragging the horse-hoe across the ground in a series of kangaroo leaps. When eventually he stopped my father gave up an obviously impossible task and went to fetch another horse, leaving me in punishment to fill in the gaps left by Caravan with spare kale plants, a much duller and more back-breaking task.

My father, commonly known as 'the Boss' or 'the Old Man', had a very great influence on my handling of horses and on my view of life in general. A born rebel, he stood six feet and was built like a boxer. He had a temper which exploded like dynamite and which had the instability of nitro-glycerine. He had black, curly hair which didn't change colour until he was over sixty. He never believed any statement or theory until he had proved it for himself, and although a deeply religious man he questioned everything and thought it out for himself. As far as the law was concerned, if he didn't agree with it or thought it stupid he would disregard it completely. One of his creeds in life was that you should never ask anybody to do something you wouldn't do yourself. Whilst at times hazardous, life was never boring with him around.

His love for animals was very deep and to him horses were, to quote his own words, 'God's supreme creation'. Whilst if he thought it deserved it he would give a horse a hiding (though not quite as severe as the ones he gave me), he could not stand to see an animal ill-treated. I once saw him knock down two gypsies who were ill-treating a pony, take the pony out of the cart, put me up on its back and take it home, the two gypsies following on behind and finally getting more out of my father for it than the pony was worth. One of my final memories of him was seeing him going into the kitchen, aged about sixty-eight, covered in mud and with a grin splitting his face in half. 'I thought I was getting old', he said, when I asked what had happened, 'but I've just had the hell of a fall and haven't hurt myself a bit, so I can't be as old as all that.'

He vividly demonstrated those qualities that are most import-ant in handling horses – determination, humour and endless patience.

The urge to do a job perfectly is extremely great in some horses. Others just want to get the job done as quickly as possible not minding how the hell it is done.

Another careful worker was Bonnie, although she walked with a limp. As a yearling she slipped a stifle and my father let her run on for another two years for the stifle to heal, but as soon as he broke her in to ride she bucked and the stifle came out again. She was left for three or four months, but it didn't heal and we were left with the unpleasant choice between using her limping, going lame on one hind leg, and having her put down. There was no choice, of course. She was happy and contented and she wasn't in pain so we worked her in harness, walking. The one job she loved was hay-making. The horse had to learn to stop at a precise spot, so that she left a neat row of hay behind her. As the driver was busy operating various levers, it didn't leave much time to drive the horse as well. So once you had gone up the field and dropped the first bundle of hay in each line, Bonnie would check at the exact spot that you had to drop the hay coming back, and so on right down the field. She would do this all day with her ears pricked, watching you and watching her lines and checking at the exact spot the whole time. The pleasure she got from doing the task perfectly was very plain to anyone. Of course, she was able to do only light work about the farm, but she did that well and enthusiastically, especially neat and fiddly little jobs that the other horses hated.

This gave me further proof that each little job the horse was doing could be a reward in itself, and that a large part of the successful handling of horses lay in finding the task that the horse did well and enjoyed doing.

2: *The Mind of a Horse*

My observations about the importance of understanding each individual horse's personality and behaviour, what one horse liked and another did not, came home to me even more forcibly when I started racing. It was soon apparent to me that horses of lesser ability were beating horses on the racecourse who were much faster and better jumpers, simply because they wanted to race and were determined to win, whereas the horses they were beating didn't want to race, so as soon as you got them up front they'd almost stop. You could see that some horses, as soon as the starter's flag was dropped, would take a hold of the bit, tear the reins out of your hand and go as fast as they could for as long as they could; whilst others, like Old Doleful, would lollop around half asleep for the first circuit, and only after about two miles get warmed up enough to start galloping. So the variation in the psychological make up of the horse is one of the important factors in racing.

What became equally obvious in observing the horses was that some horses would do anything for you, while dealing with others was like trying to get a response out of a block of wood. This in its turn led to the conclusion that there's more to communication between horse and rider than pulling a pair of reins and catching him a clout with a stick.

The third thing I found out was that teaching a horse to do something was a great deal more complex than ever the 'experts' lead you to believe. My reading told me that learning in a horse was merely the result of repetition of the same tasks over and over again. But my observation showed me that if you tried to teach a horse to do something in one way, he would learn much more quickly than if you taught him to do the same task another way. I needed, in fact, to know a great deal more about the process whereby learning in horses takes place.

The horse that first set me thinking in this direction was the same little pony that took me to school, Black Beauty. Now she could get any halter off, untie any rope, open any stable door and open most of the gates on the farm by using her head, her neck and her teeth. She could undo knots, pull back bolts or lift gates. The only gates she couldn't open were the gates that were falling to pieces and were tied into place with a dozen different pieces of string, and this was only because they were too heavy and awkward for her to shift. They were in any case no problem to her because she just jumped them. But it struck me very forcibly that she had learned to do these things simply and solely by teaching herself. And she had taught herself to do these things because she wanted to wander around the farm where and whenever she pleased. This desire was so strong that she had learnt tasks that the other horses found impossible. The corollary of this was quite simple – teaching a horse to do something new would be much easier if you could make the horse *want* to do it.

This conclusion was reinforced by my observation of polo ponies. A pony who enjoyed the game, I found, would require fewer and fewer signals from me, until it was merely a case of shifting my weight and touching his mouth to get him to do what I wanted. And even if the pony got a clout from a polo stick, which happened from time to time – not only did the pony get clouted, I got clouted by a polo stick once every week or so – it didn't diminish his enthusiasm for the game.

But to get a horse keen on something I had to teach him first of all what it was I wanted him to do : or rather, what I wanted him to want to do. And this involved learning something about horse communication. If I could learn how horses talked to each other, I would be in a better position to convey my own wishes to them.

Once I had discovered that the common idea that animals communicated using particular sounds to express particular feelings or concepts was erroneous, and began to watch how my horses conveyed their wishes and desires to each other, learning how they communicated was only a matter of study and time. I discovered that it was the tone of the vocal sound that mattered, not the sound itself; and that sign language was very important. But as well as this, I found that horses can convey their feelings and desires from one to another over great distances without using either sign or sound – just as if I was excited my horse would be excited, and if I was cool and calm I could make my horse relax. This form of communication I identified as a form of ESP, which we eventually extended to include communication by telepathy – conveying mental pictures, as well as feelings to our horses.

The results we obtained from using ESP as we developed our abilities were really quite amazing. The original work was done during training, but we found it equally useful in competition and general riding.

One of the most dramatic examples of the success of ESP was with a little Welsh cob I had. In those days transport was extremely difficult to get hold of, petrol being short, and when I was going to a hunter trial, show or gymkhana, I used to ride one horse and lead the ones who were competing. They arrived at the competition as fresh as was possible.

I rode Witch to the hunter trials at Cattistock, which was about fifteen miles away, leading three other horses with me. On the way there she behaved like an absolute cow, dancing and jogging all over the place and pulling the other horses from side to side of the road. I was really annoyed when I got there, so I gave the other three to someone to hold. She was still dancing and pulling herself, so I thought I'd get her steady before I got home by giving her a fast mile around the field. I got her settled down and galloping on, but as I came to the fence she'd no intention whatsoever of turning, and we went over the bank at a rate of knots. How she jumped it I don't know, she'd never jumped a fence in her life before, but she found about eight different legs as she landed and went away up the next field. The only way I could get back to the other horses was back over the bank, so I swung her round and put her back at the bank and she jumped it much more efficiently. I decided that since she was there and still much too lively to do anything or give me a comfortable ride home, the bitch could go in the novice class of the hunter trial.

I rode my other novice first and then came Witch's turn. I was extremely apprehensive and somewhat excited and she was as excited as she could be, so we danced down to the start and away we went. I had no hope of steadying her going into the first fence, which was a post and rail, and we went into it much too fast. With me saying my prayers and hoping for the best, we approached it. Ten yards from the fence she suddenly saw the object in front of her and half tried to refuse, but she was going too fast to stop on the slippery ground. She arched over it – this was the first proper fence she had jumped in her life – and away we went into the second fence. This was a straightforward bank, and after jumping two, she was absolutely certain that she was an expert on banks and I was reasonably confident. Over we went, getting between the flags by the skin of our teeth, since she was veering to one side. We had to turn at right angles to the next fence and to my surprise, instead of going twice round the field before I got her facing it, she swung round like an old hand and, having got the worst of the steam out of herself, she went into the gate at a good steady gallop. And so we proceeded round the course to the twelfth fence which was an extremely difficult one – you had to pop over a post and rails, go down into a quarry and jump out over another bigger post and rails at the bottom. Everyone had been having trouble with this, I'd already had one refusal on the other horse and only about two people had done it correctly and got through without refusing. I galloped Witch into it – or rather she galloped herself into it fairly fast – and as she got close she could see that she was more or less launching herself straight out into mid-air and she steadied back to a trot, popped over the first one without any difficulty, landing a little far out so that she slipped down the quarry half on her bottom. As soon as she reached the level bit at the bottom, since her hind quarters were under her, she gave a terrific spring and went over the second post and rails like a rocket. We finished the course to find that we were in fact one of the only three clear rounds of the day and I was in the jump off. But having completed the course successfully once, I decided that the little mare had done enough. By this time she had changed from being, 'that bloody-minded little bitch' that I had to hack to the hunter trials, into a good little mare and we were the best of friends.

Riding home in the half light of the evening, over fifteen miles, I had time to think about Witch's performance and analyse it. Three things were very plain, (a) she obviously had terrific natural ability, (b) she had changed within an hour or so from something that was only half broken and almost uncontrollable into an easily controlled horse and (c) her desire to gallop and jump, correctly harnessed, had turned what promised to be an extremely difficult ride into a very good ride indeed.

The thing that surprised me most of all was that because I knew my reins were more or less useless as she was more or less impossible to stop and steer, I hadn't bothered to use them, and simply by using the weight of my body, and by looking from fence to fence – i.e. using ESP – I had managed to steer her round the course. She had responded to the slight signals that I had given, but mainly to the oneness that had grown between us. But this had been possible only because she had clearly been enjoying herself, and could see the object of what she was doing. This led me to the conclusion that if you could discover the right motive for getting a horse to do something, the horse would do it with very little difficulty at all.

So, not only was I working on how best to communicate with my horses, I started studying how their minds worked – where I was successful in doing this, training became much easier, because it was merely a question of discovering the physical and mental needs and desires of the horse, and then harnessing them to the ends I wanted.

But the third leg of the triangle also had to be worked on. And that was discovering how a horse learned, other than by dull repetition. My experiences made it obvious to me that dull repetition was extremely tedious and very hard work for me as well as the horses. If I could harness my understanding of communication and motivation with some comprehension of the process whereby horses learn, I could not only make it easier to break and train a horse, but when it came to competition I could increase my horse's ability, power and will to win; or at least to co-operate in what I always wanted to do, which is to get a horse performing above his normal ability at the correct time and in the correct way.

3: *How Horses Learn*

The thing that sets the horse apart from most other domestic animals is his incredible capacity to learn. But it is the extent and kind of his learning that makes each horse into an individual being. What he's learned and how he's learned it reveals itself in all his behaviour. Through his learning capacity, combined with his ability to communicate and be communicated with – which is itself extended by learning – he acquires his habits and customs and develops his abilities. Since everything he does derives from what he has learnt, this is the key to understanding how the individual horse behaves.

The young horse may learn by imitating his mother; for example, he learns what to eat partly by trial and error, and partly by imitating and selecting food his mother eats. Early in his life he develops an attitude to man which is directly connected to the way man has behaved towards him, and his mother before him. Thus if in his early contact with man he has been ill-treated, he will after that instinctively distrust man. And if his mother has a fear and distrust of man, this will be communicated to him. I came across an example of the power of early learning while I was working on this book. I had a desperate message from a friend who lives just outside Lampeter. Would I come and help him catch his mare and foal, because he wanted to take them to Llanybyther horse sale. When I got there I discovered that the mare, though extremely nervous, was not too difficult, but the foal was absolutely terrified of all human beings. This was so unusual that I asked the owner why. It seemed that kids from a nearby housing estate had been throwing stones at the horses to make them gallop. This had gone on for the past three or four months, and had made the foal absolutely terrified of all human contact. By the time he had discovered what was happening the foal was so wild that he couldn't move it to a quieter part of the farm since he was unable to get near either the mare or the foal – they galloped round and round the field in circles rather than go out of the gate. Finally he decided to solve his problem by selling them.

We were very fortunate that there was only a short, quiet lane from the field to the farm. So we solved the problem comparatively easily. We took the owner's small daughter's pony and left it with a bucket of nuts just outside the gateway and then walked quietly down to the far end of the field, which meant that the foal tore up the field and the mare followed at a quieter pace. When they got to the gateway they saw the pony eating out in the lane. They stood watching the old pony eating for a while, then the mare walked slowly towards the gate, stood for a minute, walked through, followed by the foal, and drove the old pony away from the bucket of nuts. From there we drove them slowly into the cattle yard.

It took me about two hours before I eventually managed to get a hand on that foal. It literally shook with terror, but slowly and gently I got it quietened down just a shade, and after another hour and a half it was beginning to trust me a little bit. I stroked it gently, imitating the mother nuzzling it. And since it was a lovely cob filly it seemed a pity to send it to Llanybyther and the owner didn't take much persuading to keep it. So we loaded the mare and foal up into a trailer and took them to a quiet field at the far end of the farm, hoping that by degrees, by the time the foal was two or three years old, it would have quietened down and lost its fear of human beings.

If, on the other hand, in his early contact with man the young horse is allowed to misbehave and walk over the top of whoever is handling him, he will never develop any respect for mankind whatsoever. Over the last ten or fifteen years we have had thirty or forty horses sent to us for gentling, as unbreakable. And by far the greatest number of difficult and unmanageable horses we have seen have had this type of upbringing. Horses that have been treated like mischievous puppies when foals, and allowed to get away with biting, kicking and pushing their owners around because at that stage they're such playful, pretty little things, by the time they're yearlings, are thoroughly spoiled and badly behaved. When we get them as three- or four-year-olds, they have had no discipline whatsoever and are used to doing exactly what they want. If the owner does not move aside when the horse pushes past him, the horse bites or kicks until he does, and ends up with no respect for the human being whatever. Such horses treat their owners as subservient members of their own herd. If they tell them to get out of the way and they don't, they immediately kick or bite them. This is normal equine behaviour. This behaviour has all been learned. And if the horse is to have any kind of future, it has to be unlearned, and better behaviour substituted. How can this best be achieved?

How a horse learns is a very large subject indeed. But the study of horse psychology which is in effect the study of learning in horses, and how this knowledge may be applied in handling, can help us to be clear about what we are doing. To begin with, what is learning? It is a relatively permanent change of behaviour which occurs as a result of experience, practice or training.

This definition has three important elements. It says first that in learning there is a change in behaviour. This may be for better or worse, but if there is no change, there is no learning. The change in behaviour may also not show up immediately: if for example you are trying to teach your horse to stop on a word of command, the first time you say 'whoa' he will take no notice of you whatsoever – you'll have to stop him by other means. But, by degrees, if you quietly make him stand still every time you say 'whoa', after eight, a dozen or maybe twenty times the horse will stop automatically. Then we say that the horse has learned to stop on command. You can see the difference – his behaviour pattern has been changed by learning.

Learning can be any form of change of behaviour as the result of experience. It need not be the result of conscious training. In teaching a horse to stop on command you are changing his behaviour pattern by consciously training him to do something. But the training could be completely unconscious, the result of an outside influence – such as the weather. For example, a horse will automatically turn its backside towards wind and rain. This too is the result of training; but no one has rushed out every time it started to rain and turned the horse so that its bottom is facing into the wind. It is merely that over the course of his early life he has discovered that if he faced into the wind and rain, the wind and rain blew into his nose and eyes, so he turned away from it and pointed the part of his body that is least affected by wind and rain towards it. This is a form of learning and a form of training : it is unconscious learning, and the training has been done by Mother Nature, but nevertheless it is as much learning as when a horse learns to jump a four-foot-six fence.

The second part of this definition is that learning takes place *through experience or practice*. Other changes of behaviour, such as those which occur as he gets older, or through fatigue or injury, do not count as learning. If a horse stops because he has injured himself or because he is too tired to go on, this is not learned behaviour.

Third, the change must be relatively permanent. If it is not, it is probably due either to a transitory change in motivation, such as fatigue, or to adaptation. For example, if you move a horse abruptly from light to darkness he will immediately lack co-ordination and be unable to see, but in a very short time he will adapt to the darkened conditions and be able to move around with comparative ease and freedom. This is not because he has learned anything, but because his body has adapted to the darkened area. Here it must be stressed that such stimuli as fatigue, restriction of exercise or overfeeding may *also* lead to learned behaviour. For example, a horse that is repeatedly overworked or overtired will learn to become lazy, a horse that is kept underexercised may learn to become excitable or shy, or a horse that is overfed may become completely unmanageable. In cases such as these the horse will have to undergo a long and laborious course of retraining. This is particularly difficult, because first the horse will have to learn to forget its previous experience, and then will have to be retrained to regain its previous level of performance.

According to behaviourist theory, all learning is the result either of classical conditioning or of operant conditioning. In both a specific response to stimulus or stimulus conditioning is required. Classical and operant conditioning differ first by the nature of the stimulus, second by the kind of response learned and third by the nature of the response to reinforcement.

Conditioning means quite simply placing an animal or a human being in a situation likely to make him respond in a certain way: to subject him to a certain stimulus. And stimulus may stimulate an animal in either of two ways: it can stimulate him positively, i.e. make him want to do something – make a horse want to please you, for instance, or make him want to get home for dinner; or it can stimulate him negatively, i.e. make him want to avoid something – he moves away from a slap on the backside, or avoids incurring your anger. To both these types of stimulus he will respond by doing what you wanted him to in the first place, but the learning process can be very different.

For example, suppose you want to catch him, you call him and he comes over to your handful of nuts or oats. He learns to respond to your calling because he knows he will please you by coming to you and he'll also get a handful of nuts for doing so. So, the stimulation and response are directly connected with each other: the call stimulates him, the response is to come to you and he'll immediately be rewarded by being caressed, made a fuss of and given the nuts. We say then that he is conditioned to come to your call. The nuts and the patting are scientifically known as the reinforcement, since they reinforce the learning. If you don't pat him and give him the nuts he is less likely to come over next time you call him in the field, and in a very short time he won't bother even to look up from his grazing when you give a shout. This is a simple example of conditioning, or training: and as in all learning, it involves stimulus, response and reinforcement.

It is easy enough to illustrate the difference between classical learning and operant learning, with another example. When I'm feeding the horses I measure out the feed into the basins in the feeding house, dropping the first one, which is usually

Cuddles', first and then the second one and the third one and so on, outside the stable doors, putting the feeds in as I go back up the line. It's a very simple, quick and efficient process, but Cuddles gets his food last. This of course doesn't please Cuddles very much because (a) he's extremely greedy and (b) he's convinced that he's the most important horse on the place and therefore should be fed first. For a long time he tried to reach over the top of the stable door to get at the feed in the bucket.

On one particular morning, however, either he wasn't particularly hungry or he'd got a very bad itch under his chin, because instead of reaching out for his feed he scratched his chin on the most convenient object which happened to be the bolt of the stable door. In so doing he pushed the bolt back, the door swung open, he walked out and started his feed. Within three days he was pushing the bolt back with his chin and opening the stable door whenever I was feeding. Another day or two and he was opening it whenever he felt like it. So we pushed the catch down so that he couldn't open the stable door. When he found that he couldn't open the bolt by rubbing it with his chin he fiddled about with his lips, released the catch, opened the door and away he went again. The next stage was to put a padlock on the door. But since by nature I'm careless and lose things, I used to leave the key in the padlock, and he learned not only to turn the key in the lock but to remove the padlock from the latch and then open the latch so that he could let himself out.

This is a typical example of operant learning. At first by chance he did the correct thing, i.e. pushed the bolt back, and got an immediate reward with food. Then from learning to do it for food, he learned to do progressively more difficult tasks, each for a reward. In the beginning the reward was early breakfast, but later on it was freedom to wander round, come down and see what we were doing in front of the house, tease the other horses and make a general nuisance of himself. And of course the greatest reward of all was that he could annoy me, and when he saw me getting particularly angry he would belt back into his stable and pretend he'd been there all the time and was an innocent little horse who'd never misbehaved in his life. His behaviour had changed from that of a horse that could quite safely be shut into a stable by closing a bolt, to that of a horse who could open a stable door and go in and out whenever he wished to. The difference in behaviour pattern is quite easy to see.

The way a horse's behaviour pattern can be changed temporarily, but not learned, is equally easily illustrated, again using something that happened to Cuddles. We were out hunting near Lampeter and had to go down a steep and slippery hill. He slipped on his hind legs coming over a fence, and his hind legs shot forward underneath him so that he slipped the whole way down a hundred-and-fifty-yard slope, sitting on his bottom. It is of course completely contrary to any horse's normal behaviour, to move a hundred and fifty yards sliding on his bottom like a small boy on a toboggan. When we got to the bottom of the hill, however, he got back to his feet as if nothing had happened, and away we went again to have an extremely good hunt.

Normally Cuddles, when he's with another horse, tends to dance along with his head in the air, jingling his bit and looking at everything and generally enjoying himself, but that day, because we'd had such a hard hunt, he was extremely tired and we hacked the two and a half to three miles home with Cuddles plodding along like an old nag, with his head hanging down half way between his legs. And this, like the toboggan slide, proved to be only a temporary change of behaviour, in this case due entirely to fatigue. Since then he has never moved across country sitting on his bottom, nor, except on the odd occasion when he has been extremely tired, has he plodded along like a tired old nag. Both of these temporary changes in behaviour were due to *unlearned* behaviour patterns.

We have given an example of operant conditioning, in Cuddles' discovery of how to open his stable door. Let us now look at classical conditioning. In classical conditioning, first the stimulus is a specific event – such as a flash of light, tone or note which is briefly present, your voice giving a command or the touch of your heels. Whereas in operant conditioning the stimulus is not a specific event, it is a longer lasting situation which has several features, only one or two of which prove relevant for learning.

Second, in classical conditioning the response, like the stimulus, is a specific one. Moreover, it is usually a reflex or an innate reaction. In operant conditioning on the other hand the responses are at first varied and random.

Third, response to reinforcement differs between the two forms of learning. In classical conditioning the reinforcement – the reward or punishment – is always part of the conditioning situation, regardless of what the person or animal does. It does not depend upon the response made.

A simple example of this kind of reinforcement is used in teaching a horse to stop when you say 'whoa'. In training a horse to stop when you say 'whoa', you pull on the bit with the reins so that the horse stops, which relieves the pressure on his mouth. So, the stimulus, putting pressure on the horse's mouth with the bit, is immediately followed by the horse stopping, and as soon as he stops the stimulus is removed, that is, he is rewarded. This is a form of classical learning.

But in operant conditioning reinforcement does depend on the response. If the subject does the right thing he is reinforced positively, that is he is rewarded with titbits or by other means, if he does the wrong thing he is reinforced negatively with a punishment.

A simple example of the operant process can be used to deal with a horse which refuses to lead. The person leading the horse has a basin of food from which, if the horse leads forward, he receives a reward. If he refuses to lead forward, an assistant throws a series of well-directed missiles at his bottom until he does move forward. Here you are teaching the horse to respond to positive reinforcement, that is the food, and to avoid negative reinforcement, that is the missiles. So, in this way he is conditioned to lead. I would add that it is infinitely better to throw small pebbles at his bottom than to catch him one with a hunting crop, since you're much less likely to have a mouthful of horse's hooves as an unwanted meal.

It will be seen that a feature of operant conditioning is that the response to the horse's behaviour should be immediate, whether the response is positive, negative or both. If a horse jumps a fence, you make a fuss of him. If he doesn't jump the fence you smack his bottom, so you can see that the reinforcement depends on what he does and if he does it.

I have had to put a lot of emphasis on the two different kinds of learning, because when you are training a horse it is extremely important to know which kind of learning you are going to use. The drawback to classical learning is that if the stimulus is insufficient it will be ignored completely, so the stimulus may have to be strengthened from time to time.

Suppose you are riding a horse. If you drive your heels into the horse hard he will shoot forward. If instead you just tap him with your heels he will move a little bit faster to begin with, but you will end up having to kick, kick, kick while the horse progressively ignores you. So though classical training will improve performance slightly, it can lead to your over using it, and in a competition for instance you may end up in front of the judges and stewards – and rightly so – for ill-treating your horse. The point is that in training a horse by classical conditioning the emphasis tends to be on punishment, and this is something I abhor very strongly. Punishment, of course, is necessary from time to time but over-use of punishment is never a good thing. In fact, punishment over a long period leads to a deterioration in performance.

To illustrate this, I knew a very promising young show jumper, who tended just to tap a pole. To cure this, her owner covered the top pole of several of the jumps with hedghog skins, so that if she hit the top pole she would prick herself – a very common trick among show jumping people. But Blodwyn, being a very intelligent mare, very quickly learned that the poles in the show jumping arena itself didn't have hedgehog skins nailed to them, so while she would jump everything perfectly at home, taking no chances whatsoever, as soon as she got into competition she would have one or two down.

Negative reinforcement in classical conditioning always tends to lead to this kind of evasion, that is to say the horse will either do just enough to avoid punishment or else will find a way of avoiding punishment altogether.

Bay Star was another example of the counter-productiveness of classical conditioning. She was a very excitable mare when she came to us, with a tendency to rear straight up on to her hind legs and go over backwards. She also arrived equipped with a bridle which contained what might be described as half an ironmongery shop in place of a bit. I quickly changed this to a rubber snaffle bit and took her out exercising. She didn't go up on her hind legs once, although she carted me all over the mountain a couple of times, this being somewhat hair-raising as the mountain is a mass of humps and hollows and bogs and God knows what else! On the first occasion we were motoring along at a fair pace with me vainly trying to stop her, when she went into an old mountain dip, which meant she went head over heels. This didn't worry me very much, but it did worry her and she went very gently for the next four or five days. Then she got away from me again, this time not quite so wildly but it had been raining heavily on dry ground for the previous twenty-four hours. I let her go in a straight line for a while and then tried to pull her to the left. She set her jaw, not having any of it, so I heaved with all my might but she set her jaw even more firmly. I went on like this for about twenty yards and then I suddenly pulled her head round the other way. The pressure that she was exerting to the left was immediately reinforced by my bodyweight, which swung her round sharply. Her forefeet went from under her and again we hit the ground.

Within a fortnight she was cured completely, both of carting me and of going up on her hind legs. The reason for her rearing, it appeared, was that she hated standing still. Her previous owner had been making her stand still while she was out hunting so that he could stop and chat to people. Simply by keeping her moving, I stopped her rearing and this sweet little mare quickly learned that I wanted to go as fast as possible when we were going; but that when I said 'steady' or 'whoa' there was a definite reason for steadying.

So by working in this way, by removing her desire to rear, we cured her completely. We substituted for the classical conditioning – when she moved her mouth was hurt – to which she had been subjected, the use of the mare's natural inclinations to train her. So her training changed from being painful and unpleasant to something that she could enjoy. In actual fact, within a month I had taught her to stand still when I asked her to, and she would stand still quite happily. When she started fidgeting I walked her round a bit and she would be quite happy to stand still again. Here was a mare who, psychologically, needed movement to relieve the build up of tension within herself. When that movement was restrained she reacted by going up on her hind legs.

4: *Using Conditioning Theory: 1*

Classical conditioning gets its name because it was the first kind of conditioning to be studied experimentally, by the pioneer Russian physiologist Ivan Pavlov.

In studying the role of saliva in the digestion of food, Pavlov found, as scientists often do, that something was getting in the way. Salivation was occurring before the food was placed in the mouths of the dogs that he was using as experimental animals. The normal reflex response is that salivation takes place after an animal has taken food into its mouth. But Pavlov found that simply by bringing a dog repeatedly to a standard experimental situation, he could cause it to salivate. Realizing that some kind of learning was going on, Pavlov decided to make a systematic study of it.

For the conditioning experiment he placed a dog in a sound proof room with a one-way screen, so that he could see the dog but the dog would not be distracted by watching him. He hooked up a pan that would be swung in and out of the dog's reach, and he connected a bell to ring inside the room. Pavlov would ring the bell and then, after a few seconds, present the food. He continued pairing the bell and the food together, while measuring the amount of saliva the dog secreted in response to the bell. In this way Pavlov could chart the course of conditioning, or training, in the dog.

He discovered that there was a definite pattern connecting the amount of saliva secreted, and the length of time the dog had been in training. It finally reached the point when the dog was secreting as much saliva at the sound of the bell alone, as would be required for the digestion and eating of its food. The mean curve that was produced was then considered to be standard for all dogs, though of course some dogs had a much sharper curve because they learned more quickly and others

397

had a much flatter curve because they were slow learners.

It is quite possible similarly to plot the response in the horse to any stimulus. We discovered, for example, in our communication work with horses, that a food response (the horse saying 'where is my bloody breakfast', by whatever sound or sign it normally used to demand food) can be produced whether or not a horse is hungry. One of the experiments we have done to prove this is extremely easy to reproduce.

If, for example, you feed your horse at one o'clock sharp every day, within a very short time you will find that, at one o'clock, your horse will ask for food. Then, once you have got this conditioned response to your appearance at one o'clock established, if one day you feed him more than he needs to satisfy his hunger at, let us say, half past eleven, you will find, even if he is not hungry because you have fed him already, that he will still demand food at one o'clock. When you give it to him he may not eat it, but he still shows what might be called a conditioned food response at the time at which he has been trained to do so.

Another kind of conditioning, fear conditioning, plays a large part in training a horse. Most horses have a good many fear conditioning experiences and these fears become part of their adjustment – or very often maladjustment – to stable routine and to being ridden.

A typical case of maladjustment through fear conditioning was a three-year-old I worked with. At the age of three he had been sent away to be broken by a woman who was afraid of him, and who ill-treated him severely. When the horse returned to his owner, whom he had previously adored, he was afraid of her, and in fact of any other woman who tried to ride him, though he went quietly when ridden or handled by a man. The fear of the woman who had trained, or rather broken and mishandled him, had been transferred to all women.

This transfer of his fear of one woman to all women demonstrates the process of stimulus generalization. This means quite simply that if a horse is frightened or excited in one set of circumstances or in a particular situation, it will react in a similar way in similar circumstances or situations in the future. If, for example, a horse enjoys jumping just a small fence and then larger fences at home, then comes across strange fences somewhere else, he will expect to enjoy jumping them and will jump them freely. But if on the other hand he is frightened by a car, he will tend to be frightened by all motor vehicles until the fear has been cured.

All that is required, then, to condition fear is to equate some unnatural stimulus with some natural or unconditioned stimulus for fear. An important feature of fear conditioning is that it should happen fast. In teaching a horse in its early stages it must be remembered that the memory of fear lasts a long time, since the learning is much stronger than that which results from positive stimulation. So the use of fear conditioning may speed training considerably.

For example, salivary conditioning in dogs will take a considerable time, but from fear a dog can be taught very quickly. It will take you a week, ten days or a fortnight to train a dog to salivate when you sound a bell. If on the other hand, when you sound the bell you also administer an electric shock to the dog's feet to make it jump a low barrier, at the third or fourth sounding of the bell the dog will jump the barrier before he gets the electric shock.* This effectiveness of fear based conditioning is probably one reason why the term 'breaking' is used for the training of horses – it is easier to train a horse with fear than it is with patience and understanding.

You can see this distinction in various ways of teaching a horse to stop. The way we do it is to ride the horse we are training down the road on the heels of an already trained horse. When I say 'whoa' the trained horse in front will stop, which means that the horse I am riding will also have to stop, or walk into the backside of the other horse. I may have to repeat this twelve times before the horse I am riding will connect the word 'whoa' with stopping. But if, on the other hand, I were to adopt a different technique, that of hitting the horse across the nose every time he didn't stop, he would learn

* Peden, *Fear response in dogs*, 1954.

in one or two lessons. Fear training will always have a much quicker effect than training by example.

Since fear training is quick and easy, why do we take so much trouble to avoid it? The answer is that it is effective only when teaching the animal to perform relatively simple tasks, such as stopping on command. It is a short-term technique.

When you are training a horse you are working with a long-term end in view. You want a finished product, a co-operative, willing and enthusiastic horse, and if you use the method of avoiding pain the animal will very quickly learn the minimum that is required to do so. So you will end up at the best with a horse which is doing the absolute minimum to avoid punishment. At worst, if you are dealing with an excitable and nervous or a very strong charactered horse, you will end up with an animal that is completely unmanageable.

On the other hand, training solely for reward, if not combined with strength of purpose and discipline, will produce a disobedient horse which does only what it wants to. As in all things, a mean between too much severity and too much kindness is necessary.

From our own and countless other people's experiences, if you can get a horse to want to do what you want him to do, you will undoubtedly get the best out of your horse. You want an iron fist, but in a velvet glove. We always go as far as we can saying 'Please will you', and try to get the horse to enjoy what he is doing. But if the horse says 'No I won't' then we make him do what he is told, just using patience, and in the last resort a good hiding.

The perfect illustration of this is Charlie. We bought him at Ascot; he had been broken as a yearling and put into training. He had run as a two-year-old, three-year-old, four-year-old and five-year-old, so for the previous five years had known nothing but the training stable and training routine. From the way he went when I rode him first, I don't think he had ever been ridden except with a string of other horses. When I took him out the day after he arrived, he literally shook with fear at the idea of going out by himself. Without the feeling of security he had from working with a number of horses he was terrified at every gateway, and it took me twenty minutes of patience and coaxing to get him past a forty-gallon drum which had been left by the side of the road.

The following day when I took him out he was beginning to enjoy the novelty of so many fresh things to see, and he took no notice of the forty-gallon drum. But the direction we took that day entailed leaving the road and going down a very slight bank, through a small gateway into the forest. In Charlie's view, my polite request that he should do so was completely outrageous. When I became more insistent he proceeded to buck and kick every time I tried to make him go forward with my heels. After forty minutes, both of us were in a muck sweat and stronger methods became necessary. I got off and opened the small gate on foot, instead of doing it from the horse's back as I did normally. I got back on and turned off the road and down the bank and eventually backed him through the gateway and up on the road the other side.

Immediately we were on the road, I told him how clever and how brave he was; I got off and made a terrible fuss of him, then I got back on again and told him we had to go back through the gate. This was more than he could bear, but after a battle of only about ten minutes, we were through. Then I turned him round and went back through the gate again without very much objection on his part; and the fourth and fifth time he walked willingly backwards and forwards through it.

Normally of course, I would avoid a battle so early in my relationship with a horse. But to be quite honest, since I had been going through that gateway on a number of horses without any difficulty for the previous ten years it never occurred to me that Charlie would make an issue of it. But when he did, he had to be made to do what I told him to do. I said 'Please will you?' and he said 'No, I won't!' so he damn well had to. We would have gone through that gateway if I had had to stay all night. But of course at no time did I hit him – it became purely a battle of wills, which I had to win.

It is this battle of wills which is the essential thing with any horse. You must prove to him, without hitting him or ill-treating him in any way, that your will is stronger than his, and in a very short time, if you ask him to do something he will do it without much complaint or objection.

He will do this for a number of reasons. First, because you have established yourself within the herd hierarchy : he will see you in terms of the natural herd situation, placing you as the dominant horse to which he defers. Thus, you are making use of the training which he has undergone from birth, conditioning him to obey the dominant horse. Second, because by making his work enjoyable, you will have conditioned him to expect an enjoyable experience even after doing something he dislikes doing. Third, because by this time you should have created a bond of affection between you and the horse, he will want to please you. And last, he will have been conditioned to expect reward in the form of praise and being caressed. Thus conflict can, in most cases, be eliminated.

5: *Using Conditioning Theory: 2*

Every kind of learning known to us can be analysed satisfactorily into some combination of classical and operant conditioning; but, except for training by fear, we seldom use pure classical training in teaching a horse.

As I explained earlier, operant conditioning differs from classical conditioning in (a) the stimulus situation, (b) the response made, and (c) the relation to, and type of, the reinforcement following the response. I will now try to make these differences a little clearer. In operant conditioning the stimulus involves a whole situation, not a single brief event such as the ringing of a bell or flashing of a light, of classical conditioning. So the subject makes a variety of random responses: wanders around, looks at things, pushes them. It does not give a specific elected response as in classical conditioning. Finally one of these responses will bring a reward or avoid punishment. Put all this together and you can say that operant conditioning consists of learning to perform some random act (selected from a number of possible actions within a situation) which leads to a reward or avoidance of punishment.

Operant conditioning can be demonstrated experimentally with rats in an operant chamber. This chamber can be used in many ways. It may contain two or more levers, or two or more lights, a feeding place into which pellets can be dropped, a drinking place for water and a metal grid floor for applying electric shocks, and such a chamber allows one to study all sorts of learning. But reduced to its bare essentials it consists merely of a box with a lever protruding from one wall and a food cup below it for rewarding an animal, usually a rat, with food. Attached to the feeding lever through an electrical circuit is a device that makes a recording on paper each time the rat pushes the lever. This is called a 'Cumulative Recorder' because one response moves the pen one unit, another response another unit, a third response a third unit and so on, and the responses are cumulative, i.e. they add up. Since the paper moves at a constant speed, a steep line on the recorder means that the rat is making responses in quick succession; a flat line means that he is making few responses.

Suppose now that a hungry rat is put in an operant chamber which is hooked up to a cumulative recorder. Since the box is unfamiliar to the rat, and unfamiliar things tend to evoke fear in animals, the rat first shows signs of fear; but these signs soon fade as the box becomes more familiar. The rat starts to explore it and it does many things – it sniffs at the walls and crevices, paws at the walls and floor, stands on its hind legs and runs along the floor. Eventually, by chance, it depresses the lever, a pellet of food is released and falls into the food cup. There follows the click of the feeding mechanism and the sound of the falling food pellet. This is the rat's first correct response to the first reward in the chamber.

In the experiment we carried out with such an operant chamber, the period between the time the rat was placed in the box and the time it made its first reward response was just over a quarter of an hour – sixteen minutes, to be precise. Another minute passed before the rat noticed the food and ate it. The rat didn't learn anything from this first experience, but the food pellet, which the rat ate because it was hungry and aroused, caused it to explore with greater vigour. As luck would have it, the rat didn't strike the lever again for eighteen minutes, that is thirty four minutes after the experiment began. At forty-five minutes it made its third response and at sixty-two its fourth. At this point, the rat began to get the idea. It had, in fact, become conditioned, and responses started coming rapidly. From then on the rat alternately pushed the lever and ate the pellet as fast as it could.

This experiment illustrates the conditioning of an operant response, of the rat's operant behaviour. At the beginning of the session it was sniffing, pawing, running, standing and incidentally pressing the lever, but only one of the responses – pressing the lever – was rewarded. This response was one it learned after a few trials at pairing responses and reward. Note carefully that the rat was required to make the responses himself – it wasn't a reflex elicited by the experiment, as in classical conditioning.

You may be wondering what a rat in a wooden box in a laboratory has to do with training horses. The answer is that the process described above demonstrates the basic principles of all learning. In his meandering around the wooden box, the rat by chance touched the lever and then again by chance he touched it a second time. But the third, fourth and fifth time he touched it, he was doing it at shorter intervals because he had quickly learned which end of the cage the food was likely to be, and he was looking for more food. Seeking for food, he touched the lever; and by the time he had touched it half a dozen times, he was associating the lever with the food. Eventually he touched the lever whenever he was hungry because he knew that the lever would bring him food.

Now, this process is very closely relevant to training horses. One of the first things about learning that it demonstrates is the importance of placing the subject in a situation where he is *likely* to do the right thing – in this case, the lever near to the reward. So it is up to you, as the horse's trainer, to put your horse into the situation where he is most likely to do the right thing.

Take as an example the task of teaching a restless horse to stand still while you get on to him. If you try to do so in the middle of a field, he will be free to move around you and there is no possibility of him doing the right thing and getting praised (rewarded). You have instead increased the chances that he will do the wrong thing – knock you over, tread on your toes, which means that you are going to clobber him (because anyone who has fifteen hundredweight of horse standing on their big toe clobbers the nearest thing handy!). But if on the other hand you stand him in a corner, or, better still, a space that he must stand in square without moving, you can get on him and then praise him for standing still, so he will very quickly get the idea.

In the first of these two situations you have made training extremely difficult. In the second you have made retraining a badly behaved horse infinitely easier. Now, when he is stationary for you to get on, the next step is for you to get on him in a gateway, facing the corner of the gate. When you're on you open the gate from the horse and go on your way, and by steps from this, he will learn to stand still whenever you want to get on him.

Similarly, you can make things easier for yourself when teaching him to jump. If you take him out and put a three-foot fence, eight-foot wide, in the middle of a field and trot him into it, he will stop at the fence, go around it and do any of a number of very peculiar things. The one thing he won't do is jump the fence! But if on the other hand you take him down to a lane containing five or six poles, two feet or two feet six high, and let him follow half a dozen other horses, letting him watch them go one after another, then cantering him up the lane over the poles on the tail of the last horse, he will pop over the five or six poles without thinking about it. When you make a great fuss of him he will know that he had done the right thing – you have put him into the position where he is likely to do the right thing and get the reward.

This is operant training. In the second of these examples, the horse has had the stimulus of the excitement of cantering with other horses. He's also had the example of the other horses jumping and the stimulus of your keenness and enthusiasm, and his response to these stimuli has been rewarded. Unlike Pavlov's dogs who, when the bell rang, were fed regardless of whether or not they responded, your horse got rewarded only when he gave the correct response. This is the difference between operant and classical training.

It should by now be clear that the learning most common in everyday life is some form of operant training, though it is often combined with classical training. Here is a simple example of operant and classical learning in the natural behaviour of horses together. A group of horses in a field learn to follow the lead horse instinctively partly by classical training – because if they try to pass him he will clobber them. This may be observed when you see another horse approaching the lead horse, who will swing his head round as if to bite the offender. This has a direct link with old Papa Pavlov's dogs in boxes: instead of a bell being rung and the dogs salivating in anticipation of food, the signal is the leader's head being swung round and the response is the second horse jumping back in anticipation of a bite. But horses also learn to follow one another by operant training. Here, early training is the key, because if a foal doesn't follow its mother about it doesn't get fed, since the milk bar will have disappeared over the horizon. The foal is free to do a number of things, such as play with other foals, stand still or gallop around the countryside, but unless he follows his mother he loses the protection that his mother affords him and dies of starvation. So, operant training at the earliest stage in a horse's life teaches him to stay within a group for protection and feeding, while classical training teaches him his place in the herd. Both negative conditioning in the classical training, and positive conditioning in the operant training, are at work.

Operant conditioning, even in the horse's natural life, may be quite a complex affair. A large number of factors may be present, only one or two of which are relevant to the proper response. A perfect example of such conditioning was offered once by Chico and Spitfire. Chico was a two-year-old thoroughbred stallion, and Spitfire my old pet pony. To most people keeping a horse like Spitfire would be like keeping a lion as a pet, but to me her incredible ability, determination and her desire to excel more than made up for the fact that she was unpredictable, bad tempered and bloody-minded. I wanted to breed a really good foal from her, and since I had a nice thoroughbred two-year-old I decided that he would do the job perfectly.

For a few days I turned him out with Spitfire for an hour or so. At first she would have nothing to do with him, then she got used to him following her around while she was grazing. I knew that four or five days later she was due to come into season. Chico, when I let him out in the mornings, would canter across, screaming his head off, to where Spitfire was standing. She would put her ears back and tell him to stop fooling around, then wave a leg in his direction to tell him that if he didn't behave himself she would kick his teeth in. But, the day before she was due to come into season, when he came galloping across to her she didn't put her ears back to him and he stopped short in some surprise, rather suspecting that she was going to spring a trap, only waiting for him to come close enough for her to have a piece of his anatomy for breakfast. But she just stood there with her ears pricked, so he trotted round her with his head held high and his tail cocked up in the air two or three times, to show her what a handsome gentleman he was. She stood, moving slowly round watching him, and then he came over and sniffed her nose.

When Chico sniffed Spits' nose and got no adverse reaction, he took a step forward, arched his neck and sniffed again. She nibbled his shoulder and in return for this compliment he nibbled the back of her neck. She put her ears back and squealed, he took a step back and she took a step forward, so he nibbled her neck again and she squealed again, then he nibbled her shoulder and her front leg. This was taking too many liberties for Spits, so she bit a piece out of his backside and told him to shove off.

The following morning was a glorious May morning and you could see the mountain sprouting green shoots of grass, straight and firm like spears pointing at the sky, and the leaf buds of the laburnum trees which later crown the top of the mountain with flowers of gold were bursting out, revealing their delicate shade of green. When we got to the field Spits was waiting at the gate for Chico. I opened the gate and took him in and he very warily dodged to the other side of my body, just to make quite sure that he wasn't going to be in any trouble again. I turned him loose and he went belting round the field for a couple of minutes, then came back to say hello to Spits. She gave a low whicker which sounded very much like a sexy chuckle to me, and put her head out and sniffed Chico's nose gently. He sniffed back, walked forward and nibbled her neck. She showed her obvious pleasure by just licking his shoulder. Chico found this very pleasant, as no doubt Spitfire did, and with his teeth he caressed her neck, her back, her withers, her shoulders and down her front leg. Spits went down on one knee and squealed, Chico immediately drew back in alarm, Spits stood up and Chico nibbled her shoulders and her leg again. She took a step forward so that he was nibbling her side and then her hind leg. She turned her backside towards him, lifting her tail to one side as an invitation. Chico had no idea what was expected of him, so he leant forward over her to nibble her neck again, but since her backside was in the way he went half up on his hind legs so that he could nibble the place that he knew was acceptable, Spitfire stood still and Chico came forward.

When it was over, Spits shook herself and wandered off, but Chico, having learned that this was a pleasant occupation, pursued her and about half an hour later served her again, this time with very little fuss and very little loveplay beforehand.

This is a very simple example of how a combination of natural urges plus instruction, in this case coming from another horse, can teach a young and ignorant horse very quickly. Seen as an example of operant learning, Chico did a large number of things – he trotted in a circle, he sniffed Spitfire, he nibbled her, he walked round her – at random, but until he did exactly the right thing he got absolutely no physical satisfaction whatsoever. Spitfire, being an old and seasoned mare, of course knew exactly what she was doing and was able to help in teaching him; but even if she had been a green two-year-old filly herself, exactly the same thing would have happened, except that the two animals would have learned at the same time, so the process would have taken longer. Chico was used on a number of mares during the summer months, his son out of Spitfire being an absolute beauty, a liver chestnut with a silver mane and tail whom we immediately christened April Fire.

When a horse learns to make one response to one stimulus and another to a second stimulus, this is called discrimination learning. This kind of learning may be classical or operant. Pavlov taught his dogs to discriminate between a bell and a buzzer,

simply by reinforcing one with the giving of food and not reinforcing the other. The usual procedure was first to train a dog
to give a conditioned response, i.e. to produce saliva because
of the ring of a bell, then for the experimenter to sound a buzzer
without following it with food. At first when the buzzer was
sounded the dog salivated in response – by stimulus generalization, because the bell and buzzer sound somewhat similar. But
as trials with the buzzer went unrewarded, the dog salivated less
and less, even though it continued to salivate at the sound of the
bell. Eventually the dog would take no notice of the buzzer whatsoever, but always took notice of the bell. It had learned a
conditioned discrimination.

Operant situations can also be arranged to teach discrimination. An experimenter may wire an operant chamber to attach
different rewards to different stimuli, and the animal has to
learn by random response to distinguish the stimulus needed to
achieve a goal.

Discrimination learning is one of the most important aspects
of training a horse, because so much success in competitions, for
instance, depends on such skills as the ability to discriminate
between different tasks and obstacles, between dressage and
jumping, and between one kind of jumping and another. The
horse also has to discriminate between the moods of his rider,
the desire of his rider, the abilities of his rider and the signals
that he receives. And most important of all, he must discriminate between correct and incorrect behaviour in an emergency.
If you are in tune with your horse, he will very quickly learn
to discriminate between being correctly placed at a fence and
coming into a fence all wrong, and if he is wrong to correct
himself, and put in that extra effort required of him.

When you are indulging in competition, hunting and indeed
anything other than general hacking, this fine discrimination of
response is extremely important. Just as, when I am talking to
people about learning, communication or psychology, I speak
and behave in a completely different manner from when I am
in a jockey's tent at a point to point, so horses must learn
appropriate behaviour to different circumstances. A horse

with a fine sense of occasion was Clear Reason by High Treason. I had a string of two or three horses going at that time, and there was no question whatsoever that Clear Reason was by far the worst of them. When the others had finished the gallop, he was trailing a hundred or a hundred and fifty yards behind. When I'm training I like to train against the stop watch, and our best horse at that time was doing the two-mile gallop, which is a very stiff and difficult one, in four minutes and eight seconds. The best that Clear Reason ever did was eight and a half minutes on the gallop. Come the first race of the season though, since I'd spent a small fortune on feeding the lazy beggar, I pushed him into the lorry with the other horses. When we got there we sorted them out, and a very good maiden we had was put in the maiden's race, my best horse Argonaut was put in the open, which only left the hunt race for Clear Reason.

Clear Reason's race was the third. I had already finished second on Argonaut, and felt very unlucky not to win. Came Clear Reason's race and I was expecting rather an uncomfortable bump round, pulling up half way round the second circuit because the rest of the field had already passed the winning post. We cantered down to the start. He was a little slow starting and went into the first fence last, but he took off well back and he went on improving until half way round the second circuit of eight, when he was lying third. I just couldn't believe it, he still didn't seem to be tiring, so I tucked him in behind the two leaders and he floated round without any difficulty. Towards the end he tired because he wasn't very fit, but I finished an easy third.

I ran him twice more, doing extremely well with him and then I had an extremely good offer for him and sold him. But I always thought of him as a fine example of discrimination learning: at home he could see no reason for bothering, but on a racecourse he could see every reason for getting down and galloping. I don't think I ever had him completely tired, but since he was only a young five-year-old I never really pushed him out.

In everyday life of course a horse has to discriminate amongst ordinary objects. We are in a low flying area, which means that the air force fly over us at about fifty feet with young fools of pilots dive-bombing us, breaking the sound barrier and generally doing their best to make an infernal nuisance of themselves. Horses, to start off with, are extremely alarmed by this and tear round the field in a panic, but after it has happened two or three times, the sound of an aircraft wooshing down over their heads doesn't worry them at all, and after a month they won't even lift their heads from grazing. They have learned to discriminate between the noise of a car wooshing past, which does frighten them, and an aeroplane coming down from a great height and making considerably more noise. They have learned that an aeroplane cannot hurt them and a motor car can. In actual fact we then use their acceptance of the low flying tactics of the idiot in the cockpit to train our horses to behave quietly in traffic.

For demonstration purposes I have taken a thirteen-two pony around our cross country course without a bridle or a saddle simply by shifting my weight to direct him to the next fence – leaning forward when I wanted to go faster and leaning back when I wanted him to steady. I started that piece of training quite simply by using a bridle and a saddle but exaggerating my weight positions until I reached such a point that his discriminatory learning had taught him that the positioning of my body indicated the speed that he had to go, and what he had to do. Also, when I have finished schooling a racehorse, which is usually after the eighth or tenth time I have ridden him racing, the horse will place himself at the fence precisely – he has learnt the exact distance that he needs to take off from each fence, the difference between an open ditch and a plain fence, a plain fence and a water jump, so that he will automatically shorten or lengthen his stride to jump the fence.

A very interesting incident happened in the race on Fanny at Aintree that I describe in detail at the end of this book. Before going to Aintree I had raced her in three hunter chases. Until she tried hunter chasing, she hadn't seen a water jump, but being a very clever jumper she learned to jump the water without any difficulty whatsoever; she also learned that water jumps were twelve feet wide. When we came to Aintree she jumped the whole course precisely, except the water jump. She made no mistake whatsoever, in fact when she jumped Beecher's there were two horses on the ground, one straight in front of where she was due to land and the other slightly at an angle. She jumped, changed legs, popped over the horse lying on the ground, changed legs again and went round the second horse who was down, damn near getting me out of the saddle in the process. But the water jump was a different question altogether. She knew from her previous learning that she had to jump twelve feet – so she jumped twelve feet, dropping her hind feet in. She hadn't had a chance to discriminate between the bigger water jump at Aintree and the small water jumps she had been accustomed to jumping, and I've no doubt whatsoever that if I'd taken her round Aintree again she'd have made no mistake whatsoever at the water jump.

Motor learning, sometimes called psycho-motor learning or skilled learning, is learning how to do something well. The emphasis in motor learning is on learning *how* a particular response is executed. And motor learning in horses involves the co-ordination of responses and skills so that the movement gets as near as it can to perfection.

All forms of jumping and training involve a certain amount of motor learning, so this is one of the important branches of learning in developing the finer points of horsemanship. Development of skills can be the most important and involved side of training a horse, and a large number of books have been written by a large number of people about how this should be done. In actual fact the basic principle is extremely simple.

When we described teaching a horse to jump earlier, we suggested you canter a horse up a lane behind four or five others and pop him over some low fences, which he enjoys doing. When you follow this up over a period of a week to ten days doing it every day, before very long the horse will be dancing about with excitement as you approach the jumping lane, because he is associating the lane with (a) the pleasure of jumping with other horses and (b) the new experience of taking off from the ground and jumping fences. The sense of achievement when he has done something he had considered impossible, gives him a great deal of satisfaction. And the praise he gets from you is an added stimulus. All this adds up to him connecting jumping with pleasure. At the end of the week he will have discovered that if he hits the fence he hurts himself, so he will begin to clear the fences well, often by an exaggerated two or three feet.

In theory, if you progress from here, raising the fences by degrees, he will continue to jump and enjoy jumping until you get to the height that marks the limit of his physical capabilities. But unfortunately, chance, to a small extent, and human incompetence to a very large extent, stops most horses jumping when they get beyond about three feet. What happens is that, by chance, the horse falls : he slips when he takes off badly, and hurts himself, so he stops jumping. Pure laziness will also stop a few horses jumping.

It is with the remainder, the horses who do go on to jump to the limit of their capabilities, that human incompetence comes in. The idiot on his back – and that includes myself, of course – tries to make him jump a fence that is too big for him, or too big a spread, before he is ready. He jogs his mouth, hits him when he is doing his best or when he had made an innocent mistake. All these things conspire to make a horse nervous when jumping, which will start him refusing his fences and so stop his natural progress. This means that you have to go back to a much lower height and eventually you reach a limit of about three foot or three foot six which is the limit of what most horses and ponies can jump easily, even though their natural ability makes it possible for them to jump five or six feet. This limit of three foot to three foot six is usually due to the competence level – or incompetence level – of the rider.

We had an example of this problem with Biddy last summer. I know a fair bit about riding cross-country, having ridden cross-country all my life, but since I have started one-day eventing I have to do a certain amount of show jumping at which I am a complete ignoramus, since jumping cross-country and show jumping are two completely different sciences, both of which have to be learned from a very early age. However, it seemed to me at the beginning that riding show jumping fences was only riding cross-country fences that knocked down.

I very soon learned the error of my thinking, because show jumping, it appears, is all about related distances between your fences. You have to take them on a short, even stride, whereas when we are riding across-country we take the fences as they come, and put in a short stride where necessary to get over. On an extra big fence, either a short stride or an extra big jump gets you over the obstacle. At this, Biddy and I were doing extremely well, completing our novice cross country easily and well within the time limit, and when we took on the crack riders in open competition, we put in extremely polished performances, usually doing the fastest time of the day.

Show jumping, however, was a different cup of tea altogether. We left a large number of coloured jumps demolished from the tip of Pembrokeshire to the North of England, so both of us had to go back to school and learn something completely new.

This is just one typical example of how a fool on a horse's back can impede the performance of the inoffensive animal between his legs. But the principle of training a horse to do anything to perfection is to take it slowly and gradually, operating well within the horse's capabilities, giving variety and the feeling of achievement and having done well. At the end of each round, even if the horse makes a mistake, you go back and jump two or three much smaller fences, so that you finish up with that sense of achievement again. This applies to any form of training and any form of riding.

This sense of achievement is very difficult to attain in the more precise schooling movements. It is easy enough when teaching anything to a horse in the early stages to give him the feeling that he has done something extremely difficult. Similarly, when you're jumping a slightly larger or different fence, the sense of achieving the impossible provides him with the motive to jump something even more difficult. But when you're teaching the horse very precise movements, this is much more difficult.

Suppose you are teaching a horse to stand completely stationary. Since to most horses the release from the stationary position will be a reward, he will tend to anticipate the movement, in order to attain the reward more quickly. Similarly, teaching a horse to go from a collected walk into an extended one is complicated by the fact that he will try to trot, there being no obvious incentive to walk instead, other than the restriction of the bit. You will have to deal with this problem first by creating a situation which discourages him from trotting. Part of this preparation will be in the way you feed the horse – on molasses, boiled barley, flaked maize and a little oats for a show horse, instead of racehouse nuts or a main diet of oats. You can certainly plan the training so that it is followed by an immediate reward – for instance, dinner. But the difficulty still remains within the training itself. One remedy is to have an audience watching you when you are doing these precise movements, who applaud when the movement is done correctly and express derision when it is anticipated or performed badly.

Improvement may also follow if you produce the horse groomed, plaited and perfectly turned out when planning dressage training, then take the plaits out when the dressage training is finished. Or a method which is effective with some horses is to have a tape recorder playing music timed to coincide with the horse's movements. Punk rock and modern music do not work, and in my experience the Death March with a good drum beat, speeded up to your horse's natural movements, is best for both the collected and the extended walk.

These are just some ways you can improve your schooling of precise movements, so that apart from your own vocal and caressing rewards the learning is made easier, and a sense of achievement for doing each movement precisely (which is in itself a reward) maintained.

To put it concisely, the secret of motor learning, like that of other learning, is implanting the motive – in this case, to attain perfection. This is essential in teaching a horse to jump a show jumping fence precisely, or in achieving the perfect dressage movement. The reinforcement and reward in motor learning is the precision and perfection of the movement, not the action or the movement itself.

6: *Fear Conditioning and Avoidance*

Avoiding something – like a jump – may be a bad habit in a horse. It is an essential skill, which, like other behaviours, all animals must learn, but it is also something that we may have to get them to unlearn.

Learning to avoid another horse, object or situation is a combination of classical and operant learning, linked in a special way, and depending on something known as avoidance motivation. That is, before avoidance conditioning can occur, fear and escape conditioning must have taken place.

Fear conditioning takes place when some neutral stimulus is paired with a stimulus which naturally causes fear. I can illustrate this with Swallow, a nice palamino foal I bought a year ago as a Christmas present for my daughter. The horse I was hunting at the time was a big sixteen-hand skewball called Kerry, and he for some reason took a violent dislike to Swallow. Every time Kerry passed Swallow's stable door he would make a dive at him, and Swallow became so terrified of the big horse that he had only to hear Kerry's stable door being opened and he rushed to the back of his loose box and stood crying there until he was sure the horse had gone out of sight. He was pairing a neutral stimulus – the sound of a door opening – with something that he was afraid of, i.e. Kerry, so that the sound of the door opening would terrify Swallow even if Kerry wasn't coming out of it.

I dealt with this problem by shifting Kerry into a different box with a different sounding door – Kerry's own stable door used to stick so you had to give it a thump when you opened it, and the sound of the thump had become the signal that terrified Swallow. For two days Swallow still showed signs of terror at the sound of the empty loose box being opened, but by the fifth day he was taking no notice of it at all. But I put Kerry back in, and immediately Swallow's fear reappeared at the sound of the door opening.

The pairing of Kerry and the sound of the door had, in good Pavlovian fashion, produced a conditioned fear in Swallow. Once fear had been conditioned and Kerry's aggressiveness had been paired to the fear-producing situation, Swallow's reaction was to escape from it. This led to Swallow desiring to escape before Kerry appeared; his natural intelligence told him that Kerry was coming when his stable door was opened, so he became afraid of the sound of the stable door.

Now this tendency to be conditioned, to associate a neutral with a fear-producing experience can be of great use, when training horses. Most people for instance can induce fear in their horse simply by scolding him. This works because the horse has learned to associate the scolding with punishment, so, provided that the scolding is reinforced from time to time with punishment, the scolding alone will usually be sufficient. The noise you make scolding a horse does not hurt him, of course, but the horse associates it with a painful situation and takes evading action.

The evading action is the result of another conditioning – escape conditioning – which may have been produced by either an unconditioned stimulus or a conditioned stimulus. Escape conditioning is a special form of operant learning, as illustrated by the following experiment with dogs.

A dog was placed in a box which was divided into two halves by a low barrier. A bell was sounded and, half a second later, a shock was given, passed through the floor on one side of the box in which the dog had been placed. The dog had to jump the fence dividing the box into the other half to escape from the shock. By the third trial the dog jumped the barrier *before* any shock was administered. Thereafter, he jumped the barrier on each occasion the bell sounded. Thus to begin with, the dog jumped the fence to escape from the shock, but once it was answering to the bell it was avoiding any shock whatsoever, and not just escaping from it. The bell was arousing a fear and to avoid the fear the dog was jumping the fence, even when there was no electric shock applied.

One of the methods we use to teach a difficult horse to load in a lorry or a trailer makes use of this method of learning. We use this only if our preferred techniques – coaxing him in with a bucket of nuts, and leading him up to the trailer and lifting his feet one after another up the tail board – fail. First we make a chute with a couple of gates opening to the back of the trailer or lorry, then we lead the horse into the chute. I stand behind him with a handful of pebbles, cursing him at the same time as throwing a pebble at his bottom and I keep this up until he decides to avoid the perpetual stinging of his bottom by going into the lorry. Immediately we make a fuss of him, then take him out of the lorry and repeat the process. We do this over and over until I have only to curse him once and he dashes into the lorry like a shot rabbit.

Fear is an extremely important tool in your handling of the horse, but it is a very finely edged one. On the other hand, the horse must respect you, and a horse will not respect any animal that is below it in the social hierarchy. In a herd the horse respects the most aggressive animal, which all the other horses have to respect, so your horse must equally respect you. But it is a completely different matter if he is afraid of you. If he is afraid of you as a person, everything you are doing in his training will be undermined, and you will never get him to want to do what you want him to do. What he must fear is the fact that you will punish him if he does wrong. It is rather like the position of father and son : a son must not be afraid of his father, but he must know that if he steals the apples off his father's favourite apple tree he will have the living daylights whaled out of him. In that case he fears the punishment for theft, though he doesn't fear his father. Similarly the horse must fear the punishment for doing wrong, but must not fear the person administering it.

A friend of mine has a vile temper and on one occasion when I was riding with him, his horse shied violently and bucked. and my friend came off. I caught the horse and came back and, to my horror my friend proceeded to whale the living daylights out of the animal. I was just going to get off and, in temper myself, stop him with my fists, when he stopped hitting him. His horse walked up to him and just rubbed his head on his shoulder. The horse knew when he was caught that he was going to get a hiding; even so, when he had had the hiding, he showed no fear whatsoever of his owner – in fact great affection. The horse knew he had done wrong in bucking, accepted his punishment and that was it – over and done with. Whilst I don't like to see a horse receive a hiding, the reaction of the horse to his owner was proof of the affection between them.

There must always be this bond of affection between horse and rider so that the horse will do things simply to please the owner. He must enjoy his work – in training this is an extremely important thing. Dull and repetitive work produces a dull and bored horse. At the same time the horse must be obedient; by this I don't mean the obedience of the stern German method of horse training, but the obedience that comes from the horse's knowledge that if you tell him to do so and so, then he must do it; so he does it because it is easier to do it straight away than after a long argument, and because he has a great desire to please you.

My work with Charlie shows how fear conditioning and affection can work together, and not against each other, in horse handling. He soon had a certain amount of affection for me, though the bond of affection between us was not yet very strong. But after riding him for only a few days, Charlie knew that if I asked him to do something he had to do it. The first time I asked him to do something when he didn't want to there was an argument that took well over an hour. The next time the same sort of situation arose, the argument lasted only a minute or so because Charlie already knew, after being handled firmly but kindly for a few days, that he was going to have to do as he was told anyway. He next reached the stage where he was really enjoying his work and he saw the reason for doing what he had considered previously to be quite impossible.

The power of fear can be such that a comparatively trivial event can interact with later experiences until the fear governs a whole range of behaviour. It becomes a conditioned response to other stimuli connected with the original situation. Something quite insignificant may happen to a foal which will multiply itself by this process of association until, when you come to gentle him, the fear has grown out of all proportion. I remember a foal that was in a field where there happened to be a great number of burrs. These got caught in the foal's coat and inside his legs, so each time his owner caught him, to keep him tidy and stop the burrs irritating him, he would pull them out of the foal's coat. But of course he couldn't help pulling a little hair with each one, and this was slightly painful to the foal.

This went on about once a month right through the summer. By the autumn the very sight of anyone approaching him petrified that foal, even though his mother was quite quiet and easy to handle. So whenever he was caught a considerable struggle ensued, which only frightened the foal more. By the time I got him as a three-year-old to gentle, he was conditioned to terror of man.

Another horse I rode had been kept throughout the winter in a stable with a very narrow doorway, and whenever he came out or in, he banged his sides. So he got into the habit of going through the door in a rush. By the spring, if you opened even a twelve-foot gate for him he would go through it absolutely flat-out for fear of catching himself on either side. On one occasion he caught my knee on the gatepost, knocked me off the saddle and I got up limping on one leg with a sore backside.

The increase in fear in cases like this may be so gradual that you don't notice it at the time, but it can multiply itself until the horse is in a state of near terror. And by that time it is a problem to both horse and trainer.

Just to show you that pleasure can be a pretty powerful conditioner too, and that for your own good you shouldn't be afraid to balance things out with a little fear conditioning when necessary, let me tell you a little tale about Chico. When he was losing his coat in the spring Chico used to back up to a tree to scratch his backside, which he enjoyed doing very much indeed. He had in his paddock a favourite small tree with a low branch which scratched his back as well, and this tree would be seen shaking about all over the place while he scratched himself on it. While I was riding him idly about the field one day, we wandered over by that tree and the next thing I knew I had a branch up my backside and I was sitting half way up on his neck whilst he proceeded to scratch himself. Even though at that time he was being groomed every day and he had no excuse for an itch at all, he'd been conditioned during the spring to associate the tree with pleasure. The fact that I was sitting in the saddle, admittedly half asleep, made no difference to him. He went to his favourite tree to scratch, boosting me out of the saddle in the process.

When he discovered what he had achieved, he found an opportunity too good to be missed. Forsaking the pleasure of scratching his backside, he took full advantage of having me half way up his neck to put in two colossal bucks, depositing me neatly on a bull thistle. Arching his neck and sticking his silver tail out like a banner, he floated round the field on his toes, each strutting stride showing his satisfaction at having got the better of the old man. Painfully I got to my feet, dropped my trousers, and removed most of the thistle spikes from my bottom. Then, replacing my trousers, I caught Chico who, seeing the unaccustomed sight of me standing there without any trousers, had come over to investigate. I got back on him and allowed him to wander back to the tree. As he backed into position, being well prepared this time, I caught him two hard cuts with my stick across his backside, which, being an intelligent horse, quickly taught him that scratching his posterior when I was in the saddle was not a pleasurable occupation.

So far I have been dealing with what happens when the simple conditions for learning exist. The conditions themselves, however, can be altered in many ways to make a difference to how effective the learning is, and to how well it is retained. Learning in the horse may be of two main kinds, (a) extending the horse's natural abilities and (b) learning a new task, or straightforward learning.

Now it's no damn good teaching a horse to do something

unless he remembers what you have taught him. For example, it is no good teaching a horse one day to stop when you say 'whoa' if he doesn't remember to stop when you say 'whoa' next day. And in memory retention fear again plays a significant part. Memory retention may in fact be governed by one or more of the following factors: fear; pleasure; habit; and subconscious memory. The longest lasting form of memory retention is based on both subconscious memory and fear. Something that has frightened the horse enough to have become part of his subconscious memory will be remembered long after he has forgotten something he has enjoyed or something he has done by habit.

We had an example of the power of subconscious fear retention in Cork Beg, my wife's favourite hunter fifteen years ago. She jumped a fence after hounds one day, cantered across a field and at the last second the horse saw the very thin wire of an electric fence in front of him. He attempted to jump it, getting his front feet over, but the electric wire caught underneath his tummy. Unfortunately the wire was live, so he continued across the field with the electric wire caught on his stifle against his most tender spot, getting a shock every two or three seconds. He bucked like hell to get rid of the irritation, and deposited my wife in two feet of mud before he finally got rid of the electric wire. No permanent physical harm was done, but from then on it was literally impossible to get him to go anywhere near electric wire. You could put a piece of wire straight across the yard and put his feed two feet on the near side of it, so that he had only to go within two feet of the electric wire to get his feed; and he would go to within four or five feet and stretch his head out trying to reach it. But he would starve rather than go any nearer, and he retained this memory for over fifteen years. Until he died at the age of twenty-two, we could shut him in a stable or field simply by tying a piece of string across the gateway. And he remained one of the very few horses we failed to teach to jump barbed wire, simply because we could never get him near enough to the wire to jump.

The memory of pleasure is much shorter lived, though how much shorter is of course dependent on the degree of pleasure, and a very intense pleasure may indeed be remembered longer than a mild fear.

The behaviour of a mare we had at home called Darling is a good illustration of memory retention based on pleasure. She was bred from as a three-year-old, and she enjoyed muzzling her foal so much that for ever after, whenever she was turned out with mares and foals, she would try to steal one of the foals. We used her a lot for training young horses – she would take a yearling, two-year-old or three-year-old and treat it like a foal. Now, this passion could not be seen in terms of pure mother instinct, because other mares do not behave in this way. But Darling always had her 'baby' with her, even though the baby was sometimes two or three hands bigger than she. She looked after it and taught it to follow her as a foal would, simply and solely because mothering a foal had given her such pleasure that she sought to repeat the pleasure by looking after another immature animal. She got so attached to these substitute babies that when, at ten or eleven years old, she had her second foal, she rejected it for the first four of five hours, until we had removed the two-year-old that she was mothering at the time.

Habit retention is seen everywhere – for example your horse carries you round largely from habit, because he is used to doing it. He will form bad habits and good habits, often quite by chance. It often seems that bad habits are a damn sight more difficult to get rid of than good ones and good ones far more difficult to establish than bad, but in actual fact this is not so. The depth of, that is the length of time that the horse retains, the habit is the only real measure of the difficulty of curing it; and it seems more difficult to get rid of bad habits than good ones because most of us have allowed bad habits to develop naturally from our own bad riding. To cure these we have to improve our riding to such a standard that the habit is eliminated automatically, and this entails learning something ourselves. Since the thickness of the human skull makes the base of

Mount Everest resemble an ice cream wafer, this is a task few of us approach easily.

For instance, if to cure a vice in a horse the rider has to learn to ride with a slacker rein, while he is concentrating he may do so, so curing the fault in the horse. But when he relaxes he will subconsciously tighten his reins, thus making his horse revert to his bad habit.

The concept of subconscious memory retention, already referred to in relation to Cork Beg and his long-remembered fear of wire, applies to any continued reaction by a horse (or other animal) to an event which has itself been forgotten. Another example might be the behaviour of a mare we had some years back. We took her to the stallion and she bred a foal from him. We didn't breed from her the second year; but in the third year, when she was in season, she got out of her field and went two miles to the field where she had previously been served by the stallion (and incidentally got in with him and I had a free service, but that's another story altogether! The argument about whether I should pay for the service is still going on ten years later!). In this case the mare's memory was re-awakened by the physical changes in her body, which took her over the fence and along the road two miles, over another fence and down to where the stallion was.

So if you want your horse to remember what you are teaching him, you need to bring as many of the factors in memory retention as possible into play; but again, fear has to be treated with great care. It is an intense emotion, it can lead to avoidance, and a behaviour instilled by fear is exceptionally difficult to eradicate.

Another of the important conditions for learning is the degree of arousal – or emotional excitement – appropriate to the task. For example, when getting on a horse for the first time you want the horse to be relaxed, happy and unafraid. This means that you want a low state of arousal. On the other hand, when teaching him to jump, you may want a high state of arousal. The degree of arousal required also of course depends on the temperament of the horse; a lazy or timid horse may require a very high state of arousal to make him jump, an alert and confident horse a comparatively low one.

Arousal may be affected by several things. First, by feeding, because a horse that is starved with a staring coat and pot belly will be extremely difficult to arouse, and hence difficult to teach. But a horse that has been shut in a loose box and fed like a fighting cock will be impossible to teach, since, after he has burst through the stable door like a bullet, he will be so excited that even if he doesn't buck you off into the dung heap, he will be dancing around so much that he will be able to pay no attention to the task. So the first thing to consider is how to adapt the feeding of your horse to what you want to teach him. (This is one of the things that makes combined training so difficult, since you want him quiet and restrained enough to do the dressage and show jumping, and yet excited, fit and bold enough to complete the cross country within the time limit.)

Arousal is also affected by the situation of the horse. A string of horses walking along half asleep will tend to quieten him down, whilst the same horses galloping will make him excited and lively. Fear, stimulated by a good belt across the backside, will wake him up and turn a lethargic plug into something that is worth riding. On the other hand, the relaxation of the rider and a caressing hand and voice will steady a horse considerably.

And this brings us to the mental state of the rider which is also a factor. If the rider is a mooning young woman dreaming of marrying Prince Charles in Westminster Abbey, her horse will be relaxed, taking a mouthful of grass now and then and thinking of fresh green grass. If, on the other hand, she is petrified and wondering whether the horse is going to buck her off in front of the next lorry, she will arouse such fear and excitement in him that he probably will dump her at the next convenient spot and return home for lunch, having learned nothing other than that the quickest way to get home to dinner is to deposit the rider as soon as possible.

Normally the horse should be aroused, but not too aroused. Up to a certain point, the higher the arousal level, the better the learning. Beyond that point the horse becomes too highly excited and most forms of learning are retarded. This can actually be illustrated experimentally on a graph, showing the general relationship between arousal and learning as an inverted U-curve : learning improves as the arousal of the horse increases to a fairly high level, but beyond a certain level it deteriorates. When high arousal fades into great anxiety or emotional excitement, learning is severely hampered.

Hence, if an experimentor is training a dog or a rat to jump a low barrier in response to an electric shock, he must be careful first to make the shock strong enough to make the animal react, but then not to make it so strong that it is overcome by its emotional state and bounces around the cage without paying attention to the warning stimulus. This excessive arousal can slow learning so much that in many cases the animal will not learn at all.

A further condition that affects learning is the motivation of the horse. The relationship between arousal and motivation is circular. It is after all obvious that an aroused horse is easily motivated, and a horse insufficiently aroused will be very hard to motivate. But the horse needs to be aroused to exactly the right level if he is to show the highest response to motivation. If your horse is grazing and relaxed and you rattle a bucket and shout for him, he will come over, motivated by the bucket. Younger horses and those most difficult to catch may be motivated by the example of other horses. On the other hand, the same group of horses galloping around the field in high excitement will ignore you completely – you can shout until you're hoarse and rattle the bucket until your arms drop off. That is how the relationship between state of arousal and motivation or response works : your horse, when asleep, has no motivation to jump whatsoever; raise the level of arousal and he is keen and alert and can respond to your instructions; raise the level of arousal further so that he is wild and excited and he will demolish the fence. So, the right level of arousal is essential. It is necessary that the horse should be awake and alert to the exact level that will bring the best response to any encouragement that you may give him.

What we are setting out to do is completely to change the behaviour patterns of our horse. The natural behaviour of the horse might be summarised, rather crudely, as : to avoid danger, to eat, drink, sleep and, if the weather is bad, to find shelter. But we aim to change that behaviour pattern to such an extent that the horse will gallop three miles and jump eighteen fences in a steeplechase, to jump unnaturally high objects in the puissance competition, to perform equally unnatural antics in dressage classes and in general to submit his will to that of whichever competent or incompetent human being he may be asked to carry hunting, riding or hacking around the countryside. By training, we not only get the horse to submit to these strange activities, but actually to enjoy them. We completely alter the horse's behaviour, and we do it by conditioning. When he does what we want he gets rewarded, and by repeating the reward – the praise or whatever – each time he does what we want, the horse will come to want to please us. First, pleasing us leads to a quiet life for him, without arguments; second it produces titbits and affection. This process, of constant conditioning by reward (and some punishment), is the crux of good training.

Training of course starts with the horse's natural responses, and builds on them. It means strengthening some responses (and weakening others) by a programme of regular reinforcement.

7: *Principles of Reinforcement*

Reinforcement is a general word, covering both reward and punishment, and it is anything which strengthens a response. It reinforces the response, or in other words it promotes learning. A reward is a positive reinforcement but punishment is a negative reinforcement. In either case the reinforcement is the road to learning. If it isn't used, or isn't used in the right way, no learning will take place. The horse is an extremely pleasant and kind animal who usually wants to learn. But if the thick-headed biped, who is endeavouring to impose strange and incomprehensible practices on the horse, relies only on garbled secondhand knowledge, weakness, ignorance or brutality as his training tools, the horse will learn very little. (It is as brutal to spoil, overfeed and then ask the horse to do something that is against its natural instincts without first conditioning it to want to do that thing, as it is to starve and beat a horse into submission.)

A horse is motivated to learn partly by his own natural curiosity, partly by his natural need for activity, and partly by the fact that he wants to please his owner. It is the last response that we work hardest to reinforce: and that is why positive reinforcement, that is the encouragement of the horse to learn for a reward, is so important, because this increases his desire to learn, since it leads to something pleasant. It increases his desire to please his owner since his affection for his owner is greater and the more he learns, the more he pleases his owner. In other words, by making sure the work is enjoyable you introduce another reinforcement. In learning as many as five or six different reinforcements may be used for the same piece of learning.

On the other hand bad horsemanship, ignorance and weakness may induce a revulsion against a particular piece of learning; thus undermining both positive and negative reinforcement.

430

Jasper was an example of a conflict of this kind. Whilst a sweet, kind horse normally, he had developed a revulsion against the tedium of exercise, which was necessary to get him fit for racing. His avoidance technique, which had been allowed to develop through weak handling, was quite simple : as soon as you rode him out of the front gate he would go straight up on his hind legs, swing round and shoot back the way he had come. His desire to please was in conflict with his wish to get back to his nice warm stable. The problem was to reinforce his desire to do what we wanted him to do. This we quickly achieved by determination, patience and ending his exercise by allowing him to gallop flat out up the jumping lane with another horse. This he enjoyed, and it also cured his main vice which was refusing to jump when racing.

The more the horse enjoys learning, the more he will want to learn, whereas negative reinforcement, i.e. punishing the horse when he has done wrong, reduces his desire to learn, since learning becomes an unpleasant experience. Negative reinforcement creates its own spiral – if learning is unpleasant, the horse will avoid getting into a situation where he has got to learn, and since ill-treatment produces a revulsion for his owner, his desire to please his owner will be lessened.

I can best illustrate what I mean by enjoyment in learning, by describing one of my favourite rides. On this ride we go up to the mountain through the forest, riding through the green avenues of larch standing in neat squares, precisely spaced line after line like a squad of guards on parade, stretching twenty or thirty feet above us, their tips swaying like feather dusters brushing the clouds. We turn down through the trees, while the branches slash our faces, punishing us for invading their lines, through to a ride at the bottom where with a plunge of excitement the horses bound away over three or four fallen tree trunks ranging from eighteen inches to two feet six inches high. Then we turn right down a steep track to the river at the bottom. The horses slide the last ten yards, landing with a splash in the pool, causing a cascade of water to sparkle in the sunlight. They stop and drink, standing in the water, some up to their knees, some up to their bellies. Then the first one raises a hoof and brings it down hard into the water, soaking himself, his companions and their riders. Soon they are all playing at it until I, who have got out of the way as soon as my horse has had a drink, have decided that the whole party has got wet enough for one day.

The consequence of this game is that jumping in and out of water is, to my horses, fun and I never have any trouble jumping into rivers or lakes out hunting or at cross country. But suppose, on the other hand, I had jumped each of those same horses into water for the first time alone, and a battle had ensued, they might have disliked jumping into or over water for ever after.

This preference for positive reinforcement does not mean that a horse should be allowed to get away with wilful misbehaviour. When a horse has bitten your backside he must be punished immediately. But if on the other hand the horse accidentally steps on your foot, even though for you the pain of one equals the pain of the other, it is your own fault for getting your foot in the way, and, far from punishing him, you should make quite sure that your boot has in no way damaged the horse's hoof.

The principle is quite easy to follow. Positive reinforcement should be used to encourage a horse to learn. Negative reinforcement is used to stop him doing wrong.

When Blodwen came to us she had a reputation for kicking – and she did kick badly. After she had taken a swipe at me the first time, I put on my heaviest boots and went back up to her. As I approached her and she took another swipe at me, I dodged, then brought my foot back as hard as I could and let her have one back hard in the belly. The message got home immediately. After that I could walk in and out of her stable and she never kicked me, and very soon she was absolutely safe for anybody to approach from behind. This story clearly illustrates negative reinforcement used in the correct time and place.

About twelve months later, Blodwen was eating her dinner when Pudding escaped. Pudding, being an extremely greedy pony, tried to steal some of Blodwen's food. I saw this happening and, not wanting a battle in the stable, went to get Pudding out. Pudding saw a kick from Blodwen coming, but being rather quick on his feet, dodged to one side and I received Blodwen's well-shod hoof in my posterior, which was extremely painful. But I was, in this case, just the unfortunate bystander. Blodwen had every right to kick at Pudding for trying to steal her dinner, and Pudding, being no fool, had naturally dodged out of the way, so the kick was just my bad luck, and certainly not a case for punishing Blodwen. It is a perfect example of where negative reinforcement should not be applied.

One of the most important things to remember about negative reinforcement is that after a battle, when the horse has done what it has been asked to, a great deal of praise and reward should be given. This is so that you can replace the negative with a positive reinforcement as soon as possible, and not be forced to repeat the punishment in similar situations in future. For similar reasons, if it should be necessary to punch or beat your horse, you should make sure you swear at him at the same time as chastising him. This is so that he will link the cursing with the clout, and after a while you may be able to use the cursing alone, without the accompaniment of the clout, as punishment. After chastising him, you should go away and leave him, to give him a chance to think about it and settle down. (This also gives you the opportunity for any surgery necessary on yourself). Then, after ten or fifteen minutes, you should return and make a great fuss of the horse, so that he does not associate you with ill-treatment only.

I had a very difficult horse to gentle, called Exeter Lady. She was just awkward, lazy and bloody-minded. Eventually I got her so that I had only to curse her and she would behave instantly. She started racing the following spring, but although several jockeys rode her, none of them got beyond the second or third fence, in spite of the fact that they were waving their whips like windmills. Eventually the owner had to eat humble pie and asked me to ride her. Instead of hitting her I swore at her going into the first fence, repeating the curses at each subsequent fence. I led from the third fence, using every expletive in my vocabulary. When coming up the straight, with the favourite up on my shoulder, my language became extraordinary. Yet no time did I touch her with the whip, since I knew that her reaction would have been to stop and start bucking. The outcome of this adventure was that the stewards warned me about my language in future races, but this was more than compensated for by a winning wager at 33 to 1.

8: *Teaching By Positive and Negative Reinforcement*

Positive reinforcement, i.e. reward and praise, should be used, but not be used to excess. Biddy gets no praise whatsoever when she jumps a three-foot-six fence, since it requires no great effort on her part. But on the other hand, when Pudding jumps three foot, he is jumping to the limit of his capability. He had to put considerable effort into it and he gets the blessings of heaven showered upon him. If I praised Biddy every time she jumped a three-foot-six fence I would have no praise left to give her when she jumped four foot six or five foot. If your horse automatically comes to you and is easy to catch, a slight pat or a friendly greeting is sufficient reward; but a horse that is very difficult to catch should be praised when he lets you catch him for the first time, and made such a fuss of that he will want to be caught again. So, it must be remembered that the reward should correspond to the effort involved.

Reinforcement of course can mean something different in classical and operant conditioning. In classical conditioning, reinforcement is the presentation of the unconditioned stimulus which elicits a specific and conditioned response. In other words, to remind you of Papa Pavlov's experiment with the bells and the salivating dogs, the sound of the bell was the unconditioned stimulus, which at first caused the dog to form no saliva. But when the experiment had been repeated a number of times, the dog was emitting saliva at the sound of the bell, so the stimulus, i.e. the bell, followed by the reinforcement of the food, caused the conditioned response, the production of the saliva. The sound of the bell had become associated with the presentation of the food.

Pavlov's work is extremely important in training horses, since we are asking them to do things that are completely alien to them in response to alien stimuli. For example, a horse in the wild never jumps, but no matter which method you use to teach the horse to jump originally – what stimulus you use – you can condition him to clear three foot or three foot six without any difficulty.

The old-fashioned method of doing this was to put the horse into a jumping lane and drive him up the lane over low obstacles with a lunging whip. Sometimes the horse would be loose and sometimes on long reins, but whichever method was used the horse learnt to jump to escape the pain of the lunging whip. That is, negative reinforcement was used.

But once the horse was trained, he would continue to jump whether the fear of the lunging whip was present or not.

We, as you know, use the method of getting the horse to jump following other horses, and then we praise him after he has jumped. Here also, once he has learned to jump the fences, the horse will jump whether or not the incentive of the other horses is present. So, the conditioned response, that is jumping the fences, remains even though the stimulus is no longer there. Your conditioning treatment will have made jumping a reward in itself.

This means that it in turn can be used to reward other achievements. You can precede your jumping with a teaching session, for example to do a flying change of legs at the canter, and use the jumping as a reward for new learning. Then, if his jumping entails changing legs to jump a series of obstacles set at different angles, he will soon see the point of doing tight figures of eight so that this lesson, in turn, becomes the reward for learning to go from a walk straight into a canter and straight back to a walk. This again will improve his performance at jumping, since it will enable him to jump difficult fences set at right angles to each other.

From this it can be seen that if the process of learning is reversed so that the ultimate objective (which in this case happens to be the most enjoyable) is taught first in its simplest form, the more tedious forms of schooling can be eliminated. So the horse learns more quickly and, most important of all, enjoys his learning, and instead of dragging hours spent in a dull classroom, life becomes interesting and exciting.

If the horse's learning, or more accurately your teaching of him, is planned in such a way that each new piece of learning can be seen to increase the pleasure of previous learning, or to make a piece of learning easier to perform, you are increasing the horse's desire to learn. This in turn increases his state of arousal so that he learns each new schooling movement faster, and with greater enthusiasm and ease. A horse can see that from one initial piece of learning the whole horizon of his enjoyment is broadened. And in addition each random task of his operant learning, instead of being a matter of chance, is placed in such a situation that it becomes the obvious thing for him to do.

Let me remind you of what operant, as distinct from classical, learning is. The horse is normally being trained in a situation where a number of alternatives present themselves, only one of which is the correct one. When the horse chooses the correct response, he is rewarded, and when he does the wrong thing he is punished; or, alternatively, he is not rewarded. You can, if you want to avoid punishment, present and re-present the horse with the alternatives, and offer the reward only when the correct response is given.

This, clearly, is a slow business. So if the next thing to learn can be seen as obvious following the previous piece of learning, learning can be much quicker and more effective. The example of sequence learning described above illustrates this perfectly. The horse learns to jump by following other horses. This gives him pleasure, so he jumps by himself. In learning to do a flying change of legs he sees that turning corners to approach another fence is made easier. During his flying change schooling, he can see if he drops from a canter to a walk at the point of changing legs, changing legs becomes easier, and putting himself right when approaching a fence becomes a matter of course. So, his jumping in turn again becomes easier and more enjoyable. If each piece of learning is devised in a similar manner to suit each horse and each phase of training, the horse's learning ability increases and teaching him becomes a far easier matter.

I first used what might be termed the motivatory method of teaching a horse, with a four-year-old thoroughbred stallion we called George. He was superbly bred, but unfortunately his mother had died at his birth, so he'd never grown properly, and by the time we got him he was only 15 hands, which was not big enough to race and not even really big enough to make anything better than a second quality crossing stallion. So we bought him very cheaply and had him cut. My father wanted him to play polo on. The pony I was playing polo on had gone lame at the time, so I started to work on him. Then there was a panic because one of the boss's ponies went lame as well, so we were very short of polo ponies. This was really the chance I had been looking for. For some time, I had been working on a method of training horses using communication, psychology and learning by behaviourist principles, and I wanted an excuse to try what was nothing less than a revolutionary method of teaching horses. In this case I proposed to break and school a horse to the point where he could play a couple of chukkas of polo, all within three weeks of his being castrated. So I took him home, and got straight on his back (this was about a week after he had been cut), though for only half an hour. To start with, my wife led me on foot, then she let me go with the horse just following her, walking by her side. The second day, she led for ten minutes, then we went back to the yard and she mounted a second horse, while I rode George.

It was a lovely day and we had a very pleasant ride for about half an hour, walking most of the time, interspersed with a few strides of jogging. On the third and fourth days we increased the jogging to trotting, and on the fifth, when he was walking and trotting and responding to the bit and reins a little bit, on our way home we came to a ten-acre field, my wife's horse broke into a canter, and George followed him. Her horse started bucking a bit from pure joi de vivre; George bucked in imitation, not trying to get me off but just because he was enjoying himself. After this we were walking, trotting and cantering each day, and after about a week, when my wife couldn't come out,

I took George out by myself, along approximately the same ride. As we came near the first of the places where he was used to cantering, he started dancing about and reaching for the bit, so that I had a job to get the gate open and shut. I got the gate only half shut when he was off, really stretching out and enjoying himself, not in the delicate canter that we had been doing, but flat out. As we came towards the end of the field, I wondered what the devil I was going to do, since he was leading with his near foreleg. As we came to the hedge, I threw my weight to the right so that he turned up the hedge. The combination of my weight suddenly coming on to his right side and having to turn sharply led him in to changing legs as we went up the side of the field. I turned him back down the field the way we had come and he went back at a much steadier pace. Halfway across the field I turned him to the left, again throwing my weight and knee sharply over to the left. He changed back from his off fore to his near fore, and for ten minutes we zigzagged about the field. By the time I'd finished I had only to throw myself over and touch the reins and he was turning and changing legs just like that.

I had had great hopes for this method of training, but the spectacular results that I was getting were more than I had hoped for. I repeated the schooling the following day and to my amazement discovered that he was enjoying changing legs on command. At the end of the schooling session his behaviour was like that of a teacher's pet at school who has given all the right answers at exactly the right time: he swaggered down to the yard showing all and sundry that not only was he a very pretty horse, but he was also a very clever horse indeed. And indeed I had made a great point of telling him how clever he was.

Because he was rather tired I felt that this would be a good time to introduce him to the polo stick, which my wife brought out to me. He looked at it with very great disfavour, but I put it round my wrist and just let it hang down at my side, and rode around the field two or three times with it there. Then I started swinging it backwards and forwards very gently and slowly. Each time I swung it he shied violently to the left, but after a bit he got used to it and we just walked round hitting the tops off thistles and buttercups, and he decided that the stick wasn't going to kill him. He relaxed, and let me go on for about five or ten minutes knocking the tops off thistles on the off side, which is the normal side you carry the polo stick, before I lifted the stick over to the other side, doing near side forward and backhand strokes. This time it took him only about five minutes to decide that everything was all right, and this was just a piece of my normal half witted behaviour.

My wife rode with me the next day, and she carried the polo stick to start with, then we changed over. I took the stick, first walking, swinging backwards and forwards, and then trotting, and he took no notice of it. When we got to a place where we could canter I cantered him changing legs, then I came back and got the polo stick and did the same thing with the stick. By this time he was quite used to the polo stick and took no notice of it whatsoever, so when we got home we went on to the next stage of his schooling. We got out an old polo ball, and I tapped it about a bit, on him. At first he looked on it with disfavour, but after about half an hour, he was beginning to follow the ball's direction with his eyes when I hit it, and then to follow it himself for me to hit it forward again. Then I did a backhander and, without being asked, he spun round and trotted back to where the ball had dropped.

The following day we were due to play polo, so I took him down with us, and seeing all the strange horses and cars and trailers was a bit much for him to start with. But I went into the normal schooling routine for ten minutes or a quarter of an hour, tapping the ball about. Then I let him watch the first chukka of polo, which was a fast chukka. The sight of the galloping horses and their keenness and enjoyment fascinated him, and above all gave him some idea of the reason for his learning. I put him into the second chukka, which was a slow chukka, and he took to it like a duck to water, just loving galloping with the other ponies chasing the ball, and leaning against the other horses to ride them off the ball. It was something so new, interesting and exciting that he thought it was absolutely wonderful.

He enjoyed it so much that I let him play in a second chukka at the end of the day, by which time he was becoming a dab hand and was changing legs, twisting, turning and following the ball with the best of them. He found great pleasure in riding other ponies off the ball, so much so that he hit one much respected and ageing Colonel such an almighty clout with his shoulder that I was told in no uncertain terms the Colonel's opinion of me, my heritage and the horse I was riding.

Unfortunately for me, George proved such an apt and willing pupil and within a month had turned into such a good polo pony that my father was offered a price for him too high to refuse, and he was sold and sent up to Cowdray Park, where he played polo for many, many seasons. But this is what happens when you get a good horse – if you're lucky you keep him for a month or two and that's all, because someone else with a much bigger pocket than your own comes along and buys him off you. Whereas if you've got some useless screw who you'd be only too pleased to see the back of, nobody wants him and you're stuck with him for ever.

George's transformation from an unbroken stallion to something capable of playing polo in three weeks, and then into an extremely good polo pony in a couple of months, proved to me beyond all doubt that my theories about using communication and psychology, and making the most of the horse's learning capacity, could make schooling easy and pleasurable for me and my horses. The revolutionary method of breaking I had evolved had worked beyond our wildest dreams.

I had demonstrated first, that by being led and made a fuss of, George had learned to accept me on his back immediately. Second, by following another horse and imitating what his elder was doing, he had learned to turn and respond to the bit, so that when I pulled the left rein and his companion turned to the left he naturally responded to the bit by turning to the left; when I pulled the reins his companion stopped, so he stopped as well. He was being conditioned by association, like

Pavlov's dogs. But he was being reinforced in his learning by being told what a good and clever horse he was, and he was responding to the praise. Third, when I taught him to change legs by making use of the situation I found myself in – going at a rate of knots at a hedge – and altering my balance, I altered his balance so that he did a flying change naturally, this being the only way he could turn in the direction he was compelled towards; and by going then from his off fore, which was his unnatural leg, half-way across the field, turning him and using my weight to bring him back on to the leg with which he led naturally, he learned to do a flying change without any difficulty whatsoever. At this point I was facilitating his operant learning by putting him in a situation to encourage him to make the choice that would be rewarded.

Then, in learning to accept the polo stick, he found that (a) it didn't hurt him and (b) he got praise and reward from me. It gave an added interest to his life when the ball was introduced and he found it quite amusing to follow the white object that was bobbing about the field, and when he got to it, to find that the stick made the ball go bobbing away from him again. He quickly learned to follow the ball. And when he got down to playing polo he found the excitement and enjoyment of galloping, turning and moving with the other horses was such that he increased his own natural handiness and ability without any real teaching. He was learning from his own experience, thinking about the game and enjoying using his brain, his brawn and his speed to excel and beat the other horses. Again, of course, each time he did something well he was praised for it.

One of the amazing things that I discovered in training George, in the two months or so that I had him, was that at no time did I have to touch him with my heels and at no time did I have to hit him with a stick. Occasionally he got a clout across the legs with a polo stick, which happened from time to time when we were playing polo, but he ignored any pain or discomfort, accepting it as part of the game just as a human being accepts the bumps and bangs of the rugger field.

This was our first really successful experiment in allowing the horse to learn instead of teaching it, and it illustrated perfectly how, if each situation is presented to the horse correctly, the horse's learning speed can be increased dramatically.

To achieve the maximum results, the required response, motive and reinforcement must not only follow in correct sequence, but any reinforcement required must be immediate. You can see the sequence in any stable at feed time. When the horse is hungry (motive), you take a feed into the loose box. When he comes to the food (required response), he eats, so satisfying his hunger (reinforcement).

Above all, negative reinforcement must be immediate. To illustrate negative reinforcement paired with response and motive suppose you are dealing with a savage horse who attacks you with his teeth and front feet. The motive here is aggression caused originally by fear. You deal with it by lunging forward, punching him with your fist and roaring at him (negative reinforcement). In every case I have handled in this manner the horse has retreated, usually to the corner of the loose box (required response). In this case the negative reinforcement has diminished his motive to attack. A series of lessons of this kind will soon eliminate the motive to attack, and on your approach alone he will retire to the corner of his box. And provided that at the same time you are feeding him, watering him and spending half an hour a day in the box just chatting to him, you will arouse no further fear.

Negative reinforcement can of course be used to decrease the motive itself. A simple example often arises in shoeing a horse. One of the most annoying habits a horse can develop is to stand up on his hind legs, or hang back, when his front feet are being shoed. Here the motive is twofold, first to annoy you and second to avoid being shod in front. The response required is for the horse to stand still. The reinforcement used is to press the base of the dock against the horse's anus. If he is standing still, the pressure is light and causes little or no discomfort. If, on the other hand, the horse attempts to come backwards or rear, the pressure is increased to the maximum, causing great discomfort.

This makes the horse go forward again and stand in the correct position, providing the motive to stand still and give the correct response.

The third way negative reinforcement is used can be illustrated with a horse out hunting. If a horse looks like refusing a fence (motive, not to jump), you catch him once with your hunting crop (negative reinforcement), so he jumps the fence (correct response) and so gallops after hounds with other horses (here positive reinforcement is added to negative reinforcement).

I remember, a horse called Croix de la Lorraine, who was a useless flat race horse of considerable ability. His owner had purchased him for a fair price (since he'd twice been placed over two miles) to go hurdling. He proved a complete failure, adding to his refusals to gallop or race his insistence that he would not jump. I ended up being given a half share of him, in return for feeding him and curing him of his vices.

The first thing to do was to give him a motive to win. This I did, by galloping him with a series of slow horses throughout his training period, so that he always won. Second, I hunted him, making sure that he never jumped a fence. As soon as he got excited and was enjoying himself hunting (that is, I had induced a state of arousal in him), I would take him home. By this stage I had induced (a) a motive to gallop and beat the other horses, and (b) a state of arousal whenever he went hunting. By now he was tearing at his bit to get in front of other horses, and resisting stopping and going home when I wanted to. So I used the motive to beat other horses and his state of arousal (excitement) to jump four or five fences on my way home. The following day I was hunting, I jumped twelve or fifteen fences before going home. That was on the Monday. Even though he was still refusing to jump anything at home, I ran him in the maiden race at Sparkford Vale on the Saturday, running in a suicidally large field of 34. I led from the start to within two fences of home, where he was passed by the eventual winner. He won easily the following Saturday.

Unfortunately in his fourth race he fell and broke a leg. But in spite of this tragedy, he showed clearly how the introduction of a motive, by using the reinforcement of enjoyment and praise, together with arousal, can not only induce learning but will also lead to the required response.

Motive reinforcement and response is the key to everything that a horse does, even though the response is not always the one required or expected. Salline for instance whickers at the sound of the bucket at feeding time, welcoming her food. But she also kicks her partition. Here you have two responses to the same stimulus, the first to welcome you, the second (kicking her partition) to tell the adjacent horses to get out of the bloody way since she is eating. This is an example also of pairing a stimulus (feeding) with a response (kicking to stop other horses eating her food), even though she has been fed by herself for six months and no other horse has had the opportunity of stealing her feed.

Another example of this pairing of response is the hunter who will become excited at the sound of the hunting horn, because he associates it with hunting and pleasurable excitement, even though he has long ceased hunting. In the case of one horse I had, paired response nearly ended a racing career. Molfre loved racing, and he used to get very excited when we got to the track. One of the symptoms of his excitement was that he would break out in a sweat. He very quickly learned the preparations for racing day – the day before he was groomed and spruced up, his mane was got ready for plaiting and his tail was bandaged, and at ten o'clock at night his hay net and water were taken out of his stall.

Then as soon as he had been put into the lorry he would start to get hotter and hotter, and before we had gone twenty miles he would be in a muck sweat. Then things got worse, because the night before racing, after we had got him ready for the following day, he would spend the whole night walking round his box so that he was almost exhausted before we left for the race meeting, let alone before we started the race.

In fact, within the first four or five meetings it became obvious that the only way we could get him to a race meeting fit to run was by getting him ready not the night before, but at the last possible moment in the morning. We also took to driving him around the countryside every now and then in the Landrover and trailer, spruced up as if he were going racing, so that after a series of such excursions which ended up at home and not at the racetrack, he ceased to pair racing preparation with racing, and he never knew whether he was going racing or not until he actually got to the meeting.

In this case a horse was associating the preparations for racing with the racing itself, and exhausting himself with his own excitement. Another kind of pairing can arise when you are trying to get a lazy horse to jump. You may have to tan his backside to start with, but he will quickly learn that he has to jump and he will jump to avoid being belted, so that you do not have to touch him at all when you want him to jump: he has associated going into a fence with avoiding a bleeding bottom by jumping. Here the negative reinforcement is paired with approaching a fence. This in turn will be reinforced by the fact that he actually enjoys jumping, especially if he is jumping with other horses.

I carried this tendency to an almost comic extreme when teaching Dart to jump barbed wire. Because he approached his fences at speed he wasn't always seeing the wire, so I got into the habit of kicking him and saying 'hup', when I was approaching a wire fence. This finally reached the stage where I could gallop across a field, kick him and say 'hup', and he would jump three-foot-six, even though there was no obstacle or sign of obstacle present. I did this quite simply, first of all by putting a rail between two posts with a thin wire rope three inches above the rail, kicking and saying 'hup' on his take off stride. I then removed the rail and jumped him over the almost invisible strand of wire rope, which was by then set at three foot nine inches. I then proceeded to move the wire rope round every fence so that it was anything up to two feet above the rail which I had on the fence already. When he was jumping the wire rope on command, I started stretching it across the field between available trees and posts, which could be anything up to thirty feet apart. Eventually, I discovered the wire itself was unnecessary because he was jumping on command automatically.

A stimulus that has become associated with a primary reinforcement in this way, is called a secondary reinforcement.

Pairing the reinforcement with the response to be learned is an essential requirement for both classical and operant conditioning. Many studies have indicated that the best interval for such pairing is about half a second. Long delays between the response to be learned and the reinforcement greatly retard the learning. So the main problem is how to get the correct response and the reinforcement closely paired, and one solution to this problem is to combine a secondary reinforcement with what is called 'shaping'. Shaping is rather like the game of hunt the thimble, in which someone in a room is trying to find a hidden thimble and the spectators, who know where it is, say 'warmer' when he gets closer and 'colder' when he moves away from it. In such a case the spectators are immediately reinforcing any response in the right direction, thus strengthening that response. Shaping keeps the subject closer to his goal rather than wandering around until he accidentally finds it.

Shaping initiated by secondary reinforcement promotes very rapid learning. A simple example of this is teaching a horse to be caught. First you put food in a bucket and leave it in his field: very quickly he will learn that the appearance of the bucket in his field means that food is coming, and he will come towards you as soon as he sees the bucket. After you put the bucket down he will come to it and eat from it. But in the second stage of your shaping the reinforcement, i.e. the reward of food for coming to you, he has to eat out of the bucket in your hand. In this you are shaping him in the direction you want to go, i.e. to catch him. In the third stage he gets his reward of food only when you have your hand on him, and in the fourth stage he gets his food only when you actually catch him.

You can see how you have shaped your reinforcement. To start with he gets food for eating out of the bucket, then he gets food for allowing you to put your hand on him, and finally you have reached the desired goal which is to give food only when he is caught.

When shaping the responses of Charlie, the flat race horse I bought at Ascot, I was aiming to get him to jump steeplechase fences. When we bought him he had never even walked on rough ground, and to get him to cross a slight depression was a major task. But within a day or two he was quite happy going over slight depressions, and each time he stepped over a dip in the ground he was made a great fuss of. The next stage in shaping him to jump was to run over a very small ditch, about a foot across and six inches deep. This was quite simple for him to jump, but it took at least twenty minutes before I could get him to take his courage in both hands and step over it. After he had done this I made a terrific fuss of him and after another five minutes' coaxing he stepped back over it and back and forward until he was just stepping over it without thinking about it. Then I told him how clever he was and took him home.

The following day I got him stepping over a bigger ditch, and by the time he had finished on his second day of learning to jump he was actually jumping a ditch about two foot across and three or four feet deep. The bigger the obstacle the more he was told how clever he was. On the third day, I looked for all the little ditches I could find on the mountain and he was really enjoying popping over them.

The next stage was to get him to take off from the ground over a solid obstacle. Normally, of course, I would have had him hunting or going up a jumping lane behind other horses over a low obstacle. But with Charlie this wasn't possible, since he had been racing and was a sprinter, and when he was with other horses he would tend to try to race them. This meant that he would be thinking about racing horses and not about jumping fences, and there was a very great risk that he might fall over something and hurt himself, which would have put him off jumping for life. So, he had to learn to jump by himself.

On the fourth day I took him into the forest where I knew there was a small tree trunk about a foot high across one of the

Learning to Jump

Two horses and their riders, happy and excited, approach the jumping fences

Photographs by Terry Williams

The young horse follows the experienced one over the jumps — low, unfrightening ones at first
Soon the young horse is ready to jump on his own — he has discovered that jumping is fun

Conditioning Theory

In this experiment, the horse has been conditioned to associate the sound of the blowing of a hunting horn with the appearance of food. Immediately the horn is blown, he pops his head expectantly out of the stable door

And is rewarded with his dinner

Overcoming Fear . . . and catching your horse
A horse registering fear and alarm at the appearance of a stranger in his field

She approaches quietly and slowly, with a bucket of horse nuts

The horse approaches . . .

And allows himself to be caught and haltered

Bad Habits: 1. Napping

This horse expresses his reluctance to cross a ditch, but his rider is firm, and he steps into it

Positive Reinforcement

He is rewarded with generous praise and patting, and concludes that ditches are not unpleasant after all

Negative reinforcement (above left)

— whip to be used sparingly, if at all

Bad Habits: 2. Avoidance technique — running out:

Above, right: The horse is able to 'run out' because the rider is going into the jump on a slack rein
Below: The same jump, this time presented correctly, the horse held together with hands and heels

Eager horse

Rostellan is groomed, saddled and ready to go out. But Leslie is keeping him waiting, so he decides to let himself out of his stable, and go and find her

Hunting morning Leslie is again keeping him waiting, so he decides to —

. . . load himself in to the lorry

Mischievous horse

Here he is using his skills because he is bored and he thinks no one is looking
First he lets himself out of his stable.
Then (below, and above right) he decides to open the front door of the house . . .

and see what is going on inside

Alert horse

Looking forward to a ride

Bored, dejected and unwanted

At the horse sale

Choosing Your Horse

top right: Alone and unhappy
centre: Alert and looking
  forward to the future
bottom right: Frightened
and worried

(Below and righthand page) Horses being paraded at a horse sale
Horse and rider bored with waiting

Untouched horses in the herd

The sheer pleasure of horse and rider alone on a Welsh mountain

rides. I trotted him down the ride until we came to it. When he saw it he stopped as if it was the most frightful object he had ever seen in his life, but after about ten minutes' coaxing I managed to get him up to it. It took me another quarter of an hour to get him to step over it, and then again he was walked backwards and forwards over it until he was thinking nothing of it. I went on about another half mile to where there was a tree about eighteen inches across, lying on the ground. This time he had actually to take off, and this he did. Again I took him over it several times, and back over it again. He suddenly found that this was fun, and the fifth or sixth time when I turned him to pop over it again, he spun round on a sixpence and flew over. I told him how clever he was and that was enough for one day.

By the end of the fifth day he was jumping about two feet and really enjoying it. On the sixth day a friend took him out hunting and then Charlie began to understand what life was all about.

This is how you shape a horse – you encourage him. We started off making a fuss of him when he first stepped over a ditch a foot wide and six inches deep, but within six days he was finding that the reward for jumping was the jumping itself : we had shaped his desires so that he really wanted to jump and he was now loving his jumping and thinking it great fun.

The important thing when training a horse is that the primary end should be that the horse is enjoying doing what you want him to do. I realize of course that in every case a horse has to do a large amount of tedious work, but it must always end with the horse enjoying himself.

9: *Retraining Techniques: Weakening Learned Responses*

In training your horse you are not only looking for enthusiastic responses to what is to be learned, you also have to weaken the undesirable responses which have been previously learned. This is an important matter because responses that have been learned over a period in everyday life take a considerable period of time to weaken. Many of the habits that your horse has acquired are not desirable, and you will want first to weaken them and then to get rid of them altogether.

How can a learned response be weakened? One way is simply to allow the horse to forget it, by not allowing him to get into the situation that will provoke it. If, for example, a horse has got into the habit of bucking when you hit him, you can stop him by not hitting him. When he has ceased to associate being hit with bucking you can start using the stick on him again.

The second way to weaken the response is to extinguish it. Extinction, the key term here, is both the procedure used and the result of that procedure. The critical feature is that we stop reinforcement of the behaviour that we wish to extinguish, by punishing the response. For example, with dogs you can extinguish the behaviour pattern we described earlier as conditioned in response to the bells, by ceasing to reward the dog with food when the bell rings. If your dog salivates at the sound of the bell, you can ring the bell continually without feeding him, and he will cease to secrete saliva. Similarly with the horse who bucks when you hit him, to get him to forget about bucking, you can hit him every time he bucks when you take him out. You will extinguish the desire to buck simply by changing his association of ideas: whereas previously he associated bucking with your stopping hitting him, he will very quickly discover that his bucking makes you hit him and so he will cease to buck. With yet a third method of curing bucking, it is advisable to point the horse up a steep hill. This has two advantages; first this way it is much easier to stay on top, and second he will tire of going into orbit much more quickly. If, on the other hand, you point him down hill, even if you do not pass a rocket on its way to Mars, both you and the horse are likely to go base over apex at the bottom of the hill. I had a very vivid example of this a couple of years ago when Clancy, after jumping a large post and rail, put in a small buck of joie de vivre which took us both over the edge of a mini Mount Etna. When we hit the bottom we both of us bounced back up into the air, turned three somersaults and landed up to our bellies in freezing water.

The method of extinction we use with a bucking horse is to assume that, other than the buck of joie de vivre, a horse bucks to annoy you. To cure his bucking, we take him out riding to the bottom of a steep hill and we point his head up the hill. I drive my heels into his side and say 'right, go on buck, you beggar', and of course having two heels rudely, painfully and for no apparent reason belting his ribs makes him buck. Each time he lands from bucking, I drive my heels into his side again and repeat the process. He will do this four or five times, but of course by the time he has bucked half way up the hill he will find the effort of bucking quite considerable and since I'm telling him to buck, his natural bloody-mindedness makes him say 'right, I won't buck'. Two or three days of this treatment extinguishes all desire to buck. This method has the advantage that (a) we do it in a forest drive, which is comparatively narrow, so that he has to go straight up the hill, and (b) it's much easier to sit a buck going up hill than on the flat or downhill.

We use the same method to stop a horse kicking. When, for example, we get a horse that kicks when you touch its legs, I get in close to the horse's side, run my hand down his leg until he kicks. As he brings his leg forward towards me I push the leg away from me, so that when he kicks back he is quite likely to kick his other hock. Then I say 'good boy, kick—go on, kick again' and run my hand down his leg. I go on doing this until he is tired of kicking himself. But if, on the other hand, I was afraid of his kicking, and didn't want him to kick, the very fact of my obvious nervousness would tell the horse that I was frightened of him, which would give him an incentive to frighten me more, by kicking again : and since in my fear I wouldn't get tight into his side, I would probably end up in the ideal position for him to bash me through the stable wall. By using the horse's natural bloody-mindedness, which all horses with a vice have, and by telling him to do the thing that until then no one has ever wanted him to do, you extinguish his desire and his motive to kick, or to buck.

Where fear conditioning has been used, that is a horse has learned something because he has been frightened, it is much more difficult to extinguish the fear and the association, than it is where the learning has been by positive conditioning, i.e. where a horse has been rewarded for learning something. A horse that has been rewarded for learning will forget about it in approximately the same length of time that it has taken him to learn it, but where fear has been used it will take considerably longer to extinguish the fear than it did to instil it in the first place.

A typically stubborn example of fear conditioning was a horse called Kingsmoor. I'd seen him first in the autumn when we were hunting between Langport and Mutchenly. He stood out from the half dozen horses he was with, a big, rawboned, slashing bay horse of terrific quality, and I enquired about him from my next door neighbour. It seemed that he was an eight-year-old, and that he was unbreakable, untouchable, unmanageable. Anyone who was fool enough to try to catch him must be a fugitive from a lunatic asylum, and, if they did get to handle him, wouldn't live long anyway.

This was just my cup of tea, so I made sure that I bumped into the owner of the horse accidentally two or three weeks later, talked to him about this and that, and mentioned that I'd seen the horse and liked him. He quickly ordered me a series of double whiskies one after the other, extolling the virtues of the horse but failing to mention any of the vices that I already knew about. In the end, I bought him for a tenner, which was below his killing price at the time, the only condition being that I should catch him myself.

It wasn't until the middle of February that I could make arrangements to fetch him. I telephoned his owner, only to be told that I couldn't possibly get him because he was down on the far end of the moor and there was a mile and a half of water between him and the nearest road. The remainder of February was extremely wet, so it was the second week in March before it was anywhere near possible to fetch him. I hired a lorry and off we set to catch the horse. We got to the farm, paid for him, picked up the owner and drove a mile and a half to the nearest point to the horses we could reach in the truck.

The willow trees were just beginning to burst into bud, with their delicate greeny-yellow leaves like long thin hands in pale green gloves. There were great lakes of water, left from the flooding, shimmering silver in the sunlight. Here and there ash saplings were standing slim and slender to attention, as if saluting the sun.

The only way we could get to the horse was to walk along a ridge of high ground, and then to wade two hundred yards down a lane flooded well up above our wellingtons. We got about a quarter of the way when the lorry driver said he was damned if he was going any further, and the girlfriend I'd brought with me was wilting considerably, but since at that time we were very much in love she would put up with anything. Three parts of the way there, the owner suggested we turn back and leave it for another day. But as we were nearly there, we kept on. When we finally got to the field I had a nasty shock: the horse and five ponies had been marooned for a month on about half an acre of ground, and the spectacle that greeted us was of six living skeletons looking hardly able to move. We opened the gate on to the lane and proceeded to shepherd them towards it. We got them half way down the field when they broke back, galloping along the edge of the water, so back we squelched with our boots full of water and drove them down again. We did this three or four times before their general weakness overcame them and they allowed us to drive them on to the lane.

Here we were lucky because the big horse had naturally established his leadership, so when we came to the spot where the water was a couple of feet deep in the road, he just splashed through it. The five ponies decided it was too much of a good thing and refused to go any further. So without much difficulty I edged round them and, leaving the others to stop the big horse coming back, I drove the five ponies that we didn't want back into their field. We then drove our horse on down the road to where the lorry driver had backed the lorry into a narrow piece of the lane and arranged it very skilfully so that the horse couldn't get past. In about ten minutes we had walked him up into the lorry without frightening him, put up the tail board and set out for home.

When we got home I changed into dry clothes and my girl-friend borrowed some of my sister's. She was only five foot two and my sister was about five foot eleven, but by tucking bits in and rolling bits up she was able to make herself reasonably mobile, so we went to unload the horse. I opened the door at the front and got myself halfway in, to be met by a tornado of flying front feet and teeth. I came out through the trap door like a shot from a gun, counting myself lucky to have sustained nothing worse than a bleeding hand.

This was a horse who went for pure attack – unprovoked, and at the very sight of a man at close quarters. Clearly a certain amount of thought had to go into the next move. I had first to halter him, then to get him out of the lorry into the stable. So we backed the lorry halfway up the yard towards the stable, and dropped the tail board. Kingsmoor – that was what I had christened him – stood up in the corner of the lorry while we opened the gate. When we got to the second gate he made a rush for it. Quickly the lorry driver and I shut it hard. Then we started to open it again, slowly. Again he attacked us. This happened four or five times before I was able to open the gate enough for me to get to one of the partitions that divided the lorry. I got it unclipped and gave it a push in towards him. I did the same with the top part of the partition, and went in very very slowly, pushing the partition away from me all the time. When Kingsmoor next made an attack, I simply flung the partition back a bit so that I was protected by it, and put my hand round it to touch him. Since he was unable to get at me he was left with no choice but to let me handle him, or to go right backwards into the other half of the lorry. This he did, so I pushed the gate shut again.

At this point my father returned, so we had our usual blazing row about how incompetent I was, but since this was the first horse I had ever bought he eventually consented to allow me to make a fool of myself in my own way. Together he and I eventually got the two partition gates shut, which meant that we were in half the lorry and Kingsmoor was in the other half. By edging the gates forward until Kingsmoor was tight up against the top end of the lorry, and at considerable danger to ourselves, we got him eventually into the position I wanted him in, and I fetched a halter, a box and two plough reins. I stood on the box and leaned over the narrow space between the top of the lorry and the partition. Kingsmoor tried to bite me, but he couldn't get his head far enough round. I tried to ease the halter over the far side of his head, but he was having none of that and I couldn't reach, so I shifted the box and tried again. Kingsmoor could reach me here: he made a dive at me and I jammed the nose-band of the halter over his head, at the same time quickly putting my hand over and catching hold of the strap which I buckled up. His teeth had bruised my arm, but I suffered no other ill effects. The next thing was to tie the two plough reins together. I fed one end of them through the side of the gate and tied it to the cheek piece of the halter. The rest was easy. The two plough reins together made about thirty feet, and the far end was given a double twist round a post.

Now we were ready to open the tail board and the gate. Kingsmoor made one leap, jumping from the floor of the lorry into the yard, and went straight up the yard as if his life depended on it. Unfortunately for him, he was travelling at a fair pace when he came to the end of the halter rope, which jerked him round and his feet shot from under him. My father, who was closer than I was, made a dash and was sitting on his head before he had a chance to get up. We undid the plough rope from the post and ran it through the ring in the stable where we planned to put him, and let him get to his feet. Playing him rather like a salmon on the end of a line, we slowly got him nearer and nearer to the stable as he dashed from one end of the rope to the other. When at last we got him into the stable, we put up two slip rails so that he couldn't hang back too far or get out, and left him with a very large feed and a large amount of hay and we all went for tea, wondering what the hell we were going to do in the morning when it came to feeding him again.

What we did when we tied him up in the evening, was to run his rope through the ring on the manger, back to the side of the stable. The following morning, when it came to feeding, I untied the rope and eased it back so that he would swing round. Immediately, he made a lunge for me with his teeth. I jammed the feed bucket over his nose so that he had a mouthful of his breakfast instead of a mouthful of me. I kept the bucket there so that he couldn't bite me, and he quickly got the idea and started eating. I took it up to the manger and tied him up very short again, so that he couldn't bite me, and then slowly and quietly, while he was eating his breakfast I stroked and teased the worst of the tangles out of his coat.

After a while he relaxed a bit, and by the time an hour had passed had been convinced that fear and anger were not the only appropriate reactions to human beings.

During the night I had been thinking about Kingsmoor's aggression, and I had concluded that he was attacking people not simply out of anger, but because anger was the best form of defence against fear, and I thought that if I could eliminate the original fear I would also eliminate the anger.

This proved to be the case. When I went to him after having my breakfast, he was already less afraid of me, and although he made a couple of kicks in my direction, he didn't attack me at all. From that morning on, other than snapping at me when I was grooming his tummy or doing something that irritated him, he never attacked with his teeth and front feet again.

I took an old saddle with me which I eased on to his back and girthed up by degrees, little by little over half an hour, until it was firmly placed. I would tighten the girth one hole, make a fuss of him, and so on until I'd got the saddle on properly. Then, using the leather halter as part of the bridle, I got an old vulcanite snaffle we had, and tied it to the cheek pieces of the halter, putting the bit in his mouth. With a halter rope which I made into a rein, I now had the horse ready to ride. My father got back for dinner at about half past twelve, and I asked him to give me a hand up on to the horse, which I did in the stable, both the boss and myself keeping well out of range of his hind legs. I'd put a feed in front of him, and funnily enough when I got on him, he barely took any notice at all, so I got off and on several times, and he stood like an old horse.

We went and had lunch and when we came back I got on to Kingsmoor again and my father untied him, taking the two plough lines and knotting them round a post, then slipping one through the bit to pull Kingsmoor round, very very slowly. He came round and took a dive through the stable door, taking the skin off my knee, nearly decapitating me and tearing my coat on the top of the stable door as he went. The idea had been that my father should lead the horse, but the sudden tug of twelve hundredweight on the ploughline caused him to let go, and I was on my own.

Kingsmoor made a dash down the yard, completely ignoring my efforts to persuade him that it might be a good idea to steady down, out through the front gate and down the road towards the river. But after about five hundred yards his weakness caused him to slow a little, and before we reached the river, half a mile away, he was back to a trot, and several hundred yards further on he steadied to a walk. I let him walk on slowly, picking at the grass as he went, making a fuss of him and talking to him. After about a mile I turned round and we meandered home slowly, meeting the boss about halfway home. He had followed me in the car – evidently calculating that the car would be handy to pick up my body and take it straight to the morgue.

We got home and I rode Kingsmoor to the stable and slipped off. My father had thoughtfully put a good feed in for him, and without any difficulty at all I tied him up, took the saddle off and proceeded to rub the worst of the sweat off his soaking coat. As I moved towards his hind legs he lashed out at me, but except that he hurt himself a little when his leg hit the wall, no damage was done. Being a clever and thinking horse, he made only two tentative kicks, hitting the wall each time and not touching me, so he settled down to the serious business of eating his dinner.

I fed him at six and again at ten. The following morning, when I went in with his feed he whickered with welcome. I was under no illusion that he was welcoming me – he was merely greeting his breakfast. But over the next six or eight weeks, he gradually stopped kicking altogether. After the first week my father was feeding and handling him as well as me, and soon my sister was handling him too. Meanwhile of course he was in, and being fed well, so as he got bigger and stronger he had a few tries at bucking me off. But he wasn't too serious about it, and it was clear that once the fear syndrome had been extinguished his anger at being approached by human beings had disappeared with it, and so had his desire to misbehave. The technique we had used to extinguish the fear was to substitute, i.e. to replace it with another feeling, that of pleasure. We had made him pleased to see a human being, by making use of his desire for food. Since the appearance of the human being was always accompanied by food, he was pairing the pleasurable anticipation of eating with my appearance. This association was closely followed by others – the pairing of my appearance with the excitement of exercising, jumping, galloping and seeing new things – so that in two months he was whickering when I went into the stable whether I had food with me or not.

We had extinguished the fear and had substituted pleasure. But it is always very difficult to eliminate fear altogether, and Kingsmoor was always just that little bit frightened of strangers, and even when he left us about four months later, if a stranger went into his box, he would still hunch himself up into a corner and turn his backside towards them. On the other hand if they stood for a minute or two and talked to him quietly, he would soon relax and lengthen himself and turn his head towards them.

He went on from us to make an outstanding hunter. The man who bought him from us kept him until he died at the age of twenty-two.

It was only after he had left us that we learned his earlier history. He had been born in 1941 out of a hunter mare by a thoroughbred stallion. In 1945 someone had tried to break him, got bucked off and given him a thrashing, got kicked and given him another thrashing for that. After a week of that treatment he had gone back to his owner as unbreakable and had then been sent to someone else. By the time he got to us four people had attempted to break him – one had ended up with a broken leg – and Kingsmoor had firmly associated man with ill-treatment and pain. Yet once that fear of man had been eliminated, and once I'd managed to associate his work with pleasure, because I got him hunting and jumping as quickly as possible, his behaviour pattern changed completely. When the man I sold him to discovered his history, he found it hard to believe, and insisted for a very long time that his informant had got his horse confused with another one.

So Kingsmoor's case illustrates very dramatically both how easy it is, with ignorance, to instil fear into a horse and how difficult it is to eradicate it. Fear probably takes three or four times as long to extinguish as does any pleasurable form of learning.

Where avoidance conditioning has been established – by

which we mean a horse has learned a way of successfully avoiding a task (he avoids jumping a fence by refusing or running out) – this too is very resistant to memory extinction. In some animals it may not be extinguished after a thousand trials, if fear conditioning has been used to establish the avoidance. This was found in those experiments with dogs already described where they were required to jump over fences when a buzzer sounded. As you may remember, the dog was trained to jump when a buzzer sounded, followed by an electric shock. The dogs continued to jump the barrier even when no electric shock was administered in over a thousand trials. It turned out that the only way to decondition the dog, i.e. make him stop jumping the fence at the sound of the buzzer, was by fatigue : i.e. only when the experiment was carried on for such a time that the dog became too physically tired to jump the fence at all, did he discover that the sounding of the buzzer was not followed by an electric shock. The following day he showed no response to the buzzer.

This technique is particularly relevant to dealing with horses that shy. If you have a horse that is in the habit of shying at certain objects or at certain places, you cure him, with a great deal of patience, by coaxing him gradually to approach the object. Or you can ride him past the object when he is tired; and the horse discovers that there is after all nothing to fear.

There are horses however who shy not out of fear, but simply in order to annoy, and in this case the best cure is to erect a large number of alarming objects (plastic bags, rattling tins, etc.), then to ride or lead the horse backwards and forwards past them, using punishment as negative motivation, so that he ceases to shy because he is afraid to do so. But I must emphasize that this method is only to be used where the horse clearly uses an avoidance technique as an irritant or out of bloody-mindedness.

Use of fatigue to weaken an established conditioning is the basis of a number of methods of breaking unbreakable horses. In this country for instance the lunging method is used. In this method the horse is deprived of water for three days first, then it is lunged for half an hour to forty minutes. A horse that is 'unridable' because he bucks or rears, for instance, will be so exhausted by this treatment that he will indeed allow the monster who is breaking him, to ride him. But anybody who uses this method is, to me anyway, a monster, and I use the term 'breaking' on purpose, too.

The Irish method of ringing is similar in principle, and cruelty. Here someone takes the horse into a very boggy field and drives it round until it is so tired that it can barely move. Then the man gets on his back and rides him. And the Australians tie the horse up in the sun for twenty-four hours: they too mount it when it is in the last stages of exhaustion.

In each case the horse had been brought to the last stages of exhaustion by fatigue or thirst, and his spirit is then completely broken. Any desire to buck or fight or rear is completely extinguished.

Another way of extinguishing a response is by suppression; this is really passive avoidance learning that weakens a previously conditioned response. Suppose you had a horse that came to you and took food out of your pocket. He would continue to do so as long as there was food in your pocket. You could of course stop him by ceasing to put food in your pocket, so that he eventually gave up looking. But you could also do it by suppressing him, that is by slapping him on the nose every time he went near your pocket. Either way you would be able to cure the habit, but the thing that complicates extinction and suppression of response is the tendency of such response to recover spontaneously. The habit may recur so whilst you may for instance have cured a horse from refusing his fences by suppressing the response, he may start refusing again, if he is weakly ridden, four or even five years later.

Pavlov noticed that a day or so after a series of extinction trials on the dogs conditioned to salivate at the sound of a bell, the salivary responses bounced back even stronger than they had been at the end of the original experiments. He named this phenomenon 'spontaneous recovery'. It is a kind of forgetting in reverse, a tendency to forget that extinction training has occurred. Spontaneous recovery, the slowness of the extinction process and the ineffectiveness of some forms of punishment, all combine to make extinction training a laborious process.

We find spontaneous recovery in horses that buck. After we have taken the horse up what we call our bucking slope four or five times, he will cease to buck, but then after three or four weeks he may start to buck again. Certainly a horse that has once discovered that he can get rid of his rider and avoid work by bucking will, if he goes to a weak rider, immediately start to buck again. Many vices have this tendency to reappear when the horse passes into the hands of a weak rider.

Another factor retarding the elimination of responses is the effect of partial reinforcement. For example, if you are trying to stop a horse taking something out of your pocket, in theory you should repel the horse every time he does so. But in actual fact on some days you will be far more tolerant with the horse than you will be on others.

This inconsistency tends to make the curing of vices and habits much more difficult. Punishment of misbehaviour must be consistent for it to be effective.

It is in fact neither possible nor desirable to reward a horse with praise or titbits *every* time he does the correct thing; or to punish the horse every time he does the wrong thing. Inevitably you will be using some form of partial, or irregular, reinforcement. This can either be random, that is you praise him sometimes when he does the correct thing and punish him sometimes when he does the wrong thing; or it can be what is called interval reinforcement, which means you praise him after every fourth or fifth correct action, perhaps, but at definite intervals rather than random ones. This method is probably more effective than regular reinforcement, at the later stages of training.

Imagine a rider who, riding along, goes kick, kick, kick, kick and then tap, tap, tap with his whip, all the time the horse is walking or trotting. The horse becomes so accustomed to the accompaniment of the drum of the heels and the tap of the whip that he learns to take no notice of either. This regular reinforcement has been completely nullified by constant use. Whereas one sharp cut from the stick or an occasional well driven thump with the heels will have a far greater effect, as the horse will never be absolutely certain when he is going to be punished for being lazy.

Equally, if after each time a horse has jumped a fence you stopped and gave him titbits and made a fuss of him, apart from the fact that you would never win a jumping competition because you would be eliminated for time, your horse would come to expect praise and reward as a matter of course.

What is more, if your horse gets abundant praise and reward each time he does the smallest thing right, you will have nothing more to give him when he makes an outstanding effort. In the same way, if you beat him to within an inch of his life for minor infringements, it will be impossible to give him adequate punishment after a major crime. From this it can be seen that constant praise or punishment soon loses its value; and both partial and graduated reinforcement are essential in training a horse.

A good example of how this works was my training of Royalty, the chestnut mare that I use to hunt hounds. She loves her work : her love of the hounds and pride in being the huntsman's horse are constant reinforcements for her. As the focus of attention at the meet, she swaggers and cavorts as she leads the hounds to the first draw, then she immediately settles down to work, even though she is still a very green hunter. She will stand absolutely still when necessary, and as soon as hounds find, she is watching and listening to see where they are going. Very often she will see the fox before I do. This is all a constant reinforcement for her. On top of that, when she negotiates a particularly large obstacle I pat her neck and tell her she is a good girl, and if she does something wrong or rather stupid I may or may not curse her. Now, this is very mild cursing and the praise too will be mild, so that when she jumps a particularly big obstacle or negotiates a very difficult and boggy place, I can give her extra praise, and she knows she has done really well. And the same principle applies to the punishment, I increase the punishment according to the crime.

10: *Changing Ingrained Habits*

The elimination of bad habits is a major preoccupation among horsemen, simply because most of us are bad riders at times, and thus teaching our horses bad habits. We can, as I described in the last chapter, try to make the horse forget his bad habits. But another way is to replace an old habit with a new one, by making the horse want to do the new thing very much. Replacement with a new habit makes it much easier to eradicate a previous pattern of behaviour. If, for example, a horse's desire to buck can be changed to a desire to jump, and when he jumps he is rewarded, he will cease to want to buck – or that is what you hope anyway.

Suppose you have a horse who has been refusing to jump, you can re-site the jumps so that he is jumping towards home and he has to cross the fences to get there. Then, when you are exercising him, before taking him home you jump the fences and then he goes home to dinner. Not only are you praising him for jumping, you are changing his reluctance to jump to a desire to jump, since jumping the fences will be associated with going home. A horse that has previously refused to jump will often learn to jump very quickly this way. (Of course, here as in any lesson in jumping, the fences must be small.)

If on the other hand the behaviour to be changed is a strongly ingrained habit – ingrained because it has been well rewarded – the habit will be very difficult to eliminate either with punishment or with praise. This was obviously so in the case of Watch, who I bought in Llanybyther in February 1976 with the idea of point to pointing him. I hacked him the first couple of days, just walking and trotting to get to know him. On the third day I decided to give him a canter along the side of the forest. After about four strides he lifted his head sharply, bashing me in the face and practically knocking my teeth down

465

my throat. Using this method he wrenched the reins out *of* my hands and carted me well and truly, only stopping three miles further on, going up a very steep hill. The second time I tried to canter him, he got away from me using the same method, and I only stopped him galloping over the edge of a quarry by changing his balance and turning him base over apex into some trees. He bolted with me regularly for about two months.

This was a typical instance of insufficient negative reinforcement: he disregarded the use of the bit because the reward – galloping flat out, which he enjoyed doing – more than compensated for any pain in his mouth of iron. I cured him in two ways, first by allowing him to gallop on a loose rein at preselected places, and then by galloping him over a fixed timber one-day event course. The first couple of times we did this we went head over heels because we were taking fences too fast, so he learned to steady and place himself at his fences naturally. It was only a short step from here to my pulling the reins and saying 'whoa' as we approached each fence, since the reward for steadying when told to do so was greater enjoyment for Watch. By using this method, he responded at all times.

The treatment, before I had a complete cure, took over a year, but I eventually was able to race him with reasonable success.

Another horse who acquired an annoying habit was my wife's cob Rostellan who, by watching another horse, learned to open his stable door. This was quite an amusing trick; when he learned to open the gate out of the yard and then the gate into the house and garden, it was still quite an amusing trick. So we told him how clever he was in opening the stable door, and when he came to the front door of the house, after opening the stable door, yard gate and front gate, he was given titbits and allowed to wander around and pick at the grass on the lawn. So opening the gates became a well reinforced habit with him. But when he started not only trampling over the lawn but eating the flowers and lettuces, we decided to stop him.

This was extremely difficult, because even if we hunted him

out of the garden whenever we saw him, he was still getting rewarded, because he was getting a certain amount of the sweeter grass around the house anyway, and a certain amount of freedom before we saw him. Even though he was being punished, the habit became extremely difficult to eradicate.

Similarly, when a horse bucks and gets its rider off, it achieves not only its goal but also a certain amount of freedom, which is an additional reward. Every time it bucks its rider off the habit of bucking is reinforced – the horse achieves its goal and gets rewarded. So the habit is very hard to cure indeed. Another problem with curing a habit is that any small rewards and punishment regularly administered come to be taken for granted, so the rewards don't seem as attractive or the punishments so terrible as when they were first given. This is the phenomenon of adaptation to reinforcement, a long phrase which means quite simply that the horse gets used to constant punishment or constant reward, and ceases to take any notice.

A typical example of a horse becoming accustomed to insufficient punishment was Donna. Whilst she was an extremely good pony, being both quiet and of extremely high ability, she became sluggish and bored, mainly because she had been ridden by poor riders. They had used their whips as tickling sticks, going tap, tap, tap with them, and ridden her as if they were rowing a boat with their feet, with their heels constantly digging Donna's ribs. This had to stop. First I changed her feed to racehorse nuts, and increased her concentrates slightly. Second, after a week's increased feeding, I rode her myself for three or four days. The increased feeding had made her a little more lively and as I left the yard, I caught her two with my racing whip, one on either side of her flank.

This immediately changed a tortoise into a torpedo. I steadied her back to a walk in ten or fifteen yards and Donna danced down the road, a thing she had never done before. The laburnum trees along the hedges of our farm were just coming into bloom and when we got to the far side of the valley I turned to look at the breathtaking sight of rows and rows of pale green branches dripping with gold.

Unfortunately, Donna was impatient, so I turned to go on. Donna by now had got the idea: as soon as I slackened the reins she swung up the hill in a spanking trot. At the top, there were posts and rails leading into the forest. I had intended going past them, but Donna, determined to make the most of her new found youth and enjoyment, swung into it before I could stop her and flew over them like a bird. She cantered up the ride for about twenty yards, where we stopped to watch the rest of the party doing their best to follow us.

For the rest of the two-hour ride, Donna seized on every possible obstacle – no matter how difficult or awkward – to alleviate her excitement, and the rest of the riders had no peace. And she frightened the living daylights out of me on one occasion, by flying a tree trunk on the verge of the forestry road, which lay twenty feet below us. She flew the jump, landed on the verge, got her hocks under her and slid down the bank rather like a small boy on a toboggan.

I rode her for two more days, catching her a couple of hard ones each time she went to sleep. By this time, her nature had changed so completely that I put a very good fourteen-year-old girl who was staying with us on her, gave them a week's schooling, then entered them for a novice hunter trial, which they won with ease.

The interesting thing about this was that in spite of this experience Donna retained her previous learning, and whenever she was given a weak rider she went back to her sleepy normal self.

So far we have been dealing with responses learned by reward or punishment. Now let us look at the effect of punishment on unlearned consummatory responses. By consummatory responses we mean responses that satisfy a primary need – for food, water, or sexual activity, so the response itself is the reward. The question is, how does punishment affect this kind of response? You might think that a consummatory response, being innate, would be hard to change.

However, experiments have shown that a rat receiving a shock at its food tray quickly learns to avoid the tray, no matter how hungry it is. It seems that it will starve itself to death rather than venture back to the food to see if the shock is still there. The reason for this lies in the principle of a conditioning stimulus : if the reward or punishment and the response are close enough together in time, learning is very fast even if the response being changed is an innate one. Even more dramatic results are seen when punishment for one consummatory response is combined with rewarding another.

An experiment conducted by Solomen in 1964 illustrates this. He found that puppies who were punished when they ate meat, but allowed to eat pellets without punishment, learnt very quickly to eat only pellets and to shun meat. The learned aversion proved to be so strong that the puppies were prepared to starve to death rather than eat meat.

This principle is important in dealing with horses, because we know that certain breeds of horses do certain things naturally, but we do not necessarily appreciate how easily this ability can be affected by conditioning. A race horse for instance will race naturally; because he is bred to race. He is bred not only for his ability to race, but also for his desire to race. However, if he is punished for racing – for instance he has a very hard, tight finish and the jockey carves him up to win the race – that horse may well cease to race, at least for a while, until the desire to race has been reinforced again by another experience. This theory of reinforcement is in fact important for innate abilities and desires just as it is for learned behaviour.

Let us take a thoroughbred, as an example. He has been bred to race and to gallop, and above all he needs excitement and movement. Yet if you take even a very highly strung thoroughbred and put him into a riding string, doing dull repetitive work, he will go off his food, lose condition and pine. There are a large number of thoroughbreds like this to be seen in riding schools. But on the other hand if you deprive a thoroughbred of galloping but at the same time replace this with something else, such as show jumping or dressage work, his desire to tear away flat-out may be changed to a desire to excel in competition, channelling ability, his liveliness and excitability in a completely different direction.

The problem of changing innate behaviour in horses reminds me of an old friend, Bryn Strap, so called because his christian name was Bryn, and his constant truancy from school led him to be beaten by his headmaster with great regularity: whenever Bryn failed to give a correct answer the headmaster would simply say 'Bryn, strap!' and try to administer some knowledge through his posterior. When I met him he was a tall, slim man of forty, immaculately shaved and dressed – which was all the more remarkable because he lived in a converted cow stall with a fire in the corner, the smoke from which escaped through a hole in the roof. The furniture consisted of a rickety table, two armchairs on the verge of collapse, a pile of blankets in the corner and no washing facilities nearer than the stream which ran below the house.

His manners were impeccable, his conversation extensive and he was as straight as a very bent corkscrew. He became a very great friend of mine, mainly because he could not only talk about any subject under the sun, but he was also an orator to make Lloyd George and Aneurin Bevan seem tongue-tied. This talent, combined with an ability to lie so that not only his listener but also he himself believed implicitly in what he was saying, would no doubt have taken him far, had he had a mind for public life.

As it was, he managed to sell me an orphaned two-year-old who made a coathanger look obese. After having her home and feeding her for a year she became a very nice little mare, about fourteen-two. The only thing you could not get her to do was to eat out of a bucket. If you emptied the feed on the floor she would lick up every morsel with great gusto; but put the feed into a bucket and she would die before she ate it. Sometime later I discovered the reason for this. She had been scavenging the local rubbish dump, trying to survive the winter before we bought her, when she had got an old galvanized bucket jammed over her nose. This had remained jammed like this for a matter of four or five days, until someone had managed to catch her and take it off. This is a clear example of how consummatory behaviour can be extinguished.

Rostellan provides another illustration. Since he is a Welsh cob, his main gait is a very fast and rather high-actioned trot, but over the course of time we have changed his behaviour fundamentally. Not only does he enjoy both cantering and galloping, his motive to excel, the great pleasure he gets from competition, and his natural asset of mighty hindquarters have actually combined to make him into an extremely good jumper.

An extremely important point to be remembered with horses is that if a horse has a genetic ability to do a certain thing, it is essential that such ability can be harnessed to overcome physical deficiencies. And some abilities, if they do not suit your purpose, can also be channelled in a new direction : a horse's desire to buck can be channelled into a desire to jump, for instance. In fact it is often said that if a horse bucks he will make a good jumper, because the muscles used for bucking and jumping are the same, and the mental approach which makes him wish to dominate his rider is similar to the will to win.

If you take a horse that naturally dominates the herd and try to make him go at the back of a bunch of horses he may give you a very uncomfortable ride. But on the other hand this dominance and competitive ability can be channelled to make him into a very good horse in competition. Or it can be converted into a sense of responsibility, if he is being ridden by the person who is in charge of a string of horses, because he will then enjoy the position of authority that his rider gives him.

Chance, for instance, when we used to have people on our farm on riding holidays, always had to be twenty or thirty yards in front of the other horses. But if I rode him when I was taking a party out he was quite happy to be at the back of the field supervising the weak riders and the horses that were misbehaving. His mental dominance was being made use of.

My experience with Dart shows how a horse's natural ability can be combined with his mental desires to overcome physical deficiencies. He again was a registered Welsh cob so not a natural jumper. But he had not only Rostellan's joy in competition and need to excel, he also had an incredible desire to win. I used him almost entirely for hunter trials and cross-country events. After his second or third competition, he was never beaten. His ability to beat thoroughbreds across country on time was almost unbelievable. First his desire to jump meant that there was never any risk of him running out or refusing; and second his great ability meant that he went into every fence flat out, and where it was necessary to take the next fence at an angle, he could twist himself in midair so that when he landed he was in the correct position to take the next fence. I had great empathy with him, so that most of the time I rode with a loose rein, steering him using telepathy combined with a slight change of balance. I only ever rode him once carrying a stick, and that was in a schooling session. He had developed the habit of napping slightly towards home, when doing a flying change to the off side. It was only a very slight hesitation, but wishing to cure him of the habit before it had developed, I decided to school him carrying a whip in my left hand and tapping his shoulder at the first sign of hesitation. This I did once successfully. On the second occasion I touched him once with the stick on his shoulder, and got a hair-raising response. Dart changed without warning to the off side suddenly putting us in front of a seven-foot fence consisting of a three-foot-six bank with three-foot-six of pig wire and barbed wire on top. Dart went at it like a torpedo and attempted to fly the whole lot, which he nearly managed, but he just caught his knees on the barbed wire, and turned a somersault throwing me fifty yards into the next field. Fortunately very little damage was done – Dart scratched his knees slightly and I excavated a large hole in the ground. I never carried a stick on him again. Nevertheless, at the end of each hunter trial or cross-country competition, Dart would end up in a state of complete exhaustion.

Another way of showing how a horse's natural ability can be channelled to a new purpose would be to examine a traditional method of teaching a young horse to work in harness. The colt would be placed between two old horses, into a set of drags. When the carter said 'hold fast', the two old horses went forward, pulling the colt with them. In a very short time the colt would be responding to the carter's command at the same time as the older horses did. Because he was between two old horses he was unable to go faster than they did, and soon he was imitating his seniors, responding to commands and pulling as well as he was able to. But imitation is not the whole story. The colt was having his desire to expend his youthful energy and power satisfied, and at the same time channelled into a rewarding task. His life was made more interesting by learning from his elders and the carter. The interest and fuss made of him by the carter also satisfied a desire, and in due course created a previously non-existent motive to please.

In nearly all these examples, we have been dealing in one way or another with the horse's tendency to associate experiences, or feelings, and to learn from the association. The horse will associate certain places, certain clothes you wear and certain stable preparations with appropriate forms of activity. If you plait your horse up the night before hunting, he will associate being plaited up with hunting; if you always jump in the same place, he will associate that place with jumping.

Weeping Roger associated racing so strongly with fatigue that he would slop around the paddock at a racecourse before a race, looking as if he were in the last stages of exhaustion. He would even wander down to the start in a tottering, lethargic way. But once he got warmed up racing, it was a different story. He always finished like a bullet, and when he won he would show his triumph by dancing and bucking back to the paddock.

We measure a horse's intelligence by his ability to learn. But at times one cannot always rely on the speed at which he learns as a direct measure of intelligence, because he may be using all his ingenuity to avoid learning something. So one has to set up a structured test. One such test is based on random feeding times. Instead of feeding the horse at regular times, say at eight, one, six and ten, you divide his feeds so that you are feeding at odd times and odd intervals. You do this so that he isn't associating a particular time of day with being fed. Then you position his feed so that you can get to it without him seeing you. Whilst you are out of sight you give a signal, such as a blast from a whistle, and repeat this each time you feed him. If, after the fourth or fifth blast of the whistle, the horse associates being fed with the whistle, and shows that he expects food, after a day or two you change the signal – instead of blowing a whistle you use a bell. This time, by the second or third signal a clever horse should associate the change to the ring of the bell with getting his food. Provided the horse is a normal feeder, you can assess its intelligence by this method quite quickly.

On the first test a response after four blasts shows intelligence, five is normal and six is slow. In the second test, if he is associating the bell with food at the second signal he's intelligent, at the third signal he is of average intelligence and at the fourth signal he is of low intelligence.

A number of simple tests like this can be evolved to test a horse's intelligence and quickness to learn. But be careful that you adjust your standards according to the test you use. In the feeding tests, a response to the fifth signal on the first test would be normal. But if instead the test were based on hunting with hunting clothes, and you only hunted the horse once a week, the association would take a bit longer – seven or eight times perhaps. It is very important to remember that the motivation, response and reward should be very close together. In the feeding experiment, the whistle should be followed by the response, which should be immediately followed by the food, in that order.

It is important to assess your horse's intelligence accurately, so that you can adjust your teaching to his learning speed. If you teach a horse too quickly, you will confuse him, and thus make him awkward and bloody-minded. If on the other hand your teaching falls behind his learning ability, he will put his intelligence to other uses, such as learning avoidance techniques and making his work more interesting by devising methods of annoying you. The art is in pairing his intelligence with your teaching, so that his interest is centred entirely upon his work.

This may be monitored by observing his enjoyment and desire to excel. It should be remembered of course that a horse is not born with instant intelligence. Intelligence is something that develops : the yearling will be more intelligent than the foal, the two-year-old more intelligent than the yearling, and so on. Maximum intelligence is not reached until the horse is seven, eight or nine years old. The drawback here, of course, is that by the time the horse is between seven and nine, any bad habits that he has learned will be very difficult to erase, (a) because the habit will be ingrained; (b) because the horse will be using its intelligence to avoid relearning; and (c) since he is at his maximum strength his fighting ability will be at its highest.

So an important factor to take into account when teaching a horse, is the previous learning that he brings with him to the lesson. A horse, once he has been through the initial training period, never learns anything from scratch. His previous training and learning and that which he has acquired from other horses is built on. This effect is called the transfer of learning, and can either be a help or a hindrance. Where learning is detrimental it is called negative transfer.

We have carried out a large number of trials and experiments to evolve a set of rules that govern positive and negative transfer, and found that these depend on the similarity between the stimuli and responses present in previous training, and those involved in the current learning situation. Where the stimuli are dissimilar but the responses are identical, the direction of the transfer will be positive, but where the stimuli are identical and the responses dissimilar, the direction of the transfer will be negative. Where the stimuli are similar and the responses identical, you will get a very strong direction of transfer, and when the stimuli are identical and the responses similar you will get a less strong direction of transfer.

Thus, positive transfer occurs when a horse learns to make a similar response to different stimuli. Suppose you taught your horse to jump a fence to gain a reward. Then suppose you used your heels and a stick to drive him over a similar fence, that is you made him jump a fence to avoid punishment. Here you have two different stimuli, one reward and the other punishment, but the response required is the same in each case : to jump a fence. The horse will make use of his previous learning – to jump a fence for reward – in order to jump a fence and avoid punishment.

Negative transfer takes place when the horse learns to make dissimilar or opposite responses to similar stimuli. Suppose you have trained your horse to respond to your legs, say pressing him with your right leg to make him turn to the left. At a later date, when you are teaching him to do a half or a full pass, you will press him with your right leg to bring his quarters in so that his head is pointing to the right. Here you have an example of exactly the same stimulus being used as part of the signal to get the horse to do a directly opposite movement. In the first of these you are using your right leg to bring his head and forehind to the left, which means his hindquarters, to maintain balance, swing slightly to the right. In the second of these, using your left knee to keep his forehind straight, you are using your right leg to make him turn his hindquarters slightly to the right, to move the horse sideways at right angles to the direction he was going. The success of this negative transfer will obviously depend on the horse's understanding of the whole context within which he is working.

Where the response similarity is identical, the nearness of the new stimulus to the old determines the amount of transfer between the two. Thus in the feeding test we did for intelligence, where the first stimulus was the whistle, when you change that stimulus to another signal, the nearer your second signal is to the first, the quicker will be the response to the stimulus and therefore the quicker the learning.

Finally, where a similar but not identical response is required, positive transfer, i.e. a helpful transfer, will depend on the stimulus being as nearly identical as possible. Thus if you have been jumping rustic timber fences it will be comparatively easy to teach him to jump colour jumps, if the same aids are used. On the other hand when you get to a more advanced stage of show jumping, and precise pacing is required – which means that you are checking him instead of letting him jump the fences at the speed and in the way he enjoys – your stimuli differ, therefore your learning is much slower.

For the same reason it is easy to teach a horse to go from a trot to a canter, if the same aids are used as you used to teach him to go from a walk to a trot. If on the other hand you use completely different aids, it will be more difficult. For example, when you are teaching a horse to go from a walk to a trot, you may simply squeeze him with your legs each time his school-master (that is, the horse you are using to teach him by example) goes from a walk to a trot. But if then it becomes necessary to teach him to go from a trot to a canter when the school-master is not there, each time you squeeze him hard he bucks, it will be necessary to teach him to respond to your voice instead. You try to get him to canter when you click your tongue, since you don't want a battle with him. By clicking your tongue each time he goes into a canter naturally, he will learn to canter when you click your tongue. It will take some time, however. This is an example of teaching a horse to do the same thing (change pace) using dissimilar stimuli. But it is always quicker and easier to teach something new if you can make use of something the horse has learned already.

11: *Developing Your Horse's Memory: Spaced and Massed Practice*

There are basically two different methods of training a horse, though most people combine the two, in one way or another. One is to do your training over a very long period, and this is called spaced practice. Spaced practice in its extreme form is illustrated by the person who will spend months teaching a horse to accept the bit before mounting it.

The other method is to cram a great deal of teaching into a very short period and this is called massed practice. In its extreme form, this might mean taking an unschooled horse out before he is going to a dressage test and cramming all the necessary training into a four- or five-hour period.

Both have their advantages and disadvantages. Mass practice capitalizes on motivating the trainer, who knows he has a one-day event the following day. And it also has the great advantage that the horse will remember its lessons fresh – the curve of forgetting will be slight, between training and event.

On the other hand, since the horse has learned an awful lot in a very short time, that knowledge is very thinly implanted and will be quickly forgotten in the long term. Spaced practice has the undoubted advantage that the learning will be retained better.

There is an exception to this rule. Over a period of time, massed practice will have an advantage over spaced practice only when the thing being taught is similar to something the horse has already learnt. So it is much better to teach a horse to jump a number of jumps, one after the other, than to have him jumping one jump over and over again, until he jumps that one perfectly, before he is taken on to another, which would be the method in spaced practice training. Massed practice in this case would have the advantage because the knowledge he had

478

learned when jumping the first fence would help him jump the others.

For most forms of training, however, a steady and meaningful programme is far better than trying to teach a horse too much at one time.

Another question of strategy in training a horse is whether to use whole or part learning: whether to teach the whole of the outline of a piece of work in one go, or whether to split it up into smaller parts. With whole learning, the horse sees the complete picture and then you perfect the details. In part learning you perfect each detail, so reaching the same end product. Your decision here will depend on whether or not what you are trying to teach a horse follows on from previous training, and on how large and complicated the task is. You can then teach the whole of a relatively straightforward task, especially if parts of it are already familiar. But if the thing you are trying to teach the horse is complicated, long and unfamiliar, then it must be split up into smaller parts.

We did an experiment in whole learning on Chico, a three-year-old grey thoroughbred stallion, of 16 hands. He had been backed for five minutes as a demonstration of gentling in July, but handled no more until at the end of October when I got on his back and rode him for twenty yards, mainly to ensure that there were no great problems. The following day I saddled him and got on him, and rode him a mile to the meet, only to find that the hunt was taking place elsewhere, so though Chico had a brief sight of hounds, which proved of great interest to him, my wife and I decided to go home and Chico had no hunting that day. I got on him next a fortnight later when hounds were meeting nearby, and followed for an hour or so, steadily walking and trotting. A month later he was ridden again. We had a mile's hack to the meet and followed as close to hounds as we could get, again for an hour. There was a good meet three weeks after this, and we arrived just after hounds had found. Fortunately they swung our way and we could follow them closely for about ten minutes to a quarter of an hour. They then crossed a very deep gorge where we couldn't follow, but we caught up with them and the rest of the field a quarter of an hour later. We had to follow a line of heavy iron gates which, like the fences they were in, were unjumpable. Chico was going so well now that I was able to gallop him past the field, jump off, open gates and let the field through, remount him and gallop on to the next gate, repeating the process half a dozen times. I ended the day following Rostellan over two two-foot banks.

A month later when we took him out for the fifth and final time, we were in a piece of forestry land where we had twenty or thirty schooling fences. Fortunately, hounds found at the far end of the jumps and after about half an hour, swung back along the line of the fences. I have a habit of getting away by myself with hounds and Chico and I were by ourselves, so I cantered him up to the first fence. He tried to stop, but he was going too fast, so he did the only thing he could think of, which was to arch his back and buck. We landed safely on the other side, with Chico now reaching for his bit to catch up with the hounds.

The next fence had a hole knocked in it, so he took an extra large stride and flew it like a hurdle. He was beginning to find this new game fun, and jumped the next eight fences with improving style and ability, the last being a three-foot high tree trunk which we'd turned into a schooling steeplechase fence by packing brush against it. Twenty yards off he measured the fence, shortened his stride, accelerating in the last couple of strides and took it in a manner that would have done Red Rum credit. Since he was by now tiring, I called it a day and we went home.

From this it can be seen that, using the whole learning method, I had in five lessons taught Chico to stop, turn, gallop past other horses, allow me to jump off and on him at will and jump up to three foot.

As an interesting footnote to this experiment, I then started working him every day. The first day he went well; the second he went sluggishly, the third he went like a pig and the fourth day he spent in trying to buck me off. It took a fortnight's steady work to get him back to the excellence he had shown out hunting. This is a fine illustration of how, when a horse can see that what he is doing leads to his own enjoyment he learns quickly, but when the enjoyment ceases, and he is, as far as he is concerned, carrying out pointless work, his whole motivation is changed and his learning ability is severely retarded.

An example of part learning, on the other hand, would be a strategy used to get a horse to the stage where he is capable of jumping a complicated cross-country course. You start by teaching him to jump a series of small fences. Then you teach him to jump bigger and more complicated fences, and so on. In this case you split his learning into several parts, first teaching him to jump a series of obstacles, then teaching him to jump three-foot-nine with five-foot spreads, finally teaching him to jump a series of obstacles in awkward places *and* at awkward angles. (These obstacles are higher and wider than he would meet in competition and should be jumped faster than he would in competition, so that his competition work is infinitely easier than anything he has done at home. This is most important.)

Any piece of complicated learning should be split into small but related parts, each part following and building on the previous one. For example, when teaching a dressage test you first teach him to walk and stop, then you teach him to walk in a circle, then you teach him the transition from a walk to a trot, and so on. This will be done in two- or three-minute spells during his general exercise. Only when he is doing each of these things separately, completely correctly, should you take him into a dressage arena and link them together to make the whole. In my opinion it is only after the horse has reached a certain competence and is motivated to please you and to excel in whatever he is doing, that dressage should be attempted. In this I am against the general opinion, but I feel that a much higher standard can be reached with high motivation than may be reached from repetitive and habit-forming training.

In other words, the training programme, the method of work, must be right. But it should be used to force the trainer and the horse to respond positively.

If you can make use of the horse's motivation so that he is

actively and positively responding to your training, your results will improve startlingly. But still your method must be correct. The problem is like that of the small boy at school: if he is enjoying the subject he is learning and is taught so that he remains interested and actively working at the subject, he will do well in any examination later. But if on the other hand, he is only doing the minimum amount of work to avoid punishment, he will do badly in examination.

In the same way with horses, when you show a horse a jump, if he carries you over the jump with his own euthusiasm, then your training method is right. If he goes over the jump with the minimum of effort required to avoid being clobbered, or if he refuses or runs out, then your training programme is wrong.

Besides the characteristics of the trainer and the horse and the strategy used to train the horse, the remaining factor to take into account in teaching a horse is the nature of the task you want him to learn. Some things are very easy to teach and the horse will learn them easily; sometimes the thing you are trying to teach is very difficult and he will have great difficulty in executing a movement or jumping a particular type of fence. When your training is becoming advanced, in other words, learning becomes more difficult for the horse. Here you can make use of the horse's ability to perceive difference, you make a virtue of the specialness of the task.

A good example is the dressage test number five. Most of this test is a trotting one, but two parts are canter work, which will be completely different from the others. Now this distinctiveness can be made use of, to implant the learning in your horse's memory. When teaching show jumping in the course you will have a double and a spread fence. These will be distinctive in the horse's mind from the rest of the course. Therefore, if time is taken to split off the spread fences and the double, in teaching the whole you can give special emphasis to that part. So the most difficult and outstanding part of the training can be fixed in the horse's mind. But the fences must stand out because they are different, and not because they are difficult.

When teaching a horse to jump a double or spread fence, you start, of course, with a small double or small spread, and gradually increase the height. If you are teaching your horse with a group of other horses, you would have the main group of horses standing on the other side of the double or spread, so that he is jumping towards them. If you are teaching him by yourself, you should always have the double or spread pointing towards home, so that he has the extra motivation to jump. You will then make sure that you finish by jumping this fence and he is praised for doing so. And because it was the last fence he jumped before going home, he will associate it not only with being different (and so standing out in his mind) but also with praise and going home. His approach to it will be positive, and not negative as it would be if he were going away from home or away from the other horses.

Another technique for dealing with teaching advanced and difficult tasks is associating them where possible with training that he has gone through before. A coloured post and rails that he had been using in training for the show ring can be associated with any other post and rails that he has jumped, and you can always use his previous training in this way if you have been schooling over rustic fences, as we do. In fact, if you can split your difficult training programme into those parts that stand out, and those parts that you can associate with something the horse has done before, you should end up with very little that is new and that doesn't stand out. This part would be learned separately.

How wonderful it would be if a horse could remember everything we taught it! Every one would be such a wonderful performer. And yet it would spoil half the pleasure of riding, since there would be so little that you could teach a horse after twelve months of training! But the fact is that a horse forgets most of what you teach it, and forgets it much too rapidly for most of us.

So let us look now at the problem of forgetting. First we need to see how much he forgets or remembers; and then what changes take place in remembering and forgetting; and finally, the causes of his forgetting. When we have just finished teaching a horse something, we can be reasonably certain that at that moment he has 100 per cent retention of what we have taught him. But take him out some days later, and he may have retained only 75 per cent of what you have taught him – he has forgotten 25 per cent of what he has learned. Months later, he will probably have forgotten 75 per cent and retained only 25 per cent.

If you could look on the horse's memory as a curve and could chart what the horse remembers and forgets, you would see that he starts off at 100 per cent remembering and no forgetting, but then the amount that he remembers will drop very sharply for a time, then the curve would slowly straighten out at about 20 per cent remembering and 80 per cent forgetting. This figure is by no means fixed, but it is reasonable to assume for working purposes that a horse will retain about 20 per cent of everything you teach him. On the other hand it is a very important point to bear in mind that a horse's memory retention is at its highest when the horse's motive for remembering is greatest. This means that work he enjoys and the things that give him most pleasure will be retained in his memory bank for a very long time (four or five years), whereas dull and repetitive work will be forgotten as soon as the acquired behaviour has been replaced by something else. Our trekking ponies, for instance, will follow in line, day after day, never deviating from their position, for the period of the trekking season. But give them two or three days' hunting, and they will be prancing about like fools, their behaviour completely unrecognizable. On the other hand memory retention of something pleasurable is shown by the almost invariably long memory that a horse will have for where the feed room is! I have had a horse that I had sold, and bought back after as long as three years, walk straight to the feed room door. He had remembered that for three years, when turned loose in the yard, but had forgotten how to rein back five days after I had taught him to do so.

A horse will remember pain, as I have already stressed, far longer than he will remember pleasure. He will also remember excitement for a long time, and he will remember people for a long time as well. But the length of time a horse remembers anything depends in part on how well taught he was, the vividness and distinctiveness of his memory and on how much interference there has been since we have taught him.

From the very early stages I taught Biddy to change legs at the canter when she changed direction. This is important for any cross country work, but when we came to do a dressage test where the counter canter was needed, it was extremely difficult to teach her *not* to change legs when she changed direction. What is more, not only did she have to learn something which was completely contrary to her previous teaching, but she also had to learn that this method of cantering, i.e. the counter canter, was applicable only to the dressage arena, and that in all other situations she had to change legs, either automatically on change of direction or when I shifted my body weight.

The method of teaching her was in itself comparatively simple. When a counter canter was required in the dressage arena, if she was leading with her near fore I gave her the signals to lead on her near fore again; this reinforced that she was already leading on that leg. I combined this signal with the telepathic communication I was able to achieve with her, and her counter canter was extremely good.

I also made use of this teaching in cross country. When she was wrong at a fence, by signalling her to change legs twice I could get her to lose half a stride so that her take-off position was correct. Using the flying change in quick succession is extremely useful in slowing a horse who is going too fast – in fact on occasion I have put a bolting horse on the ground by using a rapid change of direction, so that he got his legs tied in a reef knot and went head over heels. But this is to be recommended only in dire emergencies or with horses who need a sharp and severe lesson.

Such a horse was Pippet, who came to us in the late 1940s as unridable. As soon as her feet touched grass she was gone like a shot from a gun. The first thing I tried was letting her gallop herself out round a twenty-acre field. After four attempts at this I tried facing her at a five-foot fence with a ditch on either side. In spite of my efforts to stop her she flew the lot. I didn't repeat this experiment because jumping five-foot fences with yawning ditches on horses out of control is not my idea of a way of prolonging active life!

So the next thing I tried was galloping her into a bramble bush. This stopped her, and she learned quickly to stop when faced with a sufficiently large bramble bush, but there were not enough about to make this a viable system of regular control. I finally taught her to change legs on command, and then took her into a freshly ploughed field. As soon as she started carting me I made her change legs quickly, which brought her down at once. I quickly sat on her head and made her lie still for ten minutes. After repeating the process four or five times I had only to change legs once or twice and she would come back on to her hocks completely under control. From then on she progressed to become an easily controlled and well mannered hunter.

Interference in learning is very important and is extremely difficult to cure in a horse. One of my first successes in eliminating interference involved teaching a horse to jump obstacles, many years ago.

Harry, a farmer acquaintance of mine, had bought a big slashing weight-carrying hunter for 700 gns. On his first day's hunting, being unused to our rhine country, the horse galloped into four rhines in succession, nearly drowning his owner in the process, so I got the job of getting him jumping water. Teaching him to do this was quite easy. I decided to do it on Harry's farm, for two reasons. First, it gave me considerable opportunity to spend time in the company of Harry's daughter Mary, especially as I was careful to pick market days, farm sales and any other time Harry was unlikely to be at home. Second, it was potato planting time at home and this was an excellent opportunity to avoid the backbreaking work of planting potatoes – such considerations as these are vital when you are considering the strategy of gentling horses. The actual relearning technique was simple. Since the horse naturally was a bold and brave jumper and simply had to learn to jump water, it was simply a question of preparing the ground.

The first thing I did was to get two ten-foot sheets of galvanized iron and tap them on to a wooden frame. This I placed in a gateway, and put a low eighteen-inch rail in front of it. Then I took Harry's big bay three fields away from home, where he had two big five-foot fences, and he flew them both with a leap of pleasure. Then we came to the gateway with the galvanized on the other side of the rail. He popped over the rail, landing with a crash as all four feet hit the galvanized. This had brought us back to the yard. I took his bridle off, loosened his girth and left him with a small feed of oats while Mary and I went into the house for half an hour's conversation and refreshment. Here you can see the motivation of both horse and rider.

After half an hour we went back out and took him over the same three fences, except I removed the rail in front of the galvanized. Again he jumped the first two fences perfectly. As we came towards the third fence and home, I drove him on. This time he took off five feet back from the galvanized and he flew it like a bird. Again he was put back into his stable with a small feed whilst we shifted the galvanized into a hollow in the ground in a different field. Again he had two fly fences before the hollow, thus keeping his motive of enjoyment alive. He galloped straight onto the galvanized, the clatter again alarmed him; I swung him round and put him back at the same place. This time he flew it without a mistake. From then on we proceeded to school him over any hollow or dip in the ground, one of which always contained the galvanized, until he was jumping any dip in the ground he came across. At the end of three days' very pleasant holiday he was jumping any rhine or stretch of water I put him at, so unfortunately it was back to planting potatoes.

This is why we insist that it is so important for a horse to enjoy his work, and that if he can see a reason for doing something and can understand it, he will retain the learning much longer than learning he has acquired but can see no reason for. Even interference in learning – probably the thing that has the greatest bearing on forgetting in horses (in this case, the interference of the horse's reaction to water) – can be overcome in this way.

We have seen the example of changing legs at the canter interfering with counter canter work. This is the kind of thing that happens all the time in training horses. You may teach a horse to jump properly, and then you make a mistake. Instead of giving him his head as he jumps you jag his mouth when he lands. Do this three times, and he will stop jumping because of the interference of his recent learning – that is when he jumps his mouth is hurt. Relearning then becomes a long and painful business.

Negative motivation, as we have already seen, makes a far deeper impression and is remembered far longer than positive motivation, because fear is a far stronger motivation than greed or love. And boredom and lethargy tend to reinforce forgetfulness, while alertness and activity tend to promote retention of lessons.

Alertness, then, is essential. It is stimulated by variation, boredom by repetition, and while everyone will pay lipservice to the idea that learning is enhanced by variation and alertness, it is a fact most people expect to teach by repeating the same lesson over and over again. Yet a little thought devoted to varying the work even a little will pay enormous dividends.

The last and final reason for forgetting I will deal with is outside interference. Say you are teaching a horse one thing, and his attention is diverted towards something else, he will tend to forget very quickly. This would seem to be obvious to anybody, but riders tend when training a horse to forget that a horse has a very short period of concentration – probably only four or five minutes – so that no lesson should last for more than this period. If your lesson exceeds his attention span, the horse is bound to be subject to outside interference. If, on the other hand, the horse concentrates for four or five minutes and is then allowed to relax and do something else, and come back to the lesson for another four or five minutes, all is well. If you try to increase this level of concentration, his level of memory retention will inevitably diminish.

External sensory information, such as may intrude in your lesson, can also be made to work for you. It is of course used by a horse to learn and function in everyday life. Sensory information comes to him as sensation, perceived through eyes, ears or skin. It is the brightness of a light, the pitch of a tone or the pain of a pinprick. Sensations are all stuff from which he moulds his experience. And yet his experience is much more than a series of sensations. In everyday life he is always interpreting the sensory information he receives. He interprets a sequence of sounds as a motor car, or a large green object as a tree, a square object as his stable or a cold wet sensation as rain. This process of interpreting sensations is called perception.

The fact about all perception is that it is always converting sensory information into meaning. A large red mass of certain shape is a car, a series of pressure sensations on his neck is a fly walking across him, a noise in the distance is another horse whinnying. Perception of objects is partly learned, but the basic tendency to organize stimuli into meaning is an innate property of the horse's sensory organs and nervous system. His natural ability to perceive objects, to create meaning, is called his organizing tendency.

One main organizing tendency which horses share with human beings is the ability to separate figures from their background. For instance we see objects, such as trees, standing out from the background of a field. Or one particular sound will stand out from other sounds, a gunshot from the sound of birdsong. The horse can select something, and separate it from its surroundings, with his eyes, ears, sense of smell or taste.

Another organizing tendency in the perception of objects is the ability to group stimuli into a pattern. This pattern means a person, that pattern a bramble bush. And he will group similar things together, and identify one man and another.

This ability to identify remains constant even though he may see one man standing on the horizon looking as if he is two inches high, and the other standing next to him who is six foot. Or the voice of one horse may come from half a mile away, very faintly, while the sound of another horse is bellowing in his ear: he will recognize them both as horses' voices and group them together. Similarly, he will perceive as constant qualities such as brightness, darkness, heat and cold.

There is another level of perception which horses appear to use, which human beings perhaps only occasionally share. This is extra-sensory perception, which is the ability to sense things they can neither see, touch, smell or hear. In one experience, this means the moods and emotions of his near companions. He will perceive your own moods in this way, and if you are nervous going into a particular fence, he may well refuse; or if he senses any weakness in your riding, use this knowledge to play you up.

On the other hand I find that I can use this faculty in a horse to get him to perform above his normal ability in competition or in special situations. In my demeanour and emotions I convey to the horse that the exceptional is required. I did this with Arctic Watch, the horse that ran away with me with great regularity and when racing would wrench the reins out of my hands and lead the field for as long as he was able. Once, the horse I had intended riding in the Llandeilo hunt team cross-country event went lame, and as a result Watch had to take part. My empathy with him was such that he perceived the difference in the situation and rose to the occasion. I dropped him in at the back of the team, from where I was able to observe how the rest of them were going. I found I could stop him when one of the other horses refused, to give it a lead over one of the fences, and turn him sharply to go back and catch one of the other horses that had deposited its rider. On the second half of the course I let him go on fast, to make up distance we had lost on the two leaders, by helping other people out of their difficulties. He allowed me to check him, turn and place him at each fence, catching up with the leaders long before they were finished.

This behaviour contrasted dramatically with his conduct the following Saturday when we were racing again. He pulled my arms out of their sockets to get into the lead, finishing third on this occasion. From this it can be seen that even though in both cases he was galloping with other horses, he was able to understand the difference in what was required of him, and this understanding depended entirely on the subtlety of his communication with me. Your understanding of a horse's perception, including his capacity for extra-sensory perception, can be made use of in any piece of learning, especially when teaching something new. In particular we use it in curing vices, in trying to make the horse change a bad habit for something we want him to do. And in curing each vice he has above all to perceive, after the initial treatment, that what we are trying to teach him is enjoyable.

12: *Eliminating Bad Habits: Stable Vices*

Some bad habits in horses are natural, but most of them are man-made. And unlearning a bad habit is one of the hardest tasks you can set your horse. It is a challenge to your teaching methods.

In this chapter, I propose to deal with the elimination of stable vices. These generally fall into two groups; those caused by boredom, and those caused partly by irritation and partly by the failure of the trainer to react to them before they develop.

Into the first group would fall crib biting. This clearly indicates a bored horse, hanging around a stable with nothing to see. On the other hand a horse that is difficult to groom, halter or saddle is frequently a horse with a thin skin that is easily irritated when he's being groomed, which in turn makes him kick or bite. If this is allowed to develop you end up with a horse that's almost impossible to touch. Both sets of vices are difficult to get rid of, and they require completely different methods.

Let us deal first with the group of vices caused by boredom. First it is important to eliminate the root cause, i.e. to see that the horse is no longer bored. This needs a two-pronged strategy. First, you increase his work and vary it, so making the horse more alert and interested when he is out. Then, when he is in the stable, leave the top half of the stable door open as much as possible. For most of the year he should be able to look out twenty-four hours a day, and even in bad weather he can wear extra rugs, even have a waterproof hood to keep his head and neck dry. He should also be put into a stable where he has maximum view of what is going on in the world outside – the rest of the farmyard, down at the house or, if you live in a town, the roads and houses nearby.

The main boredom stable vices are weaving, windsucking,

crib-biting and kicking the stable wall. In fact you can almost call these infectious diseases, because once one horse in the stable starts weaving or crib-biting you'll soon get others doing the same thing.

Weaving is most easily cured by turning the horse out for twelve months, but this isn't very often practicable since if you get a horse to ride or hunt you want to ride or hunt him, so you'll need to have him in. So the method I use to cure weaving is to make the horse's life as interesting as possible. Apart from leaving the stable door open, as I've already described, I give him toys to play with: I collect half a dozen Guinness cans, since these are usually plentiful about the place, and put some small stones in the bottom and then hang them on a series of strings across the door, so that when he looks out through the doorway there is just enough room for him to put his head through the middle. Now, if when he looks out he starts weaving from side to side, he's going to bash himself with the cans; but if he's bored he has only to move his head and he's got the tinkle, tinkle, tinkle of the cans to amuse him.

Within twenty-four hours of buying Salline at Llanybyther market, it became obvious that she was a very bad weaver and within another two days one of our younger horses had also started weaving. Daffyd in fact was quite easy to cure, simply by swearing at him. He quickly got the idea that weaving incurred our displeasure and probably meant that he got a stone thrown at him, though the stone, of course, never hit him, but caught the surround of the stable door a good thump. But Salline was a different case altogether. So we hung our empty Guinness cans around her door. She inspected them thoroughly, and then put out her head through the hole in the middle to see what was going on in the yard. She stood for four or five minutes, and then from habit she started weaving, first one way and then another, back again, back and forward. Then, when she was just getting into the swing of the weave, she caught herself on the face with a Guinness can. She jumped back into the stable, wondering what had happened. Ten minutes later she looked out again and started weaving again; again she hit herself. Over the following week she gradually weaved less and less, until at the end of ten days, instead of weaving, she would shake her head every five minutes or so just to hear the cans rattle. When she reached this stage we started to take down the Guinness cans. First we took down one on either side, then two, then we took them all down, by which time she was so engrossed in what was going on down at the house and in the other stables, among the cars going up the road and the sheep in the opposite field that she'd ceased to weave altogether.

The next stables vice is particularly annoying because it tends to cause so much damage. This is kicking, which appeals to horses that are stabled in wooden stalls because they find that if they lash back at the wall they get a good resounding thump. It tends to give the horse capped hocks, and the stable gets demolished very quickly. And since this often goes on especially at night, the thump, thump, thump from the stable wakes you up as well.

One cure is to hang a series of bags, half full of hay or straw, round the edge of the stable, so that when the horse kicks he's got a pretty fair chance of hitting one of them, which in turn bumps off the stable wall, giving him a bump on the backside. This is usually enough to distract the horse from bringing the loose box clattering down round his ears; though he may for a time continue to kick the bags, just to make them sway about. The worst stable kicker we ever had was old Cork Beg, and it took us a very long time trying to cure him before we hit upon this dodge.

Crib-biting, wind sucking and eating the stable are all manifestation of the same progression: the horse is bored, so first he bites at the stable door or his manger, just chewing it; then he really starts crib-biting, getting hold of the manger and scraping his teeth on it. Because at the same time he is arching his neck and inhaling air through his gullet, wind sucking then becomes a habit. This needs a great deal of time and patience to cure. So it is best to deal with the biting and chewing before it ever gets to the wind sucking stage.

The first step is comparatively simple. Since all these biting habits arise from boredom, and often happen mainly at night, you can put a piece of gorse bush, or the branch of a tree in the stable so that he's got something else to chew at, instead of the stable door.

I prefer this approach to the general recommended remedies, such as putting metal tops to all the surfaces that the horse is likely to eat, or using one of the greases and creams that are advertised, since none of these eliminate the root cause of the vice, which is boredom, though they may be useful in lessening the vice, and may be used – in fact have to be used in certain cases.

A determined crib-biter, however, may need more compli-cated treatment than the mere provision of a gorse bush. First, the important thing to do is to remove his wooden manger, or put him into a stable without a feed manger so that when you have fed him, you can take the feeding receptacle out of the stable. When you have done this, he will turn his attention to the top of the door. Here, in a minor case, you can simply put a series of tin tacks in a piece of cloth and fix this to the door so that he pricks his nose when he tries to bite the top of it. But he'll then look for something else to bite, so you proceed round the stable until you've eliminated everything that he's able to bite. Only then will some horses turn their attention to the gorse bush or branch that you've provided them with.

In very bad cases, the horse may simply tear the tin tacks off the top of the stable door, so you have to adopt much sterner methods. Here you want inch nails and a wooden batten, so that the inch nails stick out half an inch from the top of the stable door. You then do the same thing with any other surface he may want to chew.

Once the horse turns his attention to the branch you can remove the unpleasant nails or tin tacks, putting them carefully to one side in a place that you can remember so that you can put them back if he starts crib-biting again.

The same treatment will be used for the wind-sucker, except that here you may also need a six-inch wide piece of leather to strap round his neck under his chin to eliminate this very damaging vice.

Both these last two vices, wind-sucking and crib-biting, are extremely damaging to the horse's health. So both must be eliminated, and in the long run this can only be done by increasing the horse's interest in his work, combined with the toy in the stable and the obstacle to hurt him if indulges in his habit.

Here I must admit that when I allow my wife to read this book I shall remove these vital pages, just in case she tries them on me to stop me smoking! I don't relish the idea of picking up a Senior Service, putting it comfortably between my lips to take a drag and finding that I've driven a tin tack into my upper teeth.

There is an alternative way of tackling these vices, which is very effective if you have a neighbour who has an electric fence. This is simply to run an electric wire along the top of all likely surfaces, so that when the horse starts crib-biting or wind-sucking he gets an electric shock to his nose and mouth. This has the advantage over using tin tacks and nails that you are less likely to catch yourself on protruding points, but it is not always easy to find someone who will lend you an electric fencer.

The other problems I have called stable vices are not really so much stable vices as vices that happen to show themselves in the stable: kicking, biting, attacking you with the forelegs and squeezing you up against the wall of the stable. The first are forms of retaliation in response to annoyance; and the others, the really unpleasant ones, straightforward defensive aggression.

For example, if when you are grooming your horse he is tickled about his elbows, tummy or head, he will retaliate by snapping at you or flicking out with a hind leg. This is a simple reflex action of annoyance. He would do exactly the same thing to another horse who was annoying him.

On the other hand if when you enter the stable the horse comes at you with his teeth, this too is an avoidance reaction, but in this case the horse is trying to dominate you in one way or another. He may kick, present his backside towards you threatening to kick, or, in the most violent case, attack you with his front legs and his teeth.

To deal first with the pure avoidance and retaliatory reactions, there are a large number of remedies, any one of which may need to be used. Your general stance here is 'I know it's unpleasant, but you've damn well got to put up with it'. For example, when you're grooming under his armpits and he attempts to snap at you, a good hard slap on the nose will soon put him in his place. If when you're grooming his belly he leans against you, crushing you against the wall, a well directed fist into the ribs will immediately enable you to breath again. If he kicks out at you when you are grooming between his hind legs, again you slap or bring your knee up sharply, catching him in a vital and painful spot. These are pure retaliatory actions on your part for misbehaviour and if you catch a vital area you will have a well-behaved horse. The other place where horses sometimes dislike being groomed is around and between the ears. This one can be cured by tying him up extremely short so that he can't dance around, and standing on a bucket to brush between his ears. But watch it, because an extremely bad case will throw himself over backwards or sideways in temper. The only thing to do then is to resort to hand grooming the neck, ears and face. You simply run your hand up his mane, between his ears and down his face. At first you will find as soon as you get near his ears he will throw his head away from you. But you continue the process without a break until he allows you to do it without question. Then you repeat the process for several days, towards the end pausing to rub between the ears or the ticklish spot. When you have reached this stage successfully, you use a very soft small brush, and in time you will be able to graduate to a Dandy brush.

In all these cases where a horse is ticklish in a particular place, the first place you groom is that place. Not only do you groom him there first, you groom him thoroughly there until he is standing still. But it is most important to remember that if you're grooming in a ticklish spot it is only fair for you to respect it and use a soft or gentle brush, or your hand. After all, if you're ticklish about your feet and someone's tickling your toes, you too are going to go to any lengths to avoid having your toes tickled.

So far we have dealt with vices using the three basics of all horsemanship – determination, patience and understanding. But, from time to time you will get a horse that has dominated its previous owner and is really difficult to groom, or even to saddle. And here you may need some tricks. If he tends to lash out at you when you are grooming his belly, a simple trick is to put a surcingle around his middle and tie up a foreleg so that he is standing on only three legs. If he tries to kick you he goes flat on the ground and he won't attempt to do it again. After a period of time, you lower the tied leg by degrees. Only when he's got over his habit of trying to remove the vital parts of your body with the toe of his shoe and he'll stand still when you're grooming him, do you abandon the tying altogether.

If he tends to snap at you while you're grooming him or girthing him up, the simplest thing is to tie him up so that he can't reach you. In this way you hope to extinguish previous learning, that is, the habit. But if he does not forget, and still contrives to have a piece out of you, you have to extinguish the memory using fear. Extinguishing the memory by tying him up short works where the memory is not very deeply embedded. But where the habit is deeply ingrained within the horse, the only way to extinguish it is by using fear techniques. You can either hit him across the nose, or in severe cases punch his teeth in and really catch him one every time he tries to bite. This works *provided* you pay more attention to stopping him biting than you do to grooming him.

I found an extremely useful tool for doing this. It was an electric cattle goad, a device which, when you press it against an animal, emits an electric shock from the battery. I strapped it on to my arm so that whenever the horse swung his head round he touched the goad and got an electric shock to his face. This very quickly cured him of any idea that I was good eating. I tried it out on two horses and it was most effective. Unfortunately, the owner of the goad came and collected it, and since I didn't have one myself and couldn't afford to buy a new one, I went back to slapping my horses' faces.

As in all these methods of extinction where fear is used, it is absolutely essential that, having punched him, you should then make a fuss of him so that he understands that the ill treatment is for his actions and not because you don't like him. Whilst your immediate aim is to make him behave himself, your long-term aim is to make him like you and want to be with you. Handling a horse is rather like a love affair, it has its ups and downs. Things may be going right for you and the horse will be going superbly and you adore him, and then you have an argument and unless you're very careful, what starts off as a small disagreement can end as a severance of all affection.

Certainly before you can eradicate bad habits it is absolutely essential that there should be empathy and genuine affection between you and the horse. Also, biting and kicking when you are girthing or grooming or working in the stable is always caused by one of three things – boredom, irritation or fear. So the initial cause must be discovered before you can attempt to cure the vice. And once you have made the initial cure, you have still to proceed to the standard treatment of making him enjoy being groomed : that is, while you still tie him up to his manger, you put a small feed into him when you are grooming his ticklish places. So you are adding to the deterrent a pleasant experience, which he may come to associate with grooming itself; and if he is annoyed he can take out his temper by biting hard into his feed.

Another thing a horse may do in the stable is jerk his head up to stop you putting his bridle on, or grooming or clipping his head. This again is very annoying, and is one of the more difficult faults to overcome. You start off by rubbing your hand up his head and rubbing him in between the ears, holding on to the halter tightly. As he swings his head up out of your reach, you get a bucket or a box to stand on and do the same thing. You go on until you can get your hand between his ears and then you scratch the tickly place round the base of the ear, in the mane, between the ears and down under his chin. What you're doing is teaching him that what he is rebelling against can really be a pleasurable experience. Again a basin of nuts at the manger helps considerably in most cases. But the main thing is to keep at it and keep at it, maybe for an hour, maybe for two or three hours, until he allows you to do what you set out to do without objection.

Suppose a horse presents you with his backside, threatens to kick you or actually kicks at you as you go into the stable. This is caused by an ingrained fear, and it is the fear that must be eliminated. I do this quite simply to start off with, by putting him into his loose box without any straw. Then at lunchtime I walk in with a feed and a bucket of water. He turns his backside towards me and kicks out, so I take the bucket of water and the feed out again. I leave him there until the evening feed and walk in again; he will probably walk over to the corner of the stable, away from me, showing me a large amount of backside and the flash of an iron-shod hoof going past my ear. I take the water and feed out again.

By the morning, he will have been twenty-four hours without food and water and he'll be extremely hungry. One or two things then happen. Either, when I walk in with the food and water, he comes to the stable door and shoves his head into the bucket before I've got the door opened, and keeps it there while I open the door and walk in. Or he walks away. If he walks away on this, the third occasion, I stand in the open stable door. He can see the bucket of food and he's dying of hunger. He sees the bucket of water and feels as though he's spent six months in the Sahara desert. Slowly he'll turn right round – it might take half an hour or an hour – and come over to the feed. And in coming to the feed he comes to me. At no time in the case of a horse attempting to kick you do you approach the horse. He must come to you.

I have, on two occasions, had to leave the food inside and shut the stable door, standing outside until the horse comes over to the water and food. But as soon as he starts feeding or drinking I open the stable door. Within three or four days, when I go into the stable with his feed he comes to me, he has his feed and water and I make a fuss of him, and within a week or a fortnight, depending upon how deeply ingrained the vice is, when I walk into the stable the horse will remain with his head stuck over the stable door taking no notice of me whatsoever. Of course each time I go in I caress and pet him.

I have already, earlier in this book, dealt with a horse that cow-kicks at you with one leg. This is different from the horse that presents his backside or kicks you when you go into the loose box, since the cow-kick is an aggressive action as opposed to the defensive reaction of the hind-kick. To cure the cow-kicking horse you keep him tied, you will remember, so that he is unable to kick you when you enter the stable. Then you get in close to his body and make him kick, pushing his leg away from you so that he kicks at his other leg.

The final stable vice that has to be dealt with is one that is fortunately very uncommon, since most of its practitioners have already ended up in catmeat tins. This is attacking you with the teeth and front legs. The offenders are often very good stallions or mares who have not been handled a lot. If a horse attacks you with his front legs and teeth, what you do is respond in a similar manner – you roar at him at the top of your voice, lunge forward and punch him sharply on the end of the nose with a very quick uppercut. I've never yet found a horse that didn't retire immediately in surprise to the corner of his box at this, and a repetition of the treatment together with the strategy already described of going into his box only when you feed him, will in almost every case cure the horse completely. I say almost every case since I have had 100 per cent success, but I will admit that success does depend on the severity of your counter attack and on the person practising the cure. Having had a fight with the horse, you've got immediately to follow it by trying to re-establish an empathy with him. In the case of a horse that is kicking whenever you go near him, or biting or attacking you, you may do this by simply leaning over the stable door and talking to him in a sing-song voice.

One final cure that I used with great success on a horse we were sent to cure who would swing his head round and have a piece of you when you were out riding him, can also be used on horses who bite while being groomed. My technique was simple; when he bit me the second time I stopped him sharply, leant forward and fastened my teeth in his ear.

Charlie, when I was grooming him, used to take a large piece out of me. But after a course of this treatment, when I started grooming him he'd take the corner of my coat between his teeth and pull it back every time I tickled him. This to me was quite acceptable, because he himself had invented a method of telling me when I was getting too near the edge of his temper, and I would go off to groom another part and then come back to it. The horse was taking great care that he wouldn't hurt me, but he'd worked out a way to stop me tickling him unreasonably.

13: *Eliminating Bad Habits: Riding Vices*

Now that we have disposed in the previous chapter of stable vices, it is time to come on to the vices you encounter in riding your horse. All these vices are avoidance techniques of one kind or another. They stem from four causes: first pure bone idleness, second boredom, third malnutrition (which doesn't mean that the horse is starved, it just means that he is fed incorrectly), and fourth what you have taught him through your weakness and incompetence. The four causes may of course be interconnected.

Let us deal first with laziness. This can often be cured simply by changing the horse's feeding habits: what you're feeding him and the amount you're feeding him. He could be underfed. A weak, undernourished horse is clearly going to lack energy, so what you have to do is get him reasonably fit and well. Equally, he may be overfed. He will have very little desire to trot or canter if he is pig fat and off grass. And even a horse that looks in reasonable condition maybe being fed the wrong food.

I can illustrate what I mean by telling you about two horses we got last autumn. Swallow, my daughter's palamino, had been extremely ill with salmonella. He looked like a skeleton, and even when he had three parts recovered he was still extremely weak. When we backed him and rode him a little bit he was quiet and steady, but rather sluggish. Six months later, after having been fed in the meantime on horse and pony nuts and a limited amount of hay, he was jumping out of his skin and was an extremely good, if at times rather lively, ride.

Salline, on the other hand, was rather fat when we bought her. She was quite a good ride with a good walk, a good trot and easy canter, and was an easy and comfortable hunter. She stopped when we were cantering her with the merest touch of the rein, cantering easily to a fence and measuring each one precisely before jumping. But she was not very energetic. We put her on 14lb of horse and pony nuts a day up to Christmas, and as she got fitter she got a little livelier. She was still rather lazy, that is for a thoroughbred being got fit for racing, so at Christmas we followed what is our usual practice with point to point horses, and switched her from horse and pony to 18lb of racehorse nuts. Three months later she was doing an hour's exercise a day, two gallops a week and was racing fit. As soon as you started her at a canter she took hold and went straight into a good racing gallop.

These are only two examples of how altering a horse's feeding can change the whole nature and motivation of the horse. So with a sluggish or lazy horse, the first thing to do is take a very careful look at his feeding. Increase his hard protein-rich food, cut out soggy starchy food such as bran, flaked maize and sugar beet pulp, and go first on to straight horse and pony nuts, and, if that doesn't work, racehorse nuts. Restrict the amount of hay he gets. Then make sure he gets an hour's exercise a day, and you will very probably find that his whole nature will change. You will have of course to experiment to find exactly what food suits the individual horse. And your treatment will also vary according to your purpose. If you merely want to sharpen him up and make a good lively ride, you will not feed him in the same way as when you want him bouncing out of his skin and trying to jump every fence he meets. With the very large variety of foods on the market your choice is extremely wide.

If a horse tends to be lazy, fitness is the key word and that entails hard work on your part, because it involves not only proper feeding but regular and hard exercise. By that I mean an hour to an hour and a half exercise every day. And this work should be made as interesting and exciting as possible. Walking and galloping him with other horses will help. Jumping low fences will help, as will some variation in the place where you are working. You should not work the horse the same way every day: give him something different to look at every day, and when he is in his stable he should, as far as possible, always be able to look out and see what is going on.

One of the best ways to make a sluggish horse lively is to ride him in front of other horses, so that he get into the habit of being in front. And you will find very soon that when another horse comes up to pass him, he will quicken his stride to keep his pride of place. When you are cantering and galloping him, let him start racing the other horses.

Some twenty years ago a friend asked me to find something quiet, steady and grey for a friend of his, and so I went round all my contacts, and eventually found a 15.3 fat, lazy grey horse. He was quite good-looking except that he had a biggish head, so I bought him for a reasonable figure and the man who wanted him came and looked at him and rode him, hummed and hawed and hummed and hawed and said he'd let me know. About a week later he said he didn't want the horse because a friend was lending him one for the winter. I was landed with this grey fat thing that I'd christened the Zombie.

By this time I'd had him in for a fortnight and had been working him reasonably regularly. I'd groomed about a hundred-weight of hair off his coat, mane and tail, and he was looking quite tidy. But I decided that the best way to sell him again was to hunt him for a bit and then sell him, so I put him on to 18lb of oats a day and cut his hay to about 6lb, which I gave him last thing at night with his last feed. By the time I got him out hunting for the first time he was beginning to lift his head a bit and was walking along quite well. It only took half a dozen hard swipes from my hunting crop to get him to trot, and if I really caught him a couple of hard ones he'd canter!

I spent most of the first day's hunting cursing and swearing as the rest of the field disappeared over the horizon, but towards the end of the day he started cantering when the other horses were cantering. I had him out the following Saturday and worked hell out of him in between. He had about three hours' exercise a day and all the oats he could eat: about 21 or 22lb a day. The following Saturday when we neared the meet, his head and tail came up and he started swaggering. When the rest of the field set sail he set sail after them, in fact he moved so quickly that I lost my reins and nearly disappeared over his tail! But we got together before the first fence, which he thundered into sounding like a herd of elephants. When we finally reached it he was going too fast to stop, so, seeing the other horses in front of him jump, he made a very creditable attempt, landed on the other side and pounded away across the field, every stride shaking my backbone and my teeth. But he was doing his best. Much to my surprise, at the end of half a mile we were still well in the middle of the field.

After a month's hunting he was eating 24lb of oats a day, and I stopped him there. I think he would have eaten more. He was really fit and strong and his jumping had improved to such an extent that he was always in the foremost group of horses all the time. From being a slow, lazy beginner's horse, he had become an enthusiast who was tearing for his bit as soon as he got on to grass, and he went flat out at every opportunity (admittedly his flat-out was slightly faster than the pace of a tortoise, but he was doing his best); and he turned into an extremely clever weight-carrying hunter. It didn't matter how awkward a fence was, he was changing legs, twisting and turning and jumping anything that came in front of him. The only thing he didn't like was a big spread, so I kept him out of water country, hunting him mainly with the Blackmore and Taunton Vale Foxhounds. At the end of the season he'd made such a name for himself that I sold him for more than ten times the amount I'd paid for him, and his new owner changed his name from Zombie to Springbok.

Just as correct feeding can change a lazy horse into a lively one, it can calm down a horse that is too lively and gassy. In this case, instead of increasing the protein and cutting out the carbohydrate, you put the horse on to a carbohydrate diet, giving him a minimum of oats but much greater quantities of bran, flaked maize and sugar beet pulp. And instead of making his exercise more exciting, you do the opposite. You still give him his half hour to an hour exercise every day, but it's all slow, steady walking, you cut out cantering and jumping completely until the horse has steadied down and has got to the stage where you want him. Once there, you regulate his food according to the work he's doing. If he's jumping, he'll need more oats: if he's jumping cross-country he'll need a great deal of oats, while if he's show jumping he'll need fewer. We once had a show jumper who had become almost impossible in the show jumping ring. As soon as he'd got into the ring he'd tear away at a rate of knots, getting over-excited and misjudging his fences. I only had him for a month, but as soon as he came I put him on a diet of flaked maize, bran, chopped mangel and chaff, filled his hay rack so that it was always full and gave him just half an hour or forty minutes' slow exercise each day. At the end of a fortnight he was going nice and steady at home, so I put him in the open class at one of the local gymkhanas and everyone sat back to enjoy the sight of me knocking fences in all directions. He flew into the first fence, very excited, but immediately afterwards he steadied down and did a clear round.

I took him home and kept him on slow steady work with no jumping whatsoever, plus his rather bulky diet. Then I took him out again on the Wednesday and finished second. He was out again several times in the next two weeks, performing very creditably, until his owner took him home.

The trouble had been simply that his owner had been schooling the horse, jumping him every day, feeding him like a king. But, this particular horse, to show jump successfully, needed slow steady work, a rather bulky diet and most of all, no jumping between shows.

There are some horses you can't steady down no matter what you do: they will always be too slow and steady, or too fast and excitable for you. If you find yourself with one of those you will have to change him for a horse that is better suited to your purposes. But before you do so, in fact in all cases where you are trying to change the motivation and nature of the horse, question whether you are giving the project enough patience or whether your riding ability is at fault. If you are not a strong enough horseman to sort him out yourself, it is infinitely better to get someone else to do so for you, or to change him for another horse.

Allied with excitability and laziness are two other vices, nappiness and rearing. Correcting nappiness is purely a question of patience and determination, possibly combined with punishment. Of course at the first sign of nappiness, you spank his bottom and tell him to behave himself. But if you have a horse who naps and won't go out of the gate, for example he half rears and refuses to budge at all, there are two things you can do. One is to sit on his back until he eventually goes forward the way you want: the other is to turn him round, back him four or five strides in the direction you want him to go, and then turn him again and see if he will go forward; if he doesn't you make him go back again. After a very few lessons he should get the idea that if he doesn't go forwards in the direction that you want him to go, he's got to go backwards in that direction.

In its more extreme form, nappiness becomes serious rearing. If a horse rears rather than go where you want him to, you keep his head pointing the way that you are going and keep niggling at him with your heels. Whatever you do you must not let him turn round and go home. Neither is it advisable to get someone else to come behind him with a hunting crop and catch him one on the backside, because you can't always have someone running about behind you with a hunting crop. When he goes up on his hind legs and tries to swing round, the answer is really a question of good steady patience. Again, backing the horse in the direction you want to go will very often help, but if his rearing gets worse you just turn him round, point him the way you want to go, and sit it out.

In both these cases it is absolutely essential that the horse goes where you want every time, every day, consistently for a week or two. And, as in all cases of curing vices, when he has done what he's been told to do, you must go out of your way to make the work that he's doing enjoyable.

In extremely bad cases of nappiness it is advisable to start by working him with another horse, because (a) if he's following another horse he's less likely to be nappy, (b) it is then quite simple to make the work enjoyable.

One of the most important things to remember in nappiness is that a horse never naps, or very rarely naps, when you are going towards home, so if you take him on a circular ride, so that you are always, even in an indirect and roundabout way, on your way home, you will find him easier than if you go out, turn round and then come back. As circumstances allow within your circular ride you can pick a place where he can do the work that he enjoys doing – maybe galloping up a string of low fences and maybe doing a little bit of dressage and schooling : I usually find that dressage tends to make the horse more nappy rather than cure the nappiness, but horses vary and you never know beforehand what he is going to enjoy.

One particularly nappy horse we had enjoyed splashing water in the stream. He'd stand in the middle of the stream with the water flowing round his knees and splash first with one foot and then with the other, bringing his foot as hard down on the water as he could. Then he would kick back his hind leg so that he was kicking water back behind him. He got so that even when it was time to go home to dinner, which was when I was beginning to get too wet, he was reluctant to go home. And within a very short time, as soon as you put the saddle on him, he'd bustle away down the road as fast as he could. When he was half way to the river he'd break into a trot, and then a canter and he'd take an almighty leap off the bank, landing in the water with a terrific splash. The nappiness had disappeared altogether. Then, once I'd got him away from the river – which I did with a couple of hefty belts in the belly with my heel – he'd walk home until he got half way, and again he'd break into a trot to get to his dinner. Such results can be expected in previously nappy horses once they get an enthusiasm for what they are doing. Nappiness, once cured, is one of the very few vices that is in very little danger of recurring.

A form of nappiness which isn't usually classed as such is refusing at a fence. This may be because the rider doesn't really want to jump anyway, and rides into the fence saying his or her prayers and wishing he had made sure that a doctor and two ambulances were waiting to take him to hospital afterwards. If you don't enjoy jumping, don't jump: it isn't necessary for every rider to do so, nor is it desirable, because not only will they be doing something that they don't want to do but they will also be ruining what could otherwise be a perfectly good horse.

Assuming however that the cause of the refusal is not in the mind and attitude of the person on the horse's back, it may be either the memory of an unpleasant experience in jumping, or pure damn laziness. He may have been jumped too much and too often, he may have attempted to jump a fence and hurt himself in doing so, or been hurt by his rider who has jagged his mouth or come down like a ton of bricks on the back of the saddle.

In any of these cases, the only way you can get him jumping freely and well again is by renewing his motivation and getting him to enjoy jumping. Here it is extremely important that the fences should not be high and that the horse should be allowed to jump them in the way that he enjoys jumping most. Some horses stop jumping because their rider has taken so much care to place them exactly at each fence that they've got sick and tired of being pulled together in a school, and so they say 'why the hell should I jump at all'. In this case you allow the horse to breeze into his fences at a good strong gallop, and fly them. Make sure of course that the fences are easily knocked down poles or brush fences so that if his pleasure in jumping is in demolishing the fences, or if he's wrong at one, he will not hurt himself. It is of course also important that he should jump with other horses, or if this isn't possible that all his jumping should be towards home.

Someone once brought a horse up to me because he wanted to school it over my fences, and he also wanted me to tell him what was going wrong to make the horse refuse. He cantered into the first fence very slowly, placed his horse beautifully and his horse popped over it. The next fence was a little higher, 3 foot, and again he cantered in slowly, placed it perfectly and jumped it. The third fence was three-foot-six high with a four-foot spread and again he placed his horse, cantering in superbly, but at the last second the horse stopped. He didn't, and made a beautiful jump, clearing the fence but leaving the horse on the other side.

He got back on, picked up his stick and caught the horse four or five clouts going away from the fence and four or five more going back into it. The horse climbed the fence somehow, leaving his hind legs on the second half of the double, and after that he refused to jump anything else. The rider asked my advice as to what he was doing wrong.

I simply got on the horse and took him at a fairish bat round the easiest part of the course, then came up at the sixth or seventh fence, still going at a good pace, into the fence he'd had trouble with before. Three strides out I drove my heels into the horse's ribs, one – two – three with each stride, increasing the pressure with my heels until he'd taken off. He rocketed over the parallel, heaved the reins out of my hand and away over the rest of the course, ending up with the four-foot gate followed by the four-foot shark's teeth fence.

In the course of the round he'd rattled four or five fences with his feet, but he pulled up blowing smoke like a dragon, with his head and tail stuck up in the air, and dancing around all over the place. So I got off and led him round for five minutes to cool down before I had a word with his owner, who couldn't believe the fences his horse had jumped. Neither could he understand how the horse had jumped all the fences at the pace we were going without being placed correctly. The answer to both questions was quite simple. The horse was enjoying himself, he was enjoying galloping and he was enjoying flying his fences; and whilst it appeared that I wasn't placing him, I was actually checking him three or four strides out so that he was going at an extended stride, or a slightly shortened stride, into each fence. He was a horse of scope and boldness who could jump the fixed timber fences with great ease, so it was merely a question of putting in a slightly bigger jump if he was wrong at his fence.

This method of jumping of course is not ideal for show jumping, but it is extremely effective going over cross country courses, hunting or racing. And even for show jumping, it is certainly more effective than being over careful in the placing of your horse so that the horse ceases to enjoy jumping at all. After all, since you're out of it if your horse starts refusing fences, it doesn't really matter if he knocks one or two down to begin with, and once you've got him jumping freely and easily and fast you can steady him, take your fences slower, and take more care over your placing before the jump.

One thing I don't like doing with a horse that is refusing his fences, is to catch him one with a stick, even though this may occasionally be necessary. With such a horse what I do is immediately to go back to a two-foot-six jump, then canter him into the fence, and if he refuses on no account do I allow him to turn his head away from the fence. I may back him three or four strides, but if I allow him to turn away from the fence without jumping it I am allowing him a victory, whereas if I keep him facing the fence, and make him jump it from three strides or a standstill (and any horse or pony can jump three-foot to three-foot-six with three strides) then the victory is mine. Sometimes, if you are by yourself, you have to tan him, but I much prefer to have someone standing ten or fifteen yards from the fence to pelt his bottom with small stones and curse him if he refuses, so that any pain and anger is coming not from the rider but from someone else. All the rider does is make him back three strides, urge him on vocally and with the heels, and praise and reward him afterwards.

I prefer to chuck a clod of earth or a small stone at the horse's backside, rather than hit him, for any form of nappiness, and this includes rearing.

There was a time when my wife's horse, Cuddles, took to refusing straw bale fences in competition. He would refuse them once, and then he would go back and jump them beautifully, which was a damn nuisance. We cured this very quickly. Whenever we cantered him into a straw bale fence, just as he got there, a stone would hit his bottom and I would shout 'Cuddles'.

This worked very well at home then at the first competition he again stopped at the bale fence. But there were two classes so when Leslie rode him in the second class I walked down to within twenty yards of the fence and, as he went past me, I said 'Cuddles' in a not very loud voice and he went into the fence and flew it. From this stage, when he responded to my cursing him he was able to transfer the response to my wife's simply scolding him as he approached any fence he was likely to refuse. You could see him tuck his tail in – which was usually stuck out at an angle – and prepare to fly over the fence, as if to avoid any stone that might be coming in his direction, even though we had long stopped throwing them. These stones were not very painful, but they were a great indignity.

The other common vice in jumping is running out. If a horse is likely to run out at a fence you need to collect him well beforehand to make him jump the fence well. If this doesn't work, you observe which side he runs – he will tend to run out consistently to one side or the other and, usually a horse will run out on his left if he is leading on his near fore and to the right if he's leading on his off fore. So you divide the fence mentally into three before you go. As you approach it, if the horse is leading on his near fore, you jump towards the right of the fence; if he's leading on his off fore you jump towards the left – in each case so that you have the wider part of the fence on the side that the horse is likely to run out.

In extremely bad cases you have to go back to jumping a foot or eighteen inches at a very slow pace, and keep him jumping slowly and collectedly except when he's in a lane where he can't run out, when you get him going at a proper pace. You progress from small fences to big fences, from trotting into them slowly to a fast trot, then to cantering in to them and eventually, after a lot of work and a lot of patience, you will get him jumping his fences fast and with efficiency.

It is a very common belief that refusing and running out are the same vice, simply because they are both used as avoidance techniques for jumping fences. And indeed some horses use both techniques to avoid jumping. Where this is the case, it is important that refusing be eliminated first, especially with horses who enjoy galloping fast and jumping. This is done by confining your jumping to a jumping lane or to fences so wide that a horse cannot run out. When the horse is enjoying his jumping so much that he is jumping everything at a slow, collected canter you can then concentrate on curing him of running out, which after your previous schooling, should be relatively easy.

Running out can take a very long time to eradicate, mainly because, for the horse, it is so well rewarded. As he goes to the left you go to the right and that's it, he's getting two rewards : a reward for avoiding the fence, and for getting you off. The reward for running out will then reinforce his motive to run out and so make it more difficult next time. His capacity to remember this particular vice is very high indeed. No matter how well you have cured him he'll try it on again every now and then, and you just have to go back and sort the problem out every time.

One more note on napping. An amazing number of nappy cases can be brought back to the ironmonger's : that is, they are caused by wrong bitting. In my belief there are basically only three bits to use – a plain snaffle, a vulcanite snaffle and a bar snaffle with egg butt ends. Anything else, if your horse is going well and correctly, is entirely unnecessary. Too much iron-mongery in your horse's mouth is merely an indication of your incompetence in riding him.

And remember that the pleasure that horses can get out of jumping is endless, and often quite spontaneous. I remember, out on a ride one day, passing a herd of four or five ponies who happened to be grazing a corner of the mountain near a piece of forest. As we passed the ponies just before we got to our jumping lane, three or four of the younger ones followed us and when our horses streamed up the jumping lane two of the ponies did the same. After that, whenever we were up that way those two ponies would follow us to the jumping lane and then gallop up the lane taking the fences as they came. These were wild and untouched ponies, and yet because they'd followed me that day having a gallop, and seen my horses jumping the fences, whenever they saw me going to the jumping lane afterwards they would follow me just because they enjoyed jumping. One form of nappiness I haven't yet dealt with is refusal by one horse to leave a group of other horses. This is usually not so much an evasive technique as an excess of herd instinct. The horse is a herd animal and breaking that herd instinct is extremely difficult. The only way to do this is with patience and perseverance, plus the occasional clout on the backside when he is being particularly bloody-minded. One of the things to remember here is that it is much easier to ride away from a group of horses at a right angle than at an acute angle. If you ride him away at an acute angle, he will tend to nap back towards the herd so that you are forced to pull his head round again and again. But if to begin with you teach him to ride directly away from the group, using your hand, heels and voice to direct him, his learning will be much more effective.

With a young horse we usually have him ride away from the group of horses led by an older and much more experienced horse, who already knows what to do. When he has learned quite easily to ride away from the main group with one horse leading him, we ride him away from the main group with the schoolmaster following him instead. At the third stage, the schoolmaster starts with him and goes a short way with him, then he stops. When the schoolmaster stops, we take great care to make sure that the pupil keeps going. The last and final step is to ride him away from the others directly.

If this is done there should be no difficulty in teaching a horse to leave the main group. This method is also useful when you are teaching jumping: you start off with the trainee following all the other horses, then you put him in the middle of the bunch, so that he goes third or fourth, then he goes second and then first, with the other horses jumping towards him. From there it is comparatively easy to get him to jump away from the main group, especially if you jump around a circle of jumps so that after he jumps away he finds himself swinging round back to the group.

The difficulty using other horses as an incentive in teaching is of course that it tends to multiply your difficulty when you're teaching him to go away from them. And in very bad cases of resistance, or with an old and bad mannered horse, it is often necessary to point your horse in the opposite direction and send the main group of horses away from you, before attempting to ride away from them. Over a period of time you diminish the distance between you and the other horses, until you can ride directly away from the main group.

14: *Rearing, Bolting and Bucking*

I have spent a considerable time on nappiness, since it is the most common and unnecessary vice among horses, and is tolerated by altogether too many riders through sheer weakness and incompetence. But we now come to more serious vices, which in their most severe forms can make a horse virtually unridable. The first point to remember, however, is that all these vices start off as very mild conditions. For example a nappy horse may go up a little on his hind legs, then more, and unless he is stopped at this stage you end up eventually with a horse who goes straight up and over backwards. To deal with all forms of rearing, from slight nappiness to the horse that throws himself straight over backwards, the same principle applies : that no horse will rear – or it is extremely unusual for a horse to rear – unless pressure is applied to the bit. So if you have your horse on a reasonably slack rein and his head is free, he is most unlikely to rear.

Rearing is one of the most dangerous vices because, when carried to its extreme not only do you hit the ground but you hit the ground with ten hundredweight of horse on top of you.

Years ago I had a horse who reared particularly badly, and I was consulting a friend, who knew a lot about horses, about it. And he came out with the opinion 'the trouble with that beggar is that you talk to too many women'. He wouldn't elaborate any further, so I went home and thought about this, and I realized that the horse only reared when I'd stopped to chat to one of my girlfriends. What was making him rear was the fact that I was making him stand still, and he was impatient to go on. Every time he tried to go on I checked him. At first he had reacted by throwing his head up. Then he started coming up on his hind legs a little bit, and by the time I talked to my friend about him he was really going up on his hind legs.

I cured him by never making him stand still. If we were waiting outside a cover while hounds drew, instead of standing still and chatting up a bird I would walk him round and round in a circle. This didn't improve my love life but it completely cured the horse of rearing.

My advice to anyone who has a really bad rearer is, first of all, flog all the ironmongery that you've got in his mouth to the local pub to decorate the bar with, and use the money to buy a plain rubber or vulcanite snaffle, which is the softest bit possible. Then never make him stand still. Keep him walking, walking, walking, walking. And never take him away from the other horses, because as soon as you do he'll start napping, which means that he'll go up on his hind legs again. After a month or so of this treatment, when he has stopped rearing completely and has no evident desire to rear, and his urge to walk round in circles has been considerably diminished because you've never allowed him to stand still, you can start letting him stand for a minute or two when he wants to. When he stands for a minute or two when *he* wants to, you can make him stand for a minute or two when *you* want to; and so you can extend the period until he will stand quite quietly.

Since the rearer is a horse of a particular psychological make up, with a very highly developed movement motivation, you will never be able to diminish his desire for movement for very long. You can however change his feeding to a high carbohydrate and a low protein diet.

If he rears when leaving other horses, your treatment is exactly the same as for nappiness: you first ride away with another horse, and then you go first, with your accompanying horse, and by degrees come to ride away from the field alone, without rearing. This again is a painstaking process because you are probably dealing with a deeply ingrained vice which has to be eliminated and forgotten over time. Long steady walking again helps in curing a horse who wants to rear, while faster work and jumping increase the vice. Only once you have cured him can you change his work so that he goes on to enjoy the things he enjoys doing.

When you get a horse that actually goes up on his hind legs and comes over backwards, there are two ways of curing him. In the first, as he gets to the point of overbalance, you slip off over his tail, let go of the reins and grab hold of the pommel of the saddle. Then as he goes down you come back up over his tail and into the saddle again. This is the one I use myself and I find it the most successful method of all. But split-second timing and athletic ability are necessary if you are to do it successfully.

There is an easier method. As the horse rears you slide off the saddle sideways, and as he comes down you vault back on the saddle. Again this takes athletic ability, but people who are curing horses who go up on their hind legs and throw themselves over backwards need a pretty high level of physical fitness anyway. Vaulting on and off a horse is a very minor accomplishment compared with some of the things you have to do when curing a bad habit in a horse.

With horses who go up on their hind legs when you try to mount them, you merely trot the horses forward, leading him, or with someone else leading him; then swing into the saddle at the run and keep him trotting. The next stage is to vault on him when he is walking, and then to make him stand still for a second while you vault on. Only after this do you slip your foot into the stirrup and get on while he is standing still. Slowly you extend the period for which you make him stand.

Rearing is usually a vice of thoroughbreds and Arabs and other horses of high excitability and great desire for movement.

Another avoidance technique, which is fortunately uncommon but extremely annoying when you come across it, is that of the horse that lies down and rolls over on top of you. This is an easy vice to cure provided you go about it the right way. It occurs in two forms. In the first the horse simply collapses on the ground and lies down. Here you simply sit on top of him, light a cigarette and admire the scenery until he gets up again. As with all these very bad vices, extreme coolness of head and control of your temper are necessary. It's no damn good hitting a horse with a very bad vice with a stick. You can be quite sure that by the time you've got him, if he's rearing up and going over backwards or lying down and rolling on top of you, he's been flayed alive by experts to try to cure him, so you may just as well leave the stick at home and rely on your patience. Eventually if the horse is simply lying down he'll find the grass rather damp and he'll get up again. You may have to sit on him for twenty minutes, half an hour, an hour or even two hours, but he'll get up sooner or later, especially if you stop him eating the grass near his head, because he will be faced with the problem that he either gets up with you on his back or else he dies of starvation and thirst. After he's gone through this treatment two or three times he'll stop the habit.

The second form, where as well as lying down the horse rolls on top of you, is also not difficult to cure. In this case you need a very old saddle that won't come to much harm, and as soon as he lies down you take your feet out of the stirrups. Then when he rolls over, you step over his tummy so that, as he comes up the other side, he gets up under you, and you're still in the saddle. I've never had a horse that tried this trick more than two or three times. When he finds that lying down and rolling over doesn't get you out of the saddle, he decides that this particular avoidance technique is no use to him, and he puts his mind to finding something else that will dislodge you.

Allied to rearing techniques are bolting techniques. These are all extremely unpleasant, and may need a certain amount of cunning to cure. One of the most unpleasant versions is where a horse carts you and heads for the nearest tree to try to brush you off against it. This may be cured in a single lesson, but does need cunning. As soon as the horse is out of control you try vigorously to swing him away from the tree then at the last moment you pull in the opposite direction so that he gallops straight into the tree and catches his head a terrible swipe. I have never had a horse try this a second time. But it is a risky technique : you must time it right at the last moment; and in any case if the horse is going fast enough and hits the tree head on, he may knock himself out.

With all these serious vices the remedies tend to be desperate ones, because either you cure them or the horse goes straight for cats' meat. But it is also true that these horses with extreme vices are very intelligent horses, who if it is possible – and it always is *possible* – to cure them become outstanding mounts to work on.

The mistake that most people make when they're on a horse that has bolted out of control, is to try to stop him by heaving on the reins. Now there are several ways of stopping a bolting horse, but one of them is not by a steady pull on the rein. All he does is shut his lower jaw, lean on the bit and use the pressure on the reins to balance himself. So, the first thing you try when your horse carts you is to give him his head, and then give a very sharp pull on the reins, lifting your hands at the same time so that you bring his head up and his weight back on his hocks.

Once you've found that your horse tends to bolt, the best thing you can do towards a permanent cure is to pick the largest field you can find and take him into it. As soon as he starts carting, let go of the reins and say 'right boy, get on with it'. After he has carried you two or three times round the field, you start to drive him on, saying 'right, now then, you go on', and push him for another half circuit or so. Then you pull the reins and say 'whoa' and he'll stop. Instead of fighting against you, you have allowed him to have his gallop and then made him stop when you told him to. Continue this treatment, and by degrees you will find that he'll stop carting you off in the same manner, and come back under control.

If your horse, when he carts you, goes off with his head in the air, one of the things I find most effective is a draw rein with a plain bar snaffle. Ignore your normal rein and let him go a hundred or two hundred yards, then heave on the draw rein and say 'whoa', pulling hard so that you have twice the strength to use on his mouth. This technique brings the horse's head down sharply on to his chest and brings him into a collected position.

The bolter must be allowed to have a good gallop every now

and then when he wants one, because the reason that he has taken to bolting is that you have suppressed his motive to gallop to such an extent that he takes matters into his own hands.

A third method of curing a horse that bolts is to keep changing direction. You allow him to gallop flat out, and then you turn him sharply to the left, sharply to the right, left, right, left, right. Each time he comes back to you, but again each time before you turn him you give him a slack rein so that he has to balance himself in his gallop without leaning on the bit. You go across or round the outside of a field on a slack rein. Then you lean back hard on the reins, at the same time leaning to the left, turning and pulling him to the left. More galloping on slack rein, then the same to the right.

The final method I use to stop a horse bolting is to put up a series of three-foot-six solid timber fences. After he has galloped into one of these, possibly putting himself and you head over heels, you will find that as he comes to the timber fence he will check and put himself right, or stop completely. At the same time as he checks, allowing him to go in on a slackish rein but making sure that he's headed straight at the fence so that he can't swing round and run out, you check him yourself, saying 'whoa'; and lean back to bring him on to his hocks so that he jumps correctly. This allows you a chance to pick him up and steady him, and then you let him go away to the next fence. As he approaches it you check him again, say 'whoa', and very quickly he will place himself and start responding to your commands to steady and stop.

With horses that bolt, you want as far as possible to make sure that they go out of a trot into a canter when they are pointing away from home and away from other horses, so decreasing the motivation to bolt.

I used two of the above methods with Watch, whom I thoroughly enjoyed racing for two seasons. But when he arrived he was extremely bad at bolting. So on the one hand I allowed him to gallop until he was tired. I did this by galloping him uphill in a straight line for about a mile and a half, then when he tired I pushed him on for two or three hundred yards and then said 'whoa' and he'd stop.

In addition, on the racecourse, I used a draw rein to steady him every time he looked like getting away from me. It took me about two months to get him so that I could ride him at home and check him and steady him, and it took me over a year to reach the stage at racing when I could drop him in at the back of the field and he'd settle down and gallop there.

Bolting is a vice that it is possible to cure, and since you know that you're almost certainly dealing with a horse that, in the long run, will probably be one of the best you've ever ridden, provided you're able to ride him, it is well worth taking the time and trouble to cure him.

The final serious vice, and a very common one in a horse, is bucking. Straightforward bucking is comparatively simple : I've already described how you find a steep hill, point the horse up it, drive your heels hard into the tenderest part you can find and say 'right, go on, buck you beggar', and each time he comes down you drive your heels in again. Half way up the hill he will have had enough and will stop bucking, and each time he takes to bucking again you repeat the cure. A horse bucking up a hill in a straight line is very easy to sit on, and you will be encouraged by the knowledge that a horse that bucks is also a horse that can jump, because the developments of the muscles – the powerful back muscles and quarters – which predispose a horse to buck are the very ones required for any form of jumping.

There are however a large number of ways of bucking, if the vice is well ingrained, and I will deal with those in detail. One variation is bucking again and again in the same place, while turning in a circle to the left or the right. If you've got a horse that is really bucking hard in a circle, he will throw you off sideways. Here you use the basic up-the-hill technique except that you carry a good long dressage whip, and when you get your horse to the bottom of the hill, as you drive your heels in to make him buck, you bring the dressage whip sharply across his neck and cheek on the side he turns towards (usually the left) when he's bucking. This immediately makes him straighten his head, and you go on using the whip to keep him going in a straight line.

This sounds brutal, and it is very hard on the horse, but please remember that all these extreme methods are used only in circumstances where the only alternative to curing the vice, is a bullet.

One possible method, that I don't use because I happen to enjoy sitting on a horse that bucks and curing him, is to put a saddle on the horse's back, tie up one leg to the girth, then put a tight strap round the back of the saddle, take a long rein and let the horse buck like hell round in a circle. By this means you do get the worst of the buck out of the horse before you get on his back. But since bucking is an avoidance technique and he's only bucking against the saddle, you're not eliminating the avoidance technique, which has to be done in a long term cure.

Some horses have a habit of bucking in a straight line four or five times, then stopping and puts in two or three big ones in the same place. Since you usually find that such a horse bucks forward with speed, the one he gets in when he's stopped is the one that gets you off. The only way to cure this is again to use your dressage whip. As you make him buck you bring the whip down across his backside, not on the side or the shoulder, so that you're driving him forward and driving him fast, and you will find that he will buck only three or four times before he settles down and gallops. Here you're changing the motive to buck to the motive to gallop, and as soon as he has learned that once he starts bucking he's got to go forwards and keep going forwards, the vice can be cured. Also, you should put him as quickly as possible into a jumping lane and get him jumping up the lane after other horses, so that his need to buck is diverted into jumping and enjoying himself.

The other two forms of bucking, both of them very rare, are switching ends and sun fishing. Switching ends means that the horse when he bucks will turn round in mid air so that he is

facing more or less in the opposite direction; and sun fishing
means that the horse twists his hind legs round as he bucks so
that you are sitting at an angle of forty-five degrees. I've only
had one of each of these in my lifetime, among maybe 150
horses I've cured of bucking, and the only way I could cure
either was with a cradle. A cradle is very simple to make. You
cut a number of sticks exactly the length of the horse's neck.
Usually I use eight tied at equal distances so that they fit round
the horse's neck exactly. This means that the horse has to keep
his neck straight with his head pointed out. The bottom two
sticks reach from the horse's chest to his chin, so that he has to
stick his head out or he's driving the stick into his chest. This
makes it impossible for the horse to buck at all. You work him
and work him and work him, and you take a couple of inches
off the sticks every week so that at the end of about three months
he's really got a loop of sticks round his neck that aren't doing
anything. When you've got to this stage and he's enjoying being
ridden and worked, and you've got him jumping, you have
made a complete cure.

You can use this method with any horse that bucks, but I've
found that it doesn't make for a very long-term cure. In other
words it can't be used as the sole remedy. But it does enable
you to change the horse's method of bucking. From sun
fishing, switching ends and turning in circles he begins to
buck in a straight line, and it is then much simpler to cure
him.

Finally, do not forget that the sooner you can get a bucking
horse to enjoy jumping, the sooner he will forget his vice, and
the motive to jump will replace the motive to buck.

Over the last three chapters we have dealt with a variety of
vices, most of them in an extreme form. The point is that if
you understand how to cure a vice at its very worst, you have
only to scale the treatment down to cure it in its minor forms.
All vices are basically avoidance techniques: a horse who doesn't
want to do something finds a way to avoid it. And in this sense
the way to cure a horse that doesn't want to be caught but
gallops across to the other side of the field is in principle the

same as the technique for curing bucking. You first make him allow himself to be caught and then, as a second stage, you make him want to be caught. You turn the horse out into a one- or two-acre field and then just walk round and round after him until he is so tired and bored with walking that he allows you to catch him. Then you make him do this four or five times until you can catch him whenever you want to. In the second stage, when you are teaching him to want to be caught, you also feed him in the field so that he comes over to you when he sees you with a bucket and sticks his head in it. So you put your arm over his neck and he'll walk in, eating his feed out of the bucket as he goes.

You teach a horse to lead in exactly the same way – you lead him with the bucket and you have your arm over his neck. As the next stage, as you lead him with the bucket from the field, you slip a piece of string round his neck; then the end of the halter. Then you put the nosepiece of the halter over his head before he can get at the oats. And all the time you're catching him and leading him with the bucket, the halter being the incidental piece of the movement.

Within a very short time a horse that was completely un-catchable becomes one who wants to be caught and wants to come in. At times in fact I'm beset with the opposite problem: that the horses are too keen to be caught. I go up to the field and give a shout and they all come over hell for leather to get at the bucket, and they're fighting and kicking at each other to get a mouthful, so that I am in imminent danger of being tramped into the ground. This is where order and discipline come in. Over the course of four or five days I teach them that they are caught in a set order. Jack, who is usually first at the bucket, has his mouthful and I halter him and give him to some-one else to hold. I go back, catch Madam, halter her and so on. In due course the horses will come in that order to be caught, each one having his two or three mouthfuls out of the bucket, each one being petted on being caught, and order and discipline triumphs.

Thus using each piece of learning which we have talked

about in this book in its correct place and in the correct way, you will make teaching your horse far easier for yourself. By increasing his learning ability the horse will learn to do each task with much greater ease. At the same time the end target of each piece of learning must be seen by the horse, so that when he has reached goal 'a' he must be able to see goal 'b', which leads on to goal 'c', and so on. How you mix which parts of his learning ability, which you use most and in what order depends mainly, on what you want to achieve in the end, but you also have to bear in mind your own abilities and the horse's characteristics.

But be careful what you teach the horse because it can have unforeseen results. You may remember how Cuddles learned to open his stable door and come down to our front door, and knock. We were rash enough then to teach him to press down the handle of the front door, and come in to get his feed just on the porch, and then actually in the sitting-room doorway. This was extremely amusing and of course a talking point among visitors. Until one day we came home and saw to our surprise that the front door had been left open. I picked up the shopping and went in, only to find that I couldn't open the door into the sitting-room. Something seemed to be wedged against it. So we went round the back door and in through the kitchen, to find Cuddles stuck in the sitting-room unable to go forwards or backwards or to turn round. Eventually, and with difficulty I lugged half the furniture out of the kitchen, got him into the kitchen and proceeded to turn him there. Unfortunately, as he swung his hindquarters round, he burned his bottom on the Raeburn, gave a bound forward, landed on my foot and shot through the door back into the sitting-room again. He refused absolutely to go back, and it took a good quarter of an hour of heaving and shoving and persuading before we could manoeuvre him out.

15: *Choosing Your Own Horse*

By now, if you don't own a horse already, you will no doubt be itching to have a horse on which to use and practice all these skills. It is impossible to study, understand, observe and work a horse consistently, unless you own a horse yourself, because understanding a horse properly is a full time job. So the only thing for it is to buy one yourself. This usually means buying the cheapest horse possible.

Cheap horses fall roughly into three categories. In the first come the old horses with so many bumps and lumps on them that they look like cheap coat racks. My advice is to avoid those. In the second category come the horses whose previous owners have been unable to handle them. These are the horses I like, and if you have the ability (this does not necessarily mean experience), the time and the patience to work on such a horse, you may end up with something outstanding. This is the way I get most of my best horses. And since you will be buying the horse at killing price, if you are successful you will be saving a very good horse from death. If on the other hand, you find that you are unable to cope with him, you will have to sell him before he kills you. And finally, in the third category of horses that you can buy cheaply you will find the plain, weak, un-broken three-year-olds. These almost certainly are the best group of horses for the beginner to purchase from. Since they are thin and weak, your preliminary work both in riding and working will be comparatively easy. Secondly the reward in taking a plain, thin, weak three-year-old and turning him into a well mannered, fit and well turned out five-year-old, ready to take part in competition, is one of the great rewards of horse-manship. You will also be turning a very cheap animal into an expensive one.

The first thing to be sure about is the height that you want to buy. And having decided, you must know that just because someone tells you that a horse is 14.1, the horse is not necessarily 14.1. He's probably about 12.2. So invest in a tape measure, or a measuring stick, and measure the damn thing. Then knock half an inch off for the shoes, and half an inch off for bad luck, and you're somewhere around the correct height of the horse. This process will eliminate fifty per cent of the horses you've been offered.

The next step is to decide how much you can afford to keep your horse. Moorland ponies for instance are comparatively cheap to keep – at the time I am writing, you can keep a moorland pony for £3 to £5 a week, depending upon the pony and the time of the year. But a thoroughbred is going to cost you £10 to £12 a week to keep. Next, remember that the pony has to be able to carry your weight, so if you can afford to buy and feed only a small pony, that is a 13.2, you want a 13.2 stocky pony not a 13.2 with legs like matchsticks. And then, decide what you want to do with your horse; if you want to do serious competition for instance, you need something big enough, and strong enough to compete on.

So, having decided the amount you can afford, both to buy and feed the animal, and approximately the size and strength you need, your next decision is what kind of temperament you are looking for. This will have a great deal to do with your own natural ability and confidence as a horseman or horsewoman. You may indeed be a genius on a horse. But geniuses on horses are very few and far between, so have a session of severe self-criticism, and decide what you want to do, and what you can cope with. Do you want to do just a little gentle hacking, a little quiet dressage work? Or do you want to compete seriously show jumping, or one-day eventing? Do you really want to hunt, or go in for team cross-country? Each of these activities needs a different type of horse.

Finally, when you have decided the type of horse you want, there is one more thing you must remember: that ability and good looks do not necessarily go together, in fact they are unlikely to go together, and pretty colours are not going to make a good horse. If you want a horse that is going to look pretty, and mince along like a pimp in Piccadilly, that's fine, but don't expect him to turn into a superb one-day eventer or a show jumper. You may be extremely lucky and find that he will, but the chances are against you. If you took the best show jumpers, the best one-day eventers and, the best steeplechasers in the country and put them in a show class, they would make a very long line at the bottom end of the class. The judge wouldn't look at them. Ability is something that is within the horse, and is not apparent on the surface.

Colours on the other hand are not irrelevant. They can be an indication – and I emphasize the word indication – of the horse's temperament. Strong colours tend towards strong character. Weak colours tend towards weak character. Now I know that there are a large number of exceptions to this rule, so don't put too much trust in it. But palaminos, washy chestnuts and greys do tend to be weaker characters than dark chestnuts, bright bays (who tend to be excitable), dark dirty browns (who tend to be steady and honest) and blacks, who tend to be strong characters and very good horses indeed. I myself have a definite bias to blacks; I have had a great number of them, and almost without exception they have been good horses: admittedly awkward and bloody-minded but they were each strong charactered with a real determination to win.

Children's Ponies

The breed of horses also makes a difference. I have very little experience of the northern breeds, so I am not going to pass any comment on them except for the Shetland pony, of which I have had a certain amount of experience, and which I abhor as a children's pony, mainly because it is stocky and broad, which makes for a difficult ride. Exmoors can be superb and very often are, but they tend to be one-man horses. Dartmoors, depending on which part of the moor they come from, again tend to be men's horses rather than children's ponies. With all mountain ponies you must remember their history. To survive they had to live on whatever they could pick up off the mountain; then, at three or four years old, they were herded in and roughly broken, and expected straight away to pull a heavy load, carry a man all day shepherding, or go down the pit and haul ten hundredweight in a tram. Only the very toughest survived : powerful, compact ponies of 11 or 12 hands whose very bloody-mindedness was their greatest asset. The one thing that they were not bred for was carrying children. The odd one who had the temperament and kindness to carry a child was the exception. The same applies to the Welsh mountain pony: only about 20 per cent of them are suitable for children to ride. The rest of them are either too excitable, or too bloody-minded. The 20 per cent are the ones that stop, and look after their riders.

The New Forest pony falls into a different category, because he tends to be a bit bigger. My personal preference for a child's pony, no matter how small the child, is something around the 13.2 mark – by that I mean from 13 to 14 hands. I know a small child on this is going to appear to be very much over horsed, but ponies this size tend to have a much steadier and easier movement than the smaller ones, and a much more reasonable temperament. No doubt a number of people will dispute this view, but as a general rule I find the 13 to 13.2 brown pony more likely to make a good, and safe ride for the child. After all, you are going to trust your offspring to the care of the horse, and the pony has to look after the child.

The most important thing in a child's first pony then, is the animal's temperament and reliability. It doesn't matter if it's knock-kneed, cow hocked, and has a head as big as an omnibus, provided it's sweet, kind and gentle so that if the child crawls between its legs and pulls itself on by pulling the pony's ears, the pony will put up with it. And if the child falls off, the pony will stop, nuzzle it and dry its tears. As the child improves, of course, you can progress to better things.

Also in buying a 13.2, of course, you have the added advantage that you also have something that you can get on yourself. If he's being a bit awkward you can put him through a term of re-schooling and discipline, until he is only too glad to get back to his owner, and a quiet easy life again! It doesn't sound very kind to the pony, but it is useful for him to learn that if he deposits his rider and misbehaves too much someone is going to get on his back, and make him work very hard, under very strict control for the next two or three weeks!

An Adult's Horse

Here, the breed of horse you want depends on the work you want to do. If you want quiet hacking, and a certain amount of competition, my personal choice is the Welsh cob and the Welsh cob cross. This is a really good horse, who enjoys competition and has an awful lot of character and brains; and by and large, Welsh cobs have a pleasant and good disposition. But if you want something that looks pretty, and just want to hack around, you could choose an Arab or Arab cross. These are the most beautiful of horses, but as far as competition and jumping are concerned, they are not particularly good. I dislike Arabs, but that is a personal prejudice, and plenty of other people dislike Welsh cobs and thoroughbreds.

For genuine and serious competition – show jumping, eventing, or indeed anything that involves jumping and galloping – you have of course to get as near to the thoroughbred as possible. But remember here that – as with the Arab – you are buying a horse that is going to be expensive to keep and feed. This I know to my cost, because I usually have four or five thoroughbreds knocking about the place, each of whom costs at least twice as much to feed and keep as I do myself. They go like the devil, in cross country competitions and hunter trials, winning just often enough to keep me interested. But the trouble is that each one I get convinces me that he's good enough to make Red Rum look like a donkey from the sands. Then, when I run him and he doesn't make it, he then convinces me with his excuses: the going was wrong, he was not fit enough, he got crossed at a vital fence, so I race them again, and again. But I get a lot of pleasure wandering up to the stable, chatting with them, schooling them and dreaming of one day actually winning the big race.

By now you should have decided on the size of horse, and the sort of horse you want. Now comes the most important part of all, which is finding one that not only suits you, and your purse, but with whom you have an empathy. There are three ways of doing this. First of all, if you are going to a riding school regularly, you may find a horse there who goes better for you than anyone else, and who suits you down to the ground. Then, if your pocket is big enough, you may be able to buy him. Or, you may have a friend with a horse who suits you. Or you may go to a dealer (or someone who has advertised a horse, and anyone who is selling a horse is a horse dealer) and buy a horse from him. If you do this, you should insist on either a fortnight's trial, or an agreement that if the horse doesn't suit you, the dealer will have it back. In either case produce a pen and paper at once and say 'I want that in writing', because, while I'm not saying that all horse dealers (including myself) are dishonest, we tend, when selling a horse, to promise more than we intend to, and then to forget all about it afterwards.

The third way of buying a horse, which is the way I buy mine, is at public auction and, provided you don't pay a stupid price (and here you want the advice of someone who knows about horses), you can do whatever you want with it, and if, at the end of the month, you decide that it's not what you want, you can take it to another auction – not the same one, because there will be a lot of people who recognize it – and resell it.

Whether buying from a friend, a dealer, an acquaintance, or at a public auction, once you have ridden and tried your horse, if you don't feel an empathy and oneness with it, leave it alone. Whatever happens you must have a bond between you and the horse you are working with. If you don't feel this bond, don't put it off, get rid of him and get something else that does suit you. He may not suit anybody else, everyone else may say how ugly he is, or how awkward he is, or how useless he is, but if he clicks with you, and will do anything you ask him to within his ability, his appearance is of only secondary importance.

On the other hand it is of vital importance that you should have the horse vetted to make sure that he is organically sound, and that his legs are in a reasonable state, to allow him to do what you want him to do.

One of the ugliest horses I ever had – he was probably the ugliest horse I had ever seen in my life – was the most superb hunter and cross country horse I have ever ridden. Dart was 14.1 h.h., roman nosed, flat sided, long backed and bad tempered. After three months' handling, he became an absolute pet. But at the time I put him in his first hunter trial, he had jumped only half a dozen fences in his life. I had three or four other horses competing in the trial, which was about four miles away, and these had been led on with my wife's and my daughter's horses. But I had some work to finish and was going to follow later in the car. Then the car wouldn't start. So I slapped a saddle on Dart and we went hell for leather, because I was late. Having got him there, I decided to put him in the novice. He went like a bomb, being beaten in the jump off by my best horse, Fanny, and one other only because I was unable to turn him fast enough round the corner into the fifth fence. Except by Fanny, he was never beaten in a cross country again. He was an absolutely superb hunter, though as far as dressage was concerned, he thought it a waste of time, and the two or three times I rode him show jumping, he did very well but tended to sacrifice speed for precision. Nevertheless he was placed in two out of the three competitions that I rode him in.

The highlight of his career was giving a solo demonstration at the Royal Welsh Show, demonstrating the versatility of the Welsh cob. This included changing legs and doing a figure of eight, in twice his own length, jumping four foot, doing full passes, counter cantering and half passes at the canter.

Another example of looks being deceptive, is Mandryka. Seeing him in the paddock, he looks a small weedy 15 hand screw, but he is without doubt one of the best lady's point-to-pointers in the history of racing, having won over forty races. And a third example is my beloved Spitfire. No man weighing eleven stone seven, would dream of buying a pony of 12.2 as a hunter, yet she is almost certainly the best hunter I have ever ridden. Without any hesitation, I could put her at a five foot iron gate, and know that she would jump it. She would never turn her head at a fence. We could jump four foot of barbed wire and know that we'd clear it. In fact I would jump fences on her that any other horse in the British Isles would find impossible.

On one occasion when I was hunting hounds on her, hounds crossed a very deep dingle (a dingle is a Welsh term for a sunken river). It was about twenty feet below the field that I was in, and a yard or so back from the dingle was a barbed wire fence, three foot six high. I trotted Spitfire into the barbed wire fence, she jumped it, turned in mid air, landed at right angles to it, walked along the edge to a sheep path, and trotted down the sheep path into the dingle. There was a tree lying between where we came down and the sheep path on the other side. She jumped that and walked up the far side, where there was another sheep fence, three foot six high with barbed wire on top. There was about five foot in front of the fence, which was just enough for her to stand facing it, at an angle. She edged back slightly, until one foot went over the edge of the dingle, so that she knew exactly where she was, two feet from the fence. She jumped, arching over it, turning in mid air so that she landed in the field, and went straight away after hounds. The whole operation hadn't taken more than three minutes. Now there isn't another horse in the British Isles that could have negotiated that particular obstacle. Shortly after that, someone told me that it wasn't fair on the horse, and that I was going to come to serious injury myself, negotiating obstacles like that, but I said 'Don't be bloody silly, I can jump anything on this pony'. The old cow must have heard what I had said, because the next fence she came to she raced straight into it, and put me on the ground in a cow pat.

Getting to Know Your Horse

Suppose now you've chosen your horse, you've got him home and you still find he suits you. The first thing you have to do is watch and study him, not just when you're riding, but when he's in his stable and you are handling him. You have to discover whether he is a horse that stands still, in the corner of his stable or looking out of the door all day; or whether he spends his time walking round and shifting his feet. You need to know whether he drinks frequently, taking small sips, or whether he drinks half a bucket in one go; whether he eats all and anything put in front of him, or picks and chooses bits of his food. You must know whether he needs movement and interest outside, or whether he spends half his day asleep. You want to know the places he enjoys being scratched, and where he's ticklish when he's being groomed. You also need to know how he communicates with you, and other horses. All these things take time to learn. And all of them have implications for how you treat your horse. For example, if he's a horse that stands still, he's one that you will need to exercise a great deal. And if he is a horse that tends to sleep at the back of his stall, you will have to provide the stimulation to make him the alert, responsive animal he should be.

It is important to almost any horse to be able to see what is going on, so that he is mentally stimulated all the time. Ideally, he should be able to see the road, so that he can watch the cars going up and down, and to see the house, so that he can see what you are doing, and to see other animals moving around – anything that is interesting to watch and do. The more things he can see, the greater will be his enjoyment, and his readiness to respond.

Having provided him with a stimulating environment, you now need to give some thought to developing his brain, and his personality. This is really a question of a proper balance between insisting on your way and letting him have his own. Part of the time when you are working him, he must of course do what you tell him, and when he's done well and done what you've told him, he is praised for it and made a great fuss of. Then for ten minutes to a quarter of an hour, you let him do what he wants to do. If he wants to throw a couple of bucks and a fart, he's allowed to; if he wants to amble along, heaving a few mouthfuls of grass out of a hedge, he's allowed to do that. But when he's had his recreation, you say 'Right, back to work, off we go again' and then you do what you want. And so, depending on the length of the lesson, you carry on alternating work and pleasure. At certain times, of course, the things he wants to do, and the things you want to do are the same, for example when you are out hunting following hounds. But this coming together is really the end product of everything else you have done; his dressage work, his jumping, if he enjoys jumping, in his playtime, and your mutual pleasure in the excitement of galloping. It's an old, old saying, 'all work and no play makes Jack a dull boy,' but it's especially true with horses.

There is no doubt that training any horse *can* be done by repetition and habit, but full enjoyment of the horse (unless the enjoyment you get is from people saying 'Oh, isn't he well schooled' and 'doesn't she ride beautifully') is not going to come from repetition training, it is going to come from empathy and oneness between horse and rider.

The first stage in establishing this empathy with the horse, is in studying how he communicates. Most people understand some of what their horses are saying – when they say 'where's my bloody breakfast', demanding food, or when they show annoyance, anger or affection. But you can comprehend much more than this if you watch, observe and understand everything that your horse is saying, and at the same time you work mentally to get in tune with the horse. You will know when you have got in tune with the horse; when you are able, say sixty per cent of the time, to ride with a slack rein and still go where you want to go, at the pace you want to go. His movement will be reflecting the state of *your* mind, so that you'll get to the stage where you don't need to touch the reins, or make any movement at all, to turn him to the left or right, stop him, move him forward at a walk or a trot or a canter. In fact, I got to the stage with Arctic Watch, when I could take him into a field where there were three fences in a row, jump two fences and then stop, turn and go back over the two fences, without either touching the reins or moving my body. In fact in the last race I rode him I had no power in my left hand since I had injured it the week before, and since Watch's method of running a race was to go off hell for leather from the start, I was very much in his power. He was a very strong and powerful horse, and from start to finish of the race I only had minimum contact with his mouth, so I was really racing him with a completely slack rein. And yet old Watch, who was eleven years old, set off in his normal pace in the field, dropped back to the leading horse, and went stride for stride with him for a circuit and a half. This was an open race and Watch wasn't really an open race horse, and finally we dropped back to third place – apart from the fact that the old fool went straight through the last fence, we should have finished third. But the point is that there was complete mental empathy between us : he knew that I couldn't ride him – I could stay on top of him, but I couldn't steady him, turn him or place him at his jumps. Yet, except for the last, he jumped every fence perfectly. I was steadying, pacing him and jumping the old man purely by mental control.

Now this is what empathy with a horse is all about. You feel so much at one that he will make up for your deficiencies, just as when he makes a mistake, he will expect you to put him right.

If you can get a horse like Watch, Spits or any one of a dozen horses, with which I have got to that complete stage of empathy, you've got something that is of a price beyond rubies. Sometimes you gain it instantaneously with a horse but with others it takes a year, eighteen months, or even two years, but when you have achieved it, then, to use racing parlance, you can put your betting boots on, because then you've got a horse that is going to give every last ounce he has. You are going to have a horse that, when you've fought with your wife and kicked the cat, phoned the bank manager and told him exactly what you think of him and he has told you to take your overdraft elsewhere, you can get on, and he'll take you out, and he'll give a little jiggle and he'll give a little buck, and you'll suddenly find he makes you laugh and by the time you get back home, you're in a frame of mind to tell your wife you're sorry and kiss her, stroke the cat and phone the bank manager and apologize.

This is what he can do for you – he can lift you when you're depressed, he will mirror your enthusiasm in competition, he will extend himself when necessary, and above all when you take him riding, each time will be a new joy.

16: *Training Your Own Horse*

This is the point where the hard work starts. So we shall go through a guided review of schooling a horse from the beginning, from training a green three-year-old, curing vices, to developing him for competition.

The most important thing that anyone riding or working horses must remember, is that the horses are not people. They don't think like people, they don't behave like people, and their reactions are not those of human beings. A horse does not work from logic, he works and develops from previous memory. For example, if he has jumped a two foot plain rail, he will retain that in his memory, and when he sees a two-foot coloured rail, he will associate it with the rail that he has already jumped, and jump it successfully. When you are doing dressage, the horse will know from previous experience when he is to halt.

Timing and rhythm are both important in working with horses, and one of the facts that we know is that the horse has approximately the same ability as the human being to judge time. This skill as a rule develops later than it does in people but it means that when you are working a horse he will learn the rhythm and timing in the same way as you will. This is of particular importance in both dressage and show jumping, when you will often find that when you need to stand stationary for four seconds in dressage, for instance, the horse is more accurate than you are.

Now that you have bought your horse, you will want to start working him. For simplicity I am going to assume that the horse is completely unbroken when you get it.

With an unbroken horse, the first thing you want to do is to study it and get to know it. If he's never been touched he is going to be scared stiff of human beings, which means that the

540

first thing you have to do is get his confidence. This is quite simple to do because you will be feeding him, watering him, cleaning him out, and generally being with him half a dozen times a day, and walking past his stable door twenty or thirty times a day.

Once he has accepted you as a friend and likes you, you can start putting your hand on him. You will know the time to do this, because when you feed him first thing in the morning, he comes bustling over to the bucket, for his breakfast. You can put a hand on him steadily, quietly and gently – just touch him with the tips of your fingers, behind his shoulder, rub him gently and working up his back and side until you get to his neck.

When you get to his neck you pinch his mane between your fingers, scratching at the same time, to try to imitate the feeling he would get from another horse nibbling at his mane, in the field. Don't forget, this is a gesture among horses and he will accept it and accept you as a friend.

When you have got to this stage, and he has accepted you as a friend, which may take three or four days, or may take two or three weeks, you can start teaching him to lead. This does not mean slapping a halter on his head, and heaving on the rope. Teaching him to lead is quite simple. When you take his feed into him, you keep hold of the bucket. As soon as he starts eating, you walk away with the bucket so that he follows you to eat his breakfast. Once he's doing this, walking round the stable following you and the bucket, you open the stable door and, following exactly the same procedure (making sure of course that the front gate is shut first), you walk round the yard with him eating out of the bucket, always making quite sure that you end up back in the stable before he has finished his breakfast.

The next stage is when, instead of him following you with the bucket, you hold the bucket in front of you, and rest your arm across his neck, so that he walks along with his head in the bucket, and your arm over his neck. It is vital at this stage of gentling and in all the early stages, at no time to have a battle with your horse. If he says no, you step back and come back to him slowly, and gently. You keep doing this patiently, until he does what you want him to. Anger breeds anger, so if you get him upset, frightened or angry, you are going to have a difficult horse to handle.

When he is walking around quite happily with his head under your neck, you take a bit of baler twine, and loop it round his neck, still using the bucket, to induce him to go where you want. A very short time after that, you wander into the stable with a bit of baler twine, put it round his neck, and you will be able to lead him simply with a bit of string round his neck, because he's learned that walking with you is a pleasurable experience.

While you are doing this, of course, you don't leave him in the stable all day. I like to have my horses out by day and in by night, making quite sure that when they come in their feed is waiting for them, and before very long they will be waiting at the gate of the field to come in for supper. At this stage you will be putting a piece of baler twine round his neck in the field, and leading him into the stable with it.

The next stage is haltering him. Haltering is very straight-forward too. When you put the bucket of feed into him in the morning, you simply put the nose piece of the halter round the top of the bucket, so that he has to put his head through the halter, to get his head into the bucket. The whole time you are using the motivation of appeasing his hunger, to get him to want to do what you want him to do. When he puts his nose through the halter, it is a simple matter to buckle the top piece of the halter over his ears, so that he has got his head collar on. And then when you catch him in the evening, you alter the practice slightly, you bring a small feed for him, so that he has to put his head down into the bucket, through the nose piece of the halter. Again you put the halter on and lead him in with the halter.

When you have got to this stage, and he is following you quite happily on the end of the halter, you take him for a walk, wandering down the road with him leading slowly and gently, letting him pick a piece of grass here and there, so that he is enjoying learning. In fact he is learning without realizing it.

One of the pieces of research that we did in teaching a horse to lead, was with a yearling colt. During his first winter, he was in by night and out by day. Each day when he came in, he was always the last one following the other three. Quite by chance to begin with, I used to walk holding his tail. Within a month I could stop him, turn him left or right, make him walk forward or trot, simply by turning his tail, pulling it slightly, or flicking it forward. Then, at the end of about three months I wanted to halter him. I had a half hour battle to get a halter on him, and then he refused to lead, and after that it took two people a fortnight to teach him to lead with a halter. One person had to hold him by the halter, while the other gave him the signals he knew and understood, using his tail.

It is a completely erroneous belief, that a horse has to be led with a halter, and certainly in the early stages it is a mistake to go straight to leading him in this way, since it leads to a battle with the horse and puts the whole relationship on the wrong basis in the beginning. Similarly we avoid a battle when we are teaching a horse to tie, by tying him fast in a stall with a bar behind him. If he hangs back, he is pushing against the bar with his backside, and not fighting against the halter. By degrees we tighten the halter rope, and have the bar further back, until he stands when tied without any trouble at all.

When you are in the stable with him, as well as making a fuss of him, you make a habit of moving your hands all over his body, as if you are grooming him with your hands. You increase the pressure here and there, you tease out a tangle in his mane, or tail. Now you are teaching him to groom. If while you are doing this quietly, he doesn't take any notice, you can take a stable rubber, and night and morning you can rub him all over, tidying up his coat smoothly. From the stable rubber, you graduate to the soft body brush. Again each stage, each step is a small step, and the feelings he gets are pleasurable, so he knows that each new thing you are doing with him is increasing his pleasure and increasing his comfort. At this stage also, when you are grooming his far side you lean over and push him over sideways with your body. When you want him to get over, don't try to train him to move over on command, push him over, so that he gets used to being pushed around physically by you. When he's used to you leaning on top of him, get someone to give you a hand over, and still with the stable rubber or body brush in your hand, groom the far side of him whilst you are lying on his back.

The next stage is to get a bridle on him. This can be done in two ways, depending on your horse. If he's going quietly, open his mouth gently and slip the bit into his mouth, and the bridle over his head. He should take very little notice of this, but if you have difficulty, put the halter on, tie the bit to one side of the halter, slip the bit through his mouth, and tie it on to the other side.

Once you start doing any action you go on doing it, and on doing it, until he accepts it quietly without any trouble. If for example, you have difficulty putting the bridle on, you stay there putting the bridle on and off, on and off, until you can do so without difficulty.

Then, having got the bridle on, you put the saddle on. Here you treat him as if he is an old and quiet horse. You go in with the stirrups and girth flapping, put the girth over his back and slide the saddle on his back. Don't go in with the attitude that you are doing a big thing – you're doing something normal, and quite straightforward. By this stage, he should be so used to you pushing him round and handling him, that a flapping saddle is something to be looked at, because it's interesting, rather than something to be frightened about. It is advisable to have a feed in his bucket when you saddle him, but if he is frightened in any way by the saddle, he is certainly not ready for you to get on his back.

Having got the saddle on, you catch hold of the girth, and

you put one buckle on the end hole, then you put the second buckle on the second hole, and slowly girth it up, until you feel his muscles tense. Then you talk to him for five minutes until he's relaxed again, then you go on tightening one hole at a time, until you've got the saddle on absolutely firmly. You then put the reins behind the stirrups, and go away and leave him for half an hour, so that he can wander round the stable with the saddle on and the stirrup leathers flapping.

When you've got the saddle on, or when you tighten the girth, perhaps two or three per cent of horses will proceed to buck. Just stay there looking at him and talking to him, telling him that he's a stupid sod, and if he wants to buck he can buck. When he stops bucking you go over to him and lead him round. If he bucks again you let go of the bridle, and let him go on bucking. Where you have a horse that bucks when you saddle him tightly – that is a cold-backed horse – before getting on to him you should always take him out with a rope and lead him round, so that if he's going to buck against the saddle he does so whilst you are on the ground.

When your horse has got tired of bucking against the saddle, and found he can't buck it off, you lead him round again and back into the stable, then get someone to give you a leg up, and lean across the saddle. Again, if he tightens his muscles, you slip from the saddle until he's relaxed, then go up again, and go on doing this until he's completely relaxed, with you lying there. Then you take your arm, over his back and down the far side. You do this a dozen or fifteen times, until he's gone fast asleep again, and then you ease your leg over the saddle, until you're sitting on it without him taking any notice. Rub your hand down his neck, scratch his mane and all his ticklish places, and slip off again. Then you get on again, on and off, on and off until he's got used to it.

Now you are ready to take him outside. If possible you should have someone on an old, quiet horse to accompany you; but if this is not possible, someone to lead him. First place him so that he's facing into a corner, so that he can't move forward. Then get someone to give you a leg up, ease your leg over the saddle, and once he is relaxed, turn him round. The person on the old horse now walks away, and you follow him. When your horse has settled down nicely and quietly, you say 'whoa', the person on the old horse stops, and your horse stops too, because if he doesn't he's going to run into the other horse's backside. You click your tongue, the horse in front will walk on, and you will follow. You do this for a quarter of an hour or twenty minutes, preferably in a circle. Exactly the same system is followed if someone else is leading the horse. When you say 'whoa', they stop and the horse will stop. When you click your tongue, the person leading walks forward and he will walk forward. By the time you get home, when you say 'whoa' and touch the reins, he should be just about stopping.

As soon as he's walking forward when you click your tongue and squeeze lightly with your legs, and stopping when you say 'whoa' and touch the bit, then you go on to the next step, which is getting him to neck rein to the left or the right. To turn left, you carry the rein right across his neck, so that you have one rein lying across his neck, and the other one is right out. At the same time, you turn your whole body to the left, so that your left knee is pressing into the saddle in front, and your right leg is pressing into his side on the right. When he's crossed the road to the left, you turn your body the other way, bringing the reins across the neck, so that he neck reins to the right. The next thing is to teach him to turn left or turn right at the end of the road.

When you've got him walking gently, slowly and nicely, turning to the left, turning to the right, and neck reining, which should take only three or four days, you get the person on the other horse to trot four or five strides when you click your tongue. Again your horse will imitate the leading horse, trotting to catch him up. Let your trotting period increase from four or five strides, to ten or twenty yards, then to fifty yards. To start off with, you will do a slow sitting trot, and when he has settled to that you do a rising trot. By now you will be doing half an hour to forty minutes' work a day on him.

Find a nice straight piece of grass, and go from a trot into a canter. Here, very occasionally, you may find that he will put in a little buck, though this applies only to one horse in twenty. When we first canter we canter uphill anyway, not because we expect the horse to buck, but because if he does buck he will find bucking hard work, so he'll stop. Canter steadily up the hill, and by the time he gets to the top of the hill, he will be a bit puffed and tend to drop back to a trot. If you feel that he's going to drop back to a trot, you say a 'steady boy', pull on the reins and pull him back, so that he has made the transition from the canter to the trot, at your command. You treat each transition in fact in the same way : from a walk to a trot, from the trot to the canter and back again. You give the command, just as you feel that he is going to do the movement anyway.

Now you have a programme of straightforward walking, trotting, cantering, turning each day. You are in effect working on two things at once : his motivation; and his fitness. He is enjoying working and riding with other horses, enjoying imitating his elders, going to different places every day, and seeing different things. His interest is aroused, his motivation is increased. At the same time he is getting fitter, and to help him do so you increase his feeds. One of the things that I particularly abhor, is the practice of underfeeding horses when they are being broken − feeding them hay instead of corn. I always believe that if a horse is doing more work, he will need increased feeding. This may lead to a little extra trouble for you, but the important thing is that each new piece of work that the horse does at this stage he should enjoy doing.

The empathy and communication that I talked about in the last chapter, will be growing as you work. You will be getting closer and closer to the horse. Now when you are out working him you make him do a collected walk. Pull him together so that he's collected, not just slopping along any old how. You will do this for two or three minutes, half a dozen times during the ride, then you increase the length of time. Particularly before you make a transition from a walk to a trot or from a trot to a canter, or back to the walk, you pull him together and get his head in the correct position, so that the transition becomes a collected transition.

You do each thing as you feel you *can* do it. The important thing is that what you are doing with the horse, should be geared to the pace that the horse wants. You must never move too slowly, so that he gets bored with the work he is doing – ideally he wants to be doing something new each day so that he is keeping his mind active – nor too fast, expecting the horse to do more than he is ready to do.

Soon now you will be ready to start teaching him to jump. By that I don't mean that you build a series of five-foot barriers, and drive him into them hoping for the best. This is in fact the way a number of people train their horses to jump for point to pointing; they jump them over a couple of gorse bushes at home, put him into a maiden point-to-point with some fool like myself on his back, and you gallop into the first fence, and he may or may not scramble over it. And this actually works after a fashion, because after he's run in three or four point-to-points, the pleasure of racing with other horses does usually get him jumping. He learns by his mistakes, and by the bruises you collect. But this is a crude method for teaching horses to jump, rather like throwing someone in the deep end of a swimming pool.

I remember on one occasion arriving at a point-to-point to find that the owner that I rode for had a horse in the lorry which I had not seen before, belonging to his neighbour. It turned out that it was a little grey mare called Passing Cloud III, and he wanted me to ride it in the maiden. I stood in the paddock looking at the ill-kempt little weed, comparing it unfavourably with the superb sleekness and fitness of another newcomer, Four Ten, who subsequently won the Gold Cup. But I couldn't offend the owner, so up I went. I got a good start on the little mare, leading into the first fence. Twenty yards from it she slowed, looking with horror at the obstacle in front of her, but the twenty other horses were bustling past her. So she stopped at the bottom of the fence, took off like a helicopter, and somehow landed on all four feet on the other side. She was a game, gutsy little mare, and dashed away after the others at a rate of knots, adopting approximately the same technique in negotiating the next two fences. The fourth fence was the open ditch. Certain that we would come to grief here, I decided to do so in style. Three paces out I caught her a couple, so that she accelerated, and from pure good fortune she took off at the right place, and jumped it superbly. She must have been an extremely quick learner, because from then on she jumped beautifully. Since the rest of the field had been going like hell, trying to keep up with Four Ten, whilst I had been doing my best to keep my neck attached to my body, we had lost an awful lot of ground but I kept the little mare going easily at a reasonable gallop, and to my surprise, after we had gone about two miles, we started passing horses that had blown up, and whose jockeys had given up the ghost. Another half mile and we were passing the horses labouring towards the finish.

There were only four horses struggling after Four Ten, two of whom fell at the last fence, and going up the last hill the little mare sprinted past the remaining two, to finish second – though I must admit that by this time Four Ten was back in the unsaddling enclosure and his jockey was weighing in. Nevertheless the little mare won her maiden flat race a couple of weeks later, and a hunt race at the end of the season, so all in all she was a lucky ride for me. By a strange coincidence I also won that season on a very good horse called Passing Cloud IV, who was also a novice.

But by far the best way to teach a horse to jump, is in the course of your ordinary riding. You simply look out for a series of small ditches, maybe six or eight inches deep and a foot across, so that he can almost step across them. But when he sees that the horse you are with breaks into a trot and flies over, your horse too will break into a trot, come to the ditch, and either stumble over it or, more likely, arch himself and give an almighty leap. When you have finally discovered where the hell your saddle has got to, retrieved your reins and stopped, you tell him how clever he is and make a fuss of him. You do this four or five times, if possible over a different ditch each time.

You then progress to larger and larger ditches, until by the end of the ride, whenever he sees his companion pricking his ears, and starting to canter, he should be tearing after him, to join in the new game you have devised for him.

When he is jumping ditches happily and successfully, you go to the next stage of your schooling, which is finding a convenient verge eighteen inches or two feet higher than the side of the road. Again he follows his companion, popping up from the side of the road onto the verge. Following this, you teach him to jump from a higher piece of ground to a lower piece of ground, jumping down over a drop again eighteen inches to two feet.

Teaching him to jump banks like this, first up, then down, has the advantage that he has time to collect himself after doing the first half, before he does the second half, which is the drop. After half a dozen or a dozen little jumps, he is enjoying the new experience. So you start by jumping two-foot banks, still preferably from a trot; but some horses won't give you much option, and when they see their companion cantering into the bank, they will tear the reins out of your hands, and go cantering into it too.

Each of these lessons, of course, is interspersed with normal schooling. By now you should be attempting flying changes and figures of eight. These are very important when you are schooling a horse to jump, since when jumping fixed fences, one of the essential methods of putting your horse right, is to do a single or double change of leg.

Teaching a horse to do a flying change is quite simple. If your horse naturally leads with his near fore at the canter, you get him going into the canter so that he leads with his off fore, that is the leg that he does not naturally lead with. You then canter down the field, check him and turn him sharply to the near side, and in most cases he will quite naturally change legs. You use your body, of course, leaning back when you check him, and then throwing your weight onto his near fore, so that he has to adjust his balance by changing legs. When he is changing on command, from his unnatural to his natural leading leg, you will reverse the process. Best results will be obtained by working him at the canter on his off fore for three or four days beforehand, then simply starting him on his near fore, checking and turning at right angles, using your body as a counter weight.

You will notice that most of the things that I am advocating go against the dressage methods, but for hunting, cross country, and any form of speed jumping competition, if you can convey your wishes to your horse by merely shifting your body weight, you will not only be speeding up communication, but you will also be assisting his balance of movement.

When your horse is jumping ditches and banks with enjoyment and fluency, you graduate to fly fences. These should preferably be jumped towards home, and I prefer loose poles of brush, eighteen inches to two feet high. If he makes a mess of one of them, he can gallop straight through it without hurting himself. When he's tearing over these, dancing and snorting as he comes to his jumping place, you can put a rail six inches above the brush. As he progresses the rail gets higher, and when he has got to about three foot, you start him jumping straight post and rails.

When this stage has been successfully completed, and he is looking forward to his jumping as a reward for his schooling work, you can start introducing spreads. To start off with, your spread will need to be two foot nine inches high, and two foot six inches wide. This of course gets bigger and wider, until his spreads are three foot six inches to four foot apart, and his normal post and rails is three foot six to three foot nine inches. After this you introduce combinations, again dropping your fences and spread widths to below the three foot mark at the beginning.

At the same time as you are schooling your horse over fixed timber fences, you can also be schooling him to jump water. This is done by first picking a nice sunny day, riding him down to the nearest river, and letting him play in it for ten minutes. Then you ride him down the river, until you come to a nice bank to jump out from, and you jump him back in the water, so that he enjoys the splash. When you have got him enjoying jumping in and out of the river, you place a low post and rails, so that he jumps the post and rails into the river. You can put various obstacles in the river for him to jump, each time making sure that he enjoys playing in the water.

You get him to jump fences at right angles to each other, by first jumping him over one fence, and then turning him to jump another at right angles twenty or thirty yards away. By degrees, you bring them closer and closer together, until he can jump a three foot six post and a rail, turn on his hocks and jump out over another.

By this time you will have taught him to jump almost any fence that you are likely to meet, either when you are out hunting or across country. The three things that you have to remember are, first, that you have to keep within the capabilities of the horse – if you have any trouble you go back to a lower and easier fence; second you have to see that he learns to place himself and jump naturally but, at the same time, responds to the movements of your body, so that you can put him right where necessary; and third, and most important, that he enjoys his jumping and looks upon it as a reward.

There is one final fence I would say that it is necessary to learn to jump, although this is not part of normal schooling. This is barbed wire. Barbed wire is much feared in this country, and yet in Australia and New Zealand it is considered to be a normal fence, and it is really quite easy to teach your horse to jump it. You stretch a strand of plain wire over a rail at three foot, or three foot three inches. Trot him into the fence (don't canter him) and he will probably clear the lot. He may hit the wire at first, which will knock his feet back, but since he's used to jumping a three foot rail, he will clear the rail anyway, and soon learn to clear the wire as well. Then, when he is jumping this quite happily and easily, you remove the rail and put a second strand of wire below the first.

Each time before jumping wire, especially on any young horse, you walk him up to it so that he can feel the height of the wire on his chest. And you click your tongue when you want him to take off, and you say 'hup', encouraging him to jump on command. This training to jump on command is a very important part of training over wire, and you can get some horses to the point where you can canter them into a gateway with nothing in it whatsoever, kick and say 'hup' and they will jump three foot six or three foot nine. Keep to plain wire at this stage.

Whether you go on to school him over barbed wire at home, or leave it until you hunt to jump barbed wire, is purely a matter of choice. I school over plain wire at home, and then when I am hunting, if I come to barbed wire with an experienced horse I just canter up to it, kick him 'hup' and go straight over it. With a green horse I trot up to the wire, let him feel it, go back and canter into it, kick him 'hup' and over. I can say quite honestly, that other than two scratches, I have never had a horse cut jumping barbed wire. And I have only had a horse caught up in barbed wire on two occasions, and on each of these I jumped a five foot fence when hounds were running, and landed straight into a barbed wire fence standing six feet the other side – that is, in both cases I was unaware that I was jumping wire at all. This is something that is most unlikely to happen now. In those days, about twenty years ago, some herds were tuberculin tested and others were not, so a lot of dairy farms had barbed wire fences six foot out from the normal fence, to isolate their cattle from their neighbour's. Today you won't find such double fences, but you will find barbed wire fences, and these will give you no trouble, provided you school your horses properly at home.

One special situation that you may meet with cross country, is one where you jump up onto a bank, and then have to slide down off the bank and jump a fence the other side. The answer here is pure straightforward schooling at home. In our ordinary riding, we teach all our horses to slide down very steep banks, which is easy in this area, because there are a lot of steep slopes. Once we've taught a horse to slide down a bank, so that he is sitting on his hocks, we put a low rail eight or ten feet out from the bank, so he has to slide straight off his hocks, out over the rail. Again we increase the height of the rail, until he is jumping three foot six or four foot straight over without any difficulty at all.

17: *Fanny*

I first saw Fanny as a yearling. She belonged to a friend, who was selling her at the horse sale in Llanybyther. Unfortunately I was particularly hard up at the time and I couldn't buy her, but as luck would have it he didn't sell her. The following spring, I was over at his place, and I saw her again. She had grown very big and very strong, and extremely wild. He wanted to run his cob stallion with his mares, and he didn't want Fanny to produce a foal, so he asked me if I would take her for the summer, and just mess about with her generally. I said yes – he was lending me three other horses for pony trekking anyway, so I didn't have much choice, and Fanny came over three or four days later with the other horses. Her owner, when he came out of the lorry, was pouring with sweat and in a flaming temper. 'I've spent a whole day racing round a field, trying to catch that something-something-something bitch!' He'd got her partitioned off from the other three in the front of the lorry, so we let the other three out into the field, and drove the lorry back to the yard. I climbed over the partition to where Fanny was breathing fire at all and sundry.

I stood quietly for five or ten minutes, and slowly but surely she relaxed, and I put my hand on her. She flinched as though she had been touched with a red hot iron, and cowered back against the front of the lorry. Again I waited for her to relax, and again I put my hand on her. She flinched this time, but not as badly, and, slowly and gently, I caressed her side, just beside her shoulder, working my hand up her side until I got to her back and withers, then I started squeezing and scratching her mane. This she obviously enjoyed and relaxed visibly. I scratched her mane until I got to the back of her ears, and then I went back down again to her side. Then I went away, to collect an old rope halter, came back and put my hand on her

555

again. Again she flinched, but she was getting used to me and allowed me slowly to work the halter over her, up her side and over to the other side of her body, and then to work my hand up her neck, so that her head was between my body and the halter on the other side.

When I got as far as her head, I eased her nose through the halter. Scratching the side of her face, I brought the halter up and over her ears.

Having got the halter on, I attached it to a long plough line, so that we had plenty of rope to play with, undid the partition and swung it back. Then I went back to her and, just rubbing the side of her face, got a hand on the halter, and pulled her round quite easily until she was facing the back of the lorry. As soon as she saw freedom in front of her, she gave a bound forward, tearing the halter out of my hand. This I had foreseen, having twisted the line round the gate post, so that as she bounded out of the lorry, preparing to go hell for leather down the road, she came to the end of the rope within five yards and had to stop. She fought the halter for two or three minutes, then I walked up to her, talking quietly and gently. She sidled away from me, but she couldn't go back because of the halter rope, she couldn't go forward because my friend was standing there, and she couldn't go sideways because there was a bank in the way so she stood, and let me get my hand on her. Again, I went up her side and her neck and got my hand on the halter. My wife got behind her, and Fanny walked forward with my hand on the halter, just holding it loosely, while my friend undid the turn on the gatepost, and took a turn round a tree in the side of the yard instead. We progressed like this until we got to the stable door. Fanny's owner went in through the door, and took a twist round the post in the corner of the stable. Fanny looked in at the stable, looked left and right, and found it uninviting, so she hung back. I stepped back two or three paces and put my hand on her bottom. As soon as I touched her bottom she jumped forward, taking her half into the stable. I walked forwards, slapped her bottom, and in she went like a bullet. We shut the door and I put a feed, some water and hay in for her.

We left Fanny where she was for the night, and the following morning, when I went in to feed her, I found that she hadn't touched the corn, but had drunk the water and eaten the hay. Obviously she had no idea what horse and pony nuts were, and had to be taught to eat them. That was an easy lesson. All I had to do was get my daughter Paddy's old pony, Strawberry, put him in the stable and leave him ten minutes. Of course, as soon as he saw the nuts, Strawberry jammed his head in the bucket and started eating, as if it was the last meal he was ever likely to see.

I stood back a fair distance and watched Fanny, and Fanny watched Strawberry, and after a few minutes Fanny realized that whatever was in the bucket must be good to eat, so she walked over to investigate. Strawberry swung his backside over at her and told her to push off, but Fanny wasn't having any. At this sign of bad manners on Strawberry's part, she bit him hard, to show him that this was no way to treat a lady. Strawberry swung round, but didn't take his head out of the bucket, so Fanny bit him harder, this time catching hold of his ear. This brought his head up quickly, whereupon Fanny seized the opportunity and put her head in the bucket, to see what it was that Strawberry was fighting to protect.

She took a mouthful of four or five nuts, picked her head up and chewed them slowly, whereupon Strawberry put his head back into the bucket, and nothing she could do would shift him again. When she had chewed the nuts and decided that they tasted quite nice, she tried to push Strawberry away, but this time he snapped at her, and eventually, when after five or ten minutes he had finished her feed, I led him out and put another feed in for Fanny.

Fanny walked over this time and sniffed, nibbled a few and then nibbled some more, then really got down and cleared the whole lot. This was an important lesson : once she had learned that nuts were good to eat, training and handling her would be comparatively easy, because nuts could be used as a reward. When she did what I told her, she got nuts – when she didn't, she got smacked.

Three or four times a day I went into her stable, first of all stroking her and handling her. Then I took the stable rubber and scratched her in her ticklish places, untangling a hair here and a hair there, not too much at a time because untangling a tangled mane tends to be a little bit painful for the horse. Over the course of the week I got her mane reasonably tidy and the worst of the tangles out of her tail. By this time, I'd also got her used to being brushed by the body brush, and she quite enjoyed having the particularly itchy bits along her back scratched with the body brush as well.

At the end of the week, I walked in and, instead of a halter, I took the snaffle bridle with me. In my hand I had a few nuts, so she stuffed her nose into my hand to get the nuts, and it was quite simple to get my thumb into the corner of her mouth, so that as she opened her mouth I slipped the bit in and put the rest of the bridle straight over her ears and nose.

I then took the saddle, which I had already placed on the half door of the stable, and slapped it on her back as if it was a normal, everyday thing. I'd put a bucket of nuts in the corner of the stable, before I put the saddle on, so though she sidled away slightly, she went on eating. I reached under her, caught hold of the girth, and gently pulled it under her, then buckled it loosely. By degrees I tightened the girth. She didn't move or flinch in any way.

My wife gave me a leg up until I was lying across Fanny's back. This I hadn't been able to do when I was grooming her, because she was a good 15.3 and all I had been able to do was to reach across her slightly when I was handling her. But even though this was the first time I'd put my weight on her she didn't shift her head out of the bucket. Slowly and gently I rubbed her side and back, and then I brought my leg over the saddle, as far as possible making sure that I didn't touch her side with my knee or my foot as I did so.

Eventually I was sitting in the saddle with my feet one either side of her. I put one foot in one stirrup whilst my wife put the other foot into the other, and just sat there talking to

Fanny whilst she finished her feed. Then my wife opened the door and led her out of the yard and up the road.

We hadn't gone ten or fifteen yards, before I could feel that the mare was completely and utterly relaxed, and I had complete empathy with her. I said 'whoa', just touching the reins. Fanny stopped. In fact throughout the whole of her early gentling, she was one of the easiest horses I have ever dealt with.

We walked about half a mile and the mare was going so well that I risked something that I've only done four or five times in my life. Normally we ride up the hill and when we get to the top I get off and lead the horse back down, because if something is going to go wrong, it is most likely to go wrong going down hill and towards home. But in this case the mare was so relaxed and going so well, that when we got to the top of the hill, and I said 'whoa' and Fanny stopped, I simply twisted my whole body round so that my knee was pressing into the saddle on the near side, and my leg was slightly back on the off side. I took the reins over, so that the near rein was bearing on the left side of the neck, and the off rein out at a wide angle to the right. Then I turned to look down the hill and Fanny, without any hesitation, turned round and walked down.

I could hardly believe it. I had never had a horse that learned so easily and responded so well. When we had gone twenty yards I neck reined her from the left hand side of the road, to the right hand side of the road, then back and forth four or five times. I stopped every twenty or thirty yards, and then we went on again, neck reining and stopping, back into the yard.

We got to the stable door and I was going to get off, when I suddenly wondered whether, since the mare had already stopped, neck reined, turned, she would also back. So I gently tightened the reins so that her head came into her chest, squeezed her with my heels and she took a stride backwards. Leslie caught hold of her head, as I eased myself out of the saddle and on to the ground. I led her into the stable, took her saddle and bridle off, and made a terrific fuss of her. Leslie brought her feed and put it in. She saw the bucket put on the ground, brought her head back and knocked me to one side, telling me to get out of the way, because I was interfering between her and her dinner. I scratched her neck and told her how clever she was, and left her to settle down quietly.

The following day I had her out again, and half way up the hill I clicked my tongue and squeezed her with my legs and she broke into a long smooth striding trot. We trotted five or ten yards, before I pulled her back to a walk, we walked, and I trotted her again. While she was trotting I neck reined her from one side of the road to the other.

The response I was getting from the mare was beyond description. The following day we got old Cork Beg out, and Leslie rode Cork Beg while I rode Fanny. We went for a ride in the forest in a big circle, walking, trotting, neck reining, stopping, backing. I hadn't intended to do more than this, but I hadn't taken into my calculations old Cork Beg.

We came to one of the spots where Cork Beg enjoyed a gallop; we had already passed two of them and he'd behaved himself, but this time he was having fun. He heaved the reins out of Leslie's hands and he was off up the slope, like a bat out of hell. Fanny, who had been trotting gently behind him, suddenly saw Cork Beg disappearing into the distance and this was too much for her. She gave a little squeal and a very small buck, and was straight off after him. Cork Beg steadied at the top of the hill and she steadied back to a trot twenty yards before she got to him, partly because I steadied her back, and partly because she was getting tired. I could feel that she was getting blown, and it was an excellent opportunity for me to assert control. We rode on slowly and gently for another half mile, until we came to a little lane, where we had half a dozen two-foot fences forty or fifty yards apart. Leslie said 'You're never going to jump the mare?' I said 'I've never done this in my life before, but I must see whether it's possible.' Cork Beg, who had been dancing around, half bucking, tearing at his bit, heard what I said, and was gone like a shot from a gun, straight up the lane and over the fences. Fanny beetled after him, determined that she was going to miss none of the fun.

She came to the first of the little brush fences, cocked her
large ears, looked at it, steadied and I thought, 'this is it, she's
gong to stop', but not a bit of it. She steadied herself at the
exact spot, launched herself into mid air, and jumped at least
five feet. I jumped at least seven feet, and came back down
into the saddle all arms and legs. Fanny should, by all the rules
of everything that is natural, have taken the opportunity offered
her, and bucked me off there and then, but she didn't. She
was away into the next fence after Cork Beg, again steadying
and jumping perfectly, although this time she only jumped
about a foot higher than the fence, and after that she jumped
each fence without any difficulty at all, until she came to the
last one. This was a fairish tree trunk lying across the lane. It
had no ground line, which foxed her a bit, and she rapped it
hard with her front legs. Undismayed, she twisted her hind legs
under, and sorted her front legs out without any difficulty. I
steadied her back to a trot and we trotted up the road to where
the old man, Cork Beg, was waiting for us.

Fanny had had enough, and after petting and talking, and
making a fuss of her, I rode her home. I gave her owner a ring
that night to tell him how well she was doing, and also that
her feet were in a bad state – she had sand crack and she was
beginning to get a bit sore – so would he come and shoe her?
He does all his own shoeing, and I hadn't finished milking the
following morning when he was on the doorstep. He walked
into the stable, put a feed down for Fanny, and had a set of
shoes tapped on to all four feet within a quarter of an hour,
before Fanny had finished her breakfast. Other than moving
a bit while he was clenching the nails down, she took no notice
of being shod whatsoever.

I rode her for another two weeks, keeping the jumping down
to about two foot six. I know that it is supposed to be wrong
to jump a two-year-old, but on the other hand Fanny was
enjoying it, and the point in training she'd got to in the last two
weeks was where I would normally expect a horse to be after
six months. She was stopping, turning, neck reining, changing
legs at a canter, jumping two foot six and going absolutely

superbly. The only thing that she was doing wrong was that once I'd got her eating plenty of corn and a little bit fit, she would dance instead of walk. This was her expression of her keenness, and try as I would I could never really cure her of it. For the following three years, I worked and worked on this point, but except when I was getting her fit for racing as a five- and six-year-old, when she did settle down and walk slowly and steadily, she always tended to dance, mainly because she was enjoying herself so much. She was so full of enthusiasm that her excitement got the better of her discipline, and she would juggle along, wanting to get on with it, to gallop or jump.

After another fortnight, the owner came over again and we had a long consultation about the work we wanted to do with Fanny. I'd already got far further than I'd thought possible. Now she needed shoeing again and the consultation was about whether to take her shoes off and leave her, or to shoe her again and eventually we came to the decision that to get her feet right again it would be best to leave a light set of shoes on her, changing them every three weeks, and turn her out for the summer. So we turned her out and left her. By turning her out and leaving her, of course, I don't mean that I turned her out on the far end of the farm and forgot all about her. I mean that I put her in the field next to the yard, and I wandered out with a small feed for her every day. She spent a lot of time standing up by the yard, and I'd chat to her as I went by, and she'd watch what the other horses were doing, and learn how they behaved.

She went back to her owner for the winter and came to me the following spring, as a three-year-old. During that summer I worked her for a couple of hours, three or four times a week, occasionally popping over little fences, but generally developing her muscles, schooling her and getting her going sensibly and well. Then at the beginning of August, a friend of mine held a hunter trial. We had a lot of horses going and I decided to take Fanny as well, to see how she'd do, so ten days before the hunter trial we put up a set of fences, about two foot six, timber mostly, some brush and a couple of combinations. I jumped her over the first timber fence, intending to do the three smaller fences, but not a bit of it! She was over the first fence, tearing to get into the second, and she went right round the course, giving me very little choice about it – although if the mare wanted to go, I was the last person in the world to stop her. Over the next week we raised the fences until they were three foot six and four foot spreads. The spreads and the doubles were regulation size as well.

We took her up to the hunter trial and rode two other horses, including little Dart, who was there by accident – I just took him round to see how he would do. To my amazement I finished first and third, in the novice hunter trial – first on Fanny and third on Dart.

The thing that finally crowned the afternoon was the fact that my daughter Paddy, who was then ten years old, was put up on an old racing pony that we had, and I took her with me, riding Cork Beg myself, in the pairs. Since the course was in a convenient circle, we went round the pairs course absolutely flat out, steeplechasing stride for stride – neither the old mare nor the old man was going to let the other in front – and we finished third. So we had a wonderful day, and I had suddenly discovered that I had two brilliant young horses in the stable, to go campaigning with.

We took Fanny to another hunter trial in the autumn, and she was third in the open. I think I could probably have won it on her, but since the fences were very big and very strong, I took my time over them, instead of letting her battle on as she would have preferred to do, and we were beaten on time.

Again she went back to her owner for the winter, and came back to me in the spring. This time I really got down to work on her, so that she would jump, and change legs, and I reached the stage where I was purposely putting her into big fences and letting her get herself out of trouble, in this way making her an extremely good hunter, racehorse and hunter trial horse. We had her in three hunter trials, and she was unbeaten in all three of them, because by now her fencing was so good that I was just setting her alight at the start, and I could stop, check, turn and go where necessary.

I kept her that autumn and had her hunting about a dozen times, stopping just before Christmas to get her ready for point to pointing. By the end of February she was extremely fit, and I took her to the first point-to-point. She wasn't really big enough or well bred enough to make a racehorse, but I had high hopes for her because she seemed to have a fairish turn of foot, and she stayed forever. We had a very good point-to-point season with her, she was third or fourth in all of her point-to-points until the last one, which she won with ease. So we turned her away for the summer to have a good rest.

At last I had got the horse I was looking for. I had one object and one only in mind, and that was the Foxhunter's Chase at Aintree. I had always wanted to ride at Aintree, but until Fanny I'd never had a horse that I thought capable of tackling the Aintree fences. That autumn we worked on her, and in due course we had her fit and qualified. All the paper work, registrations, hunter's certificates, jockey's certificates and training permits were in order by the end of February. We took her up to Leicester for the first race. The going was very, very heavy, and it was a two and a half mile race. They went away like bats out of hell and the pace was too fast for Fanny, so I settled down well in the rear of the field for the first circuit, and the other horses started coming back to me. Three fences from home I was lying fifth in a field of thirteen. We came over the open ditch, and there was a horse lying on the ground in front of us. Fanny made a valiant effort to jump the horse as well as the fence, but the mud was just too much for us and over we went. It was the only time she ever fell racing in her life, but I was more than satisfied with her performance.

We took her to Bangor on Dee a fortnight later, and the going was very fast, and she just hadn't got the pace to keep up with them. She jumped impeccably and went well, so I went home and decided that all I could do after that was to pray hard every night that it would rain hard every night for the next fortnight. I must have offended the Almighty in some way, because it didn't, it stayed as dry as a bone. The Foxhunter's Chase at Aintree was on the Thursday and we spent the whole of the Monday, Tuesday and Wednesday getting the landrover greased and oiled – an unprecedented experience for the landrover; it nearly fell to pieces with the shock. Then we cleaned the trailer out, my wife repainted it, and Paddy never stopped grooming Fanny, so that by Wednesday we were all worn out.

I got my racing stuff packed into the back of the landrover during Wednesday and at half past three on Thursday morning the alarm went off and we got up, gave Fanny a feed and ourselves a quick cup of coffee. By half past four we were on the road for Aintree. By about half past eight we passed through Hereford, and up over the downs towards Worcester. It was a glorious morning, the birds were singing, and we stopped to get the *Sporting Life* to see our names in print for Liverpool that day. Paddy, who had woken up – she had been fast asleep in her sleeping bag in the passenger seat – proceeded to read out what they'd said about each horse. She came to Fanny: 'Third rate point-to-pointer: has won a small point-to-point, and has been placed in bad company'. But still hope springs eternal in the human breast, and at Aintree all things are possible. The rest of them might fall and we might win.

We drove on and on the endless miles to Liverpool. Eventually we came to a sign which said 'Aintree Racecourse' and every two or three miles we passed another until suddenly the signs to Aintree ended and I decided I'd gone too far. By the side of us were walls thirty feet high. Her Majesty's Prison at Walton might be where I should have been, paying for my misdeeds, but it certainly wasn't where I was supposed to be racing that day! So I turned round and retraced my steps, and finally after some searching found concealed without any sign or indication, a small gate. We went in and there at last I was at the Mecca of steeplechasing.

We got Fanny out and walked her round, and let her pick grass. Her silver mane and tail floated in the breeze looking an absolute picture, but compared with most of the other horses, she looked like a weight carrying hunter. Having attended to her wants, we put her back into the trailer and went to inspect Aintree. In some ways it was a bit shabby, and in others it was magnificent. Fanny ran in Paddy's name and as owner she was due a free lunch and a seat in the county stand, so she went off to her meal, at the expense of Mrs Mirabelle Topham, whilst I went and dumped my racing kit, and greeted my various acquaintances in the jockeys' room.

An old friend, who had a friend who had ridden at Aintree before the war, had given me a piece of invaluable advice. 'Whatever you do', he said, 'do not go and look at the course. If you stand and look at the fences, they look terrible; when you're riding them, they don't look bad at all.' So I carefully avoided the course and went to have a look round. Eventually the crowds arrived and Paddy and I, after some difficulty, eventually located Leslie and Fanny's owner, who had driven up separately. We saw the first race, and then the rest of them went to get Fanny out and ready, whilst I went in and got changed. When I was ready I sat on my bench in the jockeys' room in glum despondency: I'd been a fool to think that I could take a fairish hunter up to Aintree, and expect a poor little mare of 15.3 to jump the biggest and most severe fences in England.

But before long the call came, 'jockeys out', and we trooped out to see Fanny swagger around with her head in the air, and her silver tail floating behind her. The television cameras seemed to be focusing on her, and she seemed to be cavorting to show herself off, for the benefit of a million viewers.

'Jockeys up'. Fanny came in and I tightened her girth. Her owner gave me a leg up, and we walked round the paddock, then they filed out of the paddock and, by a bit of skulduggery, I indulged my favourite superstition, based on the old-fashioned saying 'Last out, first in'. I always find that if I don't observe this rule, I go for a burton. So I jumped off Fanny and pretended to readjust the breast plate, so that I was last out of the paddock, and we cantered down to the start.

The starter called the roll and we were walking around. He said 'Come into line' and, intending to be clever, I said 'No, no, no, I'm not ready yet,' but I couldn't catch him out, he was too old and wily a bird. So up went the tapes and away we went, but instead of getting a flying start as I intended, I lost a couple of lengths and was at the tail of the field.

Fanny was reaching for the reins and galloped into the first fence, going like a bat out of hell. She stood back and flew it like a bird, and so with the second and the third. Then came the Chair; this is supposed to be a huge fence. I looked at it afterwards and it did look huge; two of us stood on either side of it and we couldn't see each other, while the ditch was wide enough to drive a landrover down. But as we galloped into it, it looked a nice, inviting little fence. Fanny stood back and I don't think she touched a twig.

We went into the water jump. Fanny had jumped water jumps before, and knew what they were about. Unfortunately what I had forgotten to tell her, was that at Aintree it's not twelve feet of water, but fourteen feet, and she dropped her hind legs into it. We lost a length or two, but she heaved herself out and away we went in pursuit of the rest of the field, across the Melling road, and into what is the first fence of the Grand National. Each fence she measured perfectly, and each fence she jumped without touching it. We came to the open ditch before Beechers and, much to my amusement, there was a jockey sitting on top of it, looking down at his horse lying on the ground below. Fanny stood right back and skimmed it like a hurdle, and so into Beechers. She jumped Beechers and in mid air, I looked down and saw a horse lying on the ground, just where we were going to land. Fanny checked and landed short of the horse, took off and jumped him. There was another horse straight in her path, she changed legs, nearly throwing me from the saddle, and went round him and on into the next fence.

Going towards the Canal turn, I was beginning to see bodies everywhere, and instead of the sixteen starters, there were only six in front of us. She came round the Canal turn on one leg, and just popped over the corner, almost from a standstill, down the far side. I was feeling wonderful. All the difficult fences were over and done with, and we just had five or six fences to hurdle, and that was it. Each fence was about fifty yards wide and though they were big and strong, their width made them look small and inviting. We came into yet another seemingly easy fence. Fanny took off well back, and I looked down and saw what appeared to be a dirty great river beneath us; I'd forgotten that we still had Valentine's Brook to jump, and this was it. We seemed to stay suspended in mid air forever but eventually down we came, with Fanny swinging away, as if she'd popped over one of the little schooling fences at home.

We jumped the next fence, and there lying on the ground was another horse – we were sixth. Over the last three fences as if they weren't there, and up round the elbow and up the straight to the winning post. Admittedly we'd been last from the very beginning to the end, but the fact remained that I had completed a life's ambition, I had ridden round Aintree. And because I was riding one of the very best fencers in the country, I had found it extremely exhilarating and easy, and was walking on cloud nine.

We rode back to the paddock and I unsaddled. I went back to the weighing room feeling absolutely elated. So obvious was my joy and happiness, that Lord Leverhulme, who happened to be speaking to one of the other stewards, stopped me and said 'There's a picture of a very happy man'. There was only one reply; I said 'You're looking at the happiest man in England; I've just ridden the best horse in England, over the best fences in England.' He said 'Did you win?' and I said 'No, I came tailing round at the back of the field, but she is still the best horse in England, and those are still the most fantastic fences in England'.

I changed and went back to the rest of the family. We loaded Fanny, watched a couple of hurdle races and flat races, and went home. We got to Tregarron at about two o'clock in the morning, and I was almost asleep. Paddy, who was supposed to be staying awake to talk to me, would talk hard for two minutes, and then go back to sleep herself.

I drove on until I came to one of my local pubs, which being out in the country has no idea of licensing hours. By now it was nearly four o'clock and I thought, 'I'm so near asleep that if I don't get someone to drive me home, I'm going to have an accident'. So I got out and went round the back of the pub, to see if I could get a chauffeur. I was just going to go in, when it suddenly struck me that if they had been in there drinking since closing time, they were even more likely to have an accident than I was. So I went back to the landrover and drove the last ten miles home, getting back at half past four. I unloaded Fanny and put her into bed, which Leslie had got ready with food and water. Fanny walked over to the bucket, had a drink, went over to her feed bucket and tucked into it, as if it was the most normal thing in the world to be driven round the countryside for twenty-four hours and raced around Aintree. I had a quick cup of coffee and went to bed, and slept solidly until half past two that afternoon. Leslie who had got up early and done the horses and all the work, said that when she'd gone out Fanny was fast asleep, until she'd brought another bucket of water and a feed, whereupon Fanny had got up, had a drink, eaten her breakfast and laid down again.

I went out to see how she was, and there she was lying fast asleep on the floor. I felt her legs which were cool. She opened her eyes and looked at me, and I patted her shoulder and scratched her neck. I sat down in the straw between her legs, leaned back against her tummy and we talked to each other for the next half hour, about the superb time we'd had the day before. After that, for the rest of the season, Paddy, who had just passed her eighteenth birthday, rode her in Ladies' races, never being out of the first three, and I went back to riding and schooling young horses.

Eventually I managed to scrape enough money together to buy Fanny, intending to ride her round Aintree again, but unfortunately in one of her schooling races, the ground was very rough, and she put her foot in a rut, cracking the fetlock bone very slightly. It was enough to put her out for the next nine months, and we never got to Aintree again.

My racing days are over too. I had an accident a year ago and injured my spine, so that Fanny and I will not face any more fences together. Yet I had her nine years, competing and hunting, and I don't think I ever rode a better horse.

I remember on one occasion, when I was out hunting with her with the South Pembrokeshire, we breezed into a bank six foot high and six foot wide. I expected her to bank it, but not a bit of it, that wasn't Fanny's fashion. She accelerated and flew it, clearing the whole damn lot, and I found an eight foot drop on the other side. She came down, landed, changed legs and went straight away. She jumped barbed wire the way most horses jump hurdles. Nine times out of ten, when you wanted to catch her, she would come over, and almost put the halter on herself. But sometimes she would choose to trot round you in an infuriating manner, in a circle fifteen yards across, with you in the middle. You could see her roaring with laughter and saying 'Now, you stupid beggar, catch me if you can'. I would give up in disgust, go up and open the gate. Then she would trot up the road behind me, with her head on my shoulder.

She's gone now to the stallion, and we hope that she's going to produce something with a bit more pace and size than she has, and if she does and he has only half as much heart, and half as much jumping ability as his mother, he's going to be a very, very good horse indeed, and sometimes I think that even if I'm still in a wheelchair, I'll get on that horse, and I'll ride him round Aintree, come hell or high water, even if I die in the attempt.